Wicked

A Musical Biography

Paul R. Laird

THE SCARECROW PRESS, INC.
Lanham • Toronto • Plymouth, UK
2011

Published by Scarecrow Press, Inc.
A wholly owned subsidiary of The Rowman & Littlefield Publishing Group, Inc.
4501 Forbes Boulevard, Suite 200, Lanham, Maryland 20706
http://www.scarecrowpress.com

Estover Road, Plymouth PL6 7PY, United Kingdom

British Library Cataloguing in Publication Information Available

Library of Congress Cataloging-in-Publication Data

Laird, Paul R.
  Wicked : a musical biography / Paul R. Laird.
    p. cm.
  Includes bibliographical references and index.
  ISBN 978-0-8108-7751-1 (cloth : alk. paper) — ISBN 978-0-8108-7752-8 (ebook)
  1. Schwartz, Stephen. Wicked. 2. Musicals—History and criticism. I. Title.
ML410.S42L38 2011
  792.6'42—dc22   2011000510

Printed in the United States of America

CONTENTS

CONTENTS

PREFACE

My route to a book on *Wicked* was largely determined by a fortuitous meeting with a generous composer and by a delightful confluence of interests with my daughter, Caitlin, who at this writing is age 16. My first meeting with composer and lyricist Stephen Schwartz was at a conference on Leonard Bernstein's *Mass* sponsored by the Columbus (Ohio) Pro Musica Chamber Orchestra in May 2004. We were both members of a panel on the work's creation, with Schwartz recalling his role in writing the English lyrics and assisting with the dramatic structure. Schwartz proved a willing interview subject, leading to two articles and finally to a planned book on his musical theater works, which will hopefully be nearly written by the time this volume is in print. (This larger study of all of Schwartz's works will also appear from Scarecrow Press.) Multiple interviews with Schwartz in the winter of 2008 led to excellent access to primary sources that turned what would have been a single chapter on *Wicked* into this book. I am most grateful to Stephen Schwartz for allowing me the opportunity to study multiple drafts of scripts, the piano/vocal score and drafts of songs, musical materials deleted from the show, some correspondence, and the orchestral full score prepared for the original cast recording. The composer/lyricist graciously allowed this access, and it was greatly facilitated by his assistant Michael Cole, who has kindly sent many files to me, answered numerous e-mails (often within minutes or hours), and helped me speak to or correspond with other important figures in *Wicked*'s development. Stephen Schwartz has been very generous with his time in several interviews for this book (and numerous others concerning his other shows), in answering e-mail messages, and in offering useful advice on whom else I should contact. When I began to work on the larger study, Schwartz told me he could not offer any primary materials because he had not yet organized his manuscript legacy, but as I continued to visit his office, he helped make available more materials. Remarkably, I had one afternoon where I was able to go through a few boxes of *Wicked* materials and find what I might need, and then I was allowed to make copies of items that required further study. It is my hope that the book that has resulted will do justice to these opportunities and explain the creation, music, and orchestration of *Wicked* in a way that others will find useful.

I first saw *Wicked* on Broadway in March 2005, just before my first face-to-face interview with Schwartz. My knowledge of the show at that point was limited to what I had learned from some reviews, from careful listening to the original cast recording, and from reading Gregory Maguire's novel *Wicked*, which is the source for the show. The audience that night included its share of young women who were enthralled from the opening downbeat, squealing with delight at their favorite moments and sometimes producing a collective, ear-splitting roar. I enjoyed the show and learned many useful details of its creation from Schwartz that night in his New York apartment (which became part of my article on the show's creation in the second edition of *The Cambridge Companion to the Musical*[1]), but my initial impressions were influenced deeply by those enraptured young women, making me question just how much *Wicked* might have to say to adults. My feelings started to change as I did further research, but what really encouraged me to delve deeply into the musical were conversations with my daughter, Caitlin, who is simply fascinated by *Wicked*. I wanted to understand why *Wicked* had such a profound effect on Caitlin and her peers. She told me that it was the depiction of Elphaba and Glinda, who seemed so alive in Winnie Holzman's script and Schwartz's songs that Caitlin described them as "people that I know." My desire to comprehend the show's appeal to young females necessitated that I see it multiple times, and I discovered real substance based on believable human emotions in characters that grow and change. I also learned that Schwartz's score serves the drama in ways that one appreciates in the most effective musical plays. That these qualities emerge in a show based on the most popular American literary fantasy provides yet another hook that draws in audiences. This process, initiated by discussions with Caitlin, helped plant in me the strong desire to study thoroughly all of the primary sources that I had acquired and to report in a detailed manner on *Wicked*'s creation.

Acknowledgments

There are numerous others to thank for their assistance with aspects of this book. Renée Camus, formerly of Scarecrow Press, showed great enthusiasm for a project on Schwartz's musical theater and helped arrange this separate volume on *Wicked*. I had several useful conversations with her about Schwartz's shows, and she played a role in shaping both books. After her departure from Scarecrow, Stephen Ryan became my helpful editor. An interview with *Wicked*'s book writer Winnie Holzman in 2005 set me on the right path in understanding the script and provided numerous useful insights. Stephen Oremus, the show's music supervisor, granted two telephone interviews and answered numerous e-mail queries, allowing me an open window into the collaboration process. William David Brohn, the orchestrator, participated enthusiastically in a joint interview with Schwartz in New York City and also answered a few e-mail queries. A telephone interview with Herb Braha concerning *Godspell* helped clarify an aspect of Schwartz's early working methods. Carol de Giere, author of *Defying Gravity: The Creative Career of Stephen Schwartz from "Godspell" to "Wicked"* (Applause Theatre & Cinema Books, 2008) has been a friendly colleague, passing on useful advice and sharing her great enthusiasm for Schwartz's works. My work in this volume would not have been possible without her extensive research, and there are areas that I have approached in less detail in this book because of what is available in hers. I am grateful to several of my fellow musical theater scholars for counsel and helpful words as I worked on this book and made presentations involving the material at regional meetings of the American Musicological Society and College Music Society, and at the 2010 Association of Theatre in Higher Education in August 2010 in Los Angeles, the conference "Song, Stage & Screen 5" in September 2010 at the University of Winchester (UK), and the conference "Classic Broadway and Those Who Built It" hosted at the University of Colorado at Boulder in October 2010. I would especially like to thank William Everett, George Ferencz, Jane Ferencz,

Thomas Riis, Jessica Sternfeld, Scott Warfield, and Stacy Wolf for some helpful conversations and input. George Ferencz also shared his materials and experiences with me concerning his freelance work on arranging the "Vocal Selections" of *Wicked* for Hal Leonard, which allowed an interesting addition to chapter 5. Jonas Westover and Doug Reside graciously assisted me with the acquisition of some materials. I am also grateful to Scott Murphy, a music theory professor and treasured colleague at the University of Kansas, who assisted me with some questions concerning a recurring chord in Schwartz's score. Dr. Karin Pagel-Meiners kindly answered some questions concerning German translations. I am thankful to a number of my colleagues at the University of Kansas for the support and interest they have shown in my project. I would like to express my appreciation to the staffs at the New York Public Library for the Performing Arts (especially of the Billy Rose Theatre Division), the British Library, and the Victoria & Albert Theatre Collection, which I consulted in its temporary quarters at the imposing Blythe House near the Kensington (Olympia) Underground station. My research in New York City in the winter of 2008 and my research trip to London in July 2008 were funded by two generous grants from the University of Kansas General Research Fund. Beneficent funding from James P. Zakoura through the Zakoura Family Foundation (a fund of the Greater Kansas City Community Fund-ZFF) and Reach Out Kansas Inc. paid for copyright permissions for the musical examples and quotation of lyrics. Arranging the license for those musical examples was made possible by the helpful cooperation of Charmaine Ferenczi of Schreck Rose Dapello Adams & Hurwitz LLP and Jonathan Belott of Hal Leonard Inc. I appreciated my brother Doug Laird's willingness to travel to what for him is nearby New York City to take the photographs of the Gershwin Theatre and *Wicked* advertising that appear in this book.

Writing a book tends to be a solitary occupation, and it constitutes a challenging addition to a busy faculty position and family life. Research on *Wicked* has been a joint familial fascination, and I have been grateful to Caitlin and my wife, Joy, for the interest and the support they have shown as I have spent many hours on this project. I dedicate this book to my miracle girl, Caitlin, who has brought her parents extraordinary happiness.

Note

1. Paul R. Laird, "The Creation of a Broadway Musical: Stephen Schwartz, Winnie Holzman, and *Wicked*," in *The Cambridge Companion to the Musical*, 2nd edition, ed. William A. Everett and Paul R. Laird, 340–52 (Cambridge: Cambridge University Press, 2008).

MUSICAL EXAMPLES

INTRODUCTION

The explosion in musical theater scholarship in the last few decades has resulted in numerous useful sources and different approaches to the area. Detailed studies of single shows have appeared, including for example Tim Carter's work on *Oklahoma!*,[1] bruce d. mcclung's book on *Lady in the Dark*,[2] and Jim Lovensheimer's look at *South Pacific*.[3] As each of these books bears an individualistic take on its subject with varied emphases and approaches, this current study also has been conditioned by unique circumstances. My analysis of literary and musical sources includes consideration of what materials were available, certainly the largest collection of scripts and musical scores related to *Wicked* that have been considered in such detail. What emerges in the three central chapters is a fairly complete picture of the development of *Wicked*'s script, its score, and the show's orchestration. The surrounding chapters place *Wicked* in various significant contexts important for fuller understanding. The subtitle of this book is a rearrangement of mcclung's anthropomorphic description of his tome (the title reads *Lady in the Dark: Biography of a Musical*), recognizing my dual interest in contributing to our understanding of the history of *Wicked* and my emphasis on the show's music and its creation.

Chapter 1 considers the importance of L. Frank Baum's *Wizard of Oz* stories in American culture, establishing why Gregory Maguire's novel *Wicked*—where the author turns Oz on its head and makes the despised Wicked Witch of the West a sympathetic, misunderstood figure—has resonated so deeply with readers. The chapter also includes a detailed synopsis of Maguire's novel, allowing the reader useful understanding of where the show's creators started as they worked on characters and plot. Chapter 2 is a brief essay on Stephen Schwartz's career before *Wicked*. Chapter 3 is a history of the show's creation, based upon interviews with the principals involved, a schedule of the process discovered in Schwartz's office, and other sources. The chapter complements accounts provided in books by Carol de Giere and David Cote.[4] Chapter 4 illustrates *Wicked*'s script development from Schwartz's first scenario in fall 1998 to changes made three years after the successful opening. The musical analysis appears in chapter 5, including consideration of sketches, deleted songs, a comparison of two piano/vocal scores dating from just before the show opened on Broadway and a year later, and other documents. Much of the analysis is cued to the original cast recording, but there are also numerous musical examples from sketches and deleted songs. The orchestration, primarily realized by William David Brohn, is the topic of chapter 6, with a description of the approach and interesting effects from each number, also cued to the recording. Chapter 7 covers *Wicked*'s reception by New York critics, and the lens widens in chapter 8 to include a description of each of the productions around the world. There is a detailed case study of the London production, ranging from its mounting in the West End to reactions from the London critical establishment. The final chapter places *Wicked* in the context of Broadway history and modern musical theater scholarship.

This study shares the dangers inherent in all scholarship on recent works. Additional scripts and musical sources from *Wicked*'s development will appear, and principals involved in the show's creation might write their own accounts that include more details on aspects of the show. The passing of years will inevitably clarify further how *Wicked* fits into Broadway history and how the show might be remembered. Carter, mcclung, and Lovensheimer had the benefit of extensive archived materials, the temporal distance of several decades, and the efforts of numerous previous scholars to bring greater perspective to their work. Similarly, it seems certain that an entirely different book on *Wicked* could be written in the future, but there is something bracing and compelling about interviewing a show's creators, assembling a historical narrative, and initiating the work on certain primary materials. What hopefully has emerged is a worthwhile story, one that will be refined and revised by future scholars in the field.

Notes

1. Tim Carter, *Oklahoma! The Making of an American Musical* (New Haven, CT: Yale University Press, 2007).

2. bruce d. mcclung, *Lady in the Dark: Biography of a Musical* (New York: Oxford University Press, 2007).

3. Jim Lovensheimer, *South Pacific: Paradise Rewritten* (Oxford: Oxford University Press, 2010).

4. Carol de Giere, *Defying Gravity: The Creative Career of Stephen Schwartz from "Godspell" to "Wicked"* (New York: Applause Theatre & Cinema Books, 2008), and David Cote, *"Wicked": The Grimmerie; A Behind-the-Scenes Look at the Hit Broadway Musical* (New York: Hyperion, 2005).

GREGORY MAGUIRE'S NOVEL IN THE AMERICAN LAND OF OZ

On a recent trip to Italy, my family stayed in a hotel in Milan close to the central train station. Just around the corner was a bar called "Il Mago di Oz," one of countless international confirmations one might randomly encounter that prove the ubiquitous nature of the fantasy *The Wonderful Wizard of Oz* (1900). Indeed, Suzanne Rahm has stated that this first book in L. Frank Baum's series of 14 has been translated into most major languages, including Chinese, Japanese, Portuguese, Romanian, Polish, Swedish, Turkish, Russian, Czech, Hungarian, Hebrew, and Bengali.[1] Baum set out to write an American fairy tale without the touches of horror that marked the famous stories set down by the Brothers Grimm,[2] but he never could have imagined the level of success he would attain. Given the importance of Oz and its most famous characters in American popular culture, it seems trite to call it the most famous American literary fantasy, but *The Wonderful Wizard of Oz* has been a significant part of the inner life of untold millions of children and adults for over a century. Such influence is more commonly found among religious texts.

Lyman Frank Baum (1856–1919) led a peripatetic and varied existence that included time spent as an actor, a salesman, the owner of a general store, a newspaper editor, an author, and a theatrical and film producer.[3] He was a good traveling salesman who supported his family in the china and glass business before he became a writer, but his penchant for risky business ventures kept his financial life far more interesting than his family might have wished, even after he should have made his fortune

1

through the Oz stories. He was born in Chittenango, New York, the son of a successful industrialist in oil and a banker who helped his son start a touring theater company with which he spent two years performing in his own play. Baum's father also gave him a small chain of theaters to manage, but he lost those in 1884. Baum married Maud Gage that same year, and two years later he published his first book, on raising a breed of chickens. Baum worked as a salesman in the family business, but it failed after his father and brother died. In 1887, the family moved to Aberdeen, South Dakota, where over the next four years of uncertain economic times Baum lost a general store and a newspaper he had purchased. He became sympathetic with the plight of South Dakota farmers and the political Populism gaining strength in the nation's midsection before moving his family to Chicago in 1891, where he began his successful years as a traveling salesman. Baum actively supported William Jennings Bryan in the 1896 presidential campaign after hearing his "Cross of Gold" speech at the Democratic National Convention that year in Chicago. He remained interested in Bryan's political fortune in 1900, when the famous orator and Populist again lost the presidency to William McKinley.

Baum's serious literary career began in 1897, when he wrote his first children's book, *Mother Goose in Prose*, and a volume of poetry, the same year that he started a journal and founded a national organization on retail window decorating, a career path he pursued until 1902. In 1899, he published the book of verse *Father Goose* with illustrations by W. W. Denslow, with whom he simultaneously worked on *The Wonderful World of Oz*. The year it was published, Baum produced three other books for children, and he continued to write books outside of the Oz series for years, but the work for which he is most famous was an immediate success. He did not intend at first to write more Oz books, but he yielded to written requests from children and published *The Marvelous Land of Oz* in 1904. Baum obviously never had purged his system of the theater bug, because he soon became involved in theatrical presentations related to Oz. The first was an extravaganza directed by the famous Julian Mitchell that premiered in Chicago in 1902 and ran for 293 performances in New York in 1903. It was revived for another 171 Broadway performances in 1904 and 1905.[4] The show was only loosely based on the first novel, but its success awakened Baum's desire to do more such shows. In 1908 he launched a series of theatrical productions called *Fairylogues and Radio*

Plays, which were unsuccessful and caused him to declare bankruptcy in 1911. In 1913, his play *The Tik-Tok Man of Oz* had a good run in Los Angeles, and the following year he formed the Oz Film Manufacturing Company, which produced five films before it failed. Baum was on the cutting edge of seeking commercial tie-ins with plays and films associated with his children's books. Demand for the Oz books and his own financial needs caused Baum to continue to write them, and he produced one per year for the last several years of his life. He died in 1919. His publisher hired Ruth Plumly Thompson to continue the series, and she wrote 19 Oz books over the next 20 years.

Given the wealth of political allegory to be found in Gregory Maguire's novel *Wicked*, and in the musical by the same name, it is fascinating to note that Baum might have intended something similar in *The Wonderful Wizard of Oz*. He stated in his foreword that he wrote the book "solely to pleasure children of today," but elsewhere he noted that he wished to write stories that "bear the stamp of our times and depict the progressive fairies of today."[5] Given the era in which Baum wrote the book, and his interest in the presidential campaigns of William Jennings Bryan, some scholars have interpreted the first Oz book as an allegory on Populism. Henry M. Littlefield was the first to publish on the possibility in his 1964 article in *American Quarterly*.[6] He calls the story a "subtle parable," with an especially clear sign being Dorothy's silver shoes on the Yellow Brick Road, a parallel to the political movement's call for silver to join gold as a currency standard in the United States. He sees the Wicked Witch of the East's spell on the woodsman's ax, which causes it to chop off parts of his body, as comparable to the Eastern banks foreclosing on Midwestern farms, and he notes that the Wizard might be any American president between Grant and McKinley. Dorothy is "Miss Everyman," and Bryan himself is the Lion. The Wicked Witch of the West might represent a political boss who enslaves the innocent. Slaying the Wicked Witch with water might be an allegorical confirmation of the importance of water rights in agricultural America. Littlefield concludes that "the author's allegorical intent seems clear, and it gives depth and lasting interest even to children who only sense something else beneath the surface of the story."[7] Geer and Rochon added another layer to this interpretation in 1993. Their primary dispute with Littlefield was which character represents Bryan, and they posit that it is Dorothy, building a convincing case that this major

Populist figure would exist at the plot's center.[8] The novel and movie have been analyzed over the last three or four decades from many platforms, and online investigation through such tools as the Literature Resource Center reveal other allegorical interpretations, feminist critiques, gay perspectives, and other postmodern readings. Suzanne Rahm provides a brief overview of Oz's interpretive history into the 1990s.[9] Continuing scholarly fascination with the story may be seen in a 2008 collection of essays edited by Randall E. Auxier and Phillip S. Seng.[10]

Many would know Baum's world of Oz if no film based on it had ever appeared, but the famous 1939 MGM film is one of the most important documents of American popular culture. Many saw it in its original release, and then the film developed into a yearly highlight for baby boomers when network television started to show the film annually beginning in 1956.[11] In those pre-VCR days, *The Wizard of Oz* starring Judy Garland was seen more often by more people than almost any other film, and many younger people have often seen the film at home. Hollywood studios, of course, are famous for taking liberties with a novel, and director Victor Fleming and his creative team made a number of changes, especially with the look of Oz. The silver slippers changed to ruby (dulling any Populist allegory), and the Wicked Witch of the West became the green meanie played by Margaret Hamilton that has scared generations of American children (including this author who remembers meeting the dust bunnies under his bed after seeing her on a black-and-white television in the 1960s). The major change in the plot comes at the end where Dorothy wakes up in her bed, safe and sound after an extraordinary dream. In Baum's book, Dorothy taps her heels together three times in the magic slippers and is taken home with Toto, fully awake, greeted by her Auntie Em. The film is so famous that it would be redundant to describe it in additional detail here. Neil Earle has offered interesting consideration of its context when issued in 1939 and how it has since been interpreted.[12]

The history of American popular culture is replete with projects based upon Baum's story, or that have provided glosses upon aspects of it. Gregory Maguire (b. 1954), previously a successful writer of children's books, decided in the early 1990s to write a fictional exploration of evil for adults, and it turned into an account of events in Oz from the viewpoint of the Wicked Witch of the West.[13] When one reads Gregory Maguire's

Wicked and then attends the musical by the same name, it is clear that the show's creators chose the characters that they wanted to use from the novel and told their own story.[14] Winnie Holzman has stated that this was their process.[15] Maguire's story is too long and complicated for a musical, with more characters than could be developed effectively. Maguire made Oz a dark place indeed and concludes with Elphaba seeming to descend into madness before she dies, and the show's creators needed to provide more hope at the end. A complication for every adaptation of a novel into a musical is that the songs and dances limit the amount of time there is for plot development. Songs might help tell the story, but far less plot can be explicated during singing than could take place in the same amount of time with dialog. Schwartz, Holzman, and Marc Platt, the principal producer who helped devise the show's plot, therefore had a difficult task in developing Maguire's sprawling novel into a musical, but they referred to many events. They often changed a circumstance's placement and meaning, and perhaps even to whom it happened, but a detailed synopsis of the show demonstrates how much of the novel actually remains in the musical. In the following synopsis of Maguire's novel, comparisons between the novel and the show are provided parenthetically. One can almost imagine the creators at work as they craft a coherent story for the show, probably returning to the novel on countless occasions looking for material and inspiration.

Maguire divided his novel into a short prologue and four other segments that correspond to places in the Land of Oz: "Munchkinlanders," "Gillikin," "City of Emeralds," and "In the Vinkus." Elphaba is from Munchkinland, and the first section tells her family's story and chronicles her birth, events that occur years before the remainder of the story. Galinda is from Gillikin, and in the second major segment we meet her as she goes to Shiz University. The majority of this section describes events at the school involving her and her friends. In "City of Emeralds," Maguire mostly tells the story of Elphaba living in Oz's capital city, where she has an affair with Fiyero and fights in a resistance group against the Wizard. "In the Vinkus" takes place seven years later. In the interim Elphaba has been living in a convent, and she has limited memories of what has transpired. She goes to live with Fiyero's family. Dorothy enters Oz, and the famous events from Baum's story unfold, but with somewhat different intentions and consequences than in the story that we already knew.

Prologue

The Witch flies over the Yellow Brick Road looking for Dorothy and her friends. She finds them resting under a tree and descends to perch in the tree and listen to them speak. They gossip about her possible identity and her life, little of it close to the truth. Dorothy says that the Witch must be in grief from losing her sister. A storm comes, and the four hurry away. The Witch hides from the rain and waits for another time to confront Dorothy so that she can try to retrieve the magic shoes.

"Munchkinlanders"

Maguire divided this segment of the book into eight subsections covering Elphaba's conception, birth, and early childhood. The man that Elphaba regards as her father is Frex, a unionist minister who frequently leaves his wife, Melena, to preach. Melena is the granddaughter of the Eminent Thropp, leader of Munchkinland. (In the musical, Frex is governor of Munchkinland rather than a pastor, placing the Munchkinland aristocracy on the other side of the family.) On the day that Melena gives birth to Elphaba, Frex is out preaching against what he considers to be a pagan device, the Clock of the Time Dragon. His message is unpopular, and the crowd assaults him and threatens his family, but women hide Melena from the mob as she gives birth to Elphaba. The child has green skin and sharp teeth, causing much consternation. As Nanny arrives—Melena's caretaker as a child—Melena reveals to her that there had been a visiting tinker who had plied Melena with a green liquid called "Miracle Elixir" that had made her dream of "the Other World." Melena does not remember if she had sexual relations with the tinker, but as the book progresses, one learns that she did and that he was the Wizard of Oz. (The musical does not consider Elphaba's birth in as much detail, and the child's only unusual physical trait is her green skin. That she is the Wizard's daughter is an important factor in the musical, because her parentage from both worlds gives her the ability to read the Grimmerie and makes her a powerful sorceress.) Frex and Melena are distraught over Elphaba's attributes, but they are unable to alter it through religious means, and Frex will not allow them to try magic, so they reluctantly accept this unusual child.

Frex continues to travel, and Melena is unfaithful. An itinerant Quadling glassblower named Turtle Heart (who does not appear in the musical) comes to their town, and Melena begins an intense affair with him, often when Nanny takes Elphaba to play with other children. Frex falls in love with Turtle Heart as well, and they perhaps share a sexual relationship. On a day that Frex announces that he will be leaving to preach in Quadling, Melena hastily says that she is pregnant and that the father is probably Turtle Heart. (In the musical, Frex is the presumed father of Nessarose.) Frex prevails upon Melena to take medicine to try to ensure that the child will not be born green, but it causes Nessarose to be born without arms and unable to walk. (In the musical, her only disability is that she cannot walk.) As one learns later in the novel, on the day that Melana gives birth to Nessarose, Turtle Heart becomes a sacrificial victim in a pagan ritual. Before he dies, he predicts that the House of Ozma (the current rulers of Oz) has fallen as "a ruby globe . . . falls from the sky" (the future Wizard's balloon). Elphaba has also learned her first word, "Horrors," which foreshadows what she will see and experience in her life.

The consequence of these events, as one learns later, is that Frex and Melena move to Quadling, partly so that he can seek forgiveness from Turtle Heart's family for his death. The family will not grant this, which colors the remainder of Frex's life. He dotes on Nessarose, whom he knows to be Turtle Heart's daughter, and nearly ignores Elphaba. This includes making jeweled shoes for his favorite "daughter," which he sends to her at Shiz when he includes no gift for Elphaba. (Frex actively favors Nessarose over Elphaba in the musical as well; he gives her the jeweled shoes as he leaves his two daughters at Shiz, and is dismissive of Elphaba.) Later Frex and Melena have a son together named Shell, and Melena dies during childbirth. (In the musical, she dies while giving birth to Nessarose.)

"Gillikin"

Years have passed. Elphaba and Nessarose are now old enough to attend Shiz University, but this segment, called "Galinda," opens with this member of a prominent Gillikinese family heading to Shiz.[16] The school's location is in Gillikin. Galinda is on the train to Shiz and has an awkward conversation with Doctor Dillamond. (The notion of a main character meeting Doctor Dillamond on the train appeared in early versions of the musical, but it was Elphaba and/or Nessarose who were on their way to Shiz. For Elphaba, however, this was not awkward; she has high regard for him.) Galinda arrives at Crage Hall at Shiz and meets the headmistress Madame Morrible, and she learns that she will live with Elphaba. (In the musical, all meet Madame Morrible after their arrival at Shiz, and both Galinda and Elphaba are horrified to learn that they will be roommates, bringing on the song "What Is This Feeling?") Galinda convinces Elphaba to try on one of her hats, knowing that later she will be able to make fun of her with her friends. (This is an important event in the musical.) At first Elphaba and Galinda do not get along, but they eventually become friends (as in the musical). Madame Morrible has a poetry soirée where she recites a poem critical of the Talking Animals, introducing the antipathy being felt for them in Oz. The final line is "Animals should be seen and not heard." (In the musical, someone writes this on the blackboard in Doctor Dillamond's history class, causing him to cancel class for the day.) Elphaba later questions Madame Morrible about her poetry and her feelings concerning the Talking Animals. (This is Elphaba's grand cause in the musical. Madame Morrible follows the Wizard's line on Talking Animals in the musical, but one does not know this until she has become his press secretary.) Galinda and Elphaba meet Boq, a Munchkin who remembers Elphaba from his childhood. Toward the end of this segment, Madame Morrible suggests to Galinda that she study sorcery, a skill at which she becomes quite proficient in the novel. (In the musical, Elphaba intervenes with Madame Morrible to have Galinda accepted into the sorcery seminar.)

The next segment, "Boq," is narrated by this Munchkin. He has become infatuated with Galinda, whom Elphaba catches him staring at through the windows at Crage Hill. Elphaba agrees to arrange a meeting with Galinda for Boq, and there he asks her to be his friend at least, but he receives little encouragement from Galinda. (Boq also makes his infatuation with Galinda obvious in the musical, but there she convinces him to ask Nessarose to the dance as a favor to her, which Boq willingly does, thus tying him to Nessarose against his will. He has little to do with Nessarose in the novel.) Boq has no trouble speaking with Elphaba because he has known her for years, and they become friends and confidants. Elphaba assists Doctor Dillamond with his research on the tissue differences between animals, Talking Animals, and humans. Boq and other male students start to help as well by checking books out of the library for him. (In early versions of the musical, Doctor Dillamond remained a scientist, and there he is trying to determine if there is any difference between the consciousness of Talking Animals and humans. Elphaba assisted him with his research along with Fiyero, rather than Boq.) Elphaba reports to Boq and others that Doctor Dillamond has made some kind of discovery, and she describes in detail how he sang about his discovery and she joined him in song. (When Elphaba and Fiyero assist Doctor Dillamond with his discovery in early versions of the musical, Schwartz turned it into the song "As If by Magic," probably inspired by this scene.) One of Galinda's friends, Pfannee (who also appears in the musical, along with Galinda's other friend, Shenshen), sends Elphaba a fake invitation to visit Galinda at the lake. Elphaba, Boq, and Avaric (another male friend) go there, and Boq gently kisses Galinda, who is touched, but nothing further develops between them. Boq finds a codex with a picture that might be the Kumbric Witch, a historical or mythological figure in Oz related to the birth of evil, a question that greatly concerns Elphaba during the novel. At the conclusion of the segment, Doctor Dillamond is found murdered, and Ama Clutch, Galinda's chaperone, has been rendered senseless after either finding the body or witnessing the murder.

"Gillikin" concludes with "The Charmed Circle," referring to this group of friends at Shiz. In honor of Doctor Dillamond, Galinda changes her name to Glinda, what he had always called her. (In the musical, she also changes her name, an insincere gesture that she hopes might impress Fiyero.) Nessarose and Nanny arrive at Shiz and room with Glinda and Elphaba. (In earlier drafts of the musical, Elphaba went to Shiz the year before Nessarose, but in the final version they arrive at the same time; Frex sent Elphaba to take care of her sister. Nanny does not appear in the musical.) Glinda's personality has changed: she is more serious and interested in others, and she and Elphaba are now friends. (Their friendship is not caused by a dramatic event as in the musical, where it follows Galinda's reaction to her embarrassment at the dance.) Elphaba tells Glinda about her family, that Turtle Heart was killed by a mob performing a pagan rite during a drought, and that her family moved to Quadling. Nessarose is religious, like Frex, and she does not approve that Glinda studies sorcery.

Fiyero, a Winkie prince, arrives at biology class late in his first appearance at Shiz. He is part of a disturbance caused by magical dust that the professor had just produced and gets attacked by a pair of enchanted antlers. (Fiyero's arrival in the musical shakes up the Shiz student body, but there he only leads them to a party.) Soon thereafter, the professor, who has replaced Doctor Dillamond, brings a young lion cub to class, intending to show how a simple operation will prevent it from learning to speak. Elphaba and a number of other students are outraged, and two women grab the cub and carry it from the class. (A similar scene also occurs in the musical, where Elphaba unintentionally puts a spell on everyone in the room but her and Fiyero and they take the cub out. Their subsequent exchange shows that they have started to have feelings for each other.)

The "Charmed Circle" starts to spend more time together. The change in Glinda has cooled Boq's ardor for her, but they remain friends. (In the musical, Boq remains infatuated with Glinda throughout.) Frex's gift of jeweled shoes arrives for Nessarose with nothing in the package for his elder daughter, who becomes envious. (In the musical, Frex presents Nessarose with the shoes when she arrives at Shiz.) In another gathering of the friends, they learn from Nessarose that Elphaba used to please her father by singing for him. They prevail upon her to do so, and she is very good. (There is no such scene in the musical, but it is notable that on more than one occasion Maguire has characters sing.)

Ama Clutch, who has been uncommunicative since Doctor Dillamond's murder, probably from Madame Morrible's spell, dies. Madame Morrible does not wish to leave her side, fearing what she might say, but Glinda and Elphaba push her out of the room. Before she dies, Ama Clutch tells Elphaba and Glinda that Grommetik, Madame Morrible's mechanical servant, stabbed Doctor Dillamond.

Morrible provides a frugal funeral for Ama Clutch and afterward brings Elphaba, Glinda, and Nessarose to her for a private conversation. Morrible wants to know what the chaperone said before she died, but the women report that they heard nothing intelligible. Morrible offers an alternative explanation as to why Grommetik was present with the goat's body, and then she tries to influence the futures of Elphaba, Glinda, and Nessarose. She says, "My special talent is to encourage talent." (Madame Morrible states this in the musical just before she takes on Elphaba as a sorcery student.) She wants the three to be "Adepts" who will live in various areas of the country as agents for the Wizard: Glinda in her native Gillikin, Elphaba in Munchkinland where she could succeed her great-grandfather as Eminent Thropp, and Nessarose in Quadling where she grew up. Morrible forbids their response and swears them to silence concerning the matter. (The Wizard and Madame Morrible wish to make Glinda and Elphaba important figures in the government in the musical. Elphaba rebels, but Glinda allows herself to be appointed "Glinda the Good," and Nessarose succeeds her father as governor of Munchkinland.) The "Charmed Circle" goes out for a drink in honor of Ama Clutch, and the boys urge all to go to the Philosophy Club, which offers a participatory sex show. Elphaba tries to talk them out of it, but most wish to attend. She tells Glinda she cannot because they need to pack to go to the Emerald City. At the Emerald City, Glinda sees poverty and other ugly aspects of life for the first time. They have a four-minute audience with the Wizard, who is unimpressed and contentious during their discussion of Doctor Dillamond's murder and the rights of Talking Animals. Elphaba is openly defiant. She declines to return to Shiz with Glinda and prepares to go underground and work in the resistance against the Wizard. (In the musical, Elphaba invites Glinda to the Emerald City to cheer her up when Fiyero has started to avoid her. They have an audience with the Wizard, but it is Elphaba that the Wizard is more interested in because of her powers—in the novel Glinda is the better sorceress. The meeting with the Wizard leads Elphaba to rebel, and she sings "Defying Gravity.")

"City of Emeralds"

Elphaba lives in the capital city and works with a shadowy group that opposes the Wizard. (Except for the affair that she has with Fiyero, also living in the city at that time, there is little in this chapter comparable to events in the musical.) It is five years later. Fiyero finds Elphaba at prayer in a chapel to St. Glinda, but she insists that she does not know him and avoids him. Fiyero follows her home and gains entrance to where she lives. They begin an intense affair, sometimes interrupted by her resistance work, which Fiyero learns little about. He runs into Glinda and Crope, another friend from Shiz. Glinda has married and has heard nothing from Elphaba; Fiyero does not tell her that he has seen her. Glinda misses her friend, and Fiyero hears that Nessarose remains angry with Elphaba for

11

abandoning her. The Oz equivalent of Christmas is Lurlinemas, and Elphaba tells Fiyero to stay home and not try to see her on the day before the holiday. He assumes that she has been given a major assignment and stalks her, observing that she is trying to kill Madame Morrible. Unexpectedly, her target becomes surrounded by children, and Elphaba abandons the mission. Fiyero goes back to Elphaba's room to await her, but the secret police arrive and kill him. Elphaba flees to a maunt, or convent, in the order of St. Glinda. (As in the musical, Fiyero and Elphaba are genuinely in love, and their relationship is complicated by her cause. Fiyero's life is changed by his love for her in both. In the musical, rather than being killed, she transforms him into the Scarecrow so that he cannot be hurt by the Wizard's men during torture.)

"In the Vinkus"

(By this point, the creators of the musical are telling another story. The only major correlations between the remainder of the novel and the second act of the musical are as follows: Elphaba goes to Kiamo Ko, where she is in possession of the Grimmerie and has a monkey named Chistery; she visits her sister as the leader of Munchkinland and declines to stay; Nessarose has become known as the Wicked Witch of the East; Elphaba has a second audience with the Wizard; and Dorothy comes to Kiamo Ko and throws the bucket of water that kills the Witch. Other small common threads between the stories will be recognized below.)

The first chapter of this section is "The Voyage Out." Elphaba has been living in the convent for seven years. She leaves in the black clothing that becomes her famous costume and with a young boy named Liir. The Mother Maunt places them with a caravan to Vinkus, where Elphaba wishes to see that Fiyero's family is well, to face his widow Sarima, and to retire from the world. Elphaba has a poor relationship with the caravan's cook and apparently causes bees to kill her, and subsequent events convince Elphaba to disguise herself as a witch. Elphaba now has the bees, three crows, a dog named Killjoy, and a monkey, who becomes Chistery. (In the musical, Chistery joins Elphaba after she gives him wings at the Wizard's urging.) The caravan arrives at Kiamo Ko. (In the musical, Elphaba goes there because Fiyero told her she would be safe; the castle is unoccupied.)

In "The Jasper Gates of Kiamo Ko," Elphaba and her entourage present themselves at Kiamo Ko, where etiquette of the mountains demands that they be welcomed. Sarima lives with her three children, two sons and a daughter, and her four younger sisters. Sarima forbids Elphaba from telling her story and asking her for forgiveness, and her sons are cruel to Liir. Elphaba finds the Grimmerie, a book of spells brought to the castle by an elderly man who said it came from another world. Elphaba discovers that she can read some of it. (In the musical she acquires the Grimmerie by taking it from the Wizard's palace when she runs away. She reads it easily.) Elphaba teaches Chistery to talk (she encourages him to do so in the musical). In a hide-and-seek game, Manek (Sarima's second son) convinces Liir to hide in a well and forgets him there. The adults save Liir. Nanny arrives after tracing Elphaba to Kiamo Ko. Elphaba wills an icicle to fall on Manek and kill him.

In "Uprisings," Nanny tells Elphaba that Nessarose has become the Eminent Thropp. She can now stand on her own because Glinda put a spell on her shoes. (In the musical, Elphaba performs this spell.) Liir reports that a goldfish in the well told him that his father was Fiyero, which Sarima rejects. Elphaba has accepted that she is Liir's mother, but she does not remember bearing him. Soldiers from Oz arrive at the castle and board there, over Elphaba's objections. She consults the Grimmerie hoping to find a spell that will depose the Wizard, but there is nothing of interest except a picture of Yakal Snarling. Elphaba wonders if she might be Mother Yackle who gave her the broom and has appeared at other important moments in her life. Nanny reports that a potion Melena took in hopes of preventing Nessarose from being born green was purchased from a sorceress named Yackle. Elphaba receives a letter from her father inviting her to Munchkinland, and she travels there by broom. She arrives and sees her father, who wants her to help Nessarose. Elphaba watches her pray over a woodsman's ax so that it will cut off the arms of the man who uses it (which produces the Tin Woodsman), a spell requested by a woman who does not want her daughter to marry the man. She pays Nessarose with a Talking Cow and Sheep that Elphaba frees. The Sheep no longer speaks. (In the musical, Elphaba works on behalf of the Animals, who can forget how to speak when persecuted.) She decides she has no more business in Munchkinland and returns to Kiamo Ko, where she discovers that soldiers have taken Sarima and her family away, leaving Liir and Nanny.

Wicked reaches its denouement in "The Murder and Its Aftermath." The tornado from the Other World that kills Nessarose arrives bearing its house and a young girl with her dog. Back at Kiamo Ko, Elphaba sews wings on monkeys. (In the musical, the flying monkeys are produced by Elphaba's spell, requested by the Wizard.) Chistery has only learned to speak monosyllabic words without apparent understanding. (He speaks a few words in the musical.) Elphaba learns of Nessarose's death and attends the funeral. Frex tells her that she was born to curse his life and that Nessarose's disability was a result of her mother's lax morals. Glinda arrives and infuriates Elphaba when she says she gave Dorothy the be-witched, jeweled shoes. Elphaba believes that Glinda wants the shoes to fall into the Wizard's hands, and they part unhappily. (Glinda is a much larger presence in the second act of the show than she is in the second half of the novel, but in both she gives the shoes to Dorothy.) The Wizard comes to Munchkinland and orders Elphaba to appear for an audience. He asks her plans for the Eminent Thropp line and knows that she has the Grimmerie. He says that most of Sarima's family has been killed, but he shows Elphaba that he holds the daughter Nor captive. He says he will return her to Elphaba when she turns over the Grimmerie. He tells Elphaba that it is from the Other World, and he is surprised that she can read any of it. (In Elphaba's second-act audience with the Wizard in the musical, he wants her to join him and return the Grimmerie, and he frees the winged monkeys as a good-will gesture. Elphaba is about to join him when she discovers Doctor Dillamond unable to speak.) Elphaba leaves Munchkinland and searches for Dorothy on the Yellow Brick Road. She meets Boq and his family. He tells her that Dorothy is charming and harmless. Elphaba decides to complete the task that eluded her earlier, flying to Shiz to kill Madame Morrible. She enters the old lady's room, discovering that she has just died. Elphaba smashes her skull and then goes to Avaric, a fellow student at Shiz from years before, to brag of her deed. Avaric tells her about the Clock of the Time Dragon, a magical device that can unravel mysteries. Its guard is a dwarf sent from the Other World. He tells Elphaba more about Yackle and arranges a presentation from the clock, which informs her that she is the Wizard's daughter and gives her a looking glass like one from her childhood where she pretended she saw the Other World. It includes pictures of her and

Fiyero at about the time they were having the affair. Elphaba returns to Munchkinland to tell Boq that she has murdered Madame Morrible. He deplores her action and tells her that she is out of control and that she should leave Dorothy alone. (This is very much like the advice that Glinda gives Elphaba in the second act of the musical.) Elphaba flies over the Yellow Brick Road, looking for Dorothy and her three famous traveling companions, but a storm hampers her. She returns to Kiamo Ko, obsessed with obtaining Nessarose's shoes from Dorothy. She turns more inward and drinks some of the Miracle Elixir, dreaming of the Other World. Nanny remembers that Melena used to have similar dreams. Liir, who befriends the soldiers in the Wizard's garrison near Kiamo Ko, tells Elphaba that they have heard that Dorothy and her friends are coming there to murder her. Elphaba is descending into madness, but she still has some compassion, going out on her broom at night to kill a soldier who has been severely tortured by his companions and left for dead after suggesting they kidnap Dorothy and sexually assault her. Elphaba begins to wonder if Fiyero might be disguised as the Scarecrow and coming home to Kiamo Ko. (In the musical, Fiyero does become the Scarecrow.) Elphaba sends her dogs, crows, and bees after Dorothy and the Scarecrow, Tin Man, and Lion, but the band defeats them all, and the Witch discovers that the Scarecrow is not Fiyero. She finally decides to welcome Dorothy in hopes of recovering the shoes, so she has the flying monkeys bring Dorothy and the Lion. They have a tense dinner, and Elphaba asks Liir to go elsewhere with Toto and the Lion. The Witch takes Dorothy to her tower room and asks for the shoes, but they will not come off. She wildly berates Dorothy, asking her unanswerable questions about the Wizard. Dorothy says she does not wish to murder the Witch, apologizes for killing her sister, and asks for forgiveness. Elphaba is horrified by the thought and accidentally catches her skirt on fire. Dorothy hurls a bucket of water to try to save her, but instead the Witch melts. Dorothy takes the bottle of green elixir back to the Wizard. All of Oz celebrates the Witch's death (as in the musical). When the Wizard sees the bottle, he knows that Elphaba was his daughter (again, like the musical), and he leaves Oz with his balloon just before ministers overthrow him. (In the musical, Elphaba fakes her death, but that is enough to overthrow the tyrant, with Glinda's help.)

Conclusion

From both a critical and a commercial standpoint, Gregory Maguire hit a homerun in his first at bat with an adult novel. Maguire now has three novels in a series that he calls "The Wicked Years," including *Son of a Witch* and *A Lion among Men*.[17] Maguire's fantasies have turned Oz into an adult's world, addressing the nature of evil and human motivation. Four scholars approach aspects of his first novel in the series in *The Wizard of Oz and Philosophy*,[18] just the tip of the iceberg for the debate this work has spawned. The creators of the show *Wicked* could not have addressed every level of meaning that Maguire brought to his book, but the novel inspired them to produce a musical that tells a serious story and deals with similar issues. Schwartz and Holzman mined Maguire's novel for characters, events, and attitudes. How they developed their story will be addressed in detail in chapter 4, with the study of several drafts of scripts. Informing that entire process was the creative team's knowledge and impressions of Maguire's absorbing novel.

Notes

1. Suzanne Rahm, *The Wizard of Oz: Shaping an Imaginary World*, Twayne's Masterwork Studies No. 167 (New York: Twayne Publishers, 1998), 9.

2. Douglas Street, "The Wonderful Wiz That Was: The Curious Transformation of *The Wizard of Oz*," *Kansas Quarterly* 16, no. 3 (Summer 1984): 91–98; accessed through Literature Resource Center.

3. For a detailed chronology of Baum's life, see Rahm, xiii–xvi.

4. *Internet Broadway Database*, www.ibdb.com, consulted 29 January 2010.

5. John G. Geer and Thomas R. Rochon, "William Jennings Bryan on the Yellow Brick Road," *Journal of American Culture* 16, no. 4 (Winter 1993): 59–64; accessed through Literature Resource Center. Geer and Rochon cite the following for the above quotation concerning "progressive fairies": Martin Gardiner and Russell Nye, *The Wizard of Oz and Who He Was* (East Lansing, MI: Michigan State University Press, 1957), 30.

6. Henry M. Littlefield, "The Wizard of Oz: Parable on Populism," *American Quarterly* 16, no. 1 (Spring 1964): 47–58.

7. Littlefield, 58.

8. Geer and Rochon, 59–64.

9. Rahm, 19–22.

10. Randall E. Auxier and Phillip S. Seng, eds., *The Wizard of Oz and Philosophy: Wicked Wisdom of the West*, Popular Culture and Philosophy, vol. 37 (Chicago and LaSalle, IL: Open Court, 2008).

11. Rahm, 109.

12. Neil Earle, *"The Wonderful World of Oz" in American Popular Culture: Uneasy in Eden* (Lewiston/Queenston/Lampeter: Edwin Mellen Press, 1993), 115–49.

13. www.gregorymaguire.com/about/about_interview.html, consulted 30 January 2010.

14. Gregory Maguire, *Wicked: The Life and Times of the Wicked Witch of the West* (New York: ReganBooks, 1995).

15. Telephone interview with Winnie Holzman, 29 March 2005, reported in Paul R. Laird, "The Creation of a Broadway Musical: Stephen Schwartz, Winnie Holzman, and *Wicked*," in *The Cambridge Companion to the Musical*, 2nd edition, ed. William A. Everett and Paul R. Laird, 340–52 (Cambridge: Cambridge University Press, 2008), 341.

16. In this study, Glinda will be referred to by this, her more familiar name, for generic references. When naming her in a section of the story, either "Galinda" or "Glinda" will be used, whichever is correct for that moment in the plot.

17. Gregory Maguire, *Son of a Witch* (New York: ReganBooks, 2005); and *A Lion among Men* (New York: William Morrow, 2008).

18. Auxier and Seng, 289–350.

STEPHEN SCHWARTZ BEFORE *WICKED*

Composer and lyricist Stephen Schwartz would be a noted creator of musicals even if he had never conceived the idea of adapting Gregory Maguire's novel *Wicked*. Coming of age at a time when the new popular music of the 1960s began to appear in the musical theater, Schwartz was one of the first to capitalize extensively on the trend. He wrote the music and lyrics to three major hits in New York by his midtwenties: *Godspell* (1971), *Pippin* (1972), and *The Magic Show* (1974). The shows with which he was involved for the next three decades were not as successful, and for a time around 1980, Schwartz became so disillusioned with the process of creating musicals that he briefly left the field. Returning to work on *Rags* (1986) as lyricist, Schwartz later went to Hollywood where he wrote lyrics to music by Alan Menken for two animated Disney features (*Pocahontas*, 1995; *The Hunchback of Notre Dame*, 1996), and then he produced music and lyrics for the DreamWorks animated film *The Prince of Egypt* (1998). About the time of this last project, Schwartz discovered Maguire's novel, launching him on the quest that led him to the premiere of *Wicked* at the Gershwin Theatre in New York City on 30 October 2003.

Carol de Giere worked closely with Schwartz on her authorized biography of his life, *Defying Gravity: The Creative Career of Stephen Schwartz from "Godspell" to "Wicked."*[1] She offers a detailed look at Schwartz's life and work, with histories of the creation of each of his projects, major and minor. She had regular access to Schwartz for interviews, consulted primary sources, and also interviewed many of his collaborators and friends.

Those who wish for a more complete consideration of his life and career should consult de Giere's book. This chapter is an overview of Schwartz's life and work before *Wicked*, based on de Giere, but also other sources, including my own interviews with Schwartz.

Stephen Lawrence Schwartz was born in New York City on 6 March 1948, the same year as Andrew Lloyd Webber. His father, Stanley Schwartz, enrolled in graduate school in Paris in fall 1949, taking his family with him. His mother, Sheila Schwartz, was interested in music and encouraged her son's passion for it from a young age. In 1951 the family returned to New York just before a daughter, Marge, was born, and in 1954 they settled in Roslyn Heights in western Long Island, where Schwartz grew up. A neighbor and friend of his mother was George Kleinsinger, a composer who wrote the music for *Shinbone Alley*, a musical based on Don Marquis's stories of *archy and mehitabel* that had a short run in 1957. Watching the creation of this musical had a huge influence on the young Schwartz, who began to attend shows in New York City and to fantasize about his own career in writing musicals. From 1960 to 1964 he studied piano, theory, and composition at the Preparatory Division of the Juilliard School of Music, his most intensive music study. Schwartz attended Mineola High School, where he was actively involved in theatrical productions, graduating at the age of 16.

Schwartz attended Carnegie Mellon University as a theater major between 1964 and 1968, specializing in directing. It was a traditional theater department where plays were far more important than musicals, but it gave Schwartz the opportunity to work in varied corners of the dramatic craft, assisting his future work and making him a confident contributor to later productions in areas besides music and lyrics. Another significant part of his undergraduate work was the Scotch'n'Soda musicals, original works mounted each spring semester by students from throughout the university. Schwartz was heavily involved in writing the works each year. His freshman year, he helped turn a show called *Whatserface* into a full-fledged musical by composing a number of new songs. The following year he wrote the score for *Nouveau*, which included a fugue that eight years later became "The Goldfarb Variations" in *The Magic Show*. His junior year, Schwartz worked with Ron Strauss on *Pippin Pippin*, which was so successful that Schwartz went to New York after graduation to pursue leads on getting a professional production of the show. (As will be noted

below, what opened five years later as *Pippin* had a completely different story and score.) For his senior year, Schwartz wrote an opera called
Voltaire and the Witches that served as half of the Scotch'n'Soda program.
These four shows allowed Schwartz to take part in almost every aspect of
creating a musical.

After moving to New York City, Schwartz auditioned songs from
Pippin Pippin for theatrical agents and recording companies. He became an artists' and repertory agent for RCA, where his real job was to
find new talent for the company, but it also gave him an opportunity to
work in a recording studio, an experience that made it possible for him
to produce most of his original cast albums. The theatrical agent Shirley
Bernstein, brother of Leonard, signed Schwartz as a client. His first song
for a Broadway production was "Butterflies Are Free" (1969) for Leonard
Gershe's play by the same name. One of the producing organizations for
which Schwartz auditioned was that of Edgar Lansbury and Joe Beruh,
who later decided to produce *Godspell* at the off-Broadway Cherry Lane
Theater. The play had been conceived by John-Michael Tebelak as his
master's directing project at Carnegie Mellon, and from there it had been
produced at the Café La MaMa Experimental Theater. Lansbury and
Beruh deemed the show's original score as unsuitable for their production, and they remembered Schwartz playing the *Pippin* songs for them.
They hired him to write a new score, bringing the composer/lyricist by
coincidence into a show that originated at his alma mater and whose cast
was primarily former students from there. Schwartz learned of the new
assignment on his twenty-third birthday, 6 March 1971, and he produced the score by early May. In addition to his songs, Schwartz assisted
Tebelak with directing the show and the musical staging. The show's
goofy but meaningful take on the Gospel of St. Matthew with Jesus and
his followers as clowns proved enormously popular, assisted greatly by
Schwartz's lively score based on popular musical styles. Most of the texts
were from the *Episcopalian Hymnal*, such as the popular "Day by Day" and
"All Good Gifts," but Schwartz wrote lyrics for "All for the Best." *Godspell*
ran until 1975 off Broadway and then spent more than a year at Broadway
theaters before its initial New York run ended.

Soon after *Godspell* opened, Leonard Bernstein met Schwartz through
his sister Shirley and asked the young songwriter to pen the English texts
for his theater piece *Mass*, commissioned as the opening production at the

Kennedy Center for the Performing Arts Opera House in Washington, D.C. Bernstein was far behind schedule, and Schwartz helped him figure out the work's sketchy plot in addition to supplying the English lyrics. They worked together rapidly during the summer of 1971; Schwartz recalls that they would finish one song and move on to the next, leaving the lyrics in a state that Schwartz describes as "first draft."[2] The controversial, uplifting piece continues to be performed, and the lyricist worked on a new version of the lyrics in 2005.

Schwartz had continued to work on *Pippin* as well, and he finally found a producer in Stewart Ostrow. Ron Strauss was no longer involved in the project, and the new book writer was Roger Hirshon. The plot had changed from a tale of intrigue at Charlemagne's court into a modern story of youthful exploration and experimentation that took place in the early Middle Ages. When Bob Fosse became director/choreographer, his vision took over the show, and Schwartz was relegated to supplying new songs as requested. *Pippin* changed in ways that the writers had not planned, but with Fosse's singular sense of showmanship, a plot with contemporary appeal, and Schwartz's expressive and popular songs, the show was a smash and ran for over four years. The songs included "Corner of the Sky," "Love Song," and "Morning Glow," among others, these demonstrating, along with the hits from *Godspell*, that Broadway had found a young composer/lyricist who understood popular music, and he could also write effectively for dramatic situations. After opening on 23 October 1972, *Pippin* ran 1,944 performances.

In late 1973, Schwartz received a call from Lansbury and Beruh about the magician Doug Henning, asking Schwartz to go see a show he was doing in Toronto. Schwartz was impressed with Henning's youthful appeal and astonishing illusions, and he agreed to provide a new score for a musical starring Henning that Lansbury and Beruh would bring to Broadway. Bob Randall signed on to write the book; Schwartz worked closely with them as they crafted a plot and song placements that would allow Henning to do his illusions. Schwartz remembers that he agreed to do the show as long as it would open during the current season, so he admits that the writing was done very quickly, and it might have benefited from more deliberation.[3] Despite their haste, *The Magic Show* opened on 28 May 1974 and ran 1,920 performances, about half of that number after Henning left the show. The show also had a national tour with other magicians. Schwartz has allowed the show to be removed from circulation; it can no longer be licensed for performances. Schwartz's score, however, showed his continued growth as a composer with such songs as "West End Avenue" and "Lion Tamer."

After huge successes in his first three commercial projects, Schwartz entered a period in which his shows found little immediate success, and he was destined to wrestle with each for years, trying to produce what he calls a "bullet-proof" version, meaning a show that groups can license that will offer them a possible success at the level that they are able to produce it. The hope was that the show's writing would have no inherent faults.[4] Schwartz worked with collaborators on his next show, *The Baker's Wife*, for nearly thirty years to get it in this shape. The musical's model was a 1938 French film, *La femme du boulanger*, directed by Marcel Pagnol, about a small French town full of interesting, conflicting character types who become closer when they finally agree among themselves to help a new baker who came to town and saw his young wife run off with a local lothario. Joseph Stein wrote the book, and Schwartz provided music unlike anything else he had written. He allowed his work to reflect the French story and sought influences from French folk songs, Debussy, the cabaret songs associated with Edith Piaf, and French film scores. David Merrick produced *The Baker's Wife*, and he booked the show on a long pre-Broadway tour with several stops in 1976. Schwartz and Stein tinkered with the show the whole time and actors came and went, but they could not get it right, and *The Baker's Wife* never opened in New York. Further revisions of the show included a version directed by Trevor Nunn in London in 1990. Stein and Schwartz finally declared the work completed after a Paper Mill Playhouse (Milburn, NJ) production in 2005. The show is available for licensed performances.

Schwartz's next show was *Working*, based upon Studs Terkel's book by the same title, in which the writer interviewed mostly blue-collar employees about their professions. Schwartz had the idea of adapting stories from the book into a musical, on which he collaborated with long-time friend Nina Faso, who also worked on *Godspell* and, later, *Rags*. Schwartz thought that the variety of backgrounds of the show's characters necessitated the participation of other songwriters more comfortable in contrasting musical styles, so his collaborators on the score included Craig Carnelia, Micki Grant, Mary Rodgers, Susan Birkenhead, and James

Taylor. Among Schwartz's songs in the score were "It's an Art" and "Fathers and Sons." Schwartz served as director and Nina Faso as associate director. The show opened in Chicago. The producers canceled a run in Washington, D.C., and took the show straight to New York for its premiere on 14 May 1978, where it only ran for 24 performances. Schwartz disagreed with the strategy because he did not believe the show was ready. Subsequent revisions soon after the show closed produced a successful version that became popular among regional and amateur companies, and it has since been revised twice. Despite the New York disappointment, *Working* has now been a popular show for three decades.

Rags, Schwartz's next project, ran for four performances in New York. The idea originated with writer Joseph Stein, who intended the show as an indirect sequel to his hit *Fiddler on the Roof* (1964). Here Jewish immigrants arrived at Ellis Island in the years before World War I, meeting with varied experiences, but the show included no characters from *Fiddler*. Many of those experiences were bitter and realistic, making the show a hard sell for audiences. Charles Strouse wrote the score, originally working with Hal David as a lyricist, but that collaboration did not work out and Schwartz joined the project, also serving as codirector with Strouse when the first director was ousted. The show starred Teresa Stratas in her only Broadway role. It opened on 21 August 1986 after three years of work. The collaborators have continued to tinker with the show, and there have been subsequent productions, but although Schwartz is still not satisfied with it he told Strouse and Stein that he has done with it what he can until somebody fresh comes to the project, such as a new director.[5]

Schwartz's other major show of the 1980s was *Children of Eden*, which started as a pageant called *Family Tree* with a book by Charles Lisanby, performed as part of a youth rally at the shrine of Our Lady of the Snows in Belleville, IL. The show covers the story of Adam and Eve and their family in the first act, and then Noah and his family and the Flood in the second act. As they worked to develop the project for a major venue, they sought a director, and John Caird came aboard. Caird had codirected *Les Misérables* with Trevor Nunn and also worked on the English version of the book. He began to work on the book with Lisanby and sought contractual credit for doing so, which Lisanby proved unwilling to grant, and he eventually left the project. Caird and Schwartz finished what was now *Children of Eden*, expecting a production in London by the Royal Shakespeare Company. After its cancellation, they went ahead with a full-blown production in London's West End in early 1991 that ran for only about three months. Schwartz and Caird continued work on the show through some subsequent productions, including useful input from director Ernest Zulia. A version at the Paper Mill Playhouse in 1997 was extremely successful, and *Children of Eden* has become one of the most popular shows licensed by Music Theater International. The pageant nature of the show, which includes children and a large chorus, makes it ideal for amateur groups but expensive for a professional production. Schwartz's score includes a number of musical influences from popular music and some non-Western sounds, and it is also Schwartz's first score that includes extensive use of sections of songs and musical themes returning for dramatic reasons. Schwartz has cited this score as an important experience preceding *Wicked*, a score unified in a similar manner.[6]

Schwartz's work in the 1990s included three animated features. For Disney, he wrote the lyrics to *Pocahantas* (1995) and *The Hunchback of Notre Dame* (1996) to music by Alan Menken. These projects began another phase in Schwartz's career, and the popularity especially of *Pocohantas* and songs like "Color of the Wind" made him a significant figure in Hollywood musicals. Menken and Schwartz won two Academy Awards for *Pocahantas*, including Best Score and Best Original Song. Schwartz then wrote the songs for the DreamWorks animated film *The Prince of Egypt* (1998); Hans Zimmer composed the instrumental underscoring for the film. Schwartz won an Academy Award for Best Original Song for "When You Believe," and the film has been one of the most successful non-Disney animated features at the box office. Schwartz went back to Broadway with *Wicked*, which he started at about the time that *The Prince of Egypt* came out, but he returned to Hollywood with *Enchanted* (Disney, 2007), where he again served as lyricist for the music of Alan Menken.

Schwartz's most significant project following *Wicked* has been his opera *Séance on a Wet Afternoon*, based on a novel by Mark McShane and the 1964 film starring Kim Stanley. Schwartz wrote both the libretto and the music for the work, which premiered on 26 September 2009 at the Santa Barbara Opera. The role of Myra was played by Lauren Flanigan, a highly respected interpreter of modern operas. Myra is a medium that tries to gain attention from the press by involving her husband with the kidnapping of a child that she will "find" with her powers. The remainder of the cast was also effective. Schwartz's son Scott was the stage director. Schwartz's music effectively captures the plot's inherent conflicts and otherworldly nature, and the score includes a number of motives that help tie the music closely to the drama. Other performances of *Séance on a Wet Afternoon*, coproduced by the Santa Barbara Opera, have been scheduled for the New York City Opera in spring 2011 and in Australia.

Schwartz has also been connected with a number of more intimate projects, including smaller musicals, recordings as a singer/songwriter, and incidental music. *Geppetto* was first written as a one-act television musical for the Disney Channel in 2000 with a book by David J. Stern. They turned it into a two-act musical in 2006 that premiered at the Coterie Theater in Kansas City, Missouri, responding to an invitation from Music Theatre International that they create a musical that could be done by a certain number of adult actors and as many children as a director might want to use.[7] Among the other smaller musicals with which Schwartz has been involved are *Captain Louie* (first conceived and premiered in the 1980s, revised and lengthened in 2005) and *Mit Eventyr* (*My Fairy Tale*), a Danish production for which Schwartz wrote six songs. He has written a score of incidental music for his son Scott Schwartz's adaptation of Willa Cather's novel *My Antonia* into a play, a project that has developed in various stages since 2002. Schwartz has also recorded two compact discs of his own songs: *Reluctant Pilgrim* (1997) and *Uncharted Territory* (2001).

Stephen Schwartz will remain famous for the musicals *Godspell*, *Pippin*, and *Wicked*, but *Working* and *Children of Eden* are regulars on the regional and amateur circuits, and *Captain Louie* and *Geppetto* might help keep his work in front of children as well. In addition, Schwartz has written lyrics or music and lyrics for four major Hollywood releases. He has yet to win a Tony, but he has Oscars and Golden Globe awards, and he has also won Grammy Awards as producer and composer for the original cast albums of *Godspell* and *Wicked*. Material success aside, however, it is the plethora of experience reflected in this brief biography that allowed Schwartz to be in a position to capitalize on the opportunity presented by Gregory Maguire's novel *Wicked*. As soon as Schwartz heard about the concept, he believed that it had the makings of a great musical play, a process in which Schwartz was the most important figure. The remainder of this study is an account and analysis of that endeavor.

Notes

1. New York: Applause Theatre & Cinema Books, 2008.

2. Telephone interview with Stephen Schwartz, 23 July 2005, reported in Paul R. Laird, "Stephen Schwartz and Bernstein's *Mass*," in *On Bunker's Hill: Essays in Honor of J. Bunker Clark*, ed. William A. Everett and Paul R. Laird, 263–70 (Sterling Heights, MI: Harmonie Park Press, 2007), 266.

3. Personal interview with Stephen Schwartz, New York, 18 March 2008.

4. Personal interview with Stephen Schwartz, Kansas City, MO, 26 June 2006.

5. Personal interview with Stephen Schwartz, Schroon Lake, NY, 20 July 2007.

6. Personal interview with Stephen Schwartz, New York, 19 March 2008.

7. Personal interview with Stephen Schwartz, Kansas City, MO, 26 June 2006.

COLLABORATION AND CREATION
Bringing *Wicked* to the Stage

The creation of a Broadway musical is a fascinating story to those who love the genre, full of interesting personalities and weighty decisions arrived at by harried collaborators. The drawback to such stories is that our knowledge is often merely anecdotal. Interviews with writers, the director, designers, and actors yield telling details, but the creation of a musical is such a daunting and time-consuming task that none of the collaborators can remember everything they did, and an interviewer will probably never have enough time with a person to draw out all the memories. Interviews also inevitably elicit different accounts of the same event. Sometimes varied versions of a story can be resolved, but when they cannot, it leaves even more questions. Documents such as draft scripts and compositional sketches provide answers and snapshots of the process, but much of a show's creation takes place in long meetings that usually can only be glimpsed by historians through fragile memories. Joe Mantello, the show's director, effectively stated this problem in an interview with David Cote: "Once these big shows are finished, everybody has their own version of who was responsible for what, and how it all came to be."[1]

Even with the difficulties of documenting the process, however, the "creation story" for a popular show such as *Wicked* is one that fans want to hear, and writers have helped fill the void. In her biography of Schwartz, *Defying Gravity*, Carol de Giere wrote more about *Wicked* than any other show or aspect of his career.[2] She founded a fan's website on Schwartz (www.stephenschwartz.com) in 2000 and remains its webmaster. De

Giere enjoyed considerable access to Schwartz as he worked on *Wicked*, and she conducted numerous interviews with the composer and others who worked on the show. She also incorporated material available in the popular press and produced an informative account of *Wicked*'s creative process. She provides insights into how the collaborators worked and generates hints of how the show changed and who might have suggested which alterations. The book is pitched at Schwartz's fans and others interested in how musicals come to life. In *The Grimmerie*, David Cote wove together interviews with principal figures to present some of the story in the first few chapters, devoting later chapters to other material, the most helpful of which for this project are Schwartz's brief essays on the conception of each song. The book's collection of photographs is impressive. *The Cambridge Companion to the Musical* includes my essay on the show's creation based on my own interviews with Schwartz and Winnie Holzman.[3] All three of these sources approach some of the same material, and, as is inevitable with sources primarily based on interviews, there are contradictions. This chapter will include a basic recounting of *Wicked*'s creation with additional documentary material found during research at Schwartz's office in New York City.[4]

Schwartz was on a snorkeling trip in Hawaii when he first heard about Maguire's novel from singer Holly Near on 16 December 1996. Schwartz has stated that a bell goes off in his head when he hears a good idea for a musical, and that happened immediately with this story.[5] It appealed to him on a fundamental level because Schwartz loves "to take familiar characters or stories and look at them from a different point of view,"[6] part of such previous projects as *Godspell* and *Children of Eden*. Soon thereafter he asked his lawyer to find the holder of the novel's film or theatrical rights. Demi Moore had purchased the rights, and Universal Studios was in the process of developing a script. In the ensuing months, Schwartz had lunch with Winnie Holzman at Disney, who had brought them together to discuss potential projects. He mentioned *Wicked* to her but lamented that the rights had already been purchased. Holzman had discovered Maguire's book herself in 1996 and loved the concept, and she was disappointed that the rights had already been purchased. Schwartz spoke with Marc Platt of Universal Pictures about the novel in 1997, urging him to shelve the film in favor of a stage musical.[7] Platt thought that music might be what was "missing from the screenplay" and also liked the fact that in a musical a character can turn to the audience and sing about personal feelings.[8] Schwartz remembers that at one point Platt wanted to develop the project both as a film without music and as a stage musical, but the latter became the sole effort.

A notation on a detailed schedule of *Wicked*'s creation in Schwartz's office (hereafter referred to as the "office schedule") states that Holzman was first mentioned as a possibility for writing the book for *Wicked* on 20 January 1998.[9] The composer was drawn to her as a possibility because she wrote convincingly for a young woman in the 1995 television series *My So-Called Life*, which starred Claire Danes.[10] In 2000, Schwartz wrote that Holzman "is particularly good at writing female characters who are funny, real, and believable."[11] Holzman was immediately interested. Schwartz himself wrote the first scenario for the show, completing it in September 1998. This has been published by de Giere and will be considered in the next chapter.[12] Schwartz, Holzman, and Platt collaborated in a number of sessions for about a year, completing another scenario on 21 November 1999.[13] Platt recalls that they worked with major plot points on note cards and pinned them to a bulletin board in his office, trying to make sure that they had the "show scene by scene, character by character," with "a beginning, middle, and end."[14] One of Holzman's major contributions was establishing the love triangle between Elphaba, Glinda, and Fiyero, and another major aspect of the discussion was making events in Act 1 effectively prepare for Act 2.[15] It was also Holzman's idea to invent a humorous, Ozian version of English that included different endings to various known word roots (e.g., "confusifying" and "horrendible") that would humorously help an audience know that they had entered another world.[16] After Platt, Schwartz, and Holzman finished framing the story, the real writing began, but Schwartz had already started some songs. Also, Schwartz had approached Gregory Maguire in November 1998 to convince him that *Wicked* needed to be a stage musical. Maguire had known Schwartz's music from *Godspell* and *Pippin* for years and found it easy to agree as long as "fundamental questions about behavior, appearance, deception, honesty, and courage" from his novel were respected.[17]

The creators primarily pursued the show's development through a series of workshops in New York and Los Angeles between 2000 and 2003. Schwartz is a strong believer in seeing how a live audience responds to material and was the veteran of many such events. Holzman feared the readings, calling them "horrifying," but she learned from Schwartz how to make them useful.[18] By inviting "certain core people," Schwartz and Holzman could receive knowledgeable feedback, in addition to reactions from other agents and actors who attended. Before a reading, the creators decided what they might hope to learn, and afterward they studied why a scene or song might not have had the intended effect. It was always possible that it was a problem with the actor, but Holzman notes that the actors tended to be very good, so her feeling was that when a line failed it needed to be reconsidered. Songs that did not land well with the audience might have been in the wrong place, or perhaps the problem was the song itself. Holzman stated that they needed to "weigh things delicately." She concluded that the readings were a crucial part: "That's how we made the show work, by doing these things and getting the feedback and analyzing what the feedback was and moving to the next stage."

Although readings could be called the "building blocks" of *Wicked*, at this point they are difficult to describe in any detail. Schwartz, Holzman, and others involved in the show mention them in interviews, but specific memories are rare.[19] As will be shown below, there is also conflicting information about the readings in print as interview subjects misplace details. An exception to this lack of concrete information was a collection of audio clips of the songs from one complete reading once available on YouTube, described in the appendix. Labels on YouTube stated that these were from a December 2001 reading (there were two that month, on 7 and 14 December), but Schwartz and his assistant Michael Cole were not certain of that identification.[20] No matter which reading the clips were from, however, they provided a fetching look at the show during its period of creation. In the following consideration of significant events and issues in the show's creation (presented chronologically), the importance of the readings is clear.

After Schwartz, Holzman, and Platt had worked out a plot to their satisfaction, finishing on 21 November 1999, Holzman and Schwartz retreated to the opposite coasts where they lived to write in preparation for an initial reading at Universal Studios, the audience of which included Stacey Snider, chief executive officer of Universal and the person responsible for deciding whether or not *Wicked* would go forward. According to a list of the show's readings compiled by Michael Cole and the office schedule, the reading took place on 23 January 2000,[21] but Carol de Giere states that it was in the spring of 2000,[22] and Schwartz also told Cote that it was in the spring of that year.[23] Winnie Holzman served as narrator, and the reading included three songs that Schwartz had written: "No One Mourns the Wicked," "Making Good," and "As Long As You're Mine." Two of the actors were Stephanie Block as Elphaba and Raúl Esparza as Fiyero.[24] The reading had its desired effect, and the writers were told they had a viable project and could continue working.

Intensive work continued through the remainder of 2000, with the office schedule indicating that the group worked together closely during the last week in June, and then Schwartz's "writer hibernation" began on 31 July. According to de Giere, he spent the entire month of August working on songs with minimal interruptions.[25] A number of songs were ready on 30 August 2000 (a collection considered in detail in chapter 5 where it illuminates the show's musical content at this point), and then September saw concentrated preparation for a reading of the first act in Los Angeles on the 28th, with the office schedule indicating a number of meetings through September. Holzman notes that the group had a large room at Universal Studios for rehearsal for about two weeks beforehand.[26] The reading took place in the basement of the Coronet Theater in West Hollywood and included Act 1 only, lasting over two hours. Stephanie Block returned as Elphaba.[27] This was the first reading where Stephen Oremus, recently hired as music supervisor, played piano.

Work continued following this reading. In the office schedule, Schwartz documented four meetings with Holzman during the last third of January 2001, and they finished a draft of the second act on 12 February, with additional work together in the following days. A reading of the entire show at Universal Studios in Los Angeles took place on 23 February, with a further presentation, after some changes, on 2 March. Schwartz has reported that he and Holzman received useful suggestions from many who attended the first reading, allowing them to make a number of improvements before the next reading only one week later.[28] Stephanie Block returned as Elphaba, and this was the first reading where Kristin Chenoweth appeared as Glinda. She thereafter remained in the role and changed the perception of her character. Chenoweth recalls that people noticed the chemistry between her and Block, and suddenly the show was about two witches instead of one.[29] Dealing with two main female characters became one of the prime tasks for the creators for the remainder of *Wicked*'s conception.[30] Other members of the cast included David Burnham, Marian Mercer, Michelle Duffy, Alan Zachary, Melissa Fahn, Beth Wishnie, Doug Ballard, Walter O'Neil, Jeannie Kaufman, Peter Blair, and Ron Fassler.[31] Another new member of the creative team at the March reading was New York producer David Stone, who was experienced with the Broadway business. Platt remembered the "overwhelming emotional response" from the audience at one of the readings.[32] It was through these readings that the team secured the remainder of the funding for their workshop process.

Cole's list of readings compiled in 2005 cites one of the entire show in New York in the middle of 2001. This is not mentioned in de Giere, Cote, or the office schedule. Cole admitted in a note on the 2005 list that Schwartz believed it included errors. Given the lack of corroboration in other sources, this reading probably did not occur. It should also be noted that Schwartz did not mention such a reading in his quarterly reports that he wrote for Carol de Giere's website in 2001.[33]

The team began to search for a director in winter 2001. In Cote, Marc Platt states that the search for this new collaborator began after the Universal readings in February and March, but Schwartz started to contact candidates for the position shortly after the first of the year. A number of names received consideration before the creative team made a final selection. On 11 January, Schwartz wrote an e-mail to Harold Prince, gauging his interest. He later sent Prince a script and recording of the songs. On 26 March, Prince replied, stating that he admired the material but did not feel that he was the right director for the show.[34] Schwartz wrote Prince back on 29 March and expressed his disappointment, adding that the singers Prince had heard on the recording included Stephanie Block as Elphaba, Kristin Chenoweth as Galinda, Lenny Wolpe as the Wizard, Marian Mercer as Madame Morrible, and David Burnham as the Scarecrow.[35] On 18 April, Schwartz met with Marc Platt and Matthew Bourne, a choreographer who later directed *Mary Poppins* on Broadway in 2006.[36] On 8 May, Schwartz contacted Michael Blakemore, an Australian director who has worked extensively on Broadway (including *City of Angels* in 1989) and in the West End.[37] Schwartz also contacted Trevor Nunn—who had directed *The Baker's Wife*, by Schwartz and Joseph Stein, in a London production in 1989—sending a script and recording. Nunn is famous for his work on *Cats* and *Les Misérables*. He wrote back declining the proposal on 21 May, but he praised the score and the conceptions of Elphaba and Glinda.[38] Director and choreographer Susan Stroman (*Contact, The Producers*) turned down the show on 25 June, and Greg Doran of the Royal Shakespeare Company was another director under consideration.[39] According to de Giere, Schwartz became frustrated with how long it took to identify a director for *Wicked.* He believed that the project required a director who had guided big Broadway musicals before, someone like Prince, Blakemore, Nunn, or Stroman.[40] David Stone suggested Joe Mantello. He had produced previous shows that Mantello had directed, and Schwartz had seen Mantello's production of Terrence McNally's *Corpus Christi* (1998), stating, "It looked like a musical staging to me."[41] In 2000, Mantello had later directed the San Francisco Opera premiere of the opera *Dead Man Walking* (by McNally and Jake Heggie) and the musical *A Man of No Importance* at Lincoln Center in 2002.[42] His name first appears in the office schedule on 3 April 2001, and according to the same source, they chose him as director of *Wicked* on 17 July. Schwartz reports that the director "responded immediately, passionately, and enthusiastically."[43] Mantello's participation on the show started in meetings with Schwartz, Holzman, Platt, Snider, and others in early August. Further consideration of his role in *Wicked*'s creation appears below. Schwartz announced Mantello's hiring on his website in his fall 2001 report, along with the appointment of Tara Rubin as the show's casting director.[44]

The office schedule documents an intensive period of work between Schwartz and Holzman from 11 to 21 September 2001, just after the tragic attacks on the World Trade Center. De Giere reports that auditions for Elphaba were scheduled to take place on 12 September, but they were canceled. Schwartz and Holzman worked on script revisions at his home in Connecticut. The rescheduled auditions occurred on 20 September.[45] As Mantello and Idina Menzel recounted for Cote, she was the first to sing, coming in with green eye shadow and lipstick.[46] These interview responses do not make clear that Menzel had more than one audition, but de Giere clarifies that Menzel received the music for "Defying Gravity" to prepare for callbacks.[47] The office schedule indicates that callbacks for Elphaba took place on 22 October, so that is probably the date that Menzel memorably sang the first act finale, but she also cracked on a note and swore in the middle of the song.[48] She had, however, made an impression, and she won the role in October, in time to rehearse for the December readings.

The office schedule includes specific dates for working on some songs in preparation for the readings, including "We Deserve Each Other" and "Bad Situation" on 6 and 8 November as part of getting ready for the December readings. According to de Giere, Menzel also suggested during this period that she sing the last verse of "Defying Gravity" up an octave, after she had started to work on her songs with Stephen Oremus.[49] De Giere states that there was a two-week workshop at the beginning of December,[50] an intensive period of work on the show confirmed in the office schedule by rehearsals from 3 to 6 December for a reading on 7 December, a meeting in Stone's office the next day, rewrites on 10 December, and work on the reprise of "We Deserve Each Other" on 12 December. The only reading in this series of events that de Giere mentions is on 14 December, but the office schedule and Cole's 2005 list of readings both state that they took place on 7 and 14 December. The second was apparently the most important, and the audience included novelist Gregory Maguire. (The office schedule supplies evidence that Schwartz stayed in touch with Maguire; there had been a meeting on 24 March 2001.) Carol de Giere was also at the 14 December reading, and according to her report in the book, Maguire enjoyed the show along with the remainder of the audience.[51] In chapters 4 and 5, we will consider scripts and musical sources that give a more detailed idea of what the show was like at this point. The office schedule shows that the creators met after the December readings, including a production meeting on 15 December and a conference call on 20 December.

Carol de Giere reports that Schwartz and Holzman worked together on revisions for a few weeks after the first of the year.[52] This preceded their return to California for a private presentation in front of Stacey Snider and other Universal Studios executives on 17 January 2002. The result of this reading was that Universal agreed to supply most of the show's budget of $14 million.

The next major project for the creators was detailed collaboration on Act 1, which was most in need of rewriting. In his spring 2002 update on his website, Schwartz stated that he had spent the last quarter (the winter) working on revisions because "it was time to pull the show apart and put it back together" based on what they had learned from the readings, with many of the problem spots in Act 1. These emendations included changes to every song and the addition of two new songs.[53] The office schedule for March lists script meetings between Schwartz, Holzman, and Mantello, in addition to work sessions just for the composer/lyricist and book writer. Other events of the month included a casting meeting, auditions, and a meeting for Schwartz and Holzman with Arthur Laurents on 20 March. (Holzman had studied musical theater writing at New York University with Laurents in the 1980s.) They found his input useful. The famous writer of *West Side Story* and *Gypsy* had serious reservations about the show, and it helped the writers learn what needed to be changed.[54] The day they met with Laurents was in the midst of three days that Schwartz's office schedule states that he worked with Holzman, and then on 21 March, Schwartz and Holzman met with Stephen Oremus and Kristin Chenoweth, presumably about Glinda's music. At about this time, Schwartz saw the revival of *Oklahoma!* that had just opened at the Gershwin Theatre, where he noted that Will Parker simply shows up early in the show and starts his number "Everything's up to Date in Kansas City," which gave him the idea that Fiyero should introduce himself through a song.[55] More work between the two writers took place on 26–27 March, and 28 March and the first several days of April included rehearsals for the reading of the new version of Act 1 on 5 April. Few details about this reading are available, but Schwartz did state on Carol de Giere's website at the time that it "went spectacularly well," and he also noted that Joe Mantello had started to make useful suggestions about scenes and events in the script.[56] Holzman stated to Cote that the director was especially insightful about how to tell the story of the Talking Animals.[57] Actors in the reading included Idina Menzel, Kristin Chenoweth, Adam Garcia as Fiyero, and Dana Ivey as Madame Morrible.[58]

The office schedule includes no entries between the 5 April reading of Act 1 and early July, and de Giere's book is very sketchy with dates for the remainder of 2002. She includes useful description of the designers and their work on *Wicked*, discussion of how delays with the script made it impossible for *Wicked* to open in New York City by spring 2003 as had been planned, how each creator worked together to create the *coup de théâtre* that concludes the first act with "Defying Gravity," and casting decisions.[59] The office schedule allows one to tease out some of the preparations that took place in the second half of 2002. Schwartz met with Oremus and Menzel on 2 July, surely about Elphaba's songs, and then a period of intensive work with Holzman began on 8 July in preparation for a full reading of the show in New York City on 29 July, an event that de Giere barely mentions.[60] In his summer 2002 report on his website, Schwartz described this as a "private reading."[61] This was apparently the last full reading of the show; the rehearsals were from 22 to 26 July. The composer's summer 2002 update also announced that the only finalized cast member at that point was Kristin Chenoweth and that the orchestrator would be Danny Troob,[62] who had worked with Schwartz and Alan Menken on the film of *Pocahontas* and who also has an extensive list of Broadway credits.[63] Obviously this did not happen, because William David Brohn orchestrated *Wicked*. Another plan that Schwartz reported in his update was the start of rehearsals in February 2003 for an opening in San Francisco on 14 April 2003, but that actually took place two months later. The office schedule is bare for August and September except for time in the recording studio on 13 September for the second set of *Wicked* demonstration recordings, necessary for designers and others as they worked on various aspects of the show.

Mantello has described how Maguire's novel served as a resource when designing the show. The map of Oz that hangs in front of the stage as a curtain for the show came "directly from the novel."[64] He also cited the Clock of the Time Dragon over the stage as a design element that came from Maguire.[65] This device is important in the novel but is seldom alluded to in the show; however, it inspired the prominent dragon jutting out above the proscenium and the main stage setting that makes it appear that the show takes place within the Clock of the Time Dragon, with the backward face of a clock sometimes on the backdrop and that same image at times projected on the floor of the stage as a shadow. The set also includes many interlocking gears and other pieces of machinery that give the feeling of a large clock. In the novel, the device is capable of manufacturing scenes for an audience, as it does for Elphaba by showing her mother copulating with the Wizard.[66] The show begins after Elphaba's "death," and then Glinda commences the flashback that is the greater part of the musical. It would be easy for readers of the novel to imagine that the Clock of the Time Dragon provides that flashback, but many in the audience would miss this detail.

Eugene Lee, the set designer, did an interview with Cote about his conception and the set. He based his clock concept on the novel and made a model with an assistant that he showed to Mantello, who liked it with some reservations, and then Lee showed it to the writers and producers at another meeting. He estimates that perhaps three-quarters of the original model remained in the final version of the set.[67] Lee's other influence, besides Maguire's novel, included W. W. Denslow's illustrations for Baum's original book *The Wonderful Wizard of Oz*. He derived no inspiration from the MGM film.[68] Lee had trouble selling the dragon over the proscenium to the show's creators, but he stated that it turned out to be "the most fun and cheapest thing we did in the whole show."[69] Glinda's bubble, another famous stage effect in *Wicked*, resembles the pendulum of the clock; Lee believes that Mantello conceived the notion of having bubbles emanate from the platform on which Glinda descends.[70] Lee also notes that the most difficult part of any musical is the transition between scenes, which in *Wicked* are immediate. His solution was "to deal with the space as simply as possible," meaning that he produced "a very simple design at heart."[71] In *The Grimmerie*, Cote provides many photographs of the set and facsimiles of several of Lee's designs.[72]

Cote includes brief statements from lighting designer Kenneth Posner, sound designer Tony Meola, costume designer Susan Hilferty, makeup designer Joseph Dulude II, and wig designer Tom Watson. Each describes a few major challenges in the show, and the section is richly illustrated. Posner worked with 800 lighting units to provide lighting and ambience to the show's 54 scenes and locations, finding the Emerald City the most "challenging."[73] The lighting for "Defying Gravity" at the end of Act 1 includes green fractured crystals behind Elphaba to help provide the illusion of flight.[74] One of Meola's biggest headaches was finding places for all of the speakers because he usually places a cluster above the proscenium, blocked for *Wicked* by the dragon.[75] Hilferty explained the costuming look that she developed for the two main characters and several of the scenes, noting, for example, that she used remnants of animals on costumes in the Emerald City, showing how the city's population accepts the Wizard's program to persecute the animals.[76] This is just part of a carefully conceived plan for the show that she recounted here. Mantello cited W. W. Denslow's illustrations for Baum's original novel and John Galliano fashion designs as influences on Hilferty's costumes.[77] Dulude primarily described the makeup for Elphaba and Madame Morrible, but he also commented on the chorus makeup.[78] The look of each character is also dependent on the 70 wigs that Watson designed, all but one made by hand from human hair.[79] David Stone, one of the show's producers, made a useful comment on the size of the production in a video interview when he stated that there were over 30 members in the backstage crew as opposed to 28 cast members.[80]

Entries in the office schedule for the remainder of the year show how *Wicked* headed toward production. There was a meeting about the set on 2 October, the day before the writers finished another draft. There were two major meetings of the creative staff on 7 and 8 October where they presumably looked over every aspect of the show. A casting meeting on 25 October preceded a dance workshop with choreographer Wayne Cilento on the 30th. Auditions of dancers were taking place because their callbacks were on 11 November, and other auditions took place on the 12th, 18th, and 19th, with additional callbacks on the 25th. The office schedule includes no entries for December 2002, but a production schedule from Schwartz's office compiled on 29 October 2002 states that 2 to 14 December was a lab for the director and choreographer.

Choreographer Wayne Cilento was a protégé of Michael Bennett who danced in *Seesaw* and *A Chorus Line* in the 1970s and has gone on to choreograph such shows as *Joseph and the Amazing Technicolor Dreamcoat* (1982), *The Who's Tommy* (1993), *How to Succeed in Business without Really Trying* (1995), and *Aida* (2000).[81] *Wicked* does not appear to be a major dancing show, but Cilento insisted to Cote that "there's dancing nonstop."[82] Much of this is imaginative stage movement rather than what an audience would immediately identify as dancing. Cilento worked closely with Mantello, with the goal being that "you don't know where the direction starts and the choreography ends."[83] Cilento stated that he "would lay down the movement road map," consult with Mantello about it, and then the choreographer "would physicalize it with the actors."[84] Cilento also described the movement styles that he conceived for Elphaba, Glinda, and Fiyero, and how he needed to vary the movement vocabulary for George Hearn when he took over as the Wizard from Joel Grey, more of a dancer. In a video interview, Cilento acknowledged that his choreography had to be part of the Ozian world created in the show: "I knew that everything I did would have to be a little bit strange."[85] Cilento states that his major influences as a choreographer were Michael Bennett and Bob Fosse, and he notes that he built on various styles of dance for the show, but he found himself "creating another vocabulary just for *Wicked*."[86]

The show's creators apparently had animated discussions about the best method for bringing *Wicked* to Broadway. Although out-of-town tryouts were standard practice for Broadway productions through much of the twentieth century, producers in the last few decades have looked to save that expense as the costs of Broadway musicals continued to spiral. Many new shows since the so-called Golden Age of the 1950s and early 1960s have never left town during the creation stage. Instead, shows began in previews at the theater where they would open, sometimes for weeks. *Wicked* had 25 preview performances before it opened at the Gershwin Theatre on 30 October 2003,[87] but that was after a full-blown tryout run in San Francisco in June and then a production shutdown during July and most of August for rewriting before starting rehearsals in New York. Schwartz argued for an intimate production outside of New York City to see if the story and music were satisfactory, and in spring 2001 he mentioned on his website that there might be a regional production of *Wicked* in early 2002,[88] but this never took place. Mantello countered that *Wicked* was not a small show, and he needed to experience a complete rendering of it to see how it worked. Schwartz, who had lived through the long pre–New York tour of *The Baker's Wife* many years before when they had tried to work on the show while it played every night, accepted Mantello's demand on the condition that they shut down the show for revisions after the initial run.[89] Both Schwartz and Holzman have insisted that the hiatus is one of the main reasons that *Wicked* has been so successful, but it was an expensive choice. David Stone told Schwartz that it cost about $1.5 million to keep everyone under contract for the summer.[90]

For Schwartz, 2003 started with serious attention to the score. Before this moment he had found his orchestrator by asking William David Brohn, the orchestrator of *Ragtime*, one of Schwartz's favorite scores.[91] Brohn made it very easy for Schwartz, reporting that he agreed to perform the task the first time that Schwartz telephoned him.[92] There was a scenic presentation on 8 January, and then sessions concerning the music on 10, 14, and 17 January. The three meetings involved music director Stephen Oremus, director Joe Mantello, choreographer Wayne Cilento, orchestrator David William Brohn, dance arranger James Lynn Abbott, arranger Alex Lacamoire, and percussionist Gary Seligson, although not all were present at every meeting. Michael Cole perhaps described the meeting of 14 January (notated in the office schedule as the four going through the score) for de Giere when Schwartz, Brohn, Oremus, and Lacamoire discussed the entire score together, trying to decide what the *Wicked* orchestra would sound like. Cole stated that they were mostly in agreement, and the same day Schwartz had a meeting with Holzman about two scenes they were reworking.[93] Rehearsals for San Francisco were to begin on the last day of March. Orchestrations and dance arrangements did not need to be finished on that precise day, but it was during the first few months of the year that the piano/vocal version of the score was to be completed so that Brohn could start the orchestrations. The orchestration will be described in detail in chapter 6.

The office schedule provides few entries for February or March. There was another meeting with Arthur Laurents on 25 February. A production schedule from 29 October 2002 states that 17 to 28 March were preproduction dance weeks.[94] There was a rehearsal on 27 March, and then the cast began a full rehearsal schedule for San Francisco on 31 March at 890 Broadway, studios opened by Michael Bennett after his huge success with *A Chorus Line*.[95] The show's first run-through was on 2 April. Carol de Giere describes some details of the rehearsals.[96] She also reveals that Schwartz wrote the second version of "What Is This Feeling?" once the rehearsals had started, replacing a lower-energy version of the song that Mantello had disliked.[97] (How the music changed for this song placement will be considered in chapter 5.) A battle being fought behind the scenes at this point concerned changes in the script required by lawyers from Universal Studios who did not want their employer to be exposed to lawsuits for images and lines used in the show for which they did not have the copyright. It was a rough road for Schwartz and Holzman, who saw some of their work thrown out by people not directly involved in the show. Schwartz fights for what he thinks is right in such situations, a trait that he has shown in a number of his collaborations. One of the points of contention was whether or not the famous slippers could be red. The lawyers finally allowed the creators to use a red light on the slippers.[98]

Mantello has stated that a major problem in the story even as late as the San Francisco run was how to handle the Wizard's persecution of the Talking Animals and making that Elphaba's great cause.[99] The plot element had to be covered in sufficient detail for the audience to understand its importance to Elphaba, but it could not be made, as Mantello said, "so complicated that it would bore the audience."[100] As will be seen in chapter 4, Doctor Dillamond at one point was a scientist, as in the novel, performing experiments to prove that Talking Animals were worthy of respect. Laboratory scenes established his credentials, and then a funeral occurred after Dillamond's suspicious death. In an interview, Schwartz said that these plot devices approached science fiction,[101] and they finally decided instead to make Doctor Dillamond a historian who helps politicize Elphaba without requiring as much time as the scientific angle.

The San Francisco tryout was in the Curran Theater. Technical rehearsals started there on 15 May, and the first run-through of the show with orchestra—an event known as the *Sitzprobe* (German, literally "seat tryout") in musical theater and operatic parlance—took place on 23 May. The first dress rehearsal was the following day, with previews beginning on 28 May. (Carol de Giere reports that dress rehearsals for each act took two nights, meaning that the first time the show ran straight through was at the first preview.[102]) Opening night was 10 June, with the run lasting until 29 June (according to the office schedule). De Giere wrote a chapter on the San Francisco run that mostly covers the creative battles fought behind the scenes.[103] They were especially intense in San Francisco because the producers had told Schwartz and Holzman to save their notes about the show until after the first preview. When finally given the opportunity to speak, the composer had much to say. It was one of the first of a number of major skirmishes between the writers and Mantello that continued until *Wicked* opened successfully on Broadway. Schwartz and Holzman were not even contented with their changes after the premiere; as will be shown in chapters 4 and 5, revisions to the script and music continued until as much as three years after the show opened. For Schwartz, this was simply part of the collaborative process. The two writers were supportive of each other and presented a united front when meeting with other collaborators. Schwartz described his work with Holzman and their cooperation: "We really respected one another, we listened to one another; we stood firm as an authorial unit at times when there was great pressure for us not to."[104]

David Cote's interviews with *Wicked*'s creators and principals substantially illuminate the company's experiences in San Francisco. Marc Platt comments that, despite the cost, the "first-class production" there was "very constructive."[105] He also reports that the summer shutdown had been planned well before San Francisco, and it would take place no matter what the result of the run there might have been. David Stone thought that the audience there was more accepting of problems than a New York audience would have been during previews.[106] Winnie Holzman emphasized the "single-mindedness" of the experience in San Francisco, with only the show to work on, and also how the creators had to consider every element of the production as they tried to figure out why a scene or a song did not work.[107] Joe Mantello described the "tweaks" they made to the show there involving the Shiz scene in Act 1, the funeral for Doctor Dillamond in the show at that time, and their attempts to give Elphaba's characterization more "fire and irony."[108] Schwartz noted how shocking he found seeing the set, costumes, and lighting plots on stage for the first time, apparently always a difficult moment for him when preparing a show. He found himself simply avoiding Mantello so that he would not gripe about what he disliked.[109] Idina Menzel reported that actors needed to learn new lines some mornings for that night's show, and that songs got moved around during the tryout period.[110] Several figures described how successful *Wicked* was in San Francisco, despite the fact that the show was still too long and had some problems.

Carol de Giere has described the contentious summer of rewrites that preceded the Broadway opening.[111] Schwartz and Holzman wanted to work on the rewrites alone before involving the creators, a course of action that did not sit well with Mantello.[112] In a quarterly report to his website after the San Francisco run, Schwartz confessed his interest in what the critics wrote, reporting that "We've taken a lot of what they said to heart and tried to address it."[113] Schwartz and Holzman have both described the surgery performed on Elphaba's role, but they do not agree on how much was actually done, another place where we run into creators trying to remember details from the midst of a long, demanding project. Schwartz stated, "She was the difficult character to solve. . . . I seemed to know how to write her musically. It took quite a while for Winnie to get the tone for her in terms of dialog . . . and storytelling." He estimated that they changed 80 percent of Elphaba's lines during the summer shutdown.[114] Holzman believed that the changes were not so drastic, offering, "It was really more delicate than that. We would change a line here, a line there."[115] Her recollection was that most of these changes took place early in the show, clarifying Elphaba's motivations and drawing her character more carefully. Once those changes were made, it was not necessary to rewrite extensively in the second act. As will be shown in chapter 4, the scripts that Schwartz's office made available for this study unfortunately do not include any that make possible a direct comparison between the San Francisco version of the show and what opened on Broadway, but scripts consulted from earlier in *Wicked*'s development seem to show that Holzman is closer to the truth here than Schwartz. Elphaba's part in the Broadway version of the show is too similar to earlier versions for there to have been changes in 80 percent of her lines. Holzman, however, told a different story in an interview with *Playbill.com*, where she described friends who saw *Wicked* in both San Francisco and New York and were unable to point out what had been changed even though she "rewrote on every page." They were careful "so as not to disturb the things that were working."[116] One of Schwartz's main efforts during the shutdown was to solidify the score's motivic unity, working musical snippets into places where they help clarify the story, an aspect of the score that will be covered in chapter 5.

Mantello commented penetratingly on the writing process to David Cote, noting that the "book writing has to be the most accommodating . . . because it is the glue that holds everything together."[117] He gives the example that extra lines might be needed so that an actor can move to another position to make an entrance, and there are also adjustments made in the book during a show's creation because of musical needs. Mantello offered that Schwartz and Holzman probably had not received enough credit for the show's plot,[118] which some people probably think came to a greater extent from Maguire's novel than it actually did. Mantello cited how Schwartz and Holzman worked aspects of the MGM film into the plot and also how Boq and Fiyero became the Tin Woodsman and Scarecrow.[119] The transformation of Boq appears only in the musical. In the novel, Elphaba wonders if the Scarecrow might be Fiyero returning to her, but she learns this is not the case before her death.[120]

The office schedule provides a list of events that leads the countdown to the Broadway opening, a period that de Giere covered extensively.[121] There was a meeting between Schwartz, Holzman, Platt, and Mantello on 19 June 2003, perhaps one where the rewriting controversy began to become clear. The composer/lyricist knew at that point that Fiyero needed a new song of introduction, and he worked on the lyrics to "Dancing through Life" on 21 June while flying from San Francisco to Denver.

As Schwartz explained to de Giere in an interview in early July 2003, he planned to write multiple versions of the song and let his colleagues pick the one that they liked most,[122] a process that will be described in more detail in chapter 5 (see pp. 137–38). Another important part of July and August was deciding the Broadway cast, and among the most important changes was Joel Grey replacing Robert Morse as the Wizard,[123] a substitution that caused some rewriting, as will be discussed in chapter 5. Holzman finished the rehearsal draft of the script on 14 August. The first read-through of the new script with the cast took place on 25 August, starting the rehearsal process for New York. The *Sitzprobe* for the new score and orchestrations was on 26 September, and after 25 previews, *Wicked* opened on 30 October at the Gershwin Theatre. Consideration of its critical reception appears in chapter 7 (see pp. 251–59). Other late tasks that faced Schwartz before the show opened he names in his quarterly update on his website from fall 2003: working on music for the show's radio advertisements, adding "new intro verses to songs which involve reprise material" to help unify the score, and on 10 November 2003 he began to record the original cast album with the cast and orchestra.[124]

The compact disc sold very successfully and helped make *Wicked* a hit. Its recording process came at the end of this skeleton of the show's creation history, which can now be fleshed out in chapters 4 and 5 through consideration of draft scripts and musical manuscripts that date between 1998 and 2006. They prove that writing a musical is not for the lazy or faint of heart: no brainless scarecrow, heartless tin man, or cowardly lion would have wanted to stick with this process, with or without a road of yellow bricks.

Notes

1. David Cote, *"Wicked": The Grimmerie; A Behind-the-Scenes Look at the Hit Broadway Musical* (New York: Hyperion, 2005), 71.

2. Carol de Giere, *Defying Gravity: The Creative Career of Stephen Schwartz from "Godspell" to "Wicked"* (New York: Applause Theatre & Cinema Books, 2008).

3. Paul R. Laird, "The Creation of a Broadway Musical: Stephen Schwartz, Winnie Holzman, and *Wicked*," in *The Cambridge Companion to the Musical*, 2nd edition, ed. William A. Everett and Paul R. Laird, 340–52 (Cambridge: Cambridge University Press, 2008).

4. I would like to thank Stephen Schwartz and his assistant Michael Cole for the opportunity to work in his office on 20 March 2008.

5. Personal interview by the author with Stephen Schwartz, New York, 22 March 2005, reported in Laird, "The Creation of a Broadway Musical," 340.

6. "Stephen Schwartz's Update Fall 2000," www.musicalschwartz.com/schwartzscene/schwartz-scene-01-12.htm#spark01 (accessed 28 July 2010).

7. Some aspects of this chronology are difficult to establish with certainty. Material in Schwartz's office and an interview with him in Cote (p. 21) suggest that he met Platt about the project in 1997, but Carol de Giere states that Schwartz first met with Platt on 13 November 1998 (p. 287), which seems late. Schwartz has usually indicated that he spoke with Platt before inviting Holzman into the project, and that would appear to have happened before late fall 1998. De Giere states that Schwartz started to work with Holzman in 1999 (p. 292), so the chronology presented in her book is consistent. What is certain is that Schwartz finished his first scenario in September 1998, and he completed the revised version with Holzman and Platt on 21 November 1999.

8. Cote, 21.

9. Schedule of *Wicked*'s creation, an unpublished document accessed in Stephen Schwartz's office, 20 March 2008.

10. Holzman has stated (Cote, 71) that in *Wicked* she did not set out to write a story about female friendships, and she was surprised when women began to react to the show in the way that they did.

11. "Stephen Schwartz's Update Fall 2000" (accessed 28 July 2008).

12. de Giere, 503–9.

13. *Wicked* Outline 11/21/99, unpublished document made available by Stephen Schwartz's office.

14. Cote, 22. Photos of four of these note cards appear in Cote, 23.

15. de Giere, 296–98.

16. Cote includes a glossary of these words, 190–91.

17. Cote, 22.

18. Telephone interview with Winnie Holzman, 29 March 2005, reported in Laird, "The Creation of a Broadway Musical," 342. The other quotations in this paragraph are also derived from this source.

19. While working on my chapter for the second edition of *The Cambridge Companion to the Musical*, I asked both Schwartz and Holzman detailed questions about the readings, but their answers tended to be general and more about the process than specific readings. This is not surprising because there were at least nine readings, some in close succession, and they were part of a process that took four years. Few people would remember each reading in detail. Carol de Giere does not cover the readings in real detail in her book, and she attended some.

20. In two e-mail messages from Michael Cole (Stephen Schwartz's assistant) on 10 January 2010, neither Schwartz nor Cole could be certain that these clips were from December 2001, citing discrepancies between what they heard and their memories of the event.

21. Cole provided this date in an e-mail from 27 March 2005, and it also appears on a schedule of *Wicked*'s creation from Schwartz's office.

22. Carol de Giere places this reading in the spring of 2000 but does not provide a date (p. 313).

23. Cote, 22. Schwartz also remembered here that the reading was at the Coronet Theater in Los Angeles, but that seems to have been the next reading in the fall.

24. de Giere, 313–14.

25. de Giere, 314.

26. Cote, 22.

27. de Giere lists the other actors in the reading (p. 314).

28. "Stephen Schwartz's Update Spring 2001," www.musicalschwartz.com/schwartzscene/schwartz-scene-01-12.htm#spark03 (accessed 29 July 2010).

29. Cote, 24.

30. de Giere considers this issue on page 330.

31. "Stephen Schwartz's Update Spring 2001" (accessed 28 July 2010).

32. Cote, 24.

33. www.musicalschwartz.com/schwartzscene/schwartz-scene-01-12.htm (accessed 28 July 2010).

34. Unpublished e-mail from Harold Prince to Stephen Schwartz, 26 March 2001.

35. These were singers from the February and March readings, meaning that Schwartz probably did not send the recording until after 2 March.

36. Internet Broadway Database, www.ibdb.com (accessed 28 July 2010).

37. "Michael Blakemore Biography (1928–)," www.filmreference.com/film/19/Michael-Blakemore.html (accessed 28 July 2010).

38. Unpublished letter from Trevor Nunn to Stephen Schwartz, 21 May 2001.

39. Undated, unpublished letter from Greg Doran to Stephen Schwartz. Unpublished letter from Susan Stroman to Stephen Schwartz, 25 June 2001.

40. de Giere, 336.

41. Personal interview with Stephen Schwartz, New York, 22 March 2005, reported in Laird, "The Creation of a Broadway Musical," 343.

42. Cote, 25.

43. Personal interview with Stephen Schwartz, New York, 22 March 2005, reported in Laird, "The Creation of a Broadway Musical," 344.

44. Stephen Schwartz Update Fall 2001," www.musicalschwartz.com/schwartzscene/schwartz-scene-01-12.htm#spark05 (accessed 7 April 2010).

45. de Giere, 339–40.

46. Cote, 26–28.

47. de Giere, 340.

48. Cote, 26–28.

49. de Giere, 341–42.

50. de Giere, 342.

51. de Giere, 345.

52. de Giere, 346.

53. "Stephen Schwartz Update Spring 2002," www.musicalschwartz.com/schwartzscene/schwartz-scene-01-12.htm#spark07 (accessed 7 April 2010).

54. See de Giere, 330–31, for a description of this meeting.

55. de Giere, 350.

56. de Giere, 356. Interesting video confirmation of Mantello's role in work on the script may be seen in his decision to "reorder" aspects of the script on the video "*Wicked*: The Road to Broadway," an extra feature on disc 3 of *B'Way/Broadway: The American Musical*, directed by Michael Kantor (Educational Broadcasting Corporation and the Broadway Film Project, 2004).

57. Cote, 71.

58. "Stephen Schwartz Update Spring 2002," accessed 7 April 2010.

59. de Giere, 361–73.

60. de Giere, 356.

61. "Stephen Schwartz Update Summer 2002," www.musicalschwartz.com/schwartzscene/schwartz-scene-01-12.htm#spark08 (accessed 7 April 2010).

62. "Stephen Schwartz Update Summer 2002" (accessed 7 April 2010).

63. Internet Broadway Database, www.ibdb.com (consulted 30 November 2010).

64. Cote, 71.

65. Cote, 71–73.

66. Maguire, 375.

67. Cote, 91.

68. Cote, 91.

69. Cote, 92.

70. Cote, 92.

71. Cote, 92.

72. Cote, 93–114. Another useful source on the stage design, costumes, lighting, and sound design for *Wicked*, written from the standpoint of technical work in the theater, is David Barbour and David Johnson, "Hocus Pocus: Envisioning

the Fantastical Land of Oz for Broadway's *Wicked*," *Entertainment Design* 38, no. 2 (February 2004): 16–23.

73. Cote, 115.

74. Cote, 116.

75. Cote, 116.

76. Cote, 120. Hilferty described the costume production as "haute couture" in a video interview, noting that each costume is handmade for a specific actor. See "*Wicked*: The Road to Broadway," an extra feature on disc 3 of *B'Way/Broadway: The American Musical*, directed by Michael Kantor (Educational Broadcasting Corporation and the Broadway Film Project, 2004).

77. Cote, 136.

78. Cote, 128–30.

79. Cote, 131.

80. "*Wicked*: The Road to Broadway."

81. Internet Broadway Database, www.ibdb.com (consulted 31 August 2010).

82. Cote, 135.

83. Cote, 134.

84. Cote, 134.

85. "*Wicked*: The Road to Broadway."

86. "*Wicked*: The Road to Broadway."

87. Internet Broadway Database, www.ibdb.com (consulted 14 February 2010).

88. Stephen Schwartz's Update Spring 2001" (accessed 7 April 2010).

89. Personal interview with Stephen Schwartz, New York, 22 March 2005, reported in Laird, "The Creation of a Broadway Musical," 345–46.

90. Personal interview with Stephen Schwartz, New York, 22 March 2005, and telephone interview with Winnie Holzman, 29 March 2005, both reported in Laird, "The Creation of a Broadway Musical," 346.

91. Personal interview with Stephen Schwartz, New York, 22 November 2008.

92. Personal interview with William David Brohn, New York, 22 November 2008.

93. de Giere, 375.

94. This document was consulted in Schwartz's office.

95. There is considerable video footage of rehearsals in New York on 30 April and 1 May 2003 in "*Wicked*: The Road to Broadway," as well as interviews with important figures in the show's creation and footage from the premiere performance at the Curran Theater in San Francisco on 28 May 2003. The show is also covered with different footage in "Episode Six: Putting It Together (1980–2004)" of *B'Way/Broadway: The American Musical*.

96. de Giere, 376–79.

97. de Giere, 378–79, and personal interview with Stephen Schwartz, New York, 22 March 2005, reported in Laird, "The Creation of a Broadway Musical," 344. Schwartz also noted in his spring 2003 update that he and Holzman had written new material during the rehearsals in New York, including a new song. See "Stephen Schwartz Update Spring 2003," www .musicalschwartz.com/schwartzscene/schwartz-scene-01-12.htm#spark11 (accessed 7 April 2010). This song was "to solve a problem spot that has plagued us for some time."

98. For details on these legal squabbles, see de Giere, 382–85.

99. Cote, 71–73.

100. Cote, 71.

101. Personal interview with Stephen Schwartz, New York, 1 April 2008.

102. de Giere, 387.

103. de Giere, 387–98.

104. Personal interview with Stephen Schwartz, New York, 22 March 2005, reported in Laird, "The Creation of a Broadway Musical," 342. Carol de Giere provides commentary on two specific disagreements between the writers and Mantello concerning a possible scene using a crystal ball like in the MGM film (p. 338) and another about how the show might end (pp. 356–58).

105. Cote, 29.

106. Cote, 29–30.

107. Cote, 30.

108. Cote, 30.

109. Cote, 31.

110. Cote, 31.

111. de Giere, 401–10.

112. de Giere, 402.

113. *The Schwartz Scene*, no. 13 (Fall 2003), www.musicalschwartz.com/ schwartzscene/schwartz-scene-13.htm (accessed 7 April 2010).

114. Personal interview with Stephen Schwartz, New York, 22 March 2005, reported in Laird, "The Creation of a Broadway Musical," 346.

115. Telephone interview with Winnie Holzman, New York, 29 March 2005, reported in Laird, "The Creation of a Broadway Musical," 346–47.

116. Telephone interview with Winnie Holzman, New York, 29 March 2005, reported in Laird, "The Creation of a Broadway Musical," 347.

117. Cote, 71.

118. Cote, 73.

119. Cote, 73.

120. Maguire, 392.

121. de Giere, 401–18.

122. de Giere, 404–6.

123. See de Giere, 403–4.

124. "Stephen Schwartz Update Fall 2002," www.musicalschwartz.com/schwartzscene/schwartz-scene-13.htm (accessed 7 April 2010).

CHAPTER FOUR
WICKED FROM SCENARIOS TO "FINAL" SCRIPT

The previous chapter summarized the story of *Wicked*'s creation largely based upon interviews with Stephen Schwartz and others, including those by David Cote and Carol de Giere. A recurring theme in that chapter was the fragility of memory, both in terms of how much one can recall about a long and arduous process with many repetitive tasks and how different people often remember the same event with conflicting details. In this chapter we rely on existing documentation as we take a close look at how the plot and script for *Wicked* changed over time, from Schwartz's earliest scenario from 1998 to a script from December 2006, more than three years after the show opened on Broadway. We turn to other sources such as interviews and secondary accounts to help put these documents into context. I extend my heartfelt gratitude to Stephen Schwartz and his assistant Michael Cole for their assistance in making these scenarios and scripts available, and for the opportunity to find additional materials in Schwartz's office. I have not seen all of the preliminary scripts for *Wicked*, but what follows is one of the more detailed accounts of the development of a script for any Broadway musical.

This study is intended for those with great interest in how Winnie Holzman, Stephen Schwartz, and their collaborators over time developed the plot and script for the show. It is satisfying to learn, for example, that Glinda's role became larger after Kristin Chenoweth started working on the readings, and to hear anecdotes and examples of how that developed over time—a process effectively illuminated by Carol de Giere in her book—but here we take that process to another level and consult more of

53

the actual scripts to see how scenes and story points changed. It is a complex and fascinating process that did not proceed linearly. One notes how much of the final version of the show appears in Schwartz's first scenario, but also how some major issues in the plot defied resolution until late in the game. The actual scenarios and scripts silently detail the changes that took place, but they usually provide no hint as to the origin of an idea. From what has been described in the previous chapter, we can be certain that the earliest scripts document the work of Schwartz and Holzman, with perhaps additions by Platt, and that later scripts include input from Joe Mantello and others. These sources show *Wicked* growing silently as an entity shaped by unseen forces, from its rough childhood in scenarios with parenthetical question marks, through gawky adolescence in drafts of scripts, to relative maturity as it gets ready to open on Broadway. The willingness of creators in this show to rethink basic issues and revise the script was notable, and these sources cause one to admire their tenacity and to see how difficult the process really was. Even someone who believes that the *Wicked* creative team failed to produce a compelling story or script might find it enlightening to see how complex this process turned out to be.

The Two Scenarios

As we have seen, Schwartz conceived the possibility of turning Maguire's novel into a musical, and he worked on the project alone for a number of months. A tablet of paper in Schwartz's office with his handwritten comments includes what must be some of his early thoughts on the adaptation.[1] Schwartz jotted down phrases from Maguire's novel that struck him as telling descriptions of a character, object, or situation. For example, he found the following description of Galinda useful: "Galinda believed she would adorn the hall maybe with her beauty and occasional clever sayings. She had wanted a living sort of marble bust."[2] Schwartz also recorded names of plants and foods that Maguire invented for Oz, perhaps his initial recognition that the show would have to recreate a world based on Baum's and Maguire's fantasies.

In September 1998, Schwartz prepared a detailed synopsis, a document that Carol de Giere published in an appendix.[3] Its summary here will be our starting point as we begin to trace the show's development.

The opening number was called "No One Loves the Wicked" (rather than "No One Mourns the Wicked"). A narrator whose face remains in shadow tells the story, and in this first scene the audience would witness Elphaba's birth, an event common to every subsequent version. Elphaba heads to school knowing that Nessarose would join her the following year. She looks forward to accomplishing something important and winning everyone's love, especially her father's, dreaming about the possibility in the song "Good Intentions." On the train, Elphaba meets Doctor Dillamond, a goat and biology professor at her new school. He tells her about the deteriorating situation for Talking Animals, but Elphaba cannot yet believe that the Wizard is evil. Upon arriving at school, she learns that she will room with Galinda, whom she wishes to emulate. Galinda tricks Elphaba into wearing a black, peaked hat to the orientation dance, where Boq, a Munchkin, falls for Galinda. Elphaba shows up in the unstylish headgear and begins to dance herself; out of guilt Galinda joins her and they become friends. Madame Morrible accepts both girls into her sorcery class and teaches them from the Grimmerie. It is written in an unknown language that Elphaba reads easily, much to her teacher's surprise. Morrible informs the young women that they are being trained to help the Wizard. Elphaba spends the summer assisting Dillamond with his experiments. Nessarose arrives at school that autumn and falls in love with Boq. She also studies sorcery and uses a spell to make Boq love her. Fiyero arrives and bonds with Elphaba over saving a lion cub from being experimented upon in a class. Dillamond finds success with his experiment, proving that humans and Talking Animals share a similar consciousness. During the celebration, joined by Elphaba and Fiyero, passion ignites between the two young people. Madame Morrible informs Elphaba and Nessarose that they must return home because their father, Frex, is ill. Before he dies, he gives Nessarose silver shoes that help her walk and Elphaba the bottle of green elixir that her mother kept. Nessarose remains in Munchkinland as governor, and Elphaba returns to school where she finds that a fire has killed Doctor Dillamond and destroyed his work. Elphaba, however, had made a copy of his formula, and she convinces Glinda (who changes her name in most versions to honor Dillamond, who could not pronounce "Galinda") to go to the Emerald City with her to show the formula to the Wizard. They receive an audience and find that Morrible is now the Wizard's assistant. He rips up Elphaba's formula and tells the students that he treats the animals as they did where he came from, and he sings "Sentimental," about how he regards Ozians as his children. Morrible enters and suggests that Elphaba and Glinda make the Wizard's monkeys fly, but Elphaba refuses, grabs the Grimmerie, and flees. She finds herself trapped in an old room in the palace but escapes with a spell that makes a broom fly.

Act 2 opens with Elphaba going to her sister and giving her the Grimmerie in hopes that she will keep it safely from the Wizard and Madame Morrible. Glinda is there and vows to find a way to help Elphaba after her friend leaves. Elphaba leads Talking Animals in an attack on the palace, but a soldier—who turns out to be Fiyero—captures her. There is a love scene between the two that includes the song "As Long As You're Mine." They are interrupted by the Wizard's men; Elphaba escapes, but they capture Fiyero. Elphaba returns to Nessarose, finding that her sister has used the Grimmerie to become powerful, and in Elphaba's presence she tries to use a spell to make Boq love her instead of Glinda, but it backfires and Elphaba turns Boq into the Tin Man to save his life. Elphaba leaves with the Grimmerie. Madame Morrible tells the Wizard that she can still manipulate the weather, and she has an idea. Elphaba hopes that a spell from the Grimmerie might prevent Fiyero from being harmed by the Wizard's men, but she is unsure what to do; in despair she sings "Reap the Whirlwind." A winged monkey arrives to tell her about the cyclone, the house, and Nessarose's death. Elphaba flies to the site and learns about Dorothy and her dog, and that Glinda gave Dorothy her sister's shoes. Glinda urges Elphaba to surrender before things get worse, but Elphaba retreats to Fiyero's castle Kiamo Ko with the winged monkeys. Fiyero's wife leaves in fear of the Wizard. The narrator returns to describe what happens with Dorothy and her three friends. When they arrive at Kiamo Ko, Elphaba reminds the Lion how she helped save him from being experimented upon, and the Tin Man how she saved his life, but they despise her. Dorothy requests forgiveness for killing Elphaba's sister, which enrages the witch and sets in motion the events that appear to melt her. Dorothy and her friends cannot return to the Wizard with the witch's broom or the Grimmerie, which burned in the fire, but they bring back the green elixir, which informs the Wizard that they had killed his own daughter. He sentences Morrible to jail and leaves Oz in control of Dorothy's three friends and Glinda. The Scarecrow declines the offer and goes to the Badlands to be with Elphaba, who was the mysterious narrator and faked her death. They sing a reprise of "As Long As You're Mine."

It is notable how much of the plot that opened on Broadway five years later appears here. The essential arc of Elphaba's story already exists, and many actions by other characters remain. Schwartz names several songs that later appear, including "As Long As You're Mine," which he had written in the 1970s. (See chapter 5 for additional information about this song.) The major difference is that Glinda's role later becomes larger, a process that can be observed over a number of other versions of the story. In this initial take on the show's plot, Glinda tricks Elphaba into wearing the black hat, she dances with Elphaba and becomes her friend, she goes to the Emerald City with her, she vows to try to help her in the opening scene of the second act, she has the scene with Elphaba after Nessarose's death, and she becomes one of Oz's rulers after the Wizard leaves. She is the second most important character, but hardly Elphaba's equal, as she became in *Wicked*'s fully realized form. Consider, for example, that this scenario includes no songs for Glinda and how her scenes at the beginning and end of Act 2 in the Broadway version are not present. Most final song placements do not appear in this scenario.

The next scenario consulted for this study dates from 21 November 1999, after Winnie Holzman had joined the project and the writers had spent their year consulting with Marc Platt. The story changed substantially; major alterations will be explained here. Elphaba no longer narrates. Either the Scarecrow or Madame Morrible is interviewed at the opening, telling how the Wicked Witch of the West died. In a crowd scene, some sell souvenirs of Dorothy and her friends. Glinda tells the story of Elphaba's birth, and the flashback begins as Elphaba and Nessarose go to the train station to head for school, where they meet Doctor Dillamond. At Shiz, Nessarose, confined to a wheelchair, begs Madame Morrible to let her room with someone besides a sister of whom she is ashamed. As Morrible wheels Nessarose away, Elphaba shows her powers by making the wheelchair return to her. This impresses Morrible, who decides that Elphaba will room with Galinda since they will both study sorcery. As the girls unpack in their room, they note their differences but also become fascinated with each other. Events surrounding the black hat and dance are similar, but now Galinda deflects Boq's attention by suggesting that he spend time with Nessarose. The scenario describes a montage that switches between Dillamond's biology class and Morrible's sorcery semi-nar, with Dillamond gradually losing student respect as the situation for Talking Animals deteriorates. Much of the first act is similar to the previ-ous scenario, but new important plot points emerge. Galinda has fallen in love with Fiyero and is distraught at his lack of attention at Dillamond's funeral; Elphaba invites her to the Emerald City to cheer her up. They enjoy their day there together and meet the Wizard, who says he wants to hear Elphaba's concerns, but first she must demonstrate her power. She gives the monkeys wings and regrets that the transformation causes pain, but she learns that a spell cannot be undone. Elphaba runs out and Glinda follows her, but Elphaba escapes on the broom without asking her friend to join her. The possible songs mentioned for the act include a reprise of "Making Good" for Elphaba when she decides to help Dillamond with his experiment; "Success" for Elphaba, Fiyero, and Dillamond when the experiment succeeds (and when the two young people start to fall in love); a song for the Wizard to impress Elphaba and Glinda; and a scene be-tween the two young women after they leave the Wizard's presence where Elphaba announces that she will now be "wicked" since her efforts to do good have failed.

The second act of this scenario includes a few significant new elements and several possible song titles. Elphaba and Fiyero flee together after he captures her in her attack on the Wizard's palace, and they go to his room to make love and sing "As Long As You're Mine." Glinda suggests that the Wizard and Morrible use Nessarose in some way to make Elphaba appear, but she immediately regrets what she said and sings "For Goodness Sake" in self-justification. Elphaba, with Fiyero, hears Morrible's cyclone and rushes to her sister's side with Fiyero. He is captured, but she escapes and uses the Grimmerie to save him, singing "Reap the Whirlwind." Toward the end, the Scarecrow resumes the interview that started the scenario, and the act closes differently from the Broadway version in a few details.

The First Complete Draft: 12 March 2001

The next source available for this study was the first complete draft of the script, dated 12 March 2001. As noted in chapter 3, readings had recently taken place at Universal Studios on 23 February and 6 March. One can only speculate why the date on this script is after the dates of the readings, but this source probably gives a fairly accurate idea as to what the show was like for the second reading. The script includes the current lyrics but no music. Below is a summary of each scene.

Act I

Scene 1—As souvenir hawkers sell mementos of Dorothy and her friends, Madame Morrible sings that the Wizard has requested that the Wicked Witch be burned in effigy. The song "No One Mourns the Wicked" appears throughout the scene. Glinda tells Elphaba's story, beginning with her birth, much like what plays today. At the end of the scene, Elphaba appears as a young woman ready for college.

Scene 2—Elphaba and Nessarose are at the train station preparing to leave for school. Some in the crowd react to Elphaba's coloring. She meets Doctor Dillamond, who is having trouble boarding the train because of restrictions against Talking Animals. Elphaba uses her looks to frighten away the family bothering him. She sings "Making Good" to Dillamond, starting with a verse in which she identifies with him by saying people often stare at her. Dillamond asks her assistance with his scientific work and identifies its nature. Elphaba's father calls her over to help with Nessarose, and the scene concludes with her singing the "Unlimited" segment, a bitter passage much as it existed in the August 2000 version of "Making Good," covered in the next chapter.

Scene 3—The students arrive at Shiz and sing the alma mater. Madame Morrible welcomes them as Pfannee and Shenshen gush over Galinda, who brags that she will have a single room. Morrible announces that Nessarose will live with her, but as she wheels her away, Elphaba uses magic to transport her sister back to her side. Morrible is excited by Elphaba's talent and offers her a private tutorial in sorcery. She places Elphaba in Galinda's room, and the two horrified students begin letters to their parents in the song "Bad Situation," which opens with some of the same lyrics as the later "What Is This Feeling?"

Scene 4—The girls are in their dormitory room and an antagonistic dialog precedes continuation of "Bad Situation." Pfannee and Shenshen comfort Galinda with material that later occurs in "What Is This Feeling?" described in chapter 5.

Scene 5—Doctor Dillamond tries to lead his biology class in a discussion of the similarities between humans and Talking Animals, and Elphaba defends him from Galinda and others. Dillamond turns over his blackboard and finds the words "Animals should be seen and not heard." Galinda laughs with the other students, and "Bad Situation" starts anew.

Scene 6—Galinda and her friends observe Fiyero and Boq, admiring the former and dismissing the latter as a Munchkin. They wonder with whom they might attend the dance, and Galinda engineers Boq asking Nessarose (causing Elphaba embarrassment when she tries to prevent it) and her date with Fiyero.

Scene 7—Morrible shows Elphaba the Grimmerie and is shocked that she can read it. The student causes a large bouquet of flowers to appear. In gratitude to Galinda for bringing Boq and Nessarose together, she convinces Morrible to add Galinda to the class.

Scene 8—In their dormitory room, Galinda gets ready for the Frolick as her friends speak with her. They cruelly offer the black, peaked hat to Elphaba, and she gives Galinda a note from Morrible inviting her to join sorcery class. Fiyero enters and trades barbs with Elphaba as Galinda finishes getting ready. Fiyero and Galinda sing "We Deserve Each Other."

Scene 9—At the dance, Galinda learns from Morrible that it was Elphaba's idea to include her in the class. Elphaba appears in the black hat, realizing that she has been tricked, and Galinda dances with her out of guilt. The scene includes no singing.

Scene 10—Back in the dorm room, Galinda sings "Popular" to her new friend, offering to give her a makeover. She invites Elphaba to a picnic with Fiyero, who will be bringing her a date.

Scene 11—A picnic with Boq, Nessarose, Fiyero, Galinda, and Elphaba, whose date does not appear. Elphaba has been transformed by Galinda, but everybody laughs at their efforts and she runs away. Boq leaves when he cannot tell Nessarose the truth, and she blames herself for his lack of interest.

Scene 12—Madame Morrible comes to biology class to announce that Doctor Dillamond is no longer eligible to teach. A new professor enters with a lion cub on which he proposes to perform experiments. Elphaba's anger causes a spell that immobilizes everyone but her and Fiyero, and they run out with the lion cub.

Scene 13—Elphaba and Fiyero feel mutual attraction, but he leaves to release the cub and she sings "I'm Not That Girl."

Scene 14—At the train station, Elphaba tells Galinda that she is not going away for break with the gang in order to stay and work with Dillamond on his experiment. She sings a reprise of "I'm Not That Girl" to close the scene after her friends leave on the train.

Scene 15—Dillamond and Elphaba work together in the laboratory, and Fiyero returns early from break alone. The "chemistry" between Elphaba and Fiyero helps the experiment succeed, proving that animal and human consciousness are identical, and the three sing "As If by Magic," the lyrics of which include some of "Making Good." Morrible appears, and Dillamond will not let Elphaba tell her what they have achieved. Morrible says that Elphaba's father is ill and that Nessarose awaits her in the coach to leave for Munchkinland. Morrible stops the rain so that they can travel on a better night.

Scene 16—The sisters arrive in Frex's chamber. He appoints Nessarose his successor and presents her with the jeweled slippers. He gives Elphaba her mother's bottle of green elixir. Nessarose remarks that every Munchkin now must bend to her will, and Frex sings, "How I hate to go and leave you . . . ," like he did to his wife Melena in Scene 1.

Scene 17—Elphaba is on the train back to Shiz, but it stops and she learns that there has been a lab explosion at the school.

Scene 18—At Doctor Dillamond's funeral (where they sing different lyrics to the "Shiz" song), Galinda begs Elphaba to find out why Fiyero has been distant with her. Elphaba tries to get away to say a few words about the goat, but Galinda wants her to talk to Fiyero, who has arrived, and Galinda goes to do a eulogy. She blurts out that she will change her name to "Glinda," the way Dillamond pronounced it, but then later she becomes distraught when Fiyero leaves. People mistake her emotion for her feelings about Dillamond. Fiyero hands Elphaba some crystals he had saved from the experiment that proved Dillamond's success, and Elphaba tells Morrible that she must go speak to the Wizard about this. Her teacher tells her she will arrange the visit. Elphaba invites Glinda to the Emerald City with her to cheer her up.

Scene 19—The scene includes the song "One Short Day" with basically the same words as in the August 2000 version, but here they do not attend a stage show about the Wizard's arrival in Oz.

Scene 20—Elphaba and Glinda go to meet the Wizard in his chamber and are at first terrified by the disembodied head, but he comes out to greet them personally after he realizes with whom he speaks. In conversation, the girls say they saw the show *Wiz You Were Here*, even though there was no mention of it in the previous scene. Madame Morrible appears as the Wizard's new press secretary. Elphaba starts to tell him about the crystals, but the Wizard interrupts her with his song "A Sentimental Man" and asks Elphaba for a demonstration of her powers in which she will give wings to his monkey Chistery. Elphaba chants the spell from the Grimmerie and finds that she has given wings to many monkeys. The creatures are in pain, and she wants to undo the spell but learns that it is impossible. She rushes out with the Grimmerie, and Glinda pursues her, hoping to bring her back. As the Wizard calls guards to capture Elphaba, she pulls Glinda into a closet with her.

Scene 21—Elphaba and Galinda confront each other in the closet, singing a version of "I Hope You're Happy." They hear announcements declaring Elphaba a "Wicked Witch." Elphaba starts to sing "Defying Gravity," at one point asking Glinda to join her in her crusade. For a moment it looks like she might, but she declines and Elphaba flies off as the "Wicked Witch of the West."

Act 2

Scene 1—A celebration is taking place in front of the palace, with a crowd and a reporter awaiting the arrival of Glinda and Fiyero. The reporter interviews them. We learn that Glinda has been living in the palace and Fiyero is captain of the guard. They have been unable to find Elphaba. Fiyero is surprised to learn that this is his engagement party with Glinda. Reporter Punch Munchburger starts a song in which he falsely describes Glinda in an audience with the Wizard when Elphaba interferes. Others join in the song, and Fiyero is offended by some of the lies that he hears told about Elphaba. Madame Morrible appears and they briefly sing "Happy Healing Day."

Scene 2—In her chamber at the Munchkinland governor's palace, Nessarose tries to seduce Boq by saying that she needs a nap. Elphaba appears and asks to hide. She produces the Grimmerie. Nessarose complains of her condition, and Elphaba puts a spell on her shoes so she can walk.

Nessarose sings "Step by Step by Step" and puts a dangerous spell on Boq's heart when he threatens to go to Glinda. To save his life, Elphaba turns him into the Tin Man, who does not require a heart. Elphaba leaves for the Emerald City, and Nessarose blames Elphaba for Boq's condition.

Scene 3—At their engagement ball, couples dance as Glinda, Fiyero, and Morrible watch. Elphaba arrives at the Wizard's chamber upstairs, and the Wizard corners her by grabbing her broom. He asks to start afresh with her and sings "Wonderful." She is ready to accept his proposition if he will release the flying monkeys, which the Wizard does. Elphaba then discovers Dillamond, unable to speak. Fiyero and Glinda hear the commotion upstairs. Fiyero arrives first and frees Elphaba from the guards, and after Glinda comes, he leaves with Elphaba. The distraught Glinda suggests that the Wizard and Morrible use Nessarose to lure Elphaba out of hiding. They revise the plan because Elphaba is too smart for such a ruse. Alone, Glinda sings a brief reprise of "I'm Not That Girl."

Scene 4—Fiyero and Elphaba are alone in a rented room and sing "As Long As You're Mine" with quite different lyrics than the Broadway version. Elphaba hears wind and fears for Nessarose, so she flies to her. Fiyero suggests that they could meet at his family's castle at Kiamo Ko.

Scene 5—In Munchkinland, next to a smashed house, Glinda and the Munchkins send Dorothy on her way. Elphaba appears, shocking Glinda, who was mourning Nessarose's death. They argue about Glinda giving Dorothy the shoes, and about Fiyero. Guards appear to arrest Elphaba. Fiyero enters and takes Glinda hostage, allowing Elphaba to escape. The guards hang Fiyero by poles in a field, trying to force him to tell where Elphaba went.

Scene 6—At Kiamo Ko, Elphaba chants from the Grimmerie to try and save Fiyero. She sings a verse of her "Unlimited" theme where she laments all that has gone wrong, and she performs the song "No Good Deed" with different lyrics than the final version.

Scene 7—Outside the Wizard's palace, Dorothy and her friends are leaving on a mission to kill the Wicked Witch. The crowd sings a song that might be called "March of the Witch-Hunters," but the text does not appear to fit with the same melody as "No Good Deed," as in the Broadway version. Glinda confronts Morrible about her role in the cyclone that carried Dorothy's house to kill Nessarose, but Morrible reminds Glinda that she has attained the popularity she desired, so she can keep silent and play the game. The Tin Man sings verses explaining why he and the Lion want to kill the witch, very similar to the Broadway version. Glinda tries to object, but they march off as the crowd sings.

Scene 8—At Kiamo Ko, Elphaba has captured Dorothy and demands the shoes. Glinda appears and confronts Elphaba, imploring her to surrender, but Glinda also lets on that she knows the truth about Nessarose's death. Two monkeys fly in with word from Fiyero, and Elphaba lets Glinda believe that he is dead. Elphaba gives Glinda the Grimmerie and tells her never to reveal that she has it. They sing "For Good" with lyrics nearly identical to the Broadway version, except it does not start with Elphaba singing "I'm limited." Glinda hides. A chorus sings some of "No One Mourns the Wicked" as Elphaba appears to melt. Dorothy and her friends exit with the broom, and Glinda reappears, finding the bottle of green elixir.

Scene 9—Back at the Wizard's palace, Morrible waves good-bye to Dorothy and her friends. Glinda appears and shows the Wizard the green elixir bottle. He realizes that he has had his own daughter killed and sings a bit of "A Sentimental Man." Glinda tells him to leave Oz and has Morrible arrested. A photographer wants a picture of the four who killed the witch, but the Scarecrow has disappeared. He is in fact Fiyero, and he goes to Kiamo Ko where he finds Elphaba, who faked her death. They head to the Badlands where we see Elphaba trying to help Dillamond speak. At the palace, the crowd sings "No One Mourns the Wicked" (with different lyrics than those heard today), and Glinda sings a bit of "For Good" as she mourns for her friend.

Except for changes in Doctor Dillamond's role and the excision of some scenes, the sequence of events in this script is close to the version that opened on Broadway in October 2003, especially in Act 2. The opening scene's souvenir hawkers were later removed, as was the role there for Madame Morrible. The elaborate second scene in the train station disappeared and with it an initial meeting between Dillamond and Elphaba, but once his profession changed to history teacher, he did not require assistance with experiments, eliminating several plot points. In Act 1, Scene 7, Morrible discovers that Elphaba can read the Grimmerie, a disclosure that does not come until nearly the end of the act in the version we know. Scene 11, the picnic, later disappeared as some details about the relationships moved elsewhere in Act 1. The lab scene was discarded when Dillamond changed fields, and they later decided that Frex's death need not be shown, meaning that telling the audience about Morrible's power over the weather had to be relocated. Dillamond's funeral was in many subsequent versions before its removal in summer 2003. The big finale of Act 1 had yet to be conceived because only Glinda watches Elphaba fly off. There are few major differences in Act 2 between the sequence of events here and the Broadway version except for the appearance of Dorothy and her friends in Scene 9. Dialog and the songs would be rewritten, and that changed a great deal for example in Scene 1, but the creators could almost have put Act 2 aside for major plot consideration at this point.

Script Draft: 21 November 2001

The next script draft consulted for this study dates from 21 November 2001, made available by Stephen Schwartz's assistant Michael Cole, who took part in the 14 December 2001 reading for which the creators prepared this version. There was also a two-week workshop preceding this reading during which the script and score changed. The script includes music for the chorus and parts of other songs. Here we will consider the major differences between this script and the last; the music will be considered in chapter 5.

Act 1, Scene 5 begins with material from "Bad Situation," which recurs later in Scene 5 in the previous version. Also in Scene 5, material has been added at the end where Elphaba stays in the classroom to comfort Dillamond, as in the Broadway version. They discuss how Animals have been losing their rights, and Dillamond invites her to help with his experiment. She accepts and sings a short reprise of "Making Good." Act 1, Scene 6 includes dialog where Galinda speaks to Boq, convincing him to ask Nessarose to the dance. This is close to what Galinda sings to Boq in the Broadway version during "Dancing through Life." In Act 1, Scene 7, at Madame Morrible's sorcery seminar, with a crystal ball Elphaba sees Galinda telling Boq to ask Nessarose to the dance, which prompts Elphaba to convince Morrible to allow Galinda into the seminar. In Act 1, Scene 9 at the Frolick, the couples sing the "Emerald City Stomp," which combines with segments of "We Deserve Each Other," as the scene starts to move toward the lengthy musical scene that eventually became "Dancing through Life." Boq's sung exchange with Nessarose is similar to the Broadway version. Act 1, Scene 10 no longer includes any mention of Galinda's picnic with Fiyero to which she invites Elphaba. "Popular" is very much like the Broadway version at this point. Scene 11 takes place in the biology class and includes all of the action of scenes 11 and 12 of the previous version. Scenes 12 through 14 closely follow scenes 13 through 15 of the previous version, but Morrible no longer tells Elphaba that she must go to her ill father's side. Instead, she tells the students that it is past their curfew, and a moment later Doctor Dillamond answers the door and shrinks back from an unseen horror. The remainder of the act is mostly similar to the previous version.

In Act 2, Scene 1, Glinda sings a verse that opens "Couldn't be happier . . . ," an ambiguous phrase that later becomes important in the song "Thank Goodness." Scene 2 no longer includes the song "Step by Step by Step." When Elphaba arrives, she learns that her father has died, as in the Broadway version, and the action of the remainder of the scene proceeds much as one sees today. The rest of the act is not unlike the current version except, as in the previous script, the audience sees more of Dorothy and her friends than one sees today, and as will be shown in chapter 5, there are significant differences in the music.

Script from October 2002

The next draft of the *Wicked* script consulted for this study dates from October 2002, a version completed during a month when there were several meetings among the creators. The source is marked as a "workshop draft," perhaps referring to the dance workshop that took place later that month. Presentation of the complete details of this script is unnecessary, but some observations of how the show differed from what opened on Broadway a year later will be provided.

Act 1, Scene 1 is much like the show as one knows it today. Scene 2 took place at Shiz, but Galinda was there from the beginning, gawking at Elphaba. After Elphaba shows her power by making Nessarose's chair return to her from Madame Morrible, the headmistress asks for a private word with Elphaba. Morrible sings the introduction now known from "The Wizard and I." She leaves, and Elphaba sings a different introduction to her song. From there the script is marked "Lyric to follow." As will be shown in chapter 5, Schwartz worked on this song at the end of October 2002.

Scene 3 takes place in the dorm room. Galinda's friends urge her to give the hideous black hat to Elphaba and tell her it is the latest fashion, but Galinda thinks that is too mean until Elphaba makes an insulting comment to her, showing how Elphaba has more of an edge as a character here than in the Broadway version of the show. She pointedly tells Galinda that she will not try to get her into the sorcery seminar just because she gave her a hat. They sing "What Is This Feeling?" but the song was not completed at this point and includes fascinatingly different lyrics. At one point, for example, they sing together, "From the moment that I spied you/Across a crowded room . . . ," perhaps a passing reference to *South Pacific* that Schwartz later chose to delete.

Scene 4 is in Doctor Dillamond's class, and it proceeds quite differently than what one sees today. He is now a history teacher rather than a scientist. Galinda uses one of the professor's questions to take a dig at Elphaba, which Dillamond says happens too often in his class. He turns over the blackboard and finds the nasty statement used in the show today. He dismisses class when no student will take responsibility. Elphaba stays after class and speaks with Dillamond for the first time. He sings "Something Bad," the lyrics of which are different but still include the notion that at times Dillamond cannot help but bleat like a goat when enunciating a short *a*. He asks Elphaba to assist with his research because he has been banned from the library, but she is not sure if she can because she promised Morrible to concentrate on her sorcery studies. He resumes the song, expressing the hope that the reports about animals losing their ability to speak might be exaggerated (later cut), but it ends similarly to what one hears today.

Fiyero appears in Scene 5 of the draft, as in the current version, but before he enters there is a great deal more dialog between the students involving gossip about Elphaba and Boq's attempts to ingratiate himself to Galinda. When Fiyero arrives, he demonstrates that he is not a serious student and sings "Which Way's the Party?"—an ensemble number and dance. Galinda, attracted to him, must deflect Boq's attentions, and she sings slightly different lyrics to him than one hears today as she sends him to Nessarose. Elphaba interprets this as kindness to Nessarose and intervenes with Madame Morrible to get Galinda admitted to the sorcery class. In a later musical sequence, Fiyero and Galinda sing a version of "We Deserve Each Other."

Much of the next scene progresses as what one sees today, but apparently with less continuous music. It starts with Morrible asking Galinda to join her sorcery class and saying that it was Elphaba's idea. One notes in order a sung sequence between Fiyero and Boq, with the former advising the Munchkin to tell Nessarose the truth about why he asked her to the dance; the sung material between Boq and Nessarose, which is much like the show today; and a different closing where Galinda and Elphaba sing some of "We Deserve Each Other" before they start to dance together. The scene closes with an ensemble version of "Which Way's the Party?"

The next scene, with Elphaba and Galinda in their room and the song "Popular," is much like today. The following scene in class is similar, but more is made of Galinda's attempt to transform Elphaba into a green version of herself. The students laugh at Elphaba, Boq attempts to support Galinda's efforts, and Nessarose ignores Fiyero when he tells her that Boq is not for her. The scene then progresses with Morrible telling the class that Dillamond can no longer teach (Dillamond is not present; the current version is more effective as men drag the professor out), a new teacher bringing in a lion cub in a cage, and Elphaba and Fiyero rescuing the lion cub after Elphaba puts a spell on everyone else in the room.

The following scene between Elphaba and Fiyero has different dialog than what one hears now, but the essential thrust is similar and it concludes with Elphaba singing "I'm Not That Girl." In this earlier version, Fiyero and Galinda do not appear above Elphaba on the bridge as she sings the song.

The creators ultimately decided that the next important event in the plot was the two friends traveling to the Emerald City to meet the Wizard, because the next three scenes of the October 2002 version eventually disappeared. Similar to older versions, Galinda takes her friends besides Elphaba to her home over break, and Elphaba says farewell at the train station. After the train leaves, she reprises a bit of "I'm Not That Girl." In the next scene, Elphaba is in her dorm room, and Dillamond stops by to pick up books that she has checked out of the library for him. He says that he will not be silenced, and they sing a verse of "Something Bad."

Fiyero returns to campus alone and comes to Elphaba's room. Dillamond leaves, and an exchange between Fiyero and Elphaba leads to them jointly holding her crystal ball. Their mutual chemistry activates it, and they see a farm in Kansas where animals cannot speak. Elphaba realizes that they really can forget how to talk and wants to inform Dillamond. Madame Morrible, however, comes to her room to say that someone had just jumped off a bridge and that she had found Dillamond's spectacles there. Elphaba insists that he would not have committed suicide. The scene changes to Dillamond's funeral, with the cast singing the Shiz alma mater with different lyrics. The next scene is not unlike previous versions of Dillamond's funeral, with Galinda trying to get Elphaba to speak with Fiyero, who has been distant. Morrible interrupts, telling Elphaba that she has made arrangements for her to see the Wizard so that she may tell him about her suspicions concerning Dillamond's fate. Galinda announces her name change to "Glinda" in honor of the goat's memory, but she is despondent when Fiyero leaves the scene without her. Elphaba invites her to the Emerald City.

The act's four concluding scenes are mostly recognizable to those who know the current version, but some lyrics and dialog have changed. The song "One Short Day," with some different lyrics, defines the first segment. The scene in the Wizard's chamber continues to include "A Sentimental Man" and "Chance to Fly" as he convinces Elphaba to perform the spell on the monkeys, and the following conflict causes her to rush out, followed by Glinda. In the next brief scene, cut in the Broadway version, Elphaba grabs Glinda and pulls her into a closet. The act's finale is familiar, but with a few changes in text.

Act 2 opens several months later with the party for Glinda and Fiyero, now with the song "Thank Goodness" rather than "Happy Healing Day." The scene plays much like the Broadway version, with subtle changes, and the act begins with the prologue based on "No One Mourns the Wicked," as heard in today's version. The action of the important second scene in Nessarose's chamber at the Munchkinland governor's palace has changed little since the 12 March 2001 script. There are sung sections that do not appear today, including a bitter version of "We Deserve Each Other" that Nessarose sings to her image in the mirror after Elphaba has left. The subsequent action at the Wizard's palace has been reduced here from previous versions. The engagement ball proceeds as Elphaba arrives to free the monkeys; her confrontation with the Wizard occurs immediately but is wordier here than on Broadway. The conclusion of the scene, through Glinda singing a brief reprise of "I'm Not That Girl," is close to the Broadway version. Scene 4, when Fiyero and Elphaba consummate their relationship, takes place in a rented room rather than while camping in a forest, and there are significant differences in the lyrics of "As Long As You're Mine." Scene 5, at the scene where the house crushed Nessarose, changed little before the Broadway opening, and Scene 6, when Elphaba sings "No Good Deed," is similar to what one hears today except that Schwartz used the "Unlimited" material just before the verse that begins, "No good deed goes unpunished . . ." (original cast recording [hereafter "OCR"], track 16, 1'15"). In this deleted verse, Elphaba states that "the damage is unlimited," ruefully noting that Fiyero has been added to the list of people she has unintentionally harmed. It is fascinating to note that the composer ultimately decided against using this recurring material here, one of the show's more dramatic moments. As in the Broadway version, the scene that immediately follows this is the Ozians cheering on Dorothy and her friends as they go off to try and kill the Wicked Witch. In this earlier version, Dorothy appears (unlike in the final version), and there are other small differences, such as the absence of the verse that the Tin Man sings about the Lion. The next scene, when Elphaba appears to melt, includes the same major plot events. Dorothy also appears on stage here. The final scene is recognizable from the Broadway version, but the dialog includes more explanation, and Elphaba sings "I'm limited" to Fiyero when he comes and finds her. Unlike previous versions, the audience does not see Fiyero and Elphaba in the Badlands working with Doctor Dillamond at the end. Schwartz argued strenuously for this scene to appear on Broadway but did not manage to have it included.[4]

Before San Francisco:
A Script Draft from 31 March 2003

A script draft bearing the date of 31 March 2003 shows the state of the show a few months before the San Francisco opening. With a few exceptions, the scene structure is familiar from the October 2002 script, but this March draft includes a number of moments later removed, some of them showing the writers further explaining or exploring plot points or a character's feelings, perhaps more than necessary. It is these surprising moments that will be described in this script in each scene, as well as places with significantly different actions by various characters.

Act I

Scene 1—Before Frex leaves his wife, he sings the entire waltz (that is now a duet), longer here with different lyrics.

Scene 2—As everyone gathers at Shiz for the start of school, the governor of Munchkinland does not accompany his daughters, and the dialog is very different. When Elphaba unintentionally shows her powers, Madame Morrible asks what other teachers have said about her, and Elphaba reports, "Pretty bad things." Morrible gives her a crystal ball to start her sorcery study, causing Galinda to leave in frustration. After "The Wizard and I," Elphaba and Galinda sing the introduction of "What Is This Feeling?" in this scene, through Elphaba's disgusted epithet of "blonde" directed at her roommate.

Scene 3—The main part of the song begins here, probably the waltz version described in chapter 5 (see p. 134). Schwartz again provides a *South Pacific*-like moment as they sing "From the moment I espied you across a crowded room . . . " The song ends in counterpoint, as does the final version.

Scene 4—Doctor Dillamond sings "Something Bad" with Elphaba. It was a very different song at this point, with a short introduction that was later removed and the goat singing extra material about how he has been banned from the library.

Scene 5—Fiyero's song at this point is "Which Way's the Party?" (see chapter 5, pp. 180ff), and there are other plot points that do not appear in the Broadway version. Boq delivers a package to Galinda's room that contains the black, peaked hat, which Galinda offers to Elphaba in dialog rather than song. Galinda has given Nessarose the jeweled shoes (instead of her father), discovered by the audience in the scene where Elphaba speaks to Nessarose as she gets ready for her date with Boq. Elphaba tries to question Galinda's motives, but Nessarose will not hear of it and leaves.

Scene 6—The party at the Ozdust Ballroom follows, and there are minor differences with the Broadway version, but the events are similar.

Scene 7—Both dialog and the song "Popular" are similar to the known version of the scene.

Scene 8—Elphaba comes to class dressed like Galinda, causing more comment from students than one hears today. Doctor Dillamond does not appear, unlike the frantic opening of this scene on Broadway. Elphaba and Fiyero rush out with the lion cub at the conclusion.

Scene 9—At the opening, Elphaba and Fiyero briefly discuss Dillamond's firing, a point that receives no further explanation in the Broadway version. The events in the scene are familiar, but the dialog is quite different. Elphaba sings "I'm Not That Girl," but only the AABA sections, saving the final repeat of A for 9A.

Scene 9A—At the train station, Elphaba tells Galinda and Fiyero that she will not be accompanying them on break so that she can work with Doctor Dillamond. Fiyero is thrown by this, showing more interest in Elphaba at this point than occurs on Broadway. Elphaba sings the final repetition of the A section of "I'm Not That Girl," making it a reprise rather than a continuation of the song.

Scene 10—Elphaba is helping Doctor Dillamond. He hands her a crystal ball and says that she should not be avoiding her other studies. They hear a noise and are frightened, with Dillamond wondering if he should leave for the Badlands like other animals have, but he says, like Dorothy, "There's no place like home!" (This probably would have been one of the lines that Universal lawyers would have wanted removed to avoid legal problems with MGM.) Dillamond sings a reprise of "Something Bad" and goes out. Fiyero has returned early from break and enters, at first scaring Elphaba. He holds the crystal ball with her, and their "chemistry" activates it, allowing them to see animals in Kansas who cannot talk. In another evocation of *The Wizard of Oz*, Elphaba says, "Fiyero, I don't think this is Oz anymore." Madame Morrible comes and says that Dillamond seems to have committed suicide, and music starts for his funeral.

Scene 11—The events here are familiar from previous versions, with Galinda wanting Elphaba to speak with Fiyero for her while doing the funeral oration. Fiyero and Elphaba discuss the nature of love, prompting him to say that he does not believe in it. Madame Morrible gives Elphaba a letter of introduction to the Wizard, and Elphaba invites Glinda to the Emerald City to cheer her up after Fiyero has left.

Scene 12—The song "One Short Day" is incomplete in this script, with the phrase "lyrics to follow" appearing after the opening segment and at the conclusion. In dialog, the friends agree that someday they would like to live in the Emerald City and have everybody envy them, a conversation with many Ozian words that bear incorrect English endings. The show they see is unnamed, and it is described in stage instructions differently than what happens today. Clearly this scene was in a state of transition.

Scene 13—The events in this scene in the Wizard's palace are similar to the Broadway version, but much of the dialog and lyrics are different. Elphaba starts to mention her concern for the Talking Animals, and the Wizard cuts her off with "A Sentimental Man." He also sings more of "Chance to Fly" than made it into the final version.

Scene 14—Elphaba and Glinda are in the room at the top of the palace. They have a different spoken introduction to "I Hope You're Happy" that added nothing and was later cut. The sung segment for "I Hope You're Happy" is the same length as the Broadway version, with a small but significant change in the lyrics (Elphaba sings to Glinda, "you abandoned our mission" instead of "you groveled in submission"). There is also additional dialog between the two before Elphaba starts "Defying Gravity," with Glinda trying to convince her that she cannot fight the Wizard. Elphaba simply answers, "I have to," and begins the song. The lyrics of "Defying Gravity" are similar to the Broadway version, with some changes in Glinda's part. She sings something rather different to Elphaba as she gently lets her know that she will not be going with her, and she has more lines at the end as she wishes her friend happiness.

Act 2

Scene 1—The opening of the scene is very different, but not in a way that changes its meaning. After the crowd sings a verse of "Thank Goodness," Madame Morrible takes over as emcee, greeting Glinda and Fiyero as they arrive and asking Glinda that important question asked of Hollywood stars on the red carpet: "Who are you wearing?" She answers "House of Pumpkinland," a special commission from the Wizard. Once Glinda starts to sing "Thank Goodness," this version is not profoundly different than what one hears on Broadway.

Scene 2—The differences here are again a matter of what is said and not what happens. There is a discussion to open the scene between Nessarose and Boq about an invitation to Glinda's engagement party that included both of them. Nessarose, desperate to keep Boq near her, refused for both of them. Boq has discovered this and objects, but as Nessarose's servant, there is nothing he can do. Once Elphaba appears, the scene proceeds similarly to the current version but with different lyrics in many of the sung segments, and at the end Nessarose ruefully sings "We deserve each other" to the mirror.

Scene 3—The lyrics to the first part of "Wonderful" are similar to what one hears today, but the latter portion of the song is different, more of the Wizard singing responses to spoken questions from Elphaba. She challenges him about what he has done to the Talking Animals, and the Wizard answers that he has allowed them to be silenced but he has saved them "from the axe and sausage grinder," pointedly asking Elphaba in song if what she has done with the Animals has actually been "kinder." Once Elphaba discovers Doctor Dillamond, the scene is similar to what plays today.

Scene 3A—Glinda sings her short reprise of "I'm Not That Girl."

Scene 4—Elphaba and Fiyero camp in the forest. There are somewhat different lyrics to "As Long As You're Mine," and the dialog has more discussion of Glinda, but otherwise the scene is similar to the Broadway version.

Scene 5—The dialog changed some before the Broadway premiere, but the actions and outcomes in this confrontation between Glinda and Elphaba are identical.

Scene 6—Schwartz included Elphaba's "Unlimited" music in this version of "No Good Deed." Here she sings "Unlimited/The damage is unlimited . . ." as she ruefully reviews what has happened to those she cares about. This is just before she sings for the first time the chorus "No good deed." Otherwise the scene is similar.

Scene 7—The content of this scene with "March of the Witch-Hunters" includes no surprises when compared to the Broadway version.

Scene 8—There is some different dialog in this scene, but the lyrics to "For Good" are very similar to the final version.

Scene 9—The only surprises in the show's final scene in this version occur when Fiyero, now the Scarecrow, comes to find Elphaba in hiding at Kiamo Ko. He tells her that the Animals, including Doctor Dillamond, await her help in the Badlands. She sings to him "I'm limited . . ." and wonders if she can do anything, but the Scarecrow sings to her that she will just have to do the best she can.

Toward the Broadway Opening: Scripts from July 2003 to October 2003

A script from the end of a busy summer of work dates from 28 July 2003, identified on the title page as the "PRE New York Rehearsal." It is the first in a series of six late scripts (28 July 2003, 25 August 2003, 16 September 2003, 6 October 2003, the New York opening performance script, and 5 December 2006) that demonstrate what occurred before *Wicked*'s opening and then other changes made in the three years after it opened. We consider together the first five scripts.

Each of the five scripts between 28 July 2003 and the show's opening bear a similar scene structure except Act 1, Scene 6, which includes many plot developments. As shown in chapter 3, Schwartz did not finish the song "Dancing through Life" until the summer, and the creators were still struggling with how best to tell the story in that scene as they entered the final rehearsal period. What follows is a brief description of each scene found in these five scripts and some of the major changes that took place.

Act I

Scene 1—The overall structure of this opening sequence changed little during these three months. As the curtain opens, the citizens of Emerald City celebrate the Wicked Witch of the West's death. Glinda reluctantly plays the central role as she also mourns her friend. She narrates in music the story of Elphaba's conception and birth, showing how her father rejected her and suggesting that her childhood was difficult. This seems to have been the hardest part of the scene for the creators because the scripts show several major changes. The first script included the sung segments between Elphaba's parents and the midwife that one hears on the Broadway cast recording, but most of that disappeared in the next three scripts, only to be reinstated before the New York opening. The writers also at one point added comments from some of Emerald City's citizens after seeing how Elphaba came into the world, noting that everyone has difficulties in life and it does not make everyone evil. These did not appear in the Broadway opening. Each script also includes the challenge to Glinda about her friendship with the Wicked Witch of the West, commencing the flashback that is the majority of the show. The only song in the scene in all five versions is "No One Mourns the Wicked."

Scene 2—This scene changed little during these three months, and the two songs in each version are "Dear Old Shiz" to open the scene and "The Wizard and I" to close it. The major events include Elphaba arriving with her family and facing immediate rejection from her fellow students; Munchkinland's governor extravagantly gifting his daughter Nessarose with jeweled shoes and reminding Elphaba that she has only come to school to take care of her sister; Galinda arriving to immediate fanfare; Madame Morrible having no room for Elphaba and placing her with Galinda; Galinda learning that she would not get her wish to study sorcery with Madame Morrible; and Morrible stating that she would have Nessarose room with her so that she could help take care of her, a decision that prompts Elphaba unconsciously to use her powers and make Nessarose's wheelchair return to her. This makes possible her unexpected study of sorcery with Madame Morrible and the song "The Wizard and I."

Scene 3—This scene was basically set from at least the beginning of this period. Elphaba and Galinda appear on opposite sides of the stage and sing "What Is This Feeling?" The chorus joins Galinda, demonstrated by both lyrics and choreography. Elphaba scares Galinda at the end, showing her ability to fight back against adversity.

Scene 4—The debates over what role Doctor Dillamond should play, whether he should be a scientist or historian, when Elphaba would meet him, and what Elphaba's main cause for advocacy should be had been resolved before 28 July 2003, meaning that there are no major changes in this scene during these three months. We are in Doctor Dillamond's history lecture hall, where he returns essays to members of the class. The antagonism between Galinda and Elphaba is clear, and Galinda is upset by the goat's inability to pronounce her name. Someone wrote "Animals should be seen and not heard" on the reverse side of the chalkboard, causing Dillamond to cancel the remainder of class. Elphaba senses a kindred spirit and stays behind to speak with the professor. She learns how Talking Animals are suffering persecution and are losing their ability to speak in the song "Something Bad," but she is not yet ready to believe that the Wizard might be the root of the problem.

Scene 5—This scene and the next comprise the "Dancing through Life" sequence that caused the creators so much grief, but Scene 5 changed little through the five scripts. Students are studying in a court-yard with Boq staying close to Galinda when Fiyero arrives at Shiz greeted by an immediately infatuated Galinda. Fiyero is glad to learn that history class has ended and conspires in "Dancing through Life" to lead a party that evening at the Ozdust Ballroom. Part of the song includes Galinda diverting Boq's attentions to Nessarose, a smooth manipulation that Fi-yero admires.

Scene 6—The continuing adjustments being made to this scene dem-onstrate its position as the last part of the plot to be finalized. Elphaba and Galinda must be converted from antagonists to friends, a process loaded with irony in that it occurs with several misunderstandings. The scene also includes the first significant interaction between Elphaba and Nes-sarose, Galinda maliciously presenting Elphaba with the black peaked hat and telling her it is the latest fashion, Boq's inability to tell Nessarose the truth about why he asked her out and resorting instead to lies that will tie him to her against his will, Madame Morrible admitting Galinda to her sorcery class at Elphaba's instigation, and Galinda dancing with Elphaba at the Ozdust Ballroom as they initiate their friendship.

The 28 July 2003 script divided this scene into scenes 6A, 6B, and 6C. In 6A, Nessarose announces to Elphaba that she is going to the dance with Boq, a date arranged by Galinda. Elphaba cannot believe Galinda would have done this without personal gain, but Nessarose is happy and reproaches Elphaba. The scene here is entirely dialog. In 6B, Galinda's friends are with her in her room, and they discover the black, peaked hat. Elphaba comes to thank Galinda for arranging Nessarose's date, and Galinda gives her the hat to wear to the dance, singing what is on the OCR (track 6, 5'07"–5'27"). Elphaba does not realize that this is a trick and runs off to speak with Madame Morrible. In 6C, at the Ozdust Ballroom, Madame Morrible enters and surprises Galinda with a train-ing wand, causing the student to regret giving Elphaba the hat. Instead of telling Nessarose the truth, Boq tells her she is beautiful and pushes her to the dance floor. This is done with the sung passages heard on the OCR (track 6, 6'19"–7'16"). Finally Elphaba enters, realizes she has been tricked, and dances alone. Galinda joins her and they sing together a few lines from "We Deserve Each Other," a tune heard often in "Dancing through Life." The scene ends with all dancing.

In the script from 25 August 2003, the content is similar, but the order of presentation has changed. The script only includes labels for "Scene 6" and "6C." Nessarose and Elphaba open Scene 6, expressing similar sentiments but with less dialog. We then move elsewhere on stage to Galinda and her friends discussing the hat, returning to the sisters for Nessarose and Elphaba to sing their exchange as it has become famous on the recording (OCR, track 6, 4'13"–4'56"). Elphaba then goes to Galinda who gives her the hat in song, and all the students sing some of "Dancing through Life" during the transition to 6C, very similar to the previous version but Elphaba and Galinda do not sing "We Deserve Each Other" after their new understanding.

In the 16 September 2003 script, scenes 6 and 6C (their designation in each of the next three scripts) proceed more or less as known today. Instead of switching between groups at the beginning of Scene 6, Nessarose and Elphaba finish their dialog and singing before we see Galinda with her friends and their plot to give Elphaba the hat, which happens immediately when Elphaba enters the scene. Scene 6C opens with the exchange and singing between Boq and Nessarose, proceeds to Madame Morrible giving Galinda the training wand, and then to the rapprochement between Galinda and Elphaba amidst everyone dancing and singing. The 5 October 2003 version is basically the same in 6 and 6C, except the exchange between Boq and Nessarose has been eliminated, an unusual choice given the scene's importance to telling their story. Stage directions at the beginning of 6C indicate that everyone is dancing. The one major difference in the performance version from 30 October 2003 is that the scene between Boq and Nessarose has been restored at the beginning of 6C. The audience must see in Act 1 that Boq cannot tell Nessarose the truth, and that she truly loves him. Most scripts include dates on each page showing when changes were last made, and the date on page 35 of the 30 October script is the same as that of the script, perhaps meaning that the exchange between Boq and Nessarose was restored at the last moment before the opening.

Scene 7—With some changes in dialog, the content of this scene had been set much earlier in the show's conception. Galinda and Elphaba have returned to their dorm room as friends. They exchange secrets, including Elphaba's dramatic story as to why her father despises her. Galinda wants to help her friend and sings "Popular" while trying to start Elphaba's makeover. Elphaba leaves toward the end of the song believing the process to be impossible, and Galinda concludes the song alone.

Scene 8—This scene changed in a few small but significant ways during these three months. Back in the lecture hall, Doctor Dillamond has learned that he will no longer be allowed to teach, which he quickly tells the class. Madame Morrible arrives to express her sorrow, along with two officials who are there to remove Dillamond, and in the versions from October he leaves dramatically, telling the class that they are not being told the whole truth. In each script, a new teacher enters with a lion cub in a cage. In the earlier scripts the teacher threatens to show the class an operation that will prevent the cub from learning to speak, but later we are simply told that the cage will prevent this development. In each of the five versions, an enraged Elphaba unconsciously places everyone but her and Fiyero in a trance, and they grab the cub and rush out with it. There are no songs in the scene, but scores include the underscoring.

Scene 9—This is another segment that was basically set by late July and changed little thereafter. Fiyero and Elphaba flee to the outskirts of campus with the lion cub, intending to release him. Fiyero is confused and tries to make sense of Elphaba and the event, but she keeps interrupting him. During this conversation they discover feelings for each other, but Fiyero is not ready to act on his desires and flees with the cub, saying that he will release it. Elphaba sings "I'm Not That Girl," during which she sees Galinda and Fiyero together walking in the rain. After she finishes the song, Madame Morrible appears with a letter from the Wizard saying that he has granted Elphaba an audience. Her teacher stops the rain so that Elphaba may walk home. Elphaba sings a reprise of "The Wizard and I," a selection that becomes shorter as one proceeds through the five scripts. The song is fifteen lines long in the 28 July 2003 version and includes mention of how Elphaba can show the Wizard that "something bad" is happening in Oz. In the performance script, the reprise is down to only the text "And there we'll finally be: the Wizard and I," introduced by Morrible singing briefly about how Elphaba will now meet the Wizard and how her teacher wants to be proud. Morrible's sung line was added after the 5 October 2003 script, meaning that this scene was finalized fairly late.

Scene 10—This changed little between the five scripts. Elphaba is with her friends at the train station as they see her off to the Emerald City. There are problems between Galinda, Boq, and Nessarose, and the latter two leave sadly and alone. Galinda worries that Fiyero seems to have changed, and her fears are not allayed when he comes briefly to wish Elphaba well but leaves soon after Galinda tries to impress Fiyero by announcing that she will change her name to "Glinda" in Doctor Dillamond's memory. Glinda is distraught, and Elphaba invites her to the Emerald City to help cheer her up. The song "One Short Day" starts as the scene changes.

Scene 12—None of the five scripts includes Scene 11. The removal of Doctor Dillamond's funeral scene apparently changed the numbering permanently; Scene 11 also does not appear in the 5 December 2006 script to be considered below. The structure of Scene 12 does not change between the five scripts from late July 2003 to the opening. The entire scene is the song "One Short Day," including the segment of the show *Wizomania*. At the end of the song, Glinda sings that they are best friends, and a guard announces that they may see the Wizard.

Scene 13—At this climactic meeting in the Wizard's chamber, Elphaba flees after discovering the Wizard's true nature. The structure changed little between the five scripts. All start with the initial terror of the mechanical head and proceed to the friends meeting the seemingly affable Wizard. He wants Elphaba to prove herself worthy of his support, and Madame Morrible, recently promoted to press secretary, appears with the Grimmerie. Elphaba performs a levitation spell, giving wings to the Wizard's monkeys. She wants to undo the spell when she sees that they are in pain, but Morrible tells her that a spell cannot be reversed, and she suggests that the monkeys will make good spies who can report on the activities of the Talking Animals. Elphaba realizes that the Wizard has no real powers and that he needs her more than she needs him, and she dashes out with the Grimmerie. Glinda tries to catch her as the Wizard and Morrible sound the alarm. The Wizard's music in this scene changed during these three months, and it was during the summer that Joel Grey joined the cast. Schwartz edited the music with Grey in mind. In the 28 July 2003 script, the Wizard only sings "Chance to Fly." "A Sentimental Man" had existed at least since August 2000, but it had been deleted in the 28 July script. By the 25 August 2003 script, a version of "A Sentimental Man" had been restored, and much like the Broadway versions, there were only isolated references to "Chance to Fly." Those several lines are important because the Wizard uses them to promise future success for Elphaba and Glinda, and also because the song "Defying Gravity" in the next scene includes a prominent reference to "a chance to fly."

Scene 14—Schwartz had decided in his first scenario that Elphaba would escape the Wizard's palace by flying away, and the structure of the scene remains in these five scripts. She has both her tender farewell with Glinda and a defiant closing to the act in "Defying Gravity," but she has also become an outlaw.

Act 2

Prologue—Schwartz has stated that his shows tend to have more problems in the first act than the second, contrary to what one often reads concerning the creation of Broadway musicals.[5] That was certainly the case with *Wicked*, where much of Act 2 had taken a recognizable form in previous scripts. Contentment with the second act continued through the three months before the New York opening, when only minor changes took place. The prologue in each of the five scripts is a short reprise of "No One Mourns the Wicked," a vivid depiction of the fear that grips Oz.

Scene 1—No substantive changes take place in the five scripts. Dominated by the song "Thank Goodness," the scene includes an engagement announcement for Glinda and Fiyero; Madame Morrible's false account of the events in Act 1, Scene 13; Fiyero's nonchalance concerning the prospects of marrying Glinda; and Glinda's ambivalence at the conclusion.

Scene 2—These dramatic events in Nessarose's private chamber in the Munchkinland governor's palace illustrate Elphaba's outlaw status and Nessarose's selfishness. All five scripts are remarkably similar. Elphaba arrives unexpectedly at her former home to seek her father's help, but she learns that Nessarose has become governor following her father's death, supposedly caused by embarrassment over Elphaba's activities. Nessarose whines that Elphaba only wants to help others and not her own sister, inspiring Elphaba to place a spell on the jeweled shoes that allows Nessarose to walk. The governor calls Boq, whom she has been keeping as a forced servant, in hopes that her new ability will finally cause him to love her. Boq enters and is horrified to see Elphaba, but he recovers to tell Nessarose that he needs to leave for the Emerald City to try to convince Glinda not to marry Fiyero. This enrages Nessarose, who grabs the Grimmerie and puts a spell on Boq to make him love her, but instead she causes his heart to shrink. (This is a hole in the story, because Nessarose should not be able to read the book of spells. Only Elphaba is able to read it fluently because she is the child of the Wizard and Melena, from both worlds. The Wizard brought the Grimmerie to Oz from the Other World.) Elphaba saves Boq's life as she has in previous versions. She leaves for the Emerald City to try to free the flying monkeys (and probably to see Fiyero), and Nessarose tells Boq that his new condition is Elphaba's fault. There are several musical sequences in the scene, all of which are part of the song "The Wicked Witch of the East."

Scene 3—Elphaba arrives upstairs at the Wizard's chamber during a ball downstairs in honor of the engagement of Glinda and Fiyero. The Wizard surprises her and grabs her broom, blocking her escape. They argue, but through the song "Wonderful" and by releasing the flying monkeys, the Wizard nearly convinces Elphaba to join him. Elphaba, however, discovers Doctor Dillamond, unable to speak, and reneges. Fiyero, now captain of the guard, comes after hearing the commotion. At first he pretends to capture Elphaba, but then he announces that he will leave with her, just after Glinda enters. Fiyero and Elphaba flee on the broom. Madame Morrible arrives and confers with the Wizard on what should be done now to find Elphaba. The distraught Glinda suggests that they start a rumor about Nessarose being in danger, which will drive Elphaba to her side. Glinda leaves. The Wizard and Morrible agree that Elphaba is too smart for a mere rumor to work, and Morrible says that she has another plan. The one substantive change in this scene is in the introduction to the song "Wonderful." In the 28 July and 25 August versions, Elphaba sings lines before the Wizard about how she once longed to meet the Wizard and how she would love to return to more innocent days. It could have been an effective moment, but the final decision was for Joel Grey to do the lion's share of the singing in this scene, with Idina Menzel only joining him for a few lines in "Wonderful."

Scene 3A—In all five versions, Glinda sadly walks down a deserted hall in the palace singing a short reprise of "I'm Not That Girl."

Scene 4—In a scene left basically unchanged from the 28 July script on, Elphaba and Fiyero are next to a lantern in the forest. They sing "As

Long As You're Mine," where the lyrics indicate the physical nature of their love. Elphaba hears a cyclone and sees an image of a flying house. She knows that Nessarose is in danger and that she must go and protect her. Fiyero tells her about Kiamo Ko, one of his family's castles where she could hide safely. He assures her that they will be together again.

Scene 5—Elphaba arrives in Munchkinland where the house has fallen on Nessarose and finds that Glinda got there first and has given Dorothy the jeweled shoes. Glinda and Elphaba argue over the shoes and over Fiyero, and they begin to fight. The Wizard's guards arrive to arrest Elphaba, but Fiyero leaps down from a tree and takes Glinda captive, threatening to kill her if the guards do not release Elphaba. Elphaba flees at the insistence of both Fiyero and Glinda, and the guards tie Fiyero to poles in a cornfield to compel him to tell them where Elphaba has gone.

Scene 6—Elphaba is at Kiamo Ko trying to find a spell in the Grimmerie that will save Fiyero whom she assumes is being tortured. The entire scene is the song "No Good Deed," in which Elphaba reviews her disappointments, questions her own motives, and finally resolves that she will be the wicked witch that all Oz believes her to be. This scene did not change substantively between the end of July and opening night.

Scene 7—In another segment basically set from the end of July, the melody of "No Good Deed" also serves for "March of the Witch-Hunters," where the citizens of Oz serenade Dorothy and her friends as they leave to try and kill Elphaba. Boq, now the Tin Man, reveals in one verse that both he and the Cowardly Lion (the now-grown cub from Act 1, Scene 8) hold her responsible for their conditions. Glinda discovers from Madame Morrible that her mentor was responsible for Nessarose's death. Morrible reminds Glinda that she has achieved her desired prominence and should acquiesce quietly to the charade.

Scene 8—This segment, featuring Elphaba's "death," changed only in minor details during these three months. At Kiamo Ko, Elphaba has imprisoned Dorothy and threatens her if she does not return the shoes. Glinda arrives and urges Elphaba to surrender. Elphaba receives a message through the flying monkeys that obviously tells her of Fiyero's fate, but she lets Glinda believe that he has died. Elphaba agrees to surrender. They sing "For Good" about their friendship. Glinda hides and witnesses Elphaba's "death." After everyone leaves, Glinda finds the bottle of green elixir that Elphaba carried because it had belonged to her mother. Glinda had learned of it as her roommate, and she has noted that the Wizard has a similar bottle.

Scene 9—Glinda returns to the Wizard's palace and shows him the bottle. He realizes that Elphaba was his daughter, and Morrible comments that Elphaba's powers came from her mixed blood. This moment of discovery includes two short musical reprises. All five versions call for a recording of part of the Wizard's song of seduction to Melena in Act 1, Scene 1, and starting in the 16 September version, there was added a few lines from "A Sentimental Man" that the Wizard sings. Glinda orders him to leave Oz, and he exits. She has Morrible arrested. Meanwhile, at Kiamo Ko, the Scarecrow/Fiyero arrives to collect Elphaba. They leave Oz together. The celebration continues in the Emerald City with Glinda promising to try to be Glinda the Good, but also mourning the loss of her friend. The "Finale" includes segments of "No One Mourns the Wicked" and "For Good."

Emendations and Changes: The Performance Script from 5 December 2006

Although the final script from the five compared above is the performance version from the night of 30 October 2003 when *Wicked* opened in New York City, it is not the final revision consulted for this study. Stephen Schwartz's office also made available a script from 5 December 2006, which, like other scripts, includes a date on each page noting when the last changes were made. Some pages bear a date from before the show opened, but there were also steady changes made until the date of this script, the work of tenacious writers who were not yet convinced that the script was a finished document, even after *Wicked* became a hit. Schwartz has explained, for example, how he rewrote sections of "Wonderful" when George Hearn took over for Joel Grey as the Wizard, and then they made further revisions for David Garrison when he became the Wizard on tour, and then, when Ben Vereen assumed the role on Broadway, Schwartz inserted the tour ending of the song into every production.[6] The revisions that one observes in the 5 December 2006 script, however, go beyond attention to this one song. The alterations are relatively minor, never changing the meaning of a scene, but sometimes introducing a different tone for a situation or character. In several scenes, the writers restored lines that had been deleted from previous versions. Significant changes in this script following *Wicked*'s opening are mentioned below.

The creators changed a number of lines in Act 1, Scene 2, where everyone meets at Shiz. The initial exchange between Elphaba, Nessarose, and Madame Morrible underwent several alterations, and lines disappeared from Galinda's introduction to Morrible. After Elphaba has displayed her power and Morrible says that she will be the sole student in her sorcery class, lines reappeared from an early version for Galinda where she complains of a headache after failing to get her way. Act 2, Scene 5, Fiyero's entrance, includes the restoration of Fiyero's car nearly hitting Elphaba and an angry exchange between them, bringing Elphaba into an antagonistic scene with her future boyfriend. (Stephen Oremus notes that they made this change to show the combative relationship between the two earlier in the show.[7]) A number of other scenes in Act 1 include subtle changes in the 5 December 2006 version, such as one of the government officials in Scene 8 blowing a loud whistle at Doctor Dillamond before dragging him off, and in Scene 10, Galinda's condescending instructions to Elphaba on how to speak with the Wizard have been cut. In Scene 13 in the Wizard's chamber, some of his lines about the mechanical head have been deleted, and as Elphaba starts to introduce the reason for their visit to the Wizard, Glinda acts surprised that they have not come for themselves but for the Talking Animals. This made explicit Glinda's personal motives with the Wizard in a way that had seldom appeared in previous versions.

There are fewer changes in Act 2 of the 5 December 2006 script than in Act 1. This might be expected, given the fact that Act 1 had more changes at almost every stage than Act 2. In Scene 2, as Elphaba is about to leave Nessarose, restored from a previous version is Elphaba's claim that she is going to the Emerald City to rescue the flying monkeys, but Nessarose suggests that she is going to see Fiyero. Scene 3, Elphaba's meeting with the Wizard, includes many alterations from after opening night. In the new version, the audience sees Glinda and Fiyero dancing at their ball as Elphaba arrives, a restoration from a previous version. The Wizard no longer grabs Elphaba's broom to trap her at his palace; she apparently stays of her own volition. The Wizard also states that she has returned to him because she wants what everyone else does: for the Wizard to help her. In another new line, Elphaba states that she wants nothing from him. The song "Wonderful" includes a new spoken lead-in for the

Wizard that makes him sound more beneficent. Also, there are changes in the content and location of dialog before and during the song. On the OCR, they sing several lines together after Elphaba has decided to work with the Wizard (track 13, 4'19"–4'27"), but in the new version, these are split into a three-line solo exchange. Also, the moment in which the Wizard goes and moves levers to make much of the set move, designed to further charm and dazzle Elphaba, has been cut, changing some of the dialog as well. The scene also includes several more small changes in lines. The only other line change in Act 2 takes place in the last scene, where Glinda's statement to the Wizard about Elphaba ("So she was yours. All along.") is cut, but this was unnecessary because the audience can figure out from the context that the Wizard was her father.

Conclusion

When one considers where the plot of *Wicked* began in Gregory Maguire's novel and what the audience now sees on stage on Broadway and elsewhere in the world, one understands how important Stephen Schwartz, Winnie Holzman, Marc Platt, and others have been in shaping the material into the popular musical. The creators of the show acquired the rights to the story, which they interpreted as a concept and a set of memorable characters that they were then free to work with and manipulate into what they hoped would be a viable musical. The story they tell is as much by Schwartz, Holzman, and their collaborators as it is by Maguire. The other impression that one takes away from the documents analyzed in this chapter is that Schwartz and Holzman have been relentless in their pursuit of what they consider the perfect script for the show, with rewrites occurring right up until the moment the show opened on Broadway, and then additional work continuing for more than three years after the successful premiere. Schwartz and his collaborators extended the same rigor and attention to detail to the music and lyrics as well, as will be shown in the next chapter.

Notes

1. Unpublished notes consulted in Stephen Schwartz's office, 20 March 2008.
2. Schwartz paraphrased this from Gregory Maguire, *Wicked: The Life and Times of the Wicked Witch of the West* (New York: ReganBooks, 1995), 75. In the

novel's context, Galinda has recently arrived at Shiz University and is trying to find her place. She had thought of her entrance into the school as "testimony to her brilliance," but she also "supposed, glumly, that she had meant to be a sort of living marble bust."

3. Carol de Giere, *Defying Gravity: The Creative Career of Stephen Schwartz from "Godspell" to "Wicked"* (New York: Applause Theatre & Cinema Books, 2008), 503–9.

4. de Giere, 357–58.

5. Personal interview with Stephen Schwartz, New York, 1 April 2008.

6. Personal interview with Stephen Schwartz, New York, 22 March 2005, reported in Paul R. Laird, "The Creation of a Broadway Musical: Stephen Schwartz, Winnie Holzman, and *Wicked*," in *The Cambridge Companion to the Musical*, 2nd edition, ed. William A. Everett and Paul R. Laird, 340–52 (Cambridge: Cambridge University Press, 2008), 351–52.

7. Telephone interview with Stephen Oremus, 5 February 2008.

THE MUSIC AND LYRICS OF *WICKED*

S tephen Schwartz's score for *Wicked* has played a major role in the show's popularity. Although he has written several scores since the early 1970s, *Wicked* has been his most successful effort since *Godspell, Pippin,* and *The Magic Show,* placing three decades between his youthful hits and his last major Broadway triumph. Certainly other Broadway creators have enjoyed long careers—Richard Rodgers, for example, wrote scores in every decade from the 1920s to the 1970s—but it is unusual to start one's career in musical theater in New York with three hits and then not have a similar success for three decades. In terms of commercial success and the length of the run, *Wicked* is Schwartz's biggest success, and it demonstrates substantial growth in his work as a composer since the 1970s.

Schwartz's score for *Wicked* has drawn attention from other writers, including the composer himself. Schwartz wrote about the creative process and the musical choices he made for each major song in *"Wicked": The Grimmerie.*[1] Much of Schwartz's material on the music has to do with how many versions he wrote for each particular song placement and why they made those changes, but he also describes the musical quality that he desired in each song, such as his inspiration from bubblegum rock in "Popular" and his evocation of Rachmaninov in "No Good Deed." Schwartz also discussed the music from *Wicked* with Carol de Giere for her book, and she wrote about the score, including some musical description, but that is not a primary focus of her study.[2] My chapter on the creation of *Wicked* in *The Cambridge Companion to the Musical* includes material derived from Schwartz's comments on the music and a bit of analysis. All of these sources offer commentary on how Schwartz used various motives for musico-dramatic unification in the score. In the present chapter, the analysis of each number includes discussion of materials mentioned in other sources, but the primary focus will be on musical description and analysis of the salient features of each number. In addition, this chapter will include descriptions of the music from drafts, sketches, and deleted songs, most made available for this study by Schwartz's office.

Schwartz as Composer and Lyricist

Stephen Schwartz has never been shy about revealing how he works. Herb Braha, a member of the original Cherry Lane Theater cast of *Godspell*, remarked how surprised he was by Schwartz's willingness to name his models for each song in that show,[3] and the composer/lyricist has remained frank and honest about such matters throughout his career. It is a topic that we addressed in an interview in 2005, the results of which appeared in a chapter in the second edition of *The Cambridge Companion to the Musical*.[4] He usually writes music and lyrics simultaneously,[5] but for *Wicked* he found himself often writing the lyrics first because the story was "so intricate."[6] (His concern for getting the lyrics right first in *Wicked* becomes clear below upon consideration of an e-mail that he wrote to Joe Mantello about "The Wizard and I.") His experience as a lyricist has been colored by his work with other composers, including Leonard Bernstein, Charles Strouse, and Alan Menken. Usually when writing words for the music of another composer, Schwartz sets words to the tunes, and he is comfortable working in either order. For Schwartz, writing lyrics is more a craft than an art, and one becomes more proficient at it with experience. He keeps a notebook with ideas for lyrics, often with ideas jotted down as a result of conversations with collaborators, such as when he discussed song ideas with Winnie Holzman while working on *Wicked*. As Schwartz said, "It's getting a lot of raw material out there without getting in my own way, and then making choices."[7] A revealing look into Schwartz the lyricist occurred when circumstances caused him to revisit the lyrics for Bernstein's *Mass*, originally written in 1971, in 2004 and 2005. Bernstein did not get down to serious work on the score for *Mass* until the spring of that year, with the premiere looming in early September. Schwartz joined the project at about the end of May, and the two worked rapidly, moving on to the next number as soon as one was in an acceptable form. Schwartz has described those lyrics as being like a "first draft," and when the opportunity presented itself, he was gratified to have the chance to improve lyrics written at a tender age.[8] As he has continued to write lyrics, he finds that he has learned more of the craft.

Schwartz describes a method that he tends to follow in writing his own songs, but within this statement it is clear that this only describes his customary process, and it can change with different projects and conditions:

> I tend to start with a title. The title is very important to me because it helps to focus what the song is about. Then I might have a little piece of music or four lines of a lyric and then, things sort of develop together. A lot of the time the music gets finalized first and then I go back and work out how the lyric's going to fit within that, partly because I've now had so much experience working with other composers, particularly with Alan [Menken], that I've learned to work that way.[9]

As will be seen with the sketches consulted for this chapter, Schwartz often starts the music for a piece as a lead sheet with melody and chords, but he also might begin with the accompaniment or a sketch of a brief idea. His approach to emotional content in a song derives from what he calls "a certain amount of 'Method Acting,'" an effort to "become the character."[10] He finds that the choices he makes while writing a song are both conscious and emotional responses to a situation, and he continually looks back on his material with a critical eye to avoid repetition. A favorite question he asks himself is, "Am I responding in so much the same way I always respond that it is starting to become . . . just a cliché?"[11] As will be shown in this chapter, ranging over musical material written between about 2000 and even after *Wicked* opened, Schwartz tirelessly revises his own work. If he happens to settle upon a cliché, it is not from a lack of reconsideration.

Carol de Giere considered Schwartz's methods of songwriting in her book *Defying Gravity*. Her exploration of the topic revealed many of the same steps and attitudes described above. In an effort to describe his process briefly, Schwartz said to her that a songwriter should "Tell the truth and make it rhyme,"[12] a reference to how truthful he believes songs must be to the human spirit. How he works on finding song placements in a show appears in de Giere's description of *Wicked*'s creation, where Schwartz worked with Winnie Holzman and Marc Platt on the storyboard, using index cards to show song placements and scenes.[13] They worked hard at getting everything correctly in order before really starting to write the show. In her most detailed section on Schwartz as a songwriter, de Giere reports, as above, that he tries to become the character to decide what ideas the song must convey.[14] Schwartz also told de Giere that he cannot become too fond of his songs because they might be discarded when collaborators discover problems with how they work at that moment in the story.[15]

Creating the Score

A complete reconstruction of Stephen Schwartz's compositional process for the score of *Wicked* is unattainable. Schwartz has commented on his work for Carol de Giere and David Cote, and he also granted interviews for this book, but no creator could remember enough about a four-year creative venture to elucidate fully the process for any interviewer. Schwartz's memories and impressions form a starting point in describing the score's genesis for this chapter, augmented by access to drafts of songs and scripts made available by the composer. These sources do not constitute Schwartz's complete body of musical materials for the show, a collection that the composer has not organized. Considered together, however, what was available for this chapter allows the most revealing look at *Wicked*'s musical development yet assembled, also illuminating how Schwartz works and what he considered the most important musical traits in the score. As shown in chapters 3 and 4, Schwartz was involved in developing the show's plot from the beginning and worked closely with his collaborators as the details of the plot continued to evolve. For the composer/lyricist, the most important function of each song was how it would help move the story forward and tell the audience about the characters. Creation of the songs, therefore, cannot be separated from the development of the show's other aspects, meaning that this chapter will inevitably involve nonmusical sides of *Wicked*.

Most of the following materials were made available for this study by the composer or by his assistant Michael Cole:

1. A folder of Act 1 songs as they existed on 30 August 2000, after Schwartz's self-imposed "writer's hibernation" as he prepared for a reading of the act that took place on 28 September.[16] What appears in the folder for each song varies, ranging from drafts of brief sections to lead sheets for entire songs. Some also include lyric sheets, or music and lyric sheets, together providing a detailed snapshot of Schwartz's work on the show's music to that point.

2. A script used by chorus member Michael Cole as they worked toward the New York reading of the entire show on 14 December 2001. The source includes all of the choral music as it existed at that time, and some material for soloists. A useful companion to this source was a set of audio tracks on YouTube that include recordings of songs close to this version of the script. The files were identified simply as the "*Wicked* 2001 Workshop," meaning that they might emanate from the 14 December 2001 reading.[17] These video clips are described in the appendix.

3. A full piano/vocal score with revisions of each number dated between 25 March and 7 October 2003, the latter date about three weeks before *Wicked* opened on Broadway. The score carries the feeling of a document in progress, with sections crossed out and handwritten changes. This source will be compared below in detail with the score described in the next paragraph, which was the source for the detailed musical analysis of the show in this chapter.

4. A piano/vocal score of the show more or less in its Broadway version, with each musical number primarily showing revisions from October 2004, but with some changes from 21 January 2005. As shown in the previous chapter with a script that dates from three years after *Wicked* opened, work continued on the show, and alterations made after the Broadway premiere are reflected in this source.

5. A series of piano/vocal scores prepared in September and October 2008 for *The Yellow Brick Road Not Taken*, a benefit

performance of earlier versions of *Wicked* songs and deleted numbers presented on 27 October 2008 in celebration of the show's fifth anniversary on Broadway. The arrangements and orchestrations were prepared by Ben Cohn, who has worked in the Broadway orchestra and served as its assistant director.[18] At least one reference in the dialog in the opening sequence demonstrates comic awareness of the event for which they were arranged, and it is difficult to know how the music might have been changed as well. They do appear, however, to be songs from earlier in the show's development, mostly undated.

6. Other smaller documents discovered in Schwartz's office that offer interesting information or commentary on the score's development, considered below with larger sources in chronological order.

7. Investigation in Schwartz's New York office brought to light materials from a number of songs deleted from the show, which will also be considered in the last segment of the chapter. This does not include every song removed from the show, but there are several that illustrate what appeared in some song placements before Schwartz wrote the current version. Like the 30 August 2000 folder of Act 1 songs, these versions of deleted songs include various combinations of drafts of sections, complete songs, and lyric sheets. Such primary sources, considered along with various statements that Schwartz and others have made about deleted songs, demonstrate in some detail what did not appear in the final version of *Wicked*.

8. A fairly detailed look at the *Wicked* score, based upon an interview with the composer and a detailed listening to the OCR, is "*Wicked*'s Ground*break*ing Score" by Robert Vieira, a composer for musical theater. Vieira's essay appeared in 2005 in the newsletter *The Schwartz Scene* on Carol de Giere's website for the composer.[19] Vieira provided an analysis of musical and performance aspects of the score with emphasis on how Schwartz served the lyrics and the plot; material on melodic, harmonic, and rhythmic elements; and how performers ren-

dered the material. Vieira cued his discussion to time indices in the OCR and the selections that Schwartz published from the show.[20] Those interested in detailed musical considerations of this score must read Vieira's work, which will be referred to in my analysis.

Before considering any of these materials, we should identify all of the songs it has been possible to establish that Schwartz wrote for *Wicked*. They are listed in textbox 5-1, by major song placements in the show, and chronologically within each placement.

Textbox 5.1
Songs That Stephen Schwartz Wrote for Each Major Placement in *Wicked*

This is as complete a list of songs that Schwartz composed for each placement it has been possible to establish from the primary sources consulted for this study and existing secondary sources. Some songs existed in multiple versions, and it is not possible to know with certainty how many there might have been, or how many changes Schwartz might have made to a song that would have caused him to consider it a new version. When possible, a date has been provided for when a song first appears in the written record. That version should then be understood to exist in subsequent versions of the show until another song took its place. Cross-references supply where in this text each of these versions is described. Deleted song placements appear in brackets with numbers followed by a letter.

Act I

1. "Opening"
    "Good News"—sketch of eight measures of music that existed on 30 August 2000 (see p. 103); music from 21 November 2001 shows that this had become part of the opening number.
    "No One Mourns the Wicked"—lyrics existed on 30 August 2000 with possible key areas sketched in (pp. 103–4); by 12 March

2001, other segments in lyrics had been added, such as the seduction and birth scene (p. 59).

Undated versions for this placement include a brief "New Opening" (p. 169) and a fully realized "Opening" prepared in six sections that appeared in *The Yellow Brick Road Not Taken* (hereafter *YBR*; see pp. 169–70).

2. "Dear Old Shiz"

Song existed in a form fairly close to the final version on 30 August 2000; in early versions of the show, this song was after "Making Good."

3. "The Wizard and I"

"Making Good"—the lyrics and melodic line existed on 30 August 2000, and in early scripts was before "Dear Old Shiz" because it took place in the deleted train station scene (pp. 104–5); the script from 21 November 2001 included a brief reprise of this number after Doctor Dillamond invites Elphaba to help with his experiment (p. 65), and music for this reprise appeared in *YBR* (pp. 170–71).

"The Wizard and I"—lyrics for the introduction appeared in the October 2002 script, and Schwartz wrote the song in about October/November 2002 (pp. 124–25); later versions include alterations.

4. "What Is This Feeling?"

"Bad Situation"—lyrics and vocal parts with some accompaniment existed on 30 August 2000 (pp. 105–7); Schwartz suggests that there were two versions of this song (he told de Giere [p. 377] there were two versions of "Bad Situation," one of "Far Be It from Me," and two of "What Is This Feeling?"); various versions are described in chapter 5 (pp. 113–15, 171–77).

"Far Be It from Me"—name of the first section of a song that includes a later section bearing the title "Bad Situation 2001" (p. 176).

"What Is This Feeling"—the introduction exists in a form in the October 2002 script with the note that lyrics would follow; two versions including one that sounded like a Richard Rodgers waltz existed by January 2003 (p. 134; see also de Giere, 375); the current version was composed once rehearsals had started for the tryout run in San Francisco (de Giere, 378).

5. "Something Bad"

Lyrics first appear in sources consulted for this study in the October 2002 script; de Giere (p. 355) reports that Joe Mantello helped provide the context of the Talking Animal component of the plot that allowed Schwartz to write this song; later versions include alterations.

"Something Bad" could be considered a song that replaced "As If by Magic," the previous number in which Doctor Dillamond sang, but it was in a different placement (see 8a below).

6. "Dancing through Life"

"Who Could Say No to You?"—lyrics existed on 30 August 2000 (p. 107).

"Easy as Winkie Wine"—undated song extant in a music manuscript and lyric sheet (pp. 177–79) that was, like "Dancing through Life," a musical scene with several sections; de Giere (p. 349) says this was the second song in this placement.

"We Deserve Each Other"—lyrics existed in the 12 March 2001 script, and the tune associated with it and other lyrics for the song appear in most succeeding versions of this scene in segments of varying lengths and associated with several characters (pp. 114–17, 138–39, 178–79); the music also became the basis for the material in Act 2 between Boq and Nessarose (see "The Wicked Witch of the East," below, Act 2, no. 2).

"The Emerald City Stomp"—lyrics existed in the 21 November 2001 script with other segments included such as "We Deserve Each Other" (p. 65); musical sources indicate that the song existed in more than one version (pp. 114, 179).

"Which Way's the Party?"—two versions of this scene (including "We Deserve Each Other," among other segments) were consulted for this study, one bearing the revision date of 20 July 2002 (pp. 180–83), and lyrics exist in the October 2002 script (pp. 67–68) and the 31 March 2003 script (p. 71).

"Dancing through Life"—de Giere (p. 405) reports that Schwartz wrote this song in July 2003, and a version of the lyrics first appears in the 28 July 2003 script, where this musical scene has started to take its final shape (pp. 77, 137–39); this placement includes "The Ozdust Dance," a version of which had existed in "Which Way's the Party?"

7. "Popular"

Lyrics (and perhaps the music) were in nearly their finished form on 30 August 2000 (pp. 107–8), with some later alterations.

8. "I'm Not That Girl"

Lyrics (and perhaps the music) were in nearly their finished form on 30 August 2000 (p. 109), with some later alterations.

[8a. "As If by Magic"—deleted song placement]

["As If by Magic"—lyrics existed in the 12 March 2001 script, sung when Doctor Dillamond, Elphaba, and Fiyero have success with the experiment (p. 61); the musical version was sung in *YBR* (pp. 183–85); because both are intended for Doctor Dillamond, the song could be considered the forerunner of "Something Bad," despite its appearance in another song placement (see 5, above).

"Something Bad (Reprise)"—lyrics existed in the October 2002 script for the same three characters to sing, but this scene was later cut.]

[8b. "Dear Old Shiz (Reprise)"—deleted song placement]

[Lyrics existed by the 12 March 2001 script, with more complete lyrics and music in the 21 November 2001 script, but this scene was later cut. Another document lists the title of this segment as "Requiem for a Goat" (p. 123).]

9. "One Short Day"

Lyrics and vocal lines existed on 30 August 2000 (pp. 109–11), with many alterations in later versions, including a major revision under way in the 31 March 2003 script with indications in two places that lyrics will be added later (p. 73).

10. "A Sentimental Man"/"The Chance to Fly"

[On the OCR and elsewhere, this placement is known exclusively as "A Sentimental Man," but at one point "The Chance to Fly" was a separate song that followed very soon after "A Sentimental Man." They are part of the same placement for the Wizard, but Schwartz thought of them as two songs. He stated in an interview, "I basically took the two songs and mushed them together" (personal interview with Stephen Schwartz, New York, 1 April 2008).]

"A Sentimental Man"/"The Chance to Fly"—lyrics (and perhaps music) for both existed on 30 August 2000 (pp. 111–12); *YBR* included a version of each song, with "A Sentimental Man" (revisions dated 1 July 2002) coming to a cadence, and then "The Chance to Fly" starting shortly thereafter under the new title (pp. 185–88); when Schwartz conflated the songs, he retained more of "A Sentimental Man," but the lyric "chance to fly" is important; Schwartz has stated that he reworked "A Sentimental Man" after Joel Grey joined the Broadway cast, and he made further revisions when George Hearn replaced Grey, with more revisions when Ben Vereen took over the role.

11. "Defying Gravity" ("For Goodness Sake" and "I Hope You're Happy")

[Schwartz originally conceived the end of the act as two songs: the first an angry duet between Elphaba and Glinda in which they each deplore the other's behavior during their audience with the Wizard. The second song was always to be "Defying Gravity," and gradually the other song's placement became the introduction to this act's finale.]

"For Goodness Sake"—lyrics existed on 30 August 2000, including a segment that starts "I hope you're happy . . ." and carries the same meaning as the current opening of "Defying Gravity" (pp. 112–13); the sources consulted also included an undated music manuscript of a complete song called "For Goodness Sake" (pp. 187–89).

"I Hope You're Happy"—lyrics for this as a separate song existed in the 12 March 2001 script, but by the 21 November 2001 script, this sentiment had become the opening of "Defying Gravity."

"Defying Gravity"—lyrics existed in a remarkably finished form on 30 August 2000, but small alterations continued in subsequent versions (pp. 112–13).

Act 2

1. "Thank Goodness"

"Happy Healing Day"—lyrics existed in the 12 March 2001 script, and by the 21 November 2001 script the opening scene in the act included lyrics that later became part of "Thank Goodness" (pp. 62, 66).

"Thank Goodness"—lyrics exist in the October 2002 script with subsequent revisions, including the 16 September 2003 script that includes the introduction now heard in the show; de Giere states that work on "Thank Goodness" took place at the end of 2000 (p. 322), but at that point the song in this placement was "Happy Healing Day."

2. "Wicked Witch of the East"

"Step by Step by Step"—lyrics with intervening dialog and most of vocal line existed 30 August 2000, but at the time this was intended for Act 1 (pp. 108–9); the song had moved to Act 2, Scene 2, in the 12 March 2001 script; undated music manuscripts that comprise two sections of the song indicate that this also existed with the title "You've Got to Love Me" (pp. 189–90); the YBR version is different than either of the first two mentioned (pp. 190–92); de Giere (p. 351) says that Schwartz wrote a song for this placement before a reading in December 2001 and provides a manuscript facsimile (p. 353) with Nessarose singing text pleading for Elphaba to save Boq while Elphaba chants in counterpoint.

"We Deserve Each Other"—lyrics in the 12 November 2001 script demonstrate that by this point "Step by Step by Step" had been abandoned and "We Deserve Each Other" now provided the musical basis for the sequence (p. 66; de Giere suggests that this decision was made in late 2001 [pp. 351–52]); the 16 September 2003 script includes Elphaba starting to sing "Defying Gravity" to Nessarose at the beginning of the song to try to enlist her in her crusade, an idea for which there is also a musical draft, but Nessarose tells her to "shut up" (p. 189).

"The Wicked Witch of the East"—this musical scene emerged late in the process, but it included elements that had been part of the scene for months at that point; much of the scene was in place by the 16 September 2003 script, but Elphaba's reference to "Defying Gravity" early in the scene (later cut) shows that changes were still to be made in the weeks before the show opened.

3. "Wonderful"

Lyrics (and perhaps music) existed by the 12 March 2001 script, with alterations continuing in subsequent versions (p. 63).

4. "I'm Not That Girl (Reprise)"

Lyrics (and perhaps music) existed by the 12 March 2001 script (p. 63).

5. "As Long As You're Mine"

Schwartz first wrote the song in 1971 (see de Giere, 302), and the first lyrics for *Wicked* existed by the 12 March 2001 script, with alterations to lyrics continuing in subsequent versions (p. 63).

6. "No Good Deed"

Lyrics (and perhaps music) existed by the 12 March 2001 script, with alterations continuing in subsequent versions; de Giere (pp. 323–24) reports that the song's original title was "Reap the Whirlwind," a title mentioned in early scenarios.

7. "March of the Witch-Hunters"

Lyrics with some resemblance to what the song became existed by the 12 March 2001 script, but they do not appear to have been sung to the same tune as "No Good Deed" (p. 63); by 21 November 2001, the song was based on the current tune as "No Good Deed."

8. "For Good"

Lyrics existed by the 12 March 2001 script; de Giere (pp. 326–27) describes how it was written in early 2001.

9. "Finale"

This number with lyrics built from "No One Mourns the Wicked" and "For Good" existed by the 12 March 2001 script, with subsequent changes.

Act 1: Songs on 30 August 2000

Schwartz's folder of Act 1 songs from 30 August 2000 opens with the following list of titles and the characters that would sing each song:

1. "No One Mourns the Wicked"—Scarecrow, Glinda, Madame Morrible, Frex, Salesman, Midwife, and Chorus
2. "Making Good"—Elphaba
3. "Dear Old Shiz"—Students
4. "Bad Situation"—Elphaba, Galinda, Pfannee, Shenshen, and students
5. "Who Could Say No to You?"—Fiyero
6. "Popular"—Galinda
7. "I'm Not That Girl"—Elphaba
8. "Step by Step by Step"—Nessarose, Elphaba
9. "One Short Day"—Elphaba, Glinda, citizens of Oz
10. "Sentimental Man"—Wizard
11. "The Chance to Fly"—Wizard, Madame Morrible, Glinda
12. "For Goodness Sake"—Elphaba, Glinda
13. "Defying Gravity"—Elphaba, Glinda, Soldiers

At this point, more than three years before the show started its Broadway run, the majority of song placements for the first act had been decided, and most songs existed in some form. As shown in textbox 5-1, "Making Good" was replaced by "The Wizard and I" (which follows "Dear Old Shiz" in the final version), and "Bad Situation" gave way to "What Is This Feeling?" Fiyero's "Who Could Ever Say No to You?" disappeared in favor of several other possibilities before the placement became the musical sequence "Dancing through Life." Nessarose would have sung "Step by Step by Step" after Elphaba bewitched her shoes so she could walk, an event in later versions from Act 2 in the scene of "Wicked Witch of the East." A portion of "The Chance to Fly" was shortened and folded into "A Sentimental Man," and part of "For Goodness Sake" became the opening of "Defying Gravity." Description of what the folder includes for each song demonstrates how far along Schwartz was in composing the first act by the late summer of 2000.

The first musical snippet in the folder is an eight-measure sketch with the text "Good news!" in the last two measures. It is mostly bitonal in C and E major, and material like it sounds in the show today just before and during the initial vocal statement of "Good news! She's dead!" (original cast recording [hereafter "OCR"], track 1, 1'00"–1'11"). This functions as a dissonant fanfare that musically communicates early in the show that the Ozian celebration is not as unambiguously happy as it appears, one of many such telling musical cues to the drama that Schwartz provides in his score.

What appears in the 2000 folder for "No One Mourns the Wicked" is a script on which Schwartz appears to have provided chords or key areas for various sections. Much of the scene has changed, so one cannot follow the keys exactly in the current score, but he seems to have made several decisions that remained in the show. For example, he had placed the show's opening in A minor and the enactment of Elphaba's conception and birth in G major (OCR, track 1, 3'47"ff, starting with the waltz between Frex and Melena). He noted a tone cluster based on A-flat minor and A minor chords (not the tone cluster that appears in the score) as Elphaba appears from her mother, followed by C-sharp minor along with material from "As Long As You're Mine" as they discover that the baby is green (which describes what one hears on the OCR, track 1, 4'53"ff), and Schwartz also indicated that he would use an A-augmented chord over G in the bass as they announce that Elphaba is green (OCR, track 1, 5'09"–5'12"). The scene would conclude with an E major chord over A-sharp in the bass (OCR, track 1, 6'22"–6'35"), Schwartz's tribute to Bernstein's famous tritone at the end of *West Side Story*, where Bernstein places an F-sharp in the bass against a C major triad.[21] Schwartz's indication of "As Long As You're Mine" to accompany Elphaba's birth demonstrates that he had planned this early on using that song's opening motive to help unify the score. This script excerpt shows that the scene of "No One Mourns the Wicked" changed greatly over the next three years, with the souvenir hawkers, reporters, Madame Morrible, and Dorothy

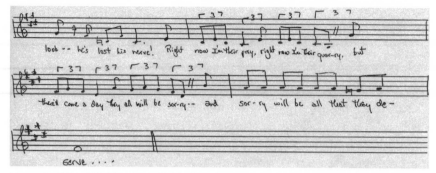

Example 5.1. "Making Good" (August 2000 folder), Introduction, mm. 7–11.

and her friends removed from the celebration. Many lyrics in segments later changed, but one section that is very much like what one now sees on stage is the birth scene. Glinda enters the scene later and shows sadness at her friend's presumed demise.

The folder includes a lyric sheet for "Making Good" in addition to the melodic line of the song, without chord symbols. Elphaba sings this at the train station in Munchkinland. She looks forward to leaving this place where she has been an object of derision and believes that those people will be sorry someday when she is able to find her "special destiny." She is angry, labeling a woman who stared at her at the train station a "hatchet-face hag" and her father "a tough old bastard"—this is a bitter Elphaba, different from the first act today. The lyric sheet includes most of the words from Elphaba's "Unlimited" stanza (addressed to Nessarose in her absence) that appears in "The Wizard and I" (OCR, track 3, 3'39"–4'19"), but those words are not set to music here. The music of "Making Good" is primarily in a sweet E major and evokes the spirit of a naive girl, perhaps out of character for part of the text. It is in 4/4 and opens with a recitative that features triplet motion, which changes tellingly to duplets as Elphaba delivers her final dismissal of those who have mistreated her: "And sorry will be all that they deserve . . ." (see example 5.1). There are then two attractive verses (see example 5.2 for an excerpt), followed by a stirring bridge where she speculates on her future accomplishments. The final stanza repeats material from the first two, but it is also different as Elphaba wonders what it will be like when her father tries to claim some credit for her future deeds. Toward the end, Schwartz moves to F major momentarily, setting up a fulfilling cadence on E major. It is possible

Example 5.2. "Making Good" (August 2000 folder), Verse, mm. 1–8.

that the song was cut partly because of the mismatch in tone between the music and the cynical lyrics.

On a lyric sheet for "Dear Old Shiz," one learns that this music was supposed to follow "Making Good" immediately. The text is the same as in the final version, and the music is similar. Schwartz wrote the August 2000 version in A minor, which makes sense after the E major of "Making Good," but the score today starts in G-sharp minor and ends in B major. Like what one hears today, this four-part chordal harmonization, with the only major departure in the final version being Galinda's melisma (OCR, track 2, 1'12"–1'17") that leads to the final cadence, was added later as her character became more important.

The folder includes complete lyrics and vocal parts, with limited piano accompaniment sketched in for "Bad Situation." According to the lyric sheet, Elphaba and Galinda are on their own sides of their dorm room, and they present their private thoughts in song, like Emile and Nellie in "Twin Soliloquies" of *South Pacific*. The roommates harbor murderous thoughts and describe each other in absolute terms. When in the room, they hope that the other might be out or sleeping, but they resolve to make the best of this "bad situation." The lyric sheet suggests a possible scene change to biology class, or something else happens that involves the two girls. The next lyrics are sung by Galinda's friends Pfannee and Shenshen, material that survived into "What Is This Feeling?" ("Dear Galinda . . . ," OCR, track 4, 1'56"–2'07"). After Galinda sings with her friends, another note in the script suggests that perhaps the scene should change here to the biology class. Other students join the song. They side with Galinda and hope to see a fight between the two roommates. The song ends with Elphaba and Galinda singing alternately with the other students in one of Schwartz's many counterpoint songs. He wrote a winning tune for "Bad Situation."

Example 5.3. "Bad Situation" (August 2000 folder), Introduction, mm. 13–16; Verse, mm. 1–9.

It opens with a verse in G minor in a rollicking 6/8, in contrast to the insulting lyrics. As the girls realize that they must make the best of this dilemma, the verse kicks in as a sort of jaunty vaudeville tune in 4/4 and B-flat major with catchy chromaticism (see example 5.3), such as at the final cadence of the verse, where the unexpected E-flat minor7 arpeggio and chromatic descent to the tonic passes through an interesting progression with a minor dominant (see example 5.4). That music is marked for repeat for the second verse and chorus, provided in the lyrics. The majority

Example 5.4. "Bad Situation" (August 2000 folder), Verse, mm. 10–14.

of the remainder of "Bad Situation" is a counterpoint segment as the other students comment and Elphaba and Galinda reprise their chorus. There is a solo interruption for Elphaba who cannot believe that she must continue to deal with the same insensitive comments that she endured in Munchkinland. Schwartz based that music on "Making Good."

All that appears in the folder for "Who Could Say No to You?" is a lyric sheet, a far cry from the long sequence that became "Dancing through Life." Fiyero was to have sung these lyrics to Galinda. He is smitten with her, unlike his cool reaction to her aggressive attention in the current version. Here he suggests that she give him "a wild goose to pursue" and desires "go trip the light fantastic tonight" with her, meaning that this scene would have also headed to a dance.

The folder includes lyrics only for "Popular," and the song was already close to its finished form. The opening verse includes one tiny change that added an attractive inner rhyme ("Though it's the toughest one I've had to face" became "Though it's the toughest case I've yet to face," OCR, track 6, 39"–44"), and in the last stanza, after Elphaba leaves, Schwartz cut the lines "I only wish/You could be as popular as me" before Galinda sings "La la la la/You'll be popular . . ." (OCR, track 6, 3'25"ff). Perhaps Schwartz made this change because the deleted line conflicted with the song's closing statement. The August 2000 version also includes a brief interruption of dialog before the stanza opening "When I see depressing creatures . . ." (OCR, track 6, 2'13"ff) that did not make the final version.

"Step by Step by Step" was for Nessarose, a character whose role became smaller as the creators realized that the core of their plot was in the interactions between Elphaba and Galinda. Nessarose's only extended musical moment in the current score takes place in "Wicked Witch of the East," which Schwartz left off the original cast album because it reveals too much of the plot. The August 2000 folder includes lyrics and intervening dialog for "Step by Step by Step" as well as much of the music, although in places Schwartz had not yet provided the piano part. The song starts after Elphaba has enchanted the silver shoes so Nessarose can walk. Instead of showing gratitude, Nessarose becomes spiteful and conniving. She asks if Elphaba could know what it has felt like to depend on her and the pity of others. She dances wildly and enumerates her "steps," involving a new wardrobe and going out to be seen. Elphaba misconstrues and sings of her happiness for her sister, but Nessarose cuts her off and begins her real planning. She learns that Elphaba does not want to be governor of Munchkinland and declares herself her father's successor, ordering that his body be removed and a coach be sent so that Elphaba can return to Shiz. Elphaba sings another verse with her music, saying that now Nessarose frightens her. Her sister ignores her and sings of how she will seek revenge on those who have wronged her, how she will impress Boq more than Galinda and achieve her dreams. Her final lyrics are biting: She can be called "a bitch . . . a beast . . . the Wicked Witch of the East." The opening verse, with no text written in, is similar music as the beginning of "Bad Situation," a musical correspondence that does not make dramatic sense. (Schwartz may have been thinking of something like the recitatives that Andrew Lloyd Webber wrote for *Joseph and the Amazing Technicolor Dreamcoat*, where many are musically similar, no matter what the dramatic situation. Schwartz did not choose to pursue such a course in *Wicked*, however.) Schwartz marked the start of the song, after the opening verse, "Shuffle," and it features an active bass line with syncopated augmented triads in the right hand that are pointedly disso-

Example 5.5. "Step by Step by Step" (August 2000 folder), mm. 5–8 of "Shuffle."

nant with the bass pattern, perhaps intended to show how the magic has brought out Nessarose's real personality. Her vocal line includes frequent use of blues thirds, syncopation, and usually ascending octave leaps as she announces her next "step" (see example 5.5). Elphaba's two passages are recitatives, the first in C major as she offers her congratulations to Nessarose, and the next with similar music in the parallel minor as she fears her sister's intentions. Schwartz notes that dialog between the sisters should be underscored with Nessarose's tune. Schwartz did not fill in the piano accompaniment for the end of the song, but the vocal part resembles what has come before.

The lyric sheet for "I'm Not That Girl" from August 2000 reveals no changes three years later in the Broadway version. Before the last verse, the sheet includes a suggestion of a possible scene with Doctor Dillamond before the final statement of the A section (OCR, track 8, 2'12") that includes a reference to Fiyero, but this was not incorporated into the show.

The August 2000 folder includes the lyric sheet (with surrounding dialog) and vocal lines for "One Short Day." This is an important scene because it shows the solid friendship between Glinda and Elphaba before they are driven apart. Details of the scene—including much of the dialog—changed substantially before the Broadway version, but its overall thrust was already in place. Glinda and Elphaba discuss the sights they want to see, and in a concern absent from the scene today, Elphaba notices that they have encountered no Talking Animals. They finally see a Talking Dog, a ticket hawker for the show *Wiz-teria*. They attend it and realize at the end of the scene, in song, that they are "best friends." It is striking to see how much the song changed over the next three years. The opening that Glinda and Elphaba sing together ("One short day in the Emerald City . . .") is similar to the Broadway version. As the girls start to list places they wish to see (see example 5.6), the lyrics and melody are substantially different than what one hears today, but the overall sound of the music is similar, operating in a fairly narrow range and based on speech rhythms—clearly the most memorable musical gesture of the song has always been intended to be the opening phrase. Following, there is another statement of "One short day . . . ," with a different text where the girls comment on how much fun they are having together. The corresponding segment in the Broadway version (OCR, track 9, 1'16"–1'36") starts with the chorus, and then the girls declare together that the city will know they have arrived. The "Wiz-teria" chorus in the August 2000 draft is tantalizingly similar to what audiences hear today in the "Wizomania" segment, but Schwartz later included several small but significant changes. (See examples 5.7a and 5.7b to compare this version with the Broadway version.) The text is basically the same, but in the draft, the initial notes are held (as opposed to the eighth notes with rests in the later version), the rhythm in the second measure is quarter notes (rather than "Whose" appearing on a dotted quarter note following an eighth rest on the downbeat), and the fourth measure of the phrase is not entirely chromatic (as in the Broadway version). Schwartz intended this segment as a parody of such Broadway composers as Jule Styne from the early 1960s.[22]

Example 5.6. "One Short Day" (August 2000 folder), mm. 10–20.

The draft ends with counterpoint between "One short day" and the "Wizteria" number, not unlike the song today, but the draft includes a shorter contrapuntal segment.

The folder from August 2000 includes only a lyric sheet with intervening dialog for the composite song "A Sentimental Man/The Chance to Fly," sung by the Wizard to impress Elphaba and Glinda. The scene opens with the Wizard's verse of "A Sentimental Man," with the first four lines similar to what opened in the show on Broadway, but most of the remainder has different lyrics where he announces that sacrifices must be made for the greater good, a reference to his policy toward Talking Animals. Dialog and a sung stanza follow, where the Wizard asks Elphaba for a gesture of allegiance in the form of giving his pet monkey Chitterly (changed to Chistery in later versions, as the name appears in Maguire's novel) temporary wings by chanting a spell from the Grimmerie. The Wizard sings "Chance to Fly," comparing the monkey's opportunity to fly with the new world that the leader will make available to Elphaba. As in the Broadway version, Elphaba succeeds, and the Wizard shows her that she also has given wings to many unseen monkeys. The Wizard and Madame Morrible cynically comment on how the flying monkeys will

Example 5.7a. "One Short Day" (August 2000 folder), mm. 1–4 of section marked "'Show' Feel."

Example 5.7b. "One Short Day" (October 2004 Broadway score), mm. 60–63.

make good spies. "Chance to Fly" continues, with Glinda and Madame Morrible singing about how they are rising in the world. Elphaba is silent and finally runs out with the Grimmerie. Glinda goes after her, and the Wizard names Morrible his press secretary and tells her to announce that Elphaba is a fugitive and that what she has done to the monkeys is proof of her wickedness. By himself, the Wizard sings another verse of "A Sentimental Man" in which he comments that he has lost a daughter and that she must be captured. Despite his plans to arrest Elphaba, he is "a sentimental man." With all of the extra music, this scene would have moved more slowly than what happens in the show today, and the extra stanzas project the Wizard as an even darker figure.

Elphaba's flight from the Wizard's throne room and escape on the broom as the chorus brands her "wicked" are two of the show's most dramatic moments, and the creators tinkered with them to enhance their effectiveness. The folder includes lyrics only for "For Goodness Sake," a song between Elphaba and Glinda later mostly deleted. It starts with an angry verse for each girl. Glinda accuses Elphaba of stubbornness in declining what the Wizard offered, and Elphaba cites what she sees as Glinda's blind ambition to work with the Wizard no matter what the consequences. After dialog where Glinda accuses Elphaba of needing to show off by performing the magical spell, they both start to sing "I hope you're happy," similar to what one hears in the Broadway version. They then, according to the script, sing in counterpoint that each knows the other is "a fake," and they alternate brief insults. The lyrics keep returning to "for goodness sake," a line that takes on the layers of multiple meanings. Most of the song became superfluous because its purpose is fulfilled far more efficiently in the current opening thirty seconds of "Defying Gravity," which includes an exchange of the lines beginning with "I hope you're happy . . . "

The folder ends with lyrics to "Defying Gravity." Although the previous song probably would have directly preceded this finale, there appears to have been something between the songs that would set up Elphaba singing "Something has changed within me." Comparison with the Broadway version of the song's major portion shows that it was in an advanced state by August 2000; most changes were only light editing. Perhaps the most significant change takes place in the "Unlimited" segment, as Elphaba tries to convince her friend to join her. In August 2000,

Elphaba sings this alone, but in the current version Glinda sings, "If we work in tandem," and then they sing together for several lines starting with "There's no fight we cannot win" (OCR, track 11, 3'18"–3'39"). Glinda's increased participation in the scene helps demonstrate how her role grew before the show opened in work done after the late summer of 2000.

The Script and Choral Score from 21 November 2001

The music interspersed in the binder with this script demonstrates how some of it was different than what an audience hears in the show today. There are revision dates for items in the folder from after the date on the title page. In the first scene, "No One Mourns the Wicked" appeared in at least six segments, with the music and the scene's dialog changing a great deal over the next two years. Among the major alterations was the deletion of interviews with Dorothy and her friends. For the conclusion of the scene, the full choral writing as it is currently known was already in place. In Act 1, Scene 2, Elphaba still sings "Making Good" (already described from August 2000), with a segment based on her "Unlimited" theme, but the lyrics that follow are less bitter than those in the previous source, stating simply that a "certain governor" will be there to take some of the credit when she becomes famous. The music for "Dear Old Shiz" is a revision from 30 November 2001. At this point, it is in A minor moving to C major, different from the Broadway score, which is G-sharp minor moving to B major, but with similar musical content. In this earlier version, the music repeats with different text for Doctor Dillamond's funeral later in the first act. The lyrics for the reprise appear to have been in a state of flux at the time. Schwartz had written the syllable "oo" from measures 5 to 8, and over that somebody wrote "so tragical," using one of the irregular endings for English adjectives and adverbs that the writers invented for Ozian speech. The reprise also carries the date 30 November 2001.

The script includes part of the music for "Bad Situation" after the chorus enters. In a moment that later was deleted, the chorus sings in sympathy with their blonde heroine: "Poor Galinda—stuck with this blight!" Schwartz set this memorably in parallel triads (E major, d-sharp minor, c-sharp minor) over an *F-sharp* pedal (mm. 42–43; see example

113

Example 5.8. "Bad Situation" (21 November 2001 script), mm. 41–44.

5.8). Frequent chromaticism occurs over the *F-sharp* pedal for several measures, and then Galinda and Elphaba sing their respective lines in counterpoint (see example 5.9). Much of the remainder of "Bad Situation" is contrapuntal, including new material that Schwartz added by hand before the score was copied. This was for Galinda and Elphaba to sing together against material in the chorus, who continue to observe the roommates trying to get along.

This script includes choral music to "The Emerald City Stomp" (the musical scene is identified in the score as "We Deserve Each Other," with four separate sections) sung in the song placement that became "Dancing through Life." Following two characters (undesignated, but most likely Galinda and Fiyero) singing "We deserve each other" to music heard today (OCR, track 6, 3'55"ff), the chorus sings the tune, whose lyrics tell one how to do the dance called the Emerald City Stomp. The many E-flat major and C major chords in the accompaniment cause considerable interplay between *E-flat* and *E-natural*, lending the song a blues cast (see example 5.10). This

Example 5.9. "Bad Situation" (21 November 2001 script), mm. 49–52.

ambiguous chromaticism is like much popular music from the early decades of the twentieth century, and Schwartz's reliance on the device throughout the song is notable. A later segment of the song opens with Boq singing different lyrics to the "We Deserve Each Other" music in which he begs Fiyero for help with Nessarose, because he is afraid that she is about to figure out that he asked her to the dance only because Galinda suggested it. Fiyero continues the tune, recommending that Boq be less kind and tell Nessarose how he really feels. In the scene's musical finale, Galinda and Fiyero sing more of "We Deserve Each Other" before the return of the refrain of "The Emerald City Stomp," which continues the dichotomy between C major/minor and E-flat major (see example 5.11) in a full choral setting. Later in the act, the script includes the lead sheet for "One Short Day," which appears to have changed little since the August 2000 version.

Example 5.10. "We Deserve Each Other, Part 1" (21 November 2001 script), mm. 29–36.

Example 5.11. "We Deserve Each Other, Part 4" (21 November 2001 script), mm. 15–18.

The next musical segment that appears in the script is the choral entrance at the end of "Defying Gravity." It begins as Elphaba begins a long note on "down" (like on the OCR, track 11, 5'27") and Glinda sings "I hope you're happy" and the chorus enters on "Look at her . . . " This version from 2001 is close to the Broadway version, except it is one-half step higher in D major rather than D-flat. Also, in this earlier score all singers hit the last note together in what Schwartz wrote, and in the Broadway ending Elphaba sings her ornament on the downbeat, resolves to the tonic on the second beat, and the choir enters on the third beat (OCR, track 11, 5'43"ff). This change apparently originated at the time of this script because over Elphaba's last two measures someone wrote "in clear," and lines and arrows indicate that the chorus enters later. Schwartz also changed the final quarter note chord in the accompaniment, which now is three octaves in unison on the tonic but included the third of the chord in the highest note in the 2001 score.

Act 2, Scene 1 includes the choral segments of the lead sheet for "Happy Healing Day" (dated 2 December 2001, during the workshop), a song later replaced by "Thank Goodness," in which Schwartz retained most of the melodic material from "Happy Healing Day," but in "Thank Goodness," there are numerous statements of the title text to a descending triadic melody. The first sixteen measures of the song (see example 5.12) from 2001 illustrate how Schwartz kept his melody, as may be heard on the OCR (track 12). The melodic outline of the first two measures, and the meter, are reminiscent of "Gloria tibi" from Leonard Bernstein's *Mass*,

Example 5.12. "Happy Healing Day" (21 November 2001 script), mm. 1–16.

certainly a possible influence for Schwartz. In an interview, he stated that the 5/8 reminded him of happy people in a village, not unlike the scene suggested here at the beginning of Act 2.[23] Segments of solo parts sung by chorus members remained similar over the next two years, including the phrase where someone suggests that animals are giving the witch food and shelter, through the call to melt her and the instrumental material that follows (OCR, track 12, 3'27"–3'45"). The ending of the song is musically recognizable, but with many different lyrics, from where Glinda sings "happy is what happens . . ." through the end of the song (OCR, track 12, 5'39"ff).

The next choral scene to include music is "No Good Deed Reprise (Witch-Hunters)" (dated 1 December 2001), demonstrating that this song shared musical material with Elphaba's solo that precedes it, which, as stated above (see chapter 4, p. 63), does not appear to have been the case in March 2001. In the Broadway score (in a revision dated October 2004), this is called "March of the Witch-Hunters." After this version, from late 2001, Schwartz changed the rhythms of the opening (see examples 5.13a and 5.13b). The song proceeds similarly in both versions through "Kill the witch" (although in the 2001 version Schwartz indicates that phrase with an *X* in place of noteheads, suggesting that it might be spoken, but the pitches on which each *X* falls are the same as in the more recent score). In the 2001 version, there is a brief choral passage that Schwartz later cut, in which the text appeals to one's sense of right and wrong, a less dramatic passage that might have seemed out of place in this

Example 5.13a. "No Good Deed Reprise (Witch-Hunters)" (21 November 2001 script), mm. 1–4.

Example 5.13b. "March of the Witch-Hunters" (October 2004 Broadway score), mm. 0–6.

strident number (mm. 14–16; see example 5.14). The version from 2001 is similar to the current score in the last eleven measures.

Schwartz wrote a brief musical segment called "The Melting," sung by a chorus to the side of the stage just before Elphaba meets her apparent end from Dorothy's bucket of water. The number changed during the course of the workshop in the first half of December because the text set to music dated 10 December changed within this 21 November script. There are a few similarities between this and number 26 in the Broadway score, also called "The Melting," but the later version is shorter.

Some of the music for the "Finale" also appears in the script. It opens similarly to the Broadway version, but then Elphaba sings "I'm limited" to

Example 5.14. "**No Good Deed Reprise (Witch-Hunters)**" (**21 November 2001 script**), mm. 12–16.

Doctor Dillamond in the Badlands, using the "Unlimited" music that appears several times in the show (e.g., OCR, track 3, 3'39"ff). An example of material cut from the show that appears in the 2001 version appears below. It is repetitious, almost hypnotic, but Schwartz might have decided that it did not carry the dramatic power needed in the finale (see example 5.15). The finale also includes the lyrics "Goodness knows, we know what goodness is . . . ," a play on a word that Schwartz used several times in the score, but perhaps he decided this was ineffective because he also cut it from "The Melting." This earlier finale is longer and might have dragged, and Elphaba and Glinda also sang a bit of "For Good" in it, as in the Broadway version. At the end, the title "Wicked" appears twice in the music, and someone wrote in afterward, "add third Wicked," meaning that the ending as we know it today sounded first during the workshop in December 2001.

Example 5.15. "Finale" (21 November 2001 script), mm. 41–52.

An Undated Song List for *Wicked*

A document from Schwartz's office is an undated list of musical numbers from *Wicked* that seems to include song titles and an order that would place sometime in 2001. Following is a transcription of the document:[24]

Act I

"No One Mourns the Wicked"

"Making Good"

"Dear Old Shiz"

"Bad Situation"—Elphaba, Galinda, Bonnie, Shenshen, and students

"We Deserve Each Other"—Galinda, Fiyero

"Popular"—Galinda

"I'm Not That Girl"—Elphaba

"As If by Magic"—Dillamond, Fiyero, Elphaba

"Requiem for a Goat"—Mourners at Shiz

"One Short Day"—Elphaba, Glinda, cast of *Wiz-teria*, and tourists

"A Sentimental Man"—Wizard

"The Chance to Fly"—Wizard, Madame Morrible, Galinda, Elphaba

"Defying Gravity"—Elphaba, Glinda, palace guards

Act 2

"Happy Healing Day"—Punch Munchburger, Morrible, citizens of Oz

"Step by Step"—Nessarose, Elphaba

"Wonderful"—Wizard, Elphaba

"I'm Not That Girl"—Glinda

"As Long As You're Mine"—Elphaba, Fiyero

"No Good Deed"—Elphaba

"March of the Witch-Hunters"—Punch Munchburger, Tin Man, citizens of Oz

"For Good"—Glinda, Elphaba

"Finale"—All

Several of these songs have already been described above in their 2001 state. Also notable are the absence of any song in the first act party dance position other than "We Deserve Each Other" (meaning perhaps that much of the scene would have occurred through dialog), the song "As If by Magic" (described below with other deleted songs; see pp. 183–85) as the victory celebration in Dillamond's lab, and the title "Requiem for a Goat" for the reprise of music from "Dear Old Shiz" at Dillamond's funeral.

Stephen Schwartz Caught in the Process of Composing

My work in Schwartz's office uncovered a fascinating document from 28 October 2002 that demonstrates in detail how Schwartz might conceive a song. As noted above, lyrics for "The Wizard and I" had yet to be written. The songwriter wrote a detailed monolog for Elphaba out of which he would write the lyrics, and he sent this to director Joe Mantello before "turning it into a song." As may be seen below, the monolog includes a number of the lines that appear in the song with only minor changes, and there is sufficient rhyme to imagine that Schwartz had already worked on the lyrics in a more poetic form. Since Schwartz specifically states that the song did not yet exist, he probably had not written the melody yet, meaning that he worked extensively on the lyrical content before starting to compose. This is not surprising when working on a book musical where each song must help advance the plot, but it is revealing to have such an intimate glimpse of Schwartz's working methods and how he approached a problem with a collaborator. To appreciate this document, one must become familiar with "The Wizard and I" and then read the following three paragraphs aloud.

> Hey Joe, because the content of this song is so key, my approach to working on it has been to try to get the content worked out and structured before I commit it into lyrics. I thought I would run by you what I have come up with (it's in sort of a vaguely rhyming stream-of-consciousness for now). If you have any thoughts about it—what you particularly like, anything you hate, anything you think is missing, what you think may be superfluous, ways to improve or clarify the structure, etc.—I'd appreciate your input before I start turning it into a song.
>
> To be clear about where this would come: It's right after Morrible has sung to her, "Many years I have waited for a gift like yours to appear; why I believe the Wizard might make you his magic grand vizier. My dear, my dear, if you work hard at your spelling with every distraction withstood, do everything I say, then I am telling you, you will make good. Miss Elphaba, you'll be making good!" Then Elphaba might sing something with this context: "Did that really just happen? Have I really understood? How could she know that has always been my secret dream, my heart's desire? To meet the Wizard? And now she says I could, if I make good. No one has ever believed in me before . . . and I can understand why. I mean, just look at me! To my father I've always been an

embarrassment and to everyone else an eyesore and a subject for harassment. And with Nessarose, well, I try and try. Now someone I've only just met, but someone who ought to know tells me this weird thing I do, which I've always tried to hide, that this is my talent. I have a talent! Whoever thought I have a talent? A gift, she called it. No one has ever believed in me before, and let's face it, I haven't even believed in myself. Now maybe I can? Maybe I do? Or at least I'm starting to. Because I know now that someday there we'll be side by side, the Wizard and me.

"And when I meet the Wizard, my life is going to change. No, my life is going to begin. Because, he's different, too. He's special, and he's so wise and insightful. He'll be able to see what no one else can—the actual me. He'll believe in me, perceive in me all my full potential. My outward appearance will be inconsequential. He'll get my jokes, the way I think, appreciate my style, he'll want me to move into the palace for awhile. And I'll help him, assist him with his wizardry chores, using my gifts and all the energy I can supply as we work together, the Wizard and I. And one day he'll say to me, 'Elphaba, my dear, a person as wonderful as you deserves to be as beautiful on the outside, too.' And I'll say, 'I don't know what to say!' And he'll say, 'Let me do what the wizards do. Your talent is so precious and your mind so superior, shouldn't you possess a matching exterior? And since people to an absurd degree seem distracted by your verdigris, here's what I'll do, I think. I'll put you, poof, in the pink.' Then everyone in Oz will see what the Wizard does, and they'll be sorry they never appreciated me before. The folks back in Munchkinland will say, 'We must have been blinded, can you forgive us Munchkins for being so small-minded?' Unlimited, my future is unlimited and I have a vision, almost like a prophecy. And I know right now it sounds crazy, and, true, the vision's hazy, but I swear someday there'll be a celebration throughout Oz that's all to do with me! And I'll feel things I never felt; I'll be so happy I could melt! As I stand beside the Wizard they'll honor and revere me, and even Nessarose will come to cheer me. I'll be the most beloved person in Oz, next to the Wizard, and next to the Wizard I will work until I die. And I'll have my dream because we'll be a team, the Wizard and I."[25]

Musical Analysis

The musical sources acquired for this study include two piano/vocal scores related to the final rehearsal process in New York and the show as it has

Table 5.1. Comparison of Revision Dates on Each Musical Number in Scores from October 2003 and October 2004

Song/Musical Number	Revision Date from Earlier Score	Later Score
Earliest date or revision for score:	25 March 2003	March 2004
Latest date or revision for score:	15 October 2003	21 January 2005
Act I		
"Opening"	7 October 2003	October 2004
"No One Mourns the Wicked"	7 October 2003	October 2004
"Elphaba's Entrance"	25 August 2003	October 2004
"Dear Old Shiz"	25 March 2003	October 2004
"Jeweled Shoes?"	24 September 2003	October 2004
"Let Her Go!"	27 May 2003	October 2004
"The Wizard and I"	25 August 2003	October 2004
"What Is This Feeling?"	25 August 2003	October 2004
"Something Bad"	25 August 2003	October 2004
"Into Courtyard" (Earlier score marked "Broadway Version")	24 September 2003	October 2004
"Dancing through Life"	19 September 2003	October 2004
"The Ozdust Dance" (Some pages carry title "We Deserve Each Other" dated 30 April 2003)	5 October 2003	October 2004
"Elphaba's Dance"	23 September 2003	October 2004
"Popular"	3 October 2003	October 2004
"After Popular"	27 May 2003	not present
"Save the Lion!" (Earlier score marked "Broadway Version")	30 September 2003	October 2004
"I'm Not That Girl"	15 September 2003	October 2004
"The Wizard and I" (Reprise)	15 September 2003	October 2004
"Into One Short Day"	3 September 2003	not present
"One Short Day"	25 August 2003	October 2004
"I Am Oz!"	24 May 2003	October 2004
"A Sentimental Man" (Later score marked "Joel Grey Version [Joel's Key]")	16 September 2003	March 2004
"Monkey Reveal" (Later score marked "Transposed" and corners of each page say "tr 10/04")	25 September 2003	July 2004
"Defying Gravity"	23 September 2003	October 2004
Act II		
"Act II Opening"	20 September 2003	October 2004
"Thank Goodness" (Part 1)	15 September 2003	October 2004
"Thank Goodness" (Part 2)	15 September 2003	October 2004
"Thank Goodness" (Part 3)	25 August 2003	October 2004
"After Thank Goodness"	17 May 2003	October 2004
"There's Elphaba!" (Handwritten in the earlier score)	no date	October 2004
"Defying Gravity" (Reprise)	23 September 2003	not present

Song/Musical Number	Revision Date from Earlier Score	Later Score
"Wicked Witch of the East—Intro"	not present	October 2004
"The Wicked Witch of the East" (Original printed title in earlier score: "We Deserve Each Other," with "The Wicked Witch of the East" handwritten as correction)	29 September 2003	October 2004
"Ballroom Transition"	25 August 2003	October 2004
"Wonderful" (Later score marked "Original Joel Grey Version/ 'old' ending/Joel's Key")	23 September 2003	March 2004
"Set Free the Monkeys"	3 October 2003	October 2004
"Dillamond Discovered"	13 September 2003	October 2004
"I'm Not That Girl" (Reprise)	25 August 2003	October 2004
"As Long As You're Mine"	25 March 2003	21 January 2005
"The Cyclone"	1 October 2003	October 2004
"Fiyero!" (Handwritten in the earlier score)	15 October 2003	October 2004
"No Good Deed"	25 August 2003	October 2004
"March of the Witch-Hunters"	1 October 2003	October 2004
"The Letter"	3 June 2003	October 2004
"For Good—Intro" (Titled "For Good (intro)" in earlier score with entire page handwritten)	no date	October 2004
"For Good"	25 August 2003	October 2004
"The Melting"	25 August 2003	October 2004
"A Sentimental Man" (Reprise)	1 October 2003	October 2004
"Finale"	1 October 2003	October 2004
"Bows/Exit"	not present	October 2004

become known to those attending it in the various places it has run. The first score chronologically dates from sometime after 15 October 2003, a bit more than two weeks before the show opened in New York. The second score is mostly from October 2004, with the latest date from early 2005 (which appears once), after Schwartz had made many adjustments to the music that have been reflected both in the Broadway version and in subsequent productions. As shown in chapter 4, the writers of *Wicked* did not rest on their laurels, continuing to revise the show's book and score after the successful opening. One gets a small sense of Schwartz's extensive revisions to the score in table 5.1, which shows the dates of the version of each song in these two scores.

The first score includes as its latest revision a handwritten version of "Fiyero!"—the music that underscores the resolution of the tight situation caused by Elphaba's arrest and Fiyero's sudden appearance to take Glinda hostage, one of several passages in the score in manuscript. The source includes many notated cuts and a number of lyrics changed by hand, showing that October 2003 was, not surprisingly, a period of considerable musical change for *Wicked*. There are even short musical numbers that had been cut from the show by the time the later score was prepared. Our primary document for musical analysis will be the later score, where clearly Schwartz had revised most numbers in October 2004 and made more changes on "As Long As You're Mine" on 21 January 2005. With the following detailed musical description derived from this document, our examination of each number will conclude with an accounting of its state in mid-October 2003, showing how each number changed from just before the opening until one year later.

The score for *Wicked* shows a composer in full command of his powers. It demonstrates Schwartz's ability to harness pop and other idioms in the service of dramatic music and his sure sense of modulation. His harmonic style includes many triads with added tones, bitonality, rich use of augmented triads in moments of dramatic tension (often with added tones or in bitonal contexts), and series of nonfunctional harmonies. As in his earlier score to *Children of Eden*, in *Wicked* Schwartz continues the frequent application of repeating musical motives to unify the score. The two main motives include what might be called the "Wicked" motive that refers to Elphaba and her destiny to be the Wicked Witch of the West (OCR, track 1, 0'00"–0'04"; six chords presented in a syncopated rhythm: a, a, Fmaj7^{+9}, Fmaj7^{+9}, G^{+4}, G^{+4} over an A pedal) and the "Unlimited" motive that at first describes Elphaba's hopes for a bright future (track 1, 0'39"–0'52") but later comes to represent acceptance of her own limitations.[26] Schwartz based the "Wicked" motive on the instrumental opening (track 15, 0'00"–0'03") of "As Long As You're Mine," a song composed in 1971 that he brought out of his "trunk" and used here. Schwartz compares the motive to Rachmaninov, a personal association perhaps caused by the chord progression, because the syncopation makes it sound more like a dramatic pop motive.[27] Vieira describes this motive as a succession of six pitches,[28] but the harmonic progression is at least as important. The first six notes of the "Unlimited" motive are from the melody of Arlen and Harburg's "Somewhere Over the Rainbow," but Schwartz changed the rhythm and the harmonic context and finished the phrase with his own material.[29] In the musical description of each song below, more unifying motives will be identified, but it is these two that Schwartz uses most prominently.

Wicked has an instrumental opening, an extended introduction to "No One Mourns the Wicked" rather than a traditional overture. The opening material involves two full statements of the "Wicked" motive built over a pedal *A* (descending to *E* on the fourth beat in the second measure, a striking gesture heard in a number of bass instruments). The motive's third occurrence is incomplete, turning into a series of nonfunctional harmonies that lands on a B major chord (OCR, track 1, 0'17"), which introduces the rapid sixteenth notes in the high instruments that later underscores the release of the flying monkeys in the second act. The long chords accompanying this are unrelated added tone triads, and the frenetic rhythmic pattern in the drums is identified as "'Monkey' Groove," which recurs at appropriate moments in the show. A monkey on stage turns the crank for the Clock of the Time Dragon and its elaborate gears, accompanied in B major and with Elphaba's "Unlimited" tune, richly scored in the orchestra. Schwartz merely plants the seed of this theme here because he soon interrupts it with rapid rising material that leads into "Moderate 2; Fanfare" (track 1, 0'59"). Three measures of bitonal material on C and E (first encountered above in sketches from August 2000[30]) introduces the choral entrances on "Good news! She's dead!" which passes through B and D major before Glinda's bubble appears. Her first sung material ("Let us be glad . . . ," track 1, 1'39", mostly over harmonies on E and B) is angular and introduces the public Glinda as a soprano, Schwartz's intentional use of Kristin Chenoweth's wide vocal range to evoke the two parts of her character. (When she belts, one hears the real, private Glinda.) She soars to an *a"* during the solo (track 1, 2'13"). The rhythm of the "Wicked" motive occurs at the end of the opening over a D-sharp pedal as Glinda describes the circumstances of Elphaba's death.

The October 2003 score transmits a few interesting points concerning this number. There is a cut of four measures in the score that would have started at 0'54" (OCR, track 1) that served as a transition between the end of the "Unlimited" motive and the triplet run that introduces the bitonal fanfare leading to the first choral entrance. Another cut of eight measures appears at 2'26" during Glinda's solo line that included a dramatic ascent from *a* to *a"* by thirds on the text "Even the wicked must die."

"No One Mourns the Wicked" follows immediately. Schwartz has stated that he was thinking about "Ding Dong, the Witch Is Dead" from the MGM film when he wrote this number.[31] He describes it as "rhythmic and explosive," and to him it sounds like Hindemith, certainly a possible influence. He also found it a good opportunity to use Kristin Chenoweth's soprano range. The melody recurs several times during the show. Set here in F-sharp minor, the full tune is in AABC form (7+7+8+6 measures). The A segment (OCR, track 1, 2'26"–2'37") is the section that recurs most often in the score. Schwartz modulates to C-sharp minor as Glinda presents B and C ("And goodness knows," track 1, 2'49"–3'11"). The chorus then repeats AA in C-sharp minor. Modulatory material underscores dialog that sets up the scene of Elphaba's conception and birth. The governor of Munchkinland and his wife sing a farewell waltz (track 1, 3'46"–4'06") in G major that is full of seventh and ninth chords that lend the sweet melody a bittersweet effect, and as the governor sings his long note at the end of the segment, the chromatic soft-shoe accompaniment for the Wizard's song of seduction begins (track 1, 4'01"). Schwartz imitates vaudeville music here. There are just a few motives in the tune, one an ascending chromatic scale, and a great deal of repetition. The accompaniment continues for several measures after the Wizard stops singing, time for the presumed sex and for Melena (the governor's wife) to appear pregnant. Glinda's narration introduces the birth. An unprepared modulation to A major following a grand pause introduces the midwife's announcement that "the baby's coming" (track 1, 4'38") in a dialog with the father that turns from speech to song. Rising major sixths in what is otherwise a conjunct passage in the vocal line create a sense of expectation, and the midwife and father sing in parallel sixths on "lovely, little" before they scream upon seeing Elphaba's unusual color. Dissonant harmonies based on parallel triads just before the vocal thirds foreshadow these strong emotions. The "Wicked" motive accompanies their reaction (track 1, 4'53") in material reminiscent of the show's opening, but now in C-sharp minor. The sung lines concerning Elphaba's coloring are angular and include extremes in range. At the text "Like a froggy, ferny cabbage" (track 1, 5'04"), the orchestra doubles the singers, emphasizing the tension. The treatment of "Green!" is an augmented triad on F over a G in the bass. As the father rejects the baby, Schwartz provides the theme of "No One Mourns the Wicked," mostly in perfect fifths, including some that are dissonant to the bass note. At "Maestoso" (track 1, 5'26"), the choir presents the A section of the song with rich use of fourths and sevenths in a Bernstein-like presentation, but the remainder of the song is less dissonant as Glinda soars above the choir with her descant. At "Deliberately" (track 1, 6'23"), Schwartz ends the opening musical segment with his *West Side Story* tribute of two statements of "Wicked!" in E major with an added ninth followed by a unison *A-sharp* in the bass. A consonant bass *E* follows the third statement of "Wicked!" concluding the song.

The October 2003 score includes a cut in the waltz that Elphaba's mother and father sing before he leaves town (track 1, 3'55"). The melodic material is similar to what has been heard in the tune to that point, and the lyrics in the cut were for the father, stating that his wife will "always be in my heart" while he is away. The text that Schwartz removed echoes sentiment heard elsewhere in the song. Several other subtle changes also occurred, such as the elimination of a grand pause just before the chorus announces that Elphaba has been born green (5'09"). The quarter rest that remains before "Green!" is sufficient silence to make the dramatic point. When the number starts its choral finale, Glinda sings a high solo line above everything else, and here the text later changed. On the OCR at 5'50" she sings "Ah," but in the earlier score she repeats "Goodness knows," as she had sung shortly before.

Glinda is about to leave the scene when an Ozian asks her if she had been friends with Elphaba. Glinda, embarrassed, initiates the flashback that forms the majority of the show. The music of "Elphaba's Entrance" starts just as the question is asked. Schwartz based this underscoring on material from the show's instrumental opening, including the ascending sixteenth note arpeggios that accompany the "Unlimited" theme, brief descending quarter note lines (also reminiscent of the "Unlimited" music), and at the end of the passage a transformation of the "Wicked" theme. The final seven measures appear on the OCR at 0'14" of track 2 as an introduction to "Dear Old Shiz." Glinda's spoken lines over this music were changed and moved in the October 2003 score in handwritten emendations.

"Dear Old Shiz" has changed little from previous versions except for Galinda's closing melisma on "old." Schwartz captures the stately sound of an alma mater with a chordal texture and chromaticism in inner parts and the text's somewhat stilted language, including the fabricated notion of hair turning "gray and sere," the latter a term usually associated with dry and withered plants. (Schwartz has stated that he simply wanted this to sound like a school song with "silly lyrics that are slightly archaic."[32]) The next number—"Jeweled Shoes?"—underscores the governor of Munchkinland presenting Nessarose with her extravagant gift and snubbing Elphaba. Schwartz based it on "Dear Old Shiz." Both the alma mater and "Jeweled Shoes?" are largely the same between the two scores under consideration here.

The next underscoring—"Let Her Go!"—accompanies Elphaba's unintentional display of magical power as she forces Nessarose's chair to return to her. Rolling eighth notes in 6/8 start in E major but move toward F minor and an inconclusive ending, while two octave leaps (*e* to *e'* and *c* to *c'*) introduce a brief transformation of the "Unlimited" motive. Marked as a cut in the October 2003 score at the end of the number are four measures in C-sharp minor based on the same material.

As Schwartz has noted, "The Wizard and I" is the show's "I want" song where the main character tells the audience about her dreams, an important song type found in many musicals.[33] Other famous examples would include Tony's "Something's Coming" from *West Side Story*, Eliza Doolittle's "Wouldn't It Be Loverly?" from *My Fair Lady*, and the title character's "Corner of the Sky" in *Pippin*. "The Wizard and I" opens with a recitative for Madame Morrible as she marvels at Elphaba's potential. Schwartz provided effective speech rhythms with the text for Morrible's introduction and Elphaba's recitative that follows. The accompaniment is primarily chordal, except for sixteenth notes under a few important words. The song's main portion starts with an Allegro designation (OCR, track 3, 1'16") and opens with driving eighth notes on a *c'* ostinato, later changing to other pitches. High *tremolos* of *g"* and *g'''* form another repeated pattern for most of the three phrases of the verse, along with syncopated held notes. Elphaba starts the main portion of the song (track 3, 1'23"–2'04") after four measures of instrumental introduction. The first two phrases, each eight measures, are thematically related and could be called A and B(A). The eighth-note *ostinato* discontinues in the C section (track 3, 1'50"–2'04"), where Schwartz accompanies Elphaba's imaginary affirmation from the Wizard with rich syncopations. Vieira describes as a major moment Schwartz's insistence on *b-flat'* in the melodic line several times (track 3, 1'44"ff), followed soon thereafter by *b-natural'* once

Elphaba is certain that the Wizard will understand her value, and Vieira traces what he finds to be important chromatic alterations in other songs as well.[34] The 24-bar AB(A)C segment soon repeats with a different text where Schwartz inserted many melodic and rhythmic differences, including abandonment of the *ostinato* accompaniment in favor of continual syncopation. In the third verse, where Elphaba fantasizes that the Wizard will change the color of her skin, Schwartz starts a step higher with a D major[9] chord (track 3, 2'48") and makes a number of other changes that significantly alters the music, but in places it remains similar, especially in the C section (track 3, 3'17"–3'34"), which he extends by repeating the last two measures. Schwartz uses a striking, unprepared modulation to G-flat major (track 3, 3'35") to introduce the first time that Elphaba sings her "Unlimited" theme, accompanied by the sixteenth note arpeggios also heard in the show's instrumental opening (track 1, 0'35"ff). After the dreamy quality of this segment, Schwartz wrote a section marked "Freely" that functions as a recitative where Elphaba builds excitement to the final "A Tempo; con moto." Elphaba sings of her vision of fame throughout Oz, based on speech rhythms. The final tempo starts as Elphaba holds the word "me" (track 3, 4'11"), mostly on a *b-flat'* as Schwartz reaches B-flat major and builds excitement with *tresillo* (3+3+2) rhythms as he barrels into B major at the end of the line with a dramatic and nonfunctional chord progression: B-flat maj7–C7–B. The final verse is analogous to the first three with a form of ABC, and there remain vestiges of the original material, but most of the verse is in a slightly higher, more exciting tessitura. Schwartz modulates to C major for the last nine measures to end in the key where he started the main portion of the song, and he ends with a fascinating cadence as Elphaba produces her powerful *c*: D-flat (add sharp 4)–B (add flat 6)–C.

Schwartz made many adjustments to "The Wizard and I" between the 25 August 2003 revision that appears in the October 2003 score and the version from one year later, including changes in the opening material between Elphaba and Madame Morrible, subtle but significant alterations to the rhythm and melody, and major adjustments to the lyrics. It is a telling example of how the songwriter feels an almost preternatural need to rework his material, perhaps even when the performers and director might want the score to be frozen. In the earlier version, Elphaba has three brief, spoken lines of reaction (with two others deleted by hand) to what

Madame Morrible sings, but by October 2004 this had been cut to her single exclamation, "The Wizard?" after her teacher suggests that Elphaba might become the Wizard's "Grand Vizier." Schwartz's fine-tuning of the song's melody was mostly in terms of the rhythms used to set the text, but he introduced a number of small but significant melodic changes at this late point in the show's genesis. A notable example in "The Wizard and I" that demonstrates his desire to place a textual accent on an accented note occurs on the text "All right, why not?" stated by Elphaba as she fantasizes that the Wizard will change her to a more acceptable color (OCR, track 3, 3'21"–3'23"). On the recording, the word "right" is accented, but in the October 2003 version, this word sounded on the second eighth note of the first beat. He also added the syncopation at the end of the measure on "I'll re-[ply]," more distinctive than "I'll re-" on the last two eighth notes of the measure heard in the earlier version. Schwartz also managed a more effective rhythmic setting on the text "vision almost like a prophe[cy]" (track 3, 3'48"–3'51"), set in the later version on equal notes except for a dotted eighth and sixteenth on "like a." In the earlier score, "vision" also occurred on a downbeat, but on an eighth note and a quarter note, and "almost" was rushed on two sixteenths, and then dotted rhythms appeared on "like a" and "pro-phe-," the latter less natural than equal eighth notes. Schwartz also made small melodic changes. A major change in lyrics appears in handwritten corrections elsewhere in the song (track 3, 2'34"–2'44"), where Schwartz crossed out the following: "But I'll be too busy to think about that,/What with Wizardly duties piled high, Working side by side . . . " The lyrics he wrote in the October 2003 version are close to what Menzel sang on the album, and Schwartz also changed the melody a bit to accommodate the new lyrics. These are representative of the many small changes made in this song.

"What Is This Feeling?" is the fifth and final song that Schwartz wrote for this spot, where the two girls consider what it will be like to share a room. He wrote it in response to Winnie Holzman's suggestion of a "falling-into-hate" song.[35] After the discarded "Bad Situation," Schwartz had written a new text (heard in this song), and he set it to a waltz somewhat like "Ten Minutes Ago" from Rodgers and Hammerstein's *Cinderella*, but the creators decided they needed another version with more energy, which resulted in this jaunty tune.[36] (Lyrics for the song exist in the 31 March 2003 script that probably represents this waltz

THE MUSIC AND LYRICS OF *WICKED*

version, but here Schwartz did not include lyrics for Galinda's friends to support her, which had been part of "Bad Situation" and were restored in the final version of "What Is This Feeling?" The lyrics to the waltz version were similar to the final version, but not identical, and they do include a contrapuntal section for Galinda and Elphaba.) Schwartz derived the three measures of introduction from the rising major sixth of Glinda's "Let us be glad . . ." of the opening number, an ironic gesture given their feelings at the moment. They alternate and sing together in the opening recitative. As they describe each other in letters to their parents, Schwartz provides humorous moments for each in Galinda's diplomatic description of Elphaba's coloring, and in Elphaba's one-word dismissal of Galinda's hair color that rhymes with "respond" from five measures before (OCR, track 4, 0'28"–0'39"). Schwartz then sets up the song with jarring, bitonal chords of punctuation. The next sixteen measures (track 4, 0'46"–1'11") function as the A portion of this counterpoint song. Schwartz forces more forward motion here with an allegro marking that corresponds to Elphaba's one-word description of her roommate as a "blonde," and he adds a more active accompaniment after seven measures. Schwartz divides the A material into witty two-measure phrases as he builds excitement, topped off by held notes on "Yes!" over an urgent accompaniment. The emphasis on C major sets up the dominant of F, to which Schwartz modulates for the B portion (track 4, 1'11"–1'56"). Its 29 measures can be divided ABA'C (7+6+7+9 measures) with some lengthy anacruses. Effective moments include the unprepared G-flat chord under "flesh begin to crawl" (Vieira finds this a good example of Schwartz's predilection for nondiatonicism, which he traces through the score[37]) and the accompanying, driving eighth notes that begin with the third phrase. Schwartz then dives into D-flat major as the student chorus enters in support of Galinda (track 4, 1'56"), singing material from an earlier version of the song described above (see p. 105). It is in two and three choral parts and thematically unrelated to the remainder of the song. Galinda's "These things are sent to try us" (track 4, 2'08"–2'13") reflects her public face in a higher range, and the rising minor sixth on "things are" might be a transformation of her earlier major sixth on "Let us be glad." In the opening number, the chorus then enters with material from the B portion of the song (transformed for the first eight measures), and the soloists start the A portion eight measures later to initiate the counterpoint (track 4,

2'27"–2'48") with many adjustments in the A tune, and then Elphaba and Galinda switch to material from the B tune in their alternations with the chorus through the end of the song. "What Is This Feeling?" provides effective musical description of the main characters, and their presentation of similar material here foreshadows their future friendship. Comparison of this version with the October 2003 score reveals far fewer changes than one finds in "The Wizard and I," with some small alterations in the rhythms of the parts that Elphaba and Galinda sing toward the end of the song to provide more energy and render what the chorus sings more easily understood.

The musical tone changes markedly in "Something Bad," where Elphaba experiences her first inkling of the cause that will lead her into conflict with the Wizard. She has sensed that Doctor Dillamond is a kindred spirit, and here she starts to learn of the persecution of the Talking Animals. Schwartz reports that part of the idea for this song came from the readings; the creators needed to explain that the Wizard's repression was causing Animals to lose their speaking ability.[38] The segment carries an eerie intensity, and Schwartz helped set the mood with an irregular form; disturbing musical ideas such the omnipresent, noodling eighth notes in the prevailing 6/8; and several modulations. The OCR includes only the number's sung portions. The opening key is C-sharp minor, but with consistent insertion of D-sharp and B into the tonic chord, creating an unsettled feeling. In the second quatrain (OCR, track 5, 0'18"ff), now on C after a sudden modulation, Schwartz alters the accent scheme while remaining in 6/8, writing the vocal line in quarter note quadruplets. Doctor Dillamond sings in a narrow range, at times almost speaking. Eight bars later (track 5, 0'28"), Schwartz changes to F minor, where he remains for much of the rest of the song, but he uses borrowed chords and the tonality remains murky. When Dillamond accidentally bleats (over a G-flat major7 chord with added augmented fourth, followed immediately by a held G-flat augmented triad, OCR, track 5, 0'45"ff), showing that he has started to lose his power of speech, the noodling mostly stops, and chords underscore the dialog. Chordal accompaniment continues when Madame Morrible arrives to find Elphaba. When she leaves, the noodling returns as Elphaba tries to reassure Doctor Dillamond in dialog. Their final duet (track 5, 1'00"–1'11"), when the professor bleats for the second time, is notated in F minor, but with E-flat minor chords as a sort of dominant substitution, and it is in E-flat minor that the accompaniment fades out, which is the first segment of number 6A, "Into Courtyard," in the score. The remainder of 6A is a brief instrumental reprise of a section of "The Wizard and I," heard as Fiyero's chauffeur drives him on stage.

"Something Bad" is longer in the October 2003 score, illustrating how Doctor Dillamond's role in the show continued to shrink, even in the last month of rehearsals. His presence and what he represented was important to establish Elphaba's great cause, but the creators seem to have discovered that one did not need to see much of him to make the point. The earlier version of the song bears the revision date of 25 August 2003. Schwartz cut the first six measures, which were mostly in B minor and in a similar mood as the rest of the song, but primarily sixteenths and in common time. Dillamond's spoken lines that open the song on the recording were added by hand in the October 2003 score, grabbing the listener far more than the bland "Miss Elphaba" that had earlier opened the song. The score also includes a cut that would have been heard at 0'45" (OCR, track 5). It was nine measures and included another of Doctor Dillamond's bleats as he tries to say "bad," meaning that Schwartz originally intended him to bleat once and then have several measures of the song's standard accompaniment without singing before he bleats again. In the recorded version he still bleats twice, but the second is toward the end of the song (1'11"). The other major change between the two versions is a segment where the melody is different and Dillamond asks Elphaba to help him in his work by checking books out of the library. Schwartz set the text with harmonic ambiguity, the melody outlining A-flat major and minor and the accompaniment migrating between D-flat minor and other keys. The earlier score shows that there were only minor changes to "Into Courtyard," which follows "Something Bad."

"Dancing through Life" is a long musical segment, a reflection of the huge amount of time that Schwartz and his collaborators spent on it and the many significant points in the plot that occur during this song and "The Ozdust Dance." Schwartz has noted that it was the last song he wrote, replacing "Which Way Is the Party?" which did not fit the personality of Norbert Leo Butz when he became Fiyero.[39] Schwartz wrote several measures of five versions of the new song in various styles (he describes them as a song that Frank Sinatra might have sung, one inspired by Gershwin's "They Can't Take That Away from Me," a Billy

Joel version, one that to Schwartz sounded too much like Sondheim, and a song like Sting might have written) and let his collaborators decide which they liked best.[40] Choreographer Wayne Cilento helped choose the Sting version, which he favored as a dance vehicle. The opening recitative includes clever rhymes, but there is little unusual about the music as Schwartz makes use of speech rhythms and one pop melisma on "know." At "A Tempo," Schwartz provides four measures of what becomes the song's primary accompaniment (OCR, track 6, 0'31"–0'39"), but entirely in treble instruments, perhaps commenting upon Fiyero's apparent lack of depth. This unusual accompaniment continues for the first eight measures of the song. Much of the tune is based on a 3+2+3 rhythm in eighth notes that fits the text well. The basic tune (OCR, track 6, 0'39"–1'16") is 18 measures long, divided into two phrases (8+10 measures). The first three bars of each phrase are similar, with the departure in the second phrase taking place on a melodic ascent on "off as I do" (track 6, 1'02"). The harmonies are predictable, with one interesting moment being the unexpected D-flat and E-flat chords on "Why think too hard—when it's so soothing?" (track 6, 0'52"–0'55"). The second stanza, based primarily on similar music, includes a more insistent bass line and accompaniment. Fiyero's invitation to the dance references 1970s disco (track 6, 2'06"–2'34"), like the main tune but varied and in C minor, with its own distinctive motives. A segment of the main tune returns, again in F major, with Fiyero singing over choral interjections. What follows had been in the show for some time: Galinda's sob story to Boq to divert his attention to Nessarose (track 6, 3'09"–3'44"). Schwartz modulates to F-sharp minor and applies his penchant for distinctive speech rhythms. When Galinda actually requests that Boq ask Nessarose to the dance, it is over a B-flat major chord, a fair distance from the F-sharp minor where the segment started, echoing the distance that Galinda has managed to move Boq. She then turns her undivided attention to Fiyero, singing the "We Deserve Each Other" material (track 6, 3'51"–4'10") that had been in the show in various places for months at this point. This material shares some of the 3+2+3 rhythm with the main tune, which helps make it seem inevitable when Schwartz modulates up a half step to E-flat and the couple sings a triumphant "Dancing through life." Underscoring based upon the main tune and unrelated motives accompanies dialog between Elphaba and Nessarose about her date for the evening, leading to Nessarose's exultation (track 6, 4'18"–4'56") that includes "We deserve each other." It is an "Allegretto," fairly relaxed, but with frequent syncopation and a balanced form of three phrases, each seven measures in length. This music becomes associated with Nessarose and Boq and returns later in this scene and in the second act. It dissolves quickly here as Elphaba assures Nessarose that she understands the reasons for her happiness. The segment was in G major, and then Schwartz modulates to D for Elphaba's foray to thank Galinda for her assistance to Nessarose, returning to G as Galinda maliciously convinces her to wear the black, peaked hat to the dance (track 6, 5'07"–5'27"). The music is like that associated with the chummy Galinda, heard as well in "Popular," strongly rhythmic with accented off-beats and syncopation, and her solo also includes "You deserve each other" material. Vieira points out that Schwartz opens the segment in the accompaniment (4'58"–4'59") with a brief quotation from "What Is This Feeling?" (track 4, 1'21"–1'22", "I loathe it all"), reminding the listener of the antipathy between the girls.[41] At the conclusion of the segment concerning Galinda giving Elphaba the hat in "Dancing through Life," "You deserve each other" appears yet again, this time in reference to Elphaba and the hat.

"The Ozdust Dance," a separate number, follows immediately on track 6 of the OCR. The first 22 measures (track 6, 5'33"–6'18") are based on "Dancing through Life," but the recording does not include two measures in the score with a harp *glissando* during which Galinda and Fiyero kiss. In the next segment, Boq tries to tell Nessarose how he really feels, but he cannot (track 6, 6'18"–7'11"). Schwartz melodically based the segment closely on what Nessarose sang earlier in the scene to Elphaba, but one step lower in F major and with a less syncopated melody. For the fourth time in the "Dancing through Life" sequence, this exchange includes "We deserve each other." There is then dance music based on "Dancing through Life" for Boq to wheel Nessarose around on the dance floor and underscore Madame Morrible's invitation to Galinda into her sorcery seminar. "Elphaba's Dance," number 8 in the score, where Galinda dances with her nemesis and they become friends, is also based upon "Dancing through Life," but little of it appears on the recording except an ensemble version of the main tune that concludes the track (track 6, 7'11"–7'32"). The stage sequence concludes with seven additional measures of exit music.

Comparison of this later score with that from October 2003 shows that Schwartz made many small, late adjustments to "Dancing through Life" and "The Ozdust Dance" between the two versions. Rewriting of rhythms in the voice line occurs frequently, with some profoundly changing the sound of a phrase. For example, the text "it's just life so keep dancing through" (1'08"–1'15") appears in a completely different setting in the earlier score, with the first five words placed in the space of a single measure (rather than one and one-half measures) and the word "dancing" treated for an entire measure with syncopation. In the next phrase, Schwartz rewrote the second and third lines of text and the melody (1'18"–1'25"), changing the lyrics from "skimming the surface, gliding where turf is smooth" to the "swaying and sweeping and always keeping cool" that one hears on the OCR. Schwartz also rewrote the melody in this passage. Among the many minor changes are alterations to the way some words are declaimed by singers. As Galinda offers Elphaba the black hat, for example, one hears Kristin Chenoweth say the words "you know black" on the recording (5'10"–5'11"), but in the October 2003 score, she was to sing those words on g'. It is a brief moment, but the contrast this allowed to the expressive Chenoweth stands out on the OCR. "The Ozdust Dance" also includes cuts and other similar, subtle changes, along with the appearance of the scene between Nessarose and Boq in a different position than in the later score, reflecting indecision on where this small exchange belonged, a matter already examined in the previous chapter in reference to the late scripts from July to October 2003 (see pp. 75–84). It is also notable that this small scene between Boq and Nessarose in the October 2003 score bears the revision date of 30 April 2003, and it is musically much like what one hears on the recording, with just a few rhythmic adjustments in the vocal line. "Elphaba's Dance" in the October 2003 score includes two cuts, but a version somewhat like one of these had been restored by October 2004.

Schwartz has stated that "Popular" was an imitation of the shallowness of bubblegum rock, demonstrating the space that Galinda's character occupies at that moment.[42] He compared the song to the Beatles repertory, but it is intentionally superficial, and he also highlighted the show's political message in "Popular." He likes the yodel effect in the song and used it because he knew Kristin Chenoweth could do it, and he admits that the song might sound somewhat like a country tune.[43] The opening recitative has a more active accompaniment and sense of forward drive than most such segments in the score because of the song's perky nature, but Schwartz still pays close attention to the lyrics in his melodic construction, writing in short phrases with several rests until the constant, rapid eighth notes on "And when someone needs a makeover, I simply have to take over" (OCR, track 7, 0'26"–0'30"). The tune, marked "Bright and Bubbly; Swing 8ths" (track 7, 1'01"–2'02"), is in AABA form (12+12+9+12 measures), in F major with small variants in the second and third A sections. Special moments include Schwartz's modulation to D-flat major (track 7, 1'34") as Galinda launches into "Don't be offended by my frank analysis" (including the clever rhyme with "personality dialysis"), returning to F major for the final A that ends with the humorous rhymes between "were . . . are" and "popul*er* . . . lar," similar to the fun that Oscar Hammerstein II had with rhymes in "Shall I Tell You What I Think of You?" in *The King and I* (such as "concubine . . . liber*tyne* . . . liber*teen*). The other major sung musical section in "Popular" is contrasting material (track 7, 2'13"–2'34", "When I see depressing creatures . . .") where Schwartz places his political comments about "great communicators" (close to Ronald Reagan's nickname), followed by a return of the A section with new text. Varied material makes up the underscoring for dialog not heard on the recording as Galinda tries to transform Elphaba. Galinda's solo after Elphaba leaves (track 7, 3'06"–3'41") includes no new melodic material.

Schwartz's tendency to continue to revise his songs appears again in a comparison of the later score with that from October 2003 for "Popular." Two distinctive changes occur between the scores in what plays on the OCR between 2:08 and 2:11. On the text "We're gonna make," Schwartz moved the first note down one-half step in the later version, placing "We're" and "make" on the same pitch (*a*) and rendering the entrance a bit more distinctive because the *a* is dissonant with the G minor7 chord that sounds under it. The recorded version also includes spiky quarter notes followed by quarter rests of "pop-u-lar," altered from half notes on each syllable in the October 2003 version (2'09"–2'11"). A typical change for Schwartz is to add more syncopation to a segment, which he did, for example, to "'specially great communicators" (2'27"–2'29") and elsewhere. Shortly thereafter, Schwartz changed "They were popular" (2'34"–2'36") from sung notes to words that are spoken, followed immediately with a substantial rewriting of the melody for the words "It's all about." The following number, "After Popular," was cut between the two scores.

"Save the Lion!"—an obvious title for its location in the show—is entirely underscoring. Schwartz marked it "Creepy," which describes the musical contents accurately: added tone chords, many tritones, augmented triads, and bitonality as Elphaba and Fiyero rush out with the lion after her spell disables everyone else in the room. Dissonant chords, tone clusters, and sixteenth notes describe their exit. This selection changed very little between the two scores.

"I'm Not That Girl," an old-style torch song, begins with underscoring for the couple's awkward conversation. The opening is based on quartal harmonies, followed by a brief motive based on the song that follows. Schwartz wanted the accompaniment to sound like a music box.[44] Schwartz marked the song "Sweetly, Non-rubato" and opens it with eight measures of instrumental introduction (OCR, track 8, 0'00"–0'21") and eighth notes in a 3+2+3 pattern that occurs several times during the song, similar to the dominant rhythm in "Dancing through Life." The songs are related dramatically. In "Dancing," Galinda and Fiyero become established as a couple, and in this number Elphaba laments that she is not the girl in that pair. This is an AABA ballad (9+9+8+12 measures) with an elastic sense of meter set in a low range for the singer and ending on *e*, a note so low that Schwartz reports Idina Menzel had to learn to place it in her voice.[45] The A sections sound conversational, with speechlike rhythms and the insertion of two bars of 6/4 in the prevailing quadruple meter. Vieira notes that he approached the matter of the 6/4 measures with Schwartz, stating that the songwriter played the passage while remaining in 4/4 time, which "robbed the song of its poignancy."[46] The accompanying chords are mainly primary triads. The B section (track 8, 1'15"–1'31"), in 6/8, is melodically more interesting. It opens in F and modulates freely and rapidly as the text speaks of the "land of What-Might-Have-Been." The third iteration of the A section is similar to the first two, and Schwartz concludes the song with a final A' (track 8, 2'12"ff), ending with great uncertainty on the dominant in a 6/4 inversion, which Schwartz admits was from the influence of folk songs performed by The Weavers and other groups that his parents listened to when he was a boy.[47] "I'm Not That Girl" includes one of Schwartz's truly inspired rhymes, pairing "winsome" with "wins him" (track 8, 1'38"–1'42"). The song is number 10 in the printed score; numbers 11 and 12 no longer exist, an indication of music removed with the cutting of Doctor Dillamond's funeral. Between the October 2003 score and this version, Schwartz made a number of minor alterations to the rhythms of the melodic line, removing a few syncopations and making a few of the speech rhythms more natural. One distinctive change took place on "She who's winsome" (track 8, 1'37"–1'39"), where in the earlier version the syllable "win-" was on just an eighth note, but later Schwartz doubled that value for the note and placed it on a syncopation, lending more exposure to the rhyme.

"The Wizard and I—Reprise" (not on the OCR) is number 13, mostly vocal underscoring for Madame Morrible's announcement to Elphaba that the Wizard wishes to meet her, and some underscoring for Elphaba's farewell at the train with her friends. Most of the latter scene, however, has no music. The opening portion includes instrumental references to "The Wizard and I," and Morrible and Elphaba both sing brief segments. The number's later underscoring also references Elphaba's earlier song. The music for this segment changed substantially between October 2003 and a year later. The earlier score seems to show that Schwartz wrote some of this number shortly before the revision date of 15 September 2003, because the first eight measures are incomplete, with chord symbols provided for the harmony. In the later score, one finds a full keyboard part. The line that Madame Morrible sings in the number today had a year before been for Elphaba: she sang to a slightly different melody "So at last, I'll meet the Wizard . . . " A handwritten change in the October 2003 score makes this a line for Morrible, like that in the show today, and then Elphaba sings how she will tell the Wizard about Doctor Dillamond, using music from "Something Bad," a segment not heard today. In addition to a number of changes to the earlier portion of the number, Schwartz used five measures of underscoring from "Into One Short Day" from the earlier score for dialog between Glinda and Elphaba about going to the Emerald City together. That number does not exist in the later score; the eight measures from the opening marked as cut in October 2003 are from "For Good," the number in the second act that confirms the friendship of Elphaba and Glinda.

"One Short Day" follows without pause. Schwartz has stated that it was the third song he wrote for *Wicked* after "No One Mourns the Wicked" and "Making Good" (replaced by "The Wizard and I"), and producer Marc Platt was waiting for an upbeat song.[48] Schwartz and Holzman had an idea for a song about Glinda and Elphaba enjoying the

Emerald City and seeing *Wizomania*, a moment that allowed Schwartz to parody *Funny Girl*. The dominant element is the opening rhythm (3+3+4 in sixteenth notes) heard many times, and numerous measures in the song include a 3+2+3 division in eighth notes (a rhythm also heard in "Dancing through Life" and "I'm Not That Girl," perhaps associating it with the two main characters). The main tune (OCR, track 9, 0'26"–1'16") is in three phrases (9+8+7 measures), each further subdivided into short groupings of two or three bars each. The first phrase is in F-sharp major with a modulation to F during the second phrase. Following a return of the opening key and the A phrase and underscoring based on similar material in D major, Glinda and Elphaba go to see *Wizomania*, an AABC tune (track 9, 1'43"–2'09") based on musical clichés such as cloying chromaticism in the vocal line, punctuation chords, a ragtime-like accompaniment in the 2/4 of the B section, and vocal *glissandi*. The opening of the segment includes a similar rhythm heard in "Don't Rain on My Parade" from *Funny Girl* (where the text begins "I'm gonna live and live now . . ."). Schwartz then combines "One Short Day" and "Wizomania" in counterpoint (track 9, 2'09"–2'22") by presenting the former in augmentation and without its signature rhythmic opening, turning a two-measure phrase in 4/4 into eight measures in 2/4 and treating the next phrase similarly. It is not one of the composer's longer counterpoint segments, changing quickly to a choral presentation of the main theme (track 9, 2'22"ff), but it is an effective addition to the song, which concludes with Elphaba and Glinda acknowledging their close friendship, confirmed in Glinda's ascending octave on "two best friends" (track 9, 2'45"–2'48"). Rapid flourishes in the chorus and orchestra conclude the tune as they are called to meet the Wizard. The next number, "I Am Oz!" underscores their entrance into the audience chamber, providing accompaniment for their terror with low tone clusters and *glissandi*.

The October 2003 score relates a number of changes in lyrics for "One Short Day" along with several musical changes similar to those described in previous songs. One major change is that the contrapuntal section lasts longer in the earlier version, with the ensemble singing another entire phrase from "Wizomania": "Whose enthuse for hot air ballooning has all of Oz honeymooning?" This line had been removed from the contrapuntal passage by the time the recording was made, and what Glinda and Elphaba sing is very much like what is in the earlier score. Another interesting musical change in the score is five measures later (2'35"–2'39") when in the later version Schwartz changes the text "then just like now, we can" from convincing speech rhythms to six equal notes on two quarter note triplets. This smooth declamation seems to ease the way for the girls to agree that they are "best friends." One of Schwartz's major lyric changes in the song between the two versions takes place in the first verse (0'31"–0'45"), where in the earlier version Elphaba and Glinda sound confrontational, telling the residents of the Emerald City, "And we're warning the city: Now that we're in here, you'll know we've been here/ Before we are done!" This was moved to the second verse (1'26"–1'34"), allowing the elimination of other lyrics that might have caused some to misunderstand the friendship between Elphaba and Glinda: "I must say: I'm so happy you're with me. The hand that I'm squeezin' is part of the reason I'm having a ball!"[49] The next number, "I Am Oz!" changed little between the two scores under consideration here.

"A Sentimental Man" is the beginning of what is nearly continuous music through the end of the first act, taking Elphaba from her exciting initial meeting with the Wizard to outlaw status as the Wicked Witch of the West. Schwartz notes that he reused the melodic snippet for the lyrics "Everyone deserves a chance to fly" in "Defying Gravity," and he calls "Sentimental Man" "falsely emotional."[50] The version in the score consulted for this analysis bears the subtitle "Joel Grey Version," revised in March 2004. The Wizard opens the song with a recitative-like passage set in 6/8 and B major marked "Freely—Colla voce" (OCR, track 10, 0'00"–0'20"). It is a sweet, predictable passage that effectively presents the emotional con job that the Wizard directs at Elphaba and Glinda. Schwartz writes "A Tempo" as the Wizard intones, "Elphaba, I'd like to raise you high" (track 10, 0'20"–0'25"), most likely a holdover from older versions that included the song "Chance to Fly." In a passage in B major, Schwartz effectively harmonizes "fly" with a G major chord (track 10, 0'30"–0'33"). An interesting set of rhymes at the end of the section pairs "ascent al-[lows]" with "parental" and "sentimental." The remainder of the number is underscoring, with a few sung passages by the Wizard and Elphaba performing a spell from the Grimmerie, but there is little that requires specific comment here except the Wizard's line that ends on "fly" in the first measure of the next number, "Monkey Reveal." Here, however, instead of the G major chord described above in a parallel passage,

145

Schwartz uses a G-flat augmented chord in the right hand over *A-flat* and *E-flat* in the left hand, an evocative moment just as the monkeys start to evince pain at their growth of wings, the event that drives Elphaba away from the Wizard.

The October 2003 score demonstrates that "Sentimental Man" remained a work in progress in the weeks leading up to the New York premiere. There are two major cuts and two added segments, one printed and another still handwritten, where Schwartz had to that point provided a partial accompaniment with chords so that the full keyboard part could be completed later. His reliance on a previously discarded version of the song may be seen twice in the earlier score where it states "come sopra *San Francisco* #15 'Sentimental Man,'" a clear reference to the song as it existed during the show's tryout and before Joel Grey assumed the part. Rewriting the song for the new Wizard involved reworking previous material.

"Monkey Reveal," number 16, is marked "Transposed" in the score, but there is no evidence as to what the previous key might have been. The B major of "Sentimental Man" has disappeared, with nothing now in the key signature, but many sharps are written in as accidentals, and one still sees B major chords (often with an added *G*, causing what could be regarded as an augmented triad with an added major seventh: G–B–D-sharp–F-sharp) in this unsettled section as the monkeys grow their wings. After 14 measures, Schwartz inserts material from the act's opening (OCR, track 1, 0'19"–0'33") with the "'Monkey' Groove." In the underscoring that follows, where Elphaba hears the Wizard and Madame Morrible agree that the flying monkeys will be effective spies and she learns that she possesses powers the Wizard does not, Schwartz mixes noodling triplets with E-flat minor and F minor chords (from "Something Bad"), tritones, and augmented triads with added tones. Finally, the Wizard returns to his "Chance to Fly" material, here in A minor and 6/8, setting up Elphaba's decision to scream "No!" and run from the room to the accompaniment of the "Wicked" motive, first in A minor and then in F-sharp minor. A modulation to D minor introduces a brief reference to the opening of "I'm Not That Girl" as Madame Morrible announces that Elphaba is a fugitive. The driving character of the music here strongly contrasts with "I'm Not That Girl," but the repeated vamp from that song allows Elphaba to say through the orchestra that she is not the girl that Madame Morrible describes. The instrumental underscoring before "Defying Gravity" includes two major statements of the "Wicked" motive in A minor and then constant eighth notes based on tritones and augmented triads with added tones. The final chord of the segment is a G-sharp major triad with an added *E* (which could also be seen as another augmented triad on E with an added major seventh: E–G-sharp–B-sharp–D-sharp), a sonority that becomes more important in Act 2 (see note 61 on pp. 209–10). Comparison of this version of the song with the October 2003 score shows that Schwartz introduced several cuts in "Monkey Reveal" along with a few other small changes, but the overall effect of the number changed little.

"Defying Gravity" follows without pause. Schwartz has stated that he originally wrote the song for Elphaba alone but then realized that Glinda needed to be a part of it, and the opening is all that is left of the song "I Hope You're Happy."[51] What remains of that song is the opening recitative of "Defying Gravity," where Glinda and Elphaba confront each · other (OCR, track 11, 0'05"–0'31") accompanied by chromatic chords of punctuation that move in parallel motion (for example, D-flat major–C minor–C-flat major) and change to sustained chords soon after Elphaba answers Glinda with her own accusation. Vieira states that the melody that sets "I hope you're happy now" is "the same musical phrase" as used with "It couldn't happen here in Oz" at the end of "Something Bad."[52] While the phrase openings are similar, their conclusions are not. The tone of "Defying Gravity" changes to one of quiet confidence with the music for underscoring that follows, which includes the syncopated instrumental motive in the bass and a brief answering flurry high in a synthesizer (ascending *do-sol-do*, descending *ti-sol-do*—perhaps a transformation of the "Unlimited" motive, *do-do-ti-sol*, with *sol* inserted in the ascending octave of *do* to *do*, and another *do* added on the end[53])—heard first on the OCR when Glinda starts to suggest that Elphaba should apologize (track 11, 0'35"–0'37"). Both the bass and treble motives sound several times during the underscoring that accompanies Madame Morrible's second announcement about Elphaba, where Morrible declares her a "Wicked Witch." Glinda and Elphaba sing more recitative as Glinda urges her to go back to the Wizard where she might still be able to realize her dreams, but Elphaba declines, stating that she "can't want it anymore" (track 11, 0'42"–1'14"). Vieira mentions the connection of this segment to "The Wizard and I," because Schwartz provides Glinda with material that sets

"When I'm with the Wizard" (track 3, 2'08"–2'10") as she sings "You can still be with the Wizard" (track 11, 0'42"–0'46").[54] Here Schwartz modulates from C-sharp minor to D-flat major, his favorite key,[55] and Elphaba sings two eight-bar phrases (A and B, each 2+2+4 measures) in which she declares her freedom from the Wizard's and society's expectations (track 11, 1'17"–1'50"), setting up the "Allegro" that starts on the last measure of B. Schwartz places it over a high, driving eighth note accompaniment that becomes associated with the title words of the song, a form of word painting as these notes "defy" any downward pull from the bass line or Elphaba's earthy voice. Elphaba's C music (track 11, 1'51"–2'06") is two similar four-measure phrases with a two-measure tag on "you can't pull me down." The melody is angular, mostly triadic, with the leaps allowing the singer to move between ranges and explore a variety of timbres. Over the two main motives of accompaniment identified above, Glinda tries to burst Elphaba's bubble (track 11, 2'06"–2'10", "delusions of grandeur") in conjunct quarter note triplets based on the accent scheme of her text, but Elphaba goes right back to her defiant A and B phrases (track 11, 2'10"–2'35"), similar to those above, but now with a new text, at a faster tempo, and with a more active accompaniment that often matches the vocal line's syncopations. The segment concludes with the C music (track 11, 2'35"–2'51") before Schwartz brings back the "Unlimited" music with its characteristic, arpeggiated sixteenth-note accompaniment (track 11, 2'48"–3'14") as Elphaba makes the broom float. In recitative, she invites Glinda to join her (track 11, 3'15"–3'27"), and for a moment it appears that her friend might as they sing the C music together (track 11, 3'27"–3'43"), but Glinda drops out as Elphaba only sings the tag "they'll never bring us down." Schwartz based the recitative that follows (track 11, 3'53"–4'22") on the chromatic, parallel chordal structures of the song's opening. The friends wish each other well over a choral accompaniment that becomes more animated with a high, driving eighth-note accompaniment as they *crescendo* toward the closing "Allegro" where Elphaba soars above the guards, physically and musically, first with a transformation of the A and B music (track 11, 4'32"–4'58") and then with a return of the C music (track 11, 4'59"–5'14"), a moment of consummate excitement where Idina Menzel suggested that much of the passage be sung an octave higher to increase the intensity.[56] The coda (track 11, 5'14"–5'50") starts with Elphaba repeating the marchlike motive as she declares that nobody in Oz can stop her, and then her final cries (which Schwartz says Menzel altered a bit and made her own[57]) with Glinda singing "I hope you're happy" and the guards performing material from "No One Mourns the Wicked," a closing that had more or less existed in this fashion since November 2001. With the stage effects, it is an unforgettable closing to the first act.

Schwartz made many small adjustments to "Defying Gravity" in the year between the October 2003 and October 2004 scores, mostly in terms of rhythmic changes in the vocal line in about 15 percent of the measures in the song. Sometimes he added more syncopation and at other times he gave the singer material based more on the basic beat, but he remains basically interested in setting a text with speech rhythms while making conspicuous use of the syncopation and brief melismas that are so much a part of pop musical sensibility. An example of how Schwartz altered vocal rhythms appears early in the song, as Glinda and Elphaba challenge each other over their contrasting behavior in the Wizard's presence. Glinda first speaks "I hope you're happy!" followed by singing "I hope you're happy now!" (0'06"–0'08") sung mostly in quarter notes on the beat, a major change from the syncopated line that appears in the October 2003 score. Schwartz made the same change for Elphaba when she sings "I hope you're happy too!" (0'15"–0'16"). These changes allow the passages to fit in better with the material around it, also mostly on the beat. Schwartz helped make Elphaba's answer parallel to Glinda's statement by having Elphaba speak her first line (0'13"–0'14") rather than sing it, as in the first score. A major addition near the opening is the treble motive described above (ascending *do-sol-do*, descending *ti-sol-do*, 0'35"–0'37"), which appears here in the later score but not in October 2003. The motive was added there before the cast recorded the OCR in November 2003. (It does appear later in the song in the earlier score.) Schwartz reworked the last thirty seconds of the song substantially by cutting much of Glinda's part, most likely to reduce the clutter with Elphaba holding long notes as her friend says "I hope you're happy" and the chorus comments on Elphaba and her wickedness and how they must capture her. In the October 2003 score, Glinda repeats her line twice, once a third higher and in an inverted, ascending motive above the staff before she sings an *a-flat"* in the last chord as the chorus sings its final "down." Schwartz cut out all but the first "I hope you're happy" in the later version, and that is also what one hears on the OCR.

To open the second act, Schwartz provides material that sounds like a continuation of "Defying Gravity," but soon the ensemble enters in unison with material from "No One Mourns the Wicked" in B-flat minor, quickly modulating to F-sharp minor, setting up new material in which soloists describe the Wicked Witch of the West's presumed activities (OCR, track 12, 0'36"–0'49"). This segment is tonally ambiguous as Schwartz uses a dissonant harmonic background, such as the bitonal combination of a D-flat7 chord and E-flat minor under "Like a terrible green blizzard . . ." and follows that with added-tone triads. The main melodic material of "No One Mourns," more or less in C minor but first with many parallel fourths, follows with new text (track 12, 0'49"–1'11"), fading out on repetitions of "Where will she strike next?" Examination of the October 2003 score reveals few differences from the source of a year later.

"Thank Goodness—Part I" follows immediately. (All three parts of the song are on track 12 of the OCR.) Schwartz has noted that his first inclination with Winnie Holzman was to open Act 2 with a number about how the Wicked Witch of the West's reputation had spread around Oz, and he spent weeks trying to write such a song at the end of 2000. They finally decided, however, to include an event where Ozians gossip about their nemesis, and this became an engagement party for Glinda and Fiyero.[58] "Thank Goodness" is a number in which Schwartz seems to show Leonard Bernstein's influence with his extensive use of 5/8. One recalls "Gloria tibi" from *Mass*, on which Schwartz worked, but the composer does not mention Bernstein's influence in this number, suggesting instead that the 5/8 meter sounded to him like a village folk dance, the effect that he tried to emulate in this celebratory ensemble number.[59] The 5/8 measures are always divided 3+2. Glinda, Madame Morrible, and the crowd sing the lines, which are primarily in regular, four-bar phrases and nearly pentatonic. The harmonies are simpler than in previous numbers, but Schwartz still occasionally uses chromaticism and nonharmonic tones. The accompaniment in both the sung passages and the underscoring for dialog is light. The measure numbers leap from 45 to 91, indicating a late cut, corresponding with an abrupt modulation from E-flat major to C major and then quickly to B-flat major in underscoring for the moment when Madame Morrible tells the surprised Fiyero that this is his engagement party. The October 2003 score reveals a cut of the number's first nine measures, meaning that Glinda begins to sing nearly immediately to bring the audience into the scene and allow a rapid transition. The only other real change between the versions is that the phrase "'Glinda' way" is sung in the earlier score and spoken in the latter, as heard on the OCR (track 12, 1'28"–1'29").

B-flat major functions as the dominant for the return of E-flat at the opening of "Thank Goodness—Part II," where the nervous Glinda tries to bring Fiyero into this plan through an avowal of their joint happiness for the crowd (OCR, track 13, 1'43"–2'14"). Her discomfort is demonstrated musically by the shifting meters, with 2/4 measures intervening on "Right, dear?" "Right here," and "True, dear?" along with 6/8 and 4/4 bars. Schwartz suddenly makes the folk song sound less joyful, and he has stated that it is here that Glinda becomes self-aware and discovers how ambivalent she feels at this "happy" moment.[60] The mixed meters also allow the passage to carry a hint of speech rhythms. Glinda somewhat regains her poise while addressing the crowd (track 13, 2'14"–2'33"), and there are fewer meter changes, but the listener knows that Glinda has lost some of her usual composure because of uncertainty about Fiyero. With simple, added-tone harmonies and a plain accompaniment, Schwartz allows this section to be about the text and his evocative use of meter. Madame Morrible then unctuously takes on her role as the Wizard's press secretary (track 13, 2'47"–3'18"), presenting an untrue version of the events in the Wizard's throne room at the end of Act 1. Schwartz provides material for Morrible in the prevailing 5/8 and moving between F-sharp minor and A major in a section that functions as recitative and includes convincing speech rhythms, switching to "Freely" in 4/4 as Morrible sings about Elphaba suddenly entering the scene. Schwartz then moves quickly to D minor as members of the crowd present outrageous claims about the Wicked Witch, a section where each new phrase is in a different key, finally landing in F minor at the choral call to "Melt her!" The following underscoring for dialog between Glinda and Fiyero is largely in 5/8 and is primarily based on material from earlier in the song.

Comparison of the later score under analysis with that from October 2003 reveals a number of subtle changes, with a few worth noting. In the earlier score, Schwartz set the words "happy ending" fairly simply (1'57"–2'00"), but in the later score, and as one hears on the recording, he spread the words out and made the rhythm more syncopated, making Glinda sound less assured. Schwartz based this upon his treatment of the word "anticipated" later in the song (4'15"–4'18"), also found in the October 2003 score. Another small but effective change between the two scores occurred on the word "concealment" (3'11"–3'12"), the last syllable of which was set to three beats in the earlier score, but Schwartz shortened it to one beat for the recording, allowing Madame Morrible to cut the note off viciously with the closed consonant on which the word ends.

"Thank Goodness—Part III" introduces little new music, based mostly on the emotionally ambiguous material with mixed meters that Glinda sang earlier (OCR, track 13, 1'43"–2'14"). Schwartz's rhythmic displacement on words like "anticipated" (track 13, 4'15"–4'18") adds strongly to this sense of disappointment, bolstered by the frequent repetition of the same melodic motives in a low tessitura until the chorus enters for the rousing ending (track 13, 5'43"–6'20") in F major. Glinda returns to her public self as she holds a *c"* for four bars at the end of the song, but the triumphant ending for the sake of the crowd does not change Glinda's transformation. Schwartz's musical and lyrical exploration of Glinda's complicated mood in this number is assisted by the effective rhymes he manages in the emotionally ambiguous section ("cost . . . lost . . . crossed"). Her ability to move on to the next word without a rest after "crossed" perhaps shows how she has started to work through her feelings. Number 18C in the score, "After Thank Goodness," is based on the previous number but is tonally unstable, starting in A but moving through F-sharp major to a cadence on C major with an added sixth degree, effective preparation for the dramatic scene to follow in Nessarose's private chamber.

The third section of this continuous song includes several minor edits of material found in the October 2003 score that show the songwriter's ear for subtle effect. Before the recording was made, he introduced a rest at the end of "anticipated" (4'18"), notating a brief break for Glinda at this ambiguous moment before she tries to change the mood with "But I couldn't be happier . . . " He did the same thing twelve measures later after "complicated" (4'37"), a parallel passage. He invested a different meaning in the word "when" at the phrase "when all your dreams come true" (5'28"–5'29") by changing it from a longer note in the earlier score to an anacrusis following a rest, placing "when" firmly into the next phrase as Glinda starts to seem more emotionally stable, and in preparation for the forced glee at the end of the song. Schwartz made a similar change to the words "when your" (5'42") later, again adding a rest and making these words an anacrusis, sweeping them into the next phrase and helping provide the needed forward motion at that moment. It also allows the singer to breathe! The October 2003 score reveals that "After Thank Goodness" was an incomplete sketch in October 2003, but it was surely close to the form one finds in the October 2004 score by the time the show opened.

"There's Elphaba" (no. 18D) is one measure in length. As Elphaba magically appears in Nessarose's mirror, Schwartz uses the bitonal structure of a G-sharp major chord against an E major chord, creating a structure incorporating two augmented triads: the *e'* of the E-major triad clashes with the *d-sharp'* of the other triad and suggests an augmented sound, and the *b-sharp* of the G-sharp chord provides the same function for the E major triad. Consciously or not, Schwartz made frequent use of augmented sounds with added tones at appropriate moments in this score. The October 2003 score shows that this measure had been composed recently, because it is handwritten without a date of composition or revision provided.

Number 18E is "Wicked Witch of the East—Intro," instrumental underscoring for the only major song in the score that does not appear on the OCR. As Elphaba learns that her father has died, Schwartz softly quotes the "Wicked" motive and the opening of "No One Mourns the Wicked." At its conclusion, Nessarose cuts off her sister to begin the selfish rant that opens the song. The material with which she begins the song had existed since at least August 2000. It is in C-sharp minor and 6/8 and marked "Angrily," composed in three phrases of four measures each, with a faster harmonic rhythm in the last phrase based on the circle of fifths as Nessarose declares, "Scrounging for scraps of pity to pick up and longing to kick up my heels." After four bars of underscoring, Elphaba starts to chant from the Grimmerie over a C-sharp pedal under augmented triads on *C*, *G*, and *E* or figures based on them, sometimes with added sevenths. Evocative underscoring accompanies Nessarose's first steps (including a combination of a C augmented triad with an added major seventh as she stands for the first time[61]) before Elphaba sings how she has finally done "something good," based on music from "Something Bad." The accompaniment includes three statements of the "Unlimited" motive, launching a segment of underscoring based on the triplet noodling from "Something

Bad" as Boq enters the room and is surprised by Elphaba's presence. The "Unlimited" motive sounds again before Boq sings to Nessarose how he wants to leave for the Emerald City to convince Glinda not to marry Fiyero. This is to the same music that Boq and Nessarose sang in Act 1, introducing rich irony because when Boq last sang the material he lied to her about how much he cared for her. For example, here he sings the text "And I've got to appeal to her, express the way I feel to her" to the same music that he had sung "Because you are so beautiful!" to Nessarose. This segment is in D-flat major, moving to C-sharp minor for Nessarose's recitative as she grabs the Grimmerie and puts a spell on Boq. Schwartz does not set Nessarose's chanting to music, placing it in dialog over bitonal underscoring that again includes augmented chords with added tones. As the section ends, it is clear that Nessarose has placed Boq's life in danger, and she blames Elphaba for showing her the Grimmerie. A contrapuntal section follows in which Nessarose sings the music that she shares with Boq while pleading for his life, while Elphaba chants another spell. The segment is in G major, a tritone away from when Boq sang the music earlier in the scene. The underscoring that follows includes Elphaba's final farewell to Nessarose, which includes a motive from Nessarose's music and then "No One Mourns the Wicked" as Elphaba says to her sister that she has done everything she can for her. Long chords, mostly bitonal and again with augmented elements, underscore the short scene between Boq and Nessarose after Elphaba's exit.

What was clearly this scene's complex development continued as Schwartz worked with the October 2003 score, which transmits two numbers for "The Wicked Witch of the East" with different titles: "Defying Gravity (Reprise)" and "We Deserve Each Other (Reprise)." The first number opens with the same ten measures as "The Wicked Witch of the East," and then a reprise of "Defying Gravity," in which Elphaba tries to enlist Nessarose in her crusade, has been cut. As shown earlier in this chapter, Schwartz had drafted such a passage months before, but here the notion of reprising his Act 1 finale finally died. The title of the next number was then crossed out by hand with the new title ("The Wicked Witch of the East") inserted. The earlier score includes a number of cuts, including one before Boq tells Nessarose that he wishes to go to the Emerald City to try to stop Glinda from marrying Fiyero and Nessarose sings "We deserve each other" to Boq once he has seen that she can now walk, thinking that her new mobility will make him love her. There are also subtle changes in the rhythms of the vocal line like those that have been described in other numbers.

The "Ballroom Transition" (no. 19A) appears on the OCR at the opening of "Wonderful" (track 13, 0'00"–0'45"). It is a dancelike, grand setting of music from "No One Mourns the Wicked" that easily makes one imagine couples whirling around a dance floor in an elegant room. Toward the end, Schwartz includes the first four notes of the "Unlimited" motive. In the October 2003 score, one learns that this dance arrangement is by Jim Abbott,[62] and four measures (including the "Unlimited" motive) were added at the end of the selection between the earlier score and the OCR recording.

"Wonderful" (no. 20) is the pivotal song in Act 2. Elphaba returns to the Wizard, and he nearly charms her into his fold, but that becomes impossible when she discovers Doctor Dillamond, who is unable to speak. Vieira applies the appellation "charm song" to this number, a term used by Lehmann Engel to describe musical theater songs where a character tries to endear himself to another character, the audience, or both.[63] The song is a musical pastiche from the early twentieth century with touches of ragtime and vaudeville that Joel Grey could present with aplomb. Schwartz states that he quotes "The Wizard and I" in the song (OCR, track 13, 4'02"–4'09", "a celebration throughout Oz that's all to do with you") and considers "Wonderful" the most political song in the score.[64] Vieira calls "Wonderful" "the only true pastiche song in *Wicked*,"[65] but it should be noted that Schwartz accessed similar influences in most of the music associated with the Wizard, including his short seduction number for Elphaba's mother at the beginning of the show ("Have another drink . . .") and "A Sentimental Man." The score consulted for this analysis includes the "Original Joel Grey Version" of "Wonderful" with the "old ending" and "Joel's key." The majority of the piece is in F major. Following underscoring for dialog in G major, the Wizard wanders into his song as speech becomes recitative (track 13, 0'46"–1'46"). Schwartz includes evocative melodic touches, such as his treatment from "Then suddenly I'm here" to "someone to believe in" (track 13, 1'11"–1'26"), where Schwartz applies primarily stepwise writing but finishes the phrase on the highest notes. The end of the recitative brings mention of the Wizard's balloon on the dominant as the accompaniment provides an extended arpeggio on a C major/minor7 chord, a decidedly vaudevillian gesture. The chorus of "Wonderful" (track 13, 1'48"–2'37") is in AA'A"B form (7+8+8+8 measures). The melody is a lively mixture of conjunct and disjunct motion, much of it built around a descent from *a* to *c-sharp*, resolving to *d*, which first sounds on the title word. The accompaniment includes *tremolo*, hints of chromaticism, oom-pah figures, and fast, ornamental scales. Related material figures in the following underscoring before the soft-shoe, during which the Wizard presents his cynical view of history (track 13, 2'55"–3'22"). Schwartz's imitation of the vaudeville sound includes the banjo accompaniment and suspension of the swinging eighth notes for the final measure on the punch line, "So we act as though they don't exist!" After the Wizard intones the dominant three times over predictable, changing harmonies, he launches back into the chorus for eleven measures before more conversational writing with chordal accompaniment, as he offers Elphaba the chance to work with him. Schwartz modulates from F to G when they start their duet based on the chorus. The dance that concludes the number, where it appears that the Wizard has brought Elphaba aboard, has a full accompaniment with more vaudeville effects, such as many *glissandi*.

The version of "Wonderful" in the October 2003 score bears the revision date of 23 September 2003. The changes between that and the later score are minor, meaning that the song existed more or less in the "Joel Grey Version" by this date. Schwartz sketched four measures of chord symbols in after measure 4 in the earlier version to serve as underscoring for dialog, which appears with a bit of added melodic motion in the later score. Schwartz cut out a segment of the song in the earlier score that would have followed the Wizard's political commentary (3'26"). It is based on the song's A material and includes the lyrics "'Wonderful,' so now I'm wonderful/If it's become the truth am I to blame? They wanted . . . " Schwartz cut this and jumped to "'Wonderful,' so I *AM* wonderful . . . ," which remains on the recording and in the more recent score. Other changes observed between the scores are insignificant.

"Set Free the Monkeys" (no. 20A) opens with Elphaba accepting the Wizard's proposition on repetitions of a single pitch, followed by a few measures of incidental music before the return of the "'Monkey' Groove" and related music heard at the opening and last scene of Act 1, but here the sixteenth notes and other figures are less regular. The harmonies are basically triadic with some augmented references and a final sonority of an E-flat augmented triad with an added major seventh, already described as one of Schwartz's favorite chords in the score for dramatic moments (see pp. 209–10, note 61). "Dillamond Discovered" includes references to "Something Bad" and the "Wicked" motive. It ends when Fiyero enters. The next underscoring is the opening of Glinda's reprise of "I'm Not That Girl," disarmingly ironic music to accompany Madame Morrible and the Wizard discussing Nessarose's fate. Glinda sings just enough of the tune—one phrase—to make the dramatic point. Schwartz has commented how unexpected it is for Glinda to reprise Elphaba's tune.[66] An interesting indication in the October 2003 score is over Elphaba's line, "You let the monkeys go." A typed note asks whether this line should be spoken, and that is how it is notated in the later score. The earlier version of "Dillamond Discovered" was just a bit longer, with one small cut notated by hand, but the two versions are very similar. Schwartz made a few significant rhythmic changes in Glinda's reprise of "I'm Not That Girl," including one that introduces a new emphasis in the song that is not part of Elphaba's earlier version. Elphaba sings "Don't start" toward the end of the song (OCR, track 8, 2'14"–2'16") after an eighth rest, parallel to other such gestures in the song, but in the reprise, Schwartz changed the rhythm for Glinda, removing the rest and placing more emphasis on "Don't" (track 14, 0'14"–0'16").

"As Long As You're Mine" follows in a direct segue. Schwartz has called this song "sexy and passionate" but also remarks that one finds a "darkness underneath it" because the happiness Elphaba and Fiyero have found will not last.[67] In the introduction, the "Wicked" motive sounds four times, softly, over an *ostinato* bass (OCR, track 15, 0'00"–0'16"). The motive also returns in the accompaniment at other points in the song. Elphaba first sings the tune (track 15, 0'16"–1'27"). It is in AABC form (8+8+8+10 measures), with conspicuous use of quarter note triplets and a consistent eighth note accompaniment and syncopation in the bass line that provides forward momentum. Following a modulation from C minor to A minor, Fiyero sings AA (track 15, 1'29"–2'00"), and then B and C sound mostly as a duet (track 15, 2'00"–2'33"), often with the pair singing in unison, not octaves. A duet restatement of B and C with a concluding tag completes the vocal lines before underscoring with two statements of the "Wicked" motive as Elphaba admits that she feels "wicked" for the first time. The audience should understand from this scene that they have consummated their relationship, confirmed by Schwartz in the lyrics of this effective duet ("I'll wake up my body, and make up for lost time . . ."). Although it was a "trunk" song, Schwartz integrated it fully in the score by making its accompaniment the "Wicked" motive.

Schwartz continued to make many changes to this song after the 25 March 2003 revision that is in the earlier score, changes that one can hear on the OCR. In the October 2003 version, he indicates that the first four measures should be played twice, doubling the introduction's length and making the "Wicked" motive heard four times instead of two, not surprising given the importance he gave it in the score as he worked on musico-dramatic unification through the summer of 2003. A particular change that occurred three times sounds first on the word "moment" (0'48"–0'50"). In the earlier score, "mo-" is set a fifth higher than "-ment," but for the recording and in the later score, Schwartz added a slur on "mo-" that drops that same fifth on two eighth notes, providing additional emphasis. This gesture already appeared in the earlier score when the duet section began (2'01"–2'02"), and Schwartz applied it elsewhere as he continued to work on the song. He subtly changed the rhythm in many places in the vocal line and also added grace notes and ornaments. The songwriter changed the lyrics several places in the October 2003 score, and more changes occurred after Schwartz was done with this score and was working on the OCR.

"The Cyclone" (no. 22A) is entirely underscoring. Schwartz again combines augmented triads with other chords (such as D+ and G major in measure 1) and also includes soft statements of the "Wicked" motive and the opening of "As Long As You're Mine" as Fiyero and Elphaba say farewell. He concludes the segment with eight measures of slow, tonally ambiguous music that closes with an augmented triad with an added major seventh, ending the scene between Fiyero and Elphaba just before the audience sees Glinda sending Dorothy and her friends on their way before she mourns Nessarose's death. As Elphaba arrives in Munchkinland, Schwartz uses the type of sixteenth note arpeggios that accompany the "Unlimited" motive. Comparison of this number with the October 2003 score reveals only a few small cuts.

"Fiyero!" (no. 22B) is two loud statements of the "Wicked" motive, the second transitioning quickly into the opening of "No Good Deed" (no. 23), perhaps the most powerful song in the score. Elphaba's many frustrations boil over as she tries to rescue Fiyero from the Wizard's men by finding an appropriate spell in the Grimmerie. Schwartz notes that the song is "structured like an opera aria," with a large range for the singer and many changes in dynamics. He also cites "complex" harmonies and fast notes in the accompaniment that remind him of Rachmaninov.[68] The vocal line starts with Elphaba's chanting, and in the verse she remains in a narrow range, but highly impassioned. The seven-measure introduction in C minor includes triplet figurations and descending quarter note scales that move in parallel fifths with the opening note of each triplet, all over a tonic pedal, but Schwartz drops the quarter note scale for the last two bars as he switches to a dominant pedal. Over this foreboding passage, Elphaba shouts her lover's name. The verse includes her chanting and desperate hope that Fiyero will survive torture. The descending scales in parallel fifths tend to correspond with her English statements while the accompaniment for the chanting is lighter. Schwartz modulates up one-half step three times during the verse, each time without harmonic preparation, using similar melodic motives in each key and building considerable tension before the chorus starts. Schwartz changes the accompaniment pattern from triplets to constant sixteenths (OCR, track 16, 1'07"), as Elphaba starts her long note on "supply" that concludes the verse. Five bars later (at 1'15"), the chorus opens in B minor as she intones "No good deed" on three consecutive quarter notes, a distinctive statement from a composer for whom syncopation seems almost habitual. Each time she sings the title words, Schwartz uses the same rhythm. The chorus opens with a 15-bar segment that breaks into two phrases, the first in seven measures (track 16, 1'15"–1'29") where she starts to sing a more angular line except for repeating "no good deed" twice, all on *f-sharp'*. The second phrase (track 16, 1'29"–1'44") complements the first, ending with a more angular statement of the title text as Schwartz modulates to G-sharp minor, this time with harmonic preparation. The chorus is in an irregular form, perhaps reflecting Elphaba's desperation. The sixteenths continue in the orchestra as she quietly names those she has lost (track 16, 1'44"–2'07")—Nessa, Doctor Dillamond, and now perhaps Fiyero— with the second, loud statement high in her range and corresponding with yet another modulation, this time up a diminished third to B-flat minor for two loud statements of the "Wicked" motive. Elphaba becomes introspective (track 16, 2'07"–2'30"), entering a passage more like recitative and without accompaniment in sixteenths (but still a strong beat) as she wonders if she has caused all of this herself. Schwartz continues to exploit dramatic modulations, in that brief passage modulating upward twice. In a dramatic gesture in the last five seconds of that brief section, Schwartz has landed on the key of F-sharp (but no third sounds in the two measures) and melodically decorates the tonic and fifth of the chord with accented nonharmonic tones a half step higher (2'25"–2'30"), setting up a return of material from the opening of the verse with the driving sixteenths. Vieira compares Schwartz's musical build-up (2'25"ff) to what sounds just before Elphaba's father and the midwife discover that Elphaba is green at her birth (OCR, track 1, 4'47"–4'50"), calling the segments "nearly identical,"[69] but they are not the same intervallically or harmonically. No new musical material appears, but Schwartz continues with the frequent modulations as Elphaba delivers her vow to never attempt to do anything "good" again, ending her portion of the song.

"Fiyero!" is longer in the October 2003 score: 16 bars with underscoring for Elphaba's escape from the site of her sister's death while Fiyero holds Glinda captive. The first twelve measures, including the "Wicked" motive and material from "As Long As You're Mine," were cut. Lines from Glinda and the Wizard's guards surrounding Fiyero's arrest indicate what this served as underscoring for, and that section of the scene includes no music in the staged version of the show. Comparison of "No Good Deed" between the two scores reveals the types of changes in vocal rhythms and the subtle rewriting of the melody that have been documented in earlier numbers. Schwartz, for example, fashioned a new melodic line for two measures late in the song that allows Elphaba to project more energy. The song reaches a level of maximum intensity just before the title text returns at 2'30". Schwartz then takes Idina Menzel into the middle of the staff for "No good deed . . ." (high for her in this song), drops her to the bottom of the staff on "All helpful urges should be circumvented," and then stays in the lower tessitura in the October 2003 score for a repeat of "No good deed goes unpunished" (2'38"ff), less effective than his final consideration, the return to the slightly higher range where Menzel packs a considerable wallop on the phrase.

Schwartz provides an ending to "No Good Deed" so that Elphaba's big scene may be applauded, but the same music continues into "March of the Witch-Hunters." Schwartz has stated that Boq's solo in this song drives home how Elphaba's deeds have been misinterpreted.[70] The song begins in E-flat minor with a brief introduction followed by a repeated three-measure phrase of simple new material based upon short notes and march rhythms (OCR, track 17, 0'00"–0'14"). The melody from "No Good Deed" follows, presented in two and four parts to a march accompaniment, based closely upon the first seven-bar phrase of the previous song's chorus (track 17, 0'14"–0'27"). A measure of vamp follows a modulation to G minor, and then Boq, now the Tin Man, begins his material in G-sharp minor (track 17, 0'27"–0'59"). Schwartz marked the recitative with active accompaniment as "conversationally." The second phrase, concerning the Cowardly Lion, is up one-half step in A minor. They are musically similar, in speech rhythms, melodically either stepwise or in broken chords. There is musical underscoring for Boq's short conversation with the Lion between the verses, including briefly an augmented triad with an added major seventh and augmented ninth (C–E–G-sharp–B–D-sharp).[71] Underscoring following Boq's verse about the Lion does not appear on the recording. It includes references to "No Good Deed" and march rhythms along with Schwartz's favorite evocative harmony of an augmented chord with an added major seventh (G-flat–B-flat–D–F) in rapid arpeggios over a perfect fifth of *E-flat* and *B-flat* in the bass, sounding just as Glinda realizes that Madame Morrible caused Nessarose's death. The song ends with the march based on "No Good Deed," now in G minor (track 17, 1'00"–1'27"). Besides a few cuts and rhythmic changes in the vocal line, the October 2003 score reveals that this number changed little before the recording or the later score.

The next music, "The Letter," is brief underscoring that sounds as Elphaba reads the message about Fiyero's fate in Glinda's presence. It includes three statements of the "Wicked" motive, the first two in A minor and the third in F-sharp minor, ending on a C-sharp minor chord with an added *F-sharp* and *B*, an indefinite ending just as Elphaba announces to Glinda that she will surrender. The number is nearly identical between the two scores.

Elphaba elicits a promise from Glinda that she will not try to clear her friend's name, which introduces "For Good—Intro" (no. 24B), a segment that opens track 18 on the OCR (0'00"–0'36"), but there are bars of music in the score missing on the recording. This segment provides the final significance of the "Unlimited" motive: to the same melodic material, Elphaba announces that she is indeed "limited" and comments on what Glinda should be able to accomplish. Vieira notes that the musico-dramatic unification continues as Elphaba sings to Glinda "And just look at you—You can do all I couldn't do" to the same music that Elphaba sang "And I've just had a vision almost like a prophecy . . ." in "The Wizard and I."[72] The segment includes some of the rising arpeggios on sixteenth notes that have accompanied this motive throughout. Underscoring (not on the OCR) from "Defying Gravity" (where the two women consider working "in tandem") accompanies Elphaba signaling Chistery to bring her the Grimmerie so she can give it to Glinda. Elphaba tells Glinda "now it is up to you" twice over added tone triads, and Schwartz executes a common-tone modulation as the *G-sharp* that Elphaba sings (over a D major triad with an added augmented fourth and major seventh) changes to an *A-flat*, the fifth in the D-flat major tonic of "For Good." It is a smooth transition into a song that forms one of the score's highlights. This introductory passage appears handwritten in the October 2003 score and is similar musically in the October 2004 score (and in what one hears on the OCR), probably an indication of Schwartz's work at unifying the score with motives during the summer of 2003.

"For Good" is in four sections.[73] Each character sings a verse, followed by a transition in which they forgive each other for their disagreements, and then a final duet based upon the material of the verses. The song expresses strong sentiments, and Schwartz filled the text with vivid imagery and handled the pacing beautifully with straightforward, approachable music. The vocal writing is intended for two pop divas, but the song is not a clumsy attempt to tug heartstrings. He based most of the vocal rhythms on those of speech, giving the women the air of sharing an intimate conversation as they express their feelings for each other, knowing that they will never see each other again. It is a moment of striking honesty and has become one of the score's most popular songs. Glinda sings the first verse, following two statements of the song's instrumental head motive based around a D-flat major arpeggio (OCR, track 18, 0'36"–0'38"), which functions elsewhere in the song as a sort of punctuation, sounding, for example, before Elphaba starts her verse. It is also the motive to which the friends sing "I have been changed." Glinda's verse divides into three phrases (8+5+10 measures). The first phrase (track 18,

0'51"–1'19") is like a recitative: diatonic, based largely around the notes of a D-flat arpeggio, drawing out the opening instrumental gesture. There is effective use of textual and musical rhyme when the same melodic gesture sets "I've heard it said" and "And we are led," the latter near the phrase's midpoint. The brief interior phrase (track 18, 1'19"–1'35") of five measures, still somewhat recitative-like, starts with similar motion as Glinda expresses her doubts about whether or not someone enters another's life for a reason (which introduces the first phrase), but Schwartz then moves boldly into sharp keys (reaching B major by the phrase's conclusion) as Glinda delivers the song's main point: that she became the person she is by befriending Elphaba. The final phrase (track 18, 1'35"–2'14"), somewhat more melodic, shares material with the first, again emphasizing the notes of the tonic chord, but with a satisfying instrumental imitation of the motive to which she sings "because I knew you." Glinda asserts that Elphaba's friendship has changed her "for good." Elphaba's verse (track 18, 2'17"–3'30") is musically similar, with rhythmic alterations to accommodate the new text. Instead of just an instrumental answer to "because I knew you," here Glinda chimes in as well, ushering in effective unison singing in the final two measures of Elphaba's verse. On the word "good," Schwartz modulates more or less to E (with several chords on F-sharp and B) for Elphaba's brief apology and Glinda's conciliatory response (track 18, 3'30"–3'52"), what might be called the B section of a large AABA in the song, but the individual sections (with an A section here including an entire verse sung by Glinda or Elphaba) seem a bit long for the listener to perceive that classic song form. This contrasting segment with the remainder of the song features the same kind of vocal writing, with careful speech rhythms and syllabic declamation, the one major exception being Glinda's brief melismatic ornament on "more" as they build for the duet return of A. In an age when many pop songs include melismas, it is striking to see how Schwartz stuck to speech rhythms in "For Good." (Vieira states that "the use of *melisma* in this song sounds completely natural,"[74] but there are few to be found.) The final A section of the proposed large form (track 18, 3'52"–5'03") includes only the final phrase of the verses sung by Glinda and Elphaba, but here the original ten-measure phrase has been extended by imitation and repetition. Schwartz returns to the home key of D-flat major as Glinda and Elphaba restate their comparisons of how their paths in life have been altered by knowing each other, with

Elphaba following Glinda in the imitation. They sing either homorhyth-mically in harmony or in unison, except for the exchanges of "because I knew you," a phrase they finally sing in unison before the final "I have been changed for good." The vocal conclusion is mostly in unison, but the verb "changed" is in harmony, with Glinda repeating the ornament from the end of the B section. The unison *D-flat* on "good" brings the song to a satisfying ending, one that will be heard for years on high school programs sung by young women who have pledged to be "best friends forever." Some might find this song maudlin, but Schwartz brought to bear excellent craftsmanship and captured the sentiment simply and elo-quently. "For Good" is one of the best demonstrations of his ability to write memorable, meaningful songs in a dramatic context. Vieira states that Schwartz does not use music from "For Good" earlier in the show,[75] but it is interesting to note that in a previous version Schwartz had used material from the song in the introductory material to "One Short Day," a high point of their friendship in Act 1, but as noted above, this segment had been cut in the October 2003 score.

The October 2003 score shows that Schwartz reconsidered many of the vocal rhythms as he finalized the song, introducing changes in more than half of the measures. Common alterations included faster anacruses, with pairs of eighth notes changed to pairs of sixteenths such as on the first two words of "Like a comet . . ." (OCR, track 18, 1'35"–1'36"), providing more energy to the opening of each phrase, and a number of long-short-short rhythms changed to triplets (such as "half-*way through the* wood" [1'47"–1'50"], complicated by the first note of the triplet on "-way" tied to the previous note). The triplets provide smoother decla-mation in a number of cases. Another effective change takes place when Glinda sings for the first time "I have been changed . . ." (2'05"–2'10"). In the earlier score, "changed" is on a quarter note tied to a dotted eighth in a 4/4 measure, and Schwartz changed it to a dotted half note in a 6/4 mea-sure, followed by a rest before "for," setting the word off more effectively. Here the listener discovers that the song's title carries multiple levels of meaning. Similar examples of subtle, useful editing abound in the song, demonstrating how Schwartz continued to search for improvements.

"The Melting" (no. 26) and "A Sentimental Man—Reprise" (no. 27) are both reprised material included at these points for musico-dramatic reasons. "The Melting" opens with a portion of "No One Mourns the

Wicked" ("And goodness knows, the wicked's lives are lonely . . .") in a three-part choral setting. Elphaba draws a curtain across the stage that shows the backlit shadow of her being drenched with water by Dorothy, and the accompanying underscoring for this shadow play is, predictably, the "Unlimited" motive (more heavily scored and with a chromatic accompaniment), with its ascending arpeggios of augmented triads in sixteenth notes, a gesture that changes to descending arpeggios over a descending (but gapped) whole-tone scale in quarter notes as Elphaba starts to "melt." Glinda witnesses this from the other side of the curtain, and the underscoring (now in D-flat major) that accompanies her search for her friend and her discovery of the green elixir bottle comes from "For Good," more or less the ten-measure segment that concludes the verses sung by each character and also concludes the song in the duet version. The last music heard in the segment is what sets "I have been changed for good." The October 2003 score reveals that this number changes little, with a minor cut and one rhythmic change in a vocal line.

Glinda returns to the Wizard's palace with Elphaba's green bottle, proof that the Wizard was her friend's father. The next music (still in D-flat major), a prerecorded excerpt from his seduction song to Melena early in the show, begins as the Wizard realizes his paternity. In a section marked "Freely," he croaks out a bit of "A Sentimental Man," only able to speak "a father" (two words designated to be sung in the October 2003 score). The underscoring that concludes the scene continues material from the same song for a moment (where he sings of treating each citizen of Oz as a "son or daughter"), but it changes to a transformation of "Wonderful" as Glinda orders him to leave Oz and he trudges off the stage a broken man. Schwartz does not end the scene in D-flat, moving to C and then to G major and E minor. Perhaps the key of "For Good" cannot be used for the Wizard to make his exit. This brief, heartfelt musical segment shows the Wizard as a pitiable character who wanted to do the right thing but lacked the ability.

The cast album does not include the entire "Finale" (no. 28). A rapid G major scale over three octaves in parallel tenths accompanies Madame Morrible being dragged off to prison on Glinda's orders, and then Schwartz repeats 24 measures of material from the opening number (OCR, track 1, 1'00"–1'29") featuring bitonal harmonies and choral settings of "Good news! She's dead!" on long notes. The story has gone full circle, and we have returned to the celebration at the show's opening, but now the music reflects truths that we know. Instead of modulating to D major at this point on the last statement of "news" (as in the opening), Schwartz goes to G minor and provides underscoring for Fiyero, now the Scarecrow, to return to Kiamo Ko for Elphaba. In a "Moderato" passage that does not appear on the OCR, Schwartz uses contemplative noodling (perhaps distantly transformed from "For Good") in the instruments in G minor and E-flat, possibly a distant transformation of "long as you're mine" from Fiyero and Elphaba's duet as Fiyero reaches the castle and knocks on the door of the chamber where Elphaba has been hiding. The underscoring for their dialog includes transformations of material from "As Long As You're Mine," "For Good" ("because I knew you"), and the "Wicked" motive, a musical cocktail that brings their relationship to its logical conclusion. The next material appears on the recording at the opening of the "Finale," a stepwise introduction (track 19, 0'00"–0'07") heard earlier with the texts "celebration throughout Oz" (from "The Wizard and I" and "Wonderful") and "now it's up to you" (from "For Good—Intro"). (Vieira suggests that Schwartz includes this motive here to underline that this is a celebration throughout Oz that has to do with Elphaba, what she foresaw, but it certainly is not an occasion that she might have desired.[76]) The ensemble enters and again starts "No One Mourns the Wicked." Underscoring follows from "No One Mourns" (material based on the setting of "the wicked die alone," track 19, 0'20"–0'42") for Glinda's announcement that she will try to rule as "Glinda the Good"; her speech is not on the OCR. The chorus answers with "Good News!" in a chordal setting (0'42"–0'46"), followed by underscoring that is not on the recording based on "No One Mourns" (as Elphaba and Fiyero agree that their existence and whereabouts must remain a secret). Schwartz placed the next ethereal "Good News!" from the chorus on the recording (0'46"–0'50"), prefacing the duet between Glinda and Elphaba from "For Good" with the choral interjections from "No One Mourns" that conclude the show (0'51"–1'37"). As previously noted, Schwartz musically defined Glinda's character with belting for the private Glinda and higher soprano writing for her public face. The two are united as she sings a solo version of "because I knew you" (1'09"–1'15"), soaring an octave from *g'* to *g"* as she proclaims a private sentiment publicly and in her higher range. The show concludes with Schwartz's evocation of the famous tritone from *West Side Story* as the *A-sharp* in the bass instruments answers the E major chords from the choir.

The October 2003 and October 2004 scores in the "Finale" transmit similar versions. In the earlier score, one cannot reconcile everything that is in the "Finale" with the remainder of the show. For example, early in the number, a dialog cue shows Chistery saying "Miss Glinda, here." This would indicate that he gives her either the Grimmerie or the bottle of green elixir, both of which should have taken place before this moment. The major musical difference between the versions is that the later score includes a crashing B major chord on the second word of "Good news!" that is not present in the earlier version. It was probably added to the later version to provide a logical conclusion to the opening choral passage. It is followed by a modulation to G minor on the same text that changes the mood for Fiyero's return to Kiamo Ko to find Elphaba, the underscoring for which follows in both versions.

Robert Vieira provides an interesting perspective on *Wicked* at the end of his essay. He suggests that the listener can leave the OCR in the player after it ends, which will cause some machines to start the disc again, and one then hears track 1 completely differently.[77] One now understands why Glinda seems so conflicted at the start of the show. She is cautious when asked if Elphaba had been her friend, but she also defends her, suggesting how hard Elphaba's life must have been. Glinda sings toward the end of the number that the wicked "die alone," and Vieira states that this line can be heard two ways. The other Ozians singing the number with Glinda would hear it as a condemnation of the Wicked Witch of the West, while Glinda could just as easily be mourning that she believes her friend did indeed perish with nobody to comfort her. As the flashback then starts and the audience meets the young, self-absorbed Galinda, one starts to appreciate the extent of her journey in the show.

Vieira's musings about how one might regard the OCR's opening track after getting to know the show demonstrates this score's complexity, where both music and lyrics make significant contributions to the storytelling. Schwartz has filled each song with characterization and unified the score with two principal motives and a number of less important ones that make meaningful appearances at telling moments in the music. The score's combination of pop, Broadway, and classical styles, good tunes, and effective lyrics has made it popular with audiences, and as has been shown, it can be analyzed both superficially and at a deeper level.

Deleted and Revised Songs

It was not possible to see all of the songs deleted from *Wicked* for the purposes of this study, but research in Schwartz's office yielded piano/vocal scores, lead sheets, and lyric sheets for several songs that are described below. Only some of these manuscripts are dated. The description below will be less detailed than the analysis applied to the October 2004 version of the piano/vocal score, but a representative sample of deleted songs will illustrate ways that the *Wicked* score might have been substantially different.

Some of these songs were part of a program called *The Yellow Brick Road Not Taken* (hereafter, *YBR*), a benefit performance for the New York Restoration Project that celebrated *Wicked*'s fifth anniversary on Broadway. It took place at the Gershwin Theatre on 27 October 2008.[78] Schwartz and Holzman provided deleted material for this event, along with earlier versions of musical segments that remained in the show. The songs were arranged and orchestrated by Ben Cohn, a keyboard player in the Broadway pit orchestra for *Wicked* and its associate director.[79] Schwartz made available these scores for this study. Few bear dates of revision from before *Wicked* opened; most of the dates on the scores refer to when Cohn arranged the songs for the benefit. It is therefore difficult to know when each of these songs existed in this state. Indeed, it cannot be established whether or not any of the songs ever existed in precisely the version one sees in these scores, although one assumes that Cohn retained most aspects of Schwartz's drafts. It should be noted, however, that there are new spoken lines in Cohn's scores that poke gentle fun at some of the material performed for the benefit. For example, in the fourth segment of the "Opening" in *YBR*, one of the "Fanatics" asks Galinda if this was really how the show opened at the time. Clearly Cohn and others who worked on the benefit desired to make the show entertaining, but one would expect that the basic thrust of each number remained, since the show's raison d'être was to present material cut from *Wicked*. Material from *YBR* will serve below as a point of comparison for some of the deleted songs, and other songs that appeared in the benefit will be described briefly.

A two-page manuscript from the office, in Schwartz's hand, is a draft of a "New Opening," which Schwartz called a "predraft." It starts with two statements of the "Wicked" motive in the keyboard part, but little of the remainder of the accompaniment appears except for chord symbols and some transformations of the "Wicked" motive, primarily in eighth notes. The lyrics, sung by some of the Ozian populace that one sees at the beginning of the show, start out almost pleadingly, asking if the Wicked Witch is dead, and then switch to descriptions of how she died. The short musical lines are punchy, with chromatic passages and affective intervals, ending with matching dramatic gestures: a melodic descent on lyrics about how she melted "like last year's dirty snow" and an ascending gesture on how the news must be spread. As may be seen in the following musical example, the setting of "witchy cider" is also evocative, with the use of *c-natural* conflicting with the A[7] chord. This would have constituted a very different opening for *Wicked*! (See example 5.16.)

YBR included a full version of the show's opening, printed in six separate but continuous sections. They bear no dates of revision. As was

Example 5.16. **"New Opening" (Undated draft, and not used in the show), mm. 5–11.**

the case in earlier scripts, the scene opens with souvenir hawkers selling wares for the occasion. The first eight measures are like the opening of the staged version, but Schwartz then skipped the "'Monkey' Groove" and jumped to the initial statement of "Unlimited" without the sixteenth notes that accompany today. Glinda sings "Let us be glad," but the lyrics have changed, as have those after the choir enters. Major segments are comparable with the OCR, but other material is quite different. Madame Morrible announces that the Wizard would like effigies of the Wicked Witch burned, and then the Scarecrow describes what it was like to watch the Wicked Witch melt. Most of this material later disappeared from the show. The Scarecrow sings "No One Mourns the Wicked" as a solo, with some of the lyrics similar to the OCR. The crowd sees Glinda, who, following an exchange based on the above-mentioned jocular question about the material, begins to sing "Who would love the wicked?" based on the familiar music of "No One Mourns," answered by the chorus and Madame Morrible. The next section, Part 5, is Elphaba's conception scene, with a major difference being that only her father sings during the waltz where he says farewell to his wife. Part 6 is the birth, and it includes both different lyrics and music, like scalar material on such lines as "I see a nose!" unlike the wider, more expectant leaps that appear on the OCR.[80] The whole scene includes material that could be edited and rewritten. For example, Elphaba's father takes the time to say "I can't bear to look at it. Get it out of my sight," words that could easily be deleted and still have the feeling of disgust conveyed. This earlier version of the scene has a choral closing like that on the OCR, but many of the lyrics are different, and there are segments that were later cut, such as the lyrics "They make their bed not of rose, but of thorns . . . " Schwartz stated in an interview that this passage was in the show as late as the San Francisco run; they cut it during the summer of 2003. The scene ends with Schwartz's tribute to *West Side Story* on three statements of the show's title.

"Making Good" is one of the songs deleted from *Wicked* that has become well known. The OCR issued in 2008 for the fifth anniversary of the show's premiere includes bonus tracks,[81] among them Stephanie Block singing this song in a version slightly different than what was heard in *YBR*, and that version is substantially different than what is described above in the August 2000 music (see pp. 104–5). For example, in late summer of 2000, Schwartz did not include the "Unlimited" section that became an important part of Elphaba's musical identity in *Wicked*, but it is a prominent part of the *YBR* version and what Block sings on the anniversary OCR, and a segment much like it remains in "The Wizard and I," the song that replaced "Making Good." The *YBR* version corresponds closely with the anniversary OCR sung by Block for the first minute and seven seconds. At that point, *YBR* includes a statement of "You'll be making good" followed by seven measures of instrumental interlude. By cutting those for the recording, Schwartz delays the satisfaction of hearing the title text and jumps breathlessly to the second verse. After that cut, the music of the final 2 minutes and 53 seconds on the recording is similar to *YBR*, with changed lyrics. For example, Elphaba sings on the anniversary OCR that "Maybe I can make world hunger cease" instead of "maybe economic expertise," as in *YBR*, and she is much harder on her father on the recording, referring to him as a "tough old bastard" rather than "a certain governor" who will come to claim credit for her once she becomes famous. "Making Good" is a top-drawer Schwartz song that musical theater performers will sing, but it would not have worked as well in *Wicked* as its replacement because it is too general in theme. Elphaba only has a dream of being famous and successful, but she does not even know in what field; in "The Wizard and I," she believes she will hitch her wagon directly to the Wizard, setting the story on a more direct trajectory from early in Act 1. *YBR* also included a reprise of "Making Good" that opens with the "Unlimited" material and then includes only a few bars of the song.

As noted above, "Bad Situation" was Schwartz's first attempt at the musical meeting between the mismatched roommates, the song placement that became "What Is This Feeling?" The materials consulted for "Bad Situation" included an undated version of the song with vocal lines, most of the piano accompaniment and chord symbols, and a lyric sheet dated 10 January 2001 that bears a rather different text. The song is in several sections, opening with 16 measures in 6/8 sung by Elphaba and Galinda in unison and dialog as they regard each other closely for the first time. Their gossipy banter is in the second phrase of eight measures, opening in this manner (see example 5.17). Similar alternation also appears in "What Is This Feeling?" Schwartz concludes the 6/8 with both young women pausing to realize that they must make this work, and they open the main part of the song with a 14-bar section in 4/4 that carries the jaunty feeling of a 1930s song. Schwartz makes rich use of chromatic

Example 5.17. "Bad Situation" (*Yellow Brick Road*), mm. 9–15.

harmonies, especially with the juxtaposition of A-flat major and E minor chords in the first inversion (see measure 18 of example 5.18). Such harmonic motion and gentle syncopation continue throughout the segment. Other students interrupt, singing the same material heard on the OCR (track 4, 1'56"–2'13"); in this score only the vocal lines and chords appear. Here it is partly a dialog between two of Galinda's friends, but on the OCR it is a chorus. In "Bad Situation," Galinda enters into a contrapuntal section with her friends based on her previous 4/4 segment. Schwartz was in good form as a lyricist here, matching "engage us" with "contagious" (part of Galinda's hope that Elphaba might become ill). The duet between the girls, with some solo interjections, follows (see example 5.19). That section then ends indecisively with "Underscoring?" meaning that some dialog would have been a transition between Galinda's section and what follows for Elphaba, which is in E major with rich syncopation, certainly not as interesting as the song that finally occupied this slot. Galinda's friends jump in again, but with different material. This shows that although Schwartz changed the song, the creators had already decided that

Example 5.18. "Bad Situation" (*Yellow Brick Road*), mm. 16–24.

this scene would include material for Galinda and Elphaba that contrasted with that presented by Galinda's friends, a general description that also fits "What Is This Feeling?" That later song closes with a contrapuntal sequence, as did "Bad Situation," where the final segment starts with a modulation up one step. The two roommates sing together, and the friends interject comments based upon similar musical material, with the spice coming from the choral suggestion that what they really hope to see

Example 5.19. "Bad Situation" (*Yellow Brick Road*), mm. 52–59.

is a fight between Galinda and Elphaba. The 1930s feeling of the song continues, which would have caused a problem in the staged version of the show because music of this ilk is associated more with the Wizard.

Another version for this placement from Schwartz's office appears to be a continuous musical scene, but whether that is what was intended is difficult to know because Schwartz tends to draft songs in short segments, with double bars at the end of each. The first section of "Far Be It from Me" is similar to the current opening of "What Is This Feeling?" (through Elphaba's insulting declaration of "Blonde"), in D major rather than the D-flat of the Broadway score and notated differently, but it is clear that Schwartz had already formulated that section in his mind. When Elphaba insults Galinda by reference to her hair color, however, in this version she does so just as Schwartz modulates into B-flat major and moves into a waltz meter. The roommates fall all over each other to be polite as they try to ascertain which bed the other desires. They bid each other good night, and the accompaniment ties a bow on the segment with a rapid

Example 5.20. "Far Be It from Me" (Undated, deleted material), mm. 37–47.

scale in F Mixolydian, a combination of F and E-flat major chords, and a grace note on *e-natural*" resolving quickly to *f*", an ironically sweet ending to a section full of barely repressed hostility. The saccharine quality in the music and waltz meter continues into the next section, where Elphaba and Galinda sing pointed insults to each other, which appeared in an early version of the show in dialog (see chapter 4, p. 59). (See example 5.20.) The next excerpt is entitled "Bad Situation 2001," including solo segments for Elphaba and Galinda and then a brief segment where each tries to explain their roommate situation to others. Galinda sings in B major and 6/8 with touches that remind one of youthful rock from the 1950s, such as the extension of final syllables at the end of the word onto different pitches, as may be seen in the following example on "tragedy-ee-ee" (see example 5.21). Schwartz described Galinda's character in "Popular" with bubblegum pop, and here he did something similar. The segment includes several examples of hemiola. "Part 2" is Elphaba's solo, in 4/4 with added tones in the chords and irregular rhythms in the vocal line that carry more of a feeling of speech rhythms, presenting Elphaba with her usual gritty honesty. She tries to be reasonable, suggesting that Galinda might have a "good heart"—while also hoping that it might "stop beating." Schwartz

Example 5.21. "Bad Situation 2001" (Undated, deleted material), mm. 4–9.

makes considerable use of quarter note triplets in this section, perhaps inspired by the 6/8 feeling of Galinda's previous section. Elphaba's segment concludes as Galinda starts to tell Pfannee and Shenshen about all that she is suffering, and they are receptive. Elphaba tries to tell Nessarose, but the song concludes with her sister saying she wants to hear nothing. It is a weak ending for a scene that fell on the cutting room floor.

YBR includes different material for "Bad Situation," but this is a song where it is difficult to know how accurately YBR represents a true stage of the creative process. One file presents the "Correct 5th Anniversary Lyrics," a title that declares the document to date from 2008, and the date of revision on the musical score is 27 September 2008. The score is different from the "office version" just described in a number of details. An interesting section in YBR is a pep talk that Elphaba and Galinda sing to themselves in which they declare that they will try to make this situation work because it would be difficult to progress in school while jailed for murder. When Galinda speaks with her friends, Boq delivers a package with the black, peaked hat in it. Galinda offers it to Elphaba, who states when she will change her mind about wearing it: "When monkeys fly!"

Following that confrontation in *YBR* is Galinda's friends singing the familiar "Dear Galinda, you are just too good . . . " Most of the music in this version of the song resembles the "office version" described above, with the ending another combination of the two main characters singing "Bad Situation" together and Galinda's friends interjecting material, sometimes approaching a counterpoint song.

"Easy as Winkie Wine" followed "Who Could Say No to You?" in the song placement that finally became "Dancing through Life," and the materials in Schwartz's office included undated lyric sheets and a piano/vocal score for the number. The lyrics in both sources are identical. The thrust of the scene is that Fiyero wants to convince Boq that asking Galinda to the Frolick is as "Easy as Winkie Wine," a popular phrase from his area in Oz. He escorts Boq to Galinda, who immediately agrees, but then she engineers that Boq would go with Nessarose and Galinda with Fiyero. She gets her way and makes it look like she looked out for everyone else. Elphaba and Madame Morrible watch it all through the crystal ball from the sorcery seminar. In the first segment, Fiyero sets the scene in Schwartz's typical recitative style, and then the more active, syncopated accompaniment of the verse begins predictably just as Fiyero intones the word "wine." Fiyero sings two similar 16-bar phrases in D major in which he outlines his easygoing philosophy and counsels Boq that "Girls are for fun, and not for pining over." Schwartz based his syncopated melody largely around the tonic triad, a pop song "easy" on the ears. Fiyero takes Boq over to Galinda, and as she begins her scheming, there is a modulation to F major. The feeling of the song changes little, and there is melodic material shared between sections. Once Galinda starts her sob story for Nessarose, the key center is D minor. The text is different than heard on the OCR, but it transmits an identical intent. It is set mostly in triplets and is like recitative, as may be seen in the following example (see example 5.22). Boq falls for the bait, and Fiyero expresses his admiration for Galinda using melodic material from his main portion of the song (see example 5.23). They sing together, concluding on the title text. It is an effective scene, but the song perhaps does not convey sufficient character or leave room for enough dramatic action to be the solution for this placement. *YBR* includes a version of "Easy as Winkie Wine" that is very close to what has been described except for the key centers and other details.

Example 5.22. "Easy as Winkie Wine" (Undated, deleted material), mm. 95–99.

The next segment, "We Deserve Each Other," is a replacement for "Easy as Winkie Wine" from sometime in 2001; the title was cut off in the copying process, and all that can be read is the year. This material includes a five-page script excerpt with much of the scene and two pages of printed score called "We Deserve Each Other (New End)." The script includes material similar to the staged version and unknown lyrics. (The *YBR* materials contain a musical version close to these five pages of script with music similar to that described here.) Galinda and Fiyero declare their joint perfection (as in OCR, track 6, 3'58"–4'02"), singing that they

Example 5.23. **"Easy as Winkie Wine" (Undated, deleted material), mm. 110–12.**

"deserve each other." The scene changes to Nessarose brushing her hair for her date with Boq and singing of how she has tied her hair in blue bows for him, and that they also "deserve each other." Boq arrives, and they share awkward dialog; the scene then jumps to the dance where all do "The Emerald City Stomp." Fiyero advises Boq to tell Nessarose the truth, but he cannot, and then Boq and Nessarose sing the sequence on the OCR (track 6, 6'18"–7'08") where he tries and fails to tell her the truth just before he takes her to the dance floor. The script includes brief mention of other dialog scenes, such as Galinda thanking Madame Morrible for letting her in the sorcery seminar. The script jumps to the end of the scene, where Galinda has rescued Elphaba on the dance floor by dancing with her, and the five—Elphaba, Galinda, Fiyero, Boq, and Nessarose— all sing how they "deserve each other" as they conclude with everyone doing "The Emerald City Stomp." The two pages of music include brief material based on the music to "We Deserve Each Other" as Galinda tells Elphaba that the hat she gave her fits her style. A sudden modulation from F-sharp to A-flat major brings in the music of "The Emerald City Stomp" described above in the choral music from the 21 November

2001 script (see p. 114). *YBR* includes dialog between Fiyero and Galinda later cut from the show that would have made Galinda seem even more manipulative and bloodless: Fiyero tells her that he feels awkward with the girl that his best friend loves, but she answers that she will never love Boq and that everyone expects her to be with Fiyero. She will not disappoint her crowd.

Schwartz's office also yielded a manuscript in his hand of music for the same scene, some with just the vocal line(s) and others with a single line of accompanying instrumental parts and chord symbols. The segments represented on these pages include Boq asking Fiyero for help with Nessarose, Fiyero advising him to tell her the truth, a version of the scene between Boq and Nessarose where he cannot tell her the truth and dances with her (much like in the OCR), and the five friends (as above) singing how they "deserve each other" as the chorus provides the end of "The Emerald City Stomp." Fiyero's answer to Boq illustrates a telling segment that did not make it into the show (see example 5.24).

Yet another printed version of the scene that combines most elements described above is also called "We Deserve Each Other," set here in four distinct but continuous sections. "Part 1" opens with Fiyero and Galinda admiring each other, with lyrics and music that do not appear elsewhere. It does include, as in the staged and recorded version, "You're perfect! You're perfect! So we're perfect together!" (OCR, track 6, 3'59"ff), but the music is different. They twice sing "We deserve each other" to the usual music, and the segment ends with everyone doing "The Emerald City Stomp." Part 2 is another rendering of the scene where Fiyero tells Boq that he must be honest with Nessarose, with some interjections of the same dance. Part 3 is close to the staged version of Boq and Nessarose as he asks her to dance rather than telling her the truth, and Part 4 is again the five friends singing how they "deserve each other" before the final time through "The Emerald City Stomp."

A later version of this scene included the song "Which Way's the Party?" deleted late in the creative process because it did not sound believable when sung by Norbert Leo Butz.[82] The materials in Schwartz's office included two printed versions of the musical scene. The first was undated, and which character is singing is not identified, but clearly Fiyero starts. His opening recitative begins in F-sharp major, moving to A major in the tenth bar. The recitative is somewhat pedestrian in both music and lyrics,

Example 5.24. "We Deserve/Emerald City Stomp—end" (Undated, deleted material), mm. 10–25.

with Fiyero commenting that all of the academic pressure at Shiz causes him to ask an important question, which is the song's title. At that moment Schwartz begins the main body of the song with an active accompaniment under a syncopated, largely stepwise melody (see example 5.25). The 16-measure melody ends by answering the question: "The party is here!" Schwartz modulates to C minor after an instrumental interlude and then includes a section that begins "Let's go down to the Ozdust Ballroom . . ." that is melodically similar to the OCR (track 6, 2'06"–2'34"). The accompaniment is different and the lyrics are changed (for example, "Leave the books on the shelves, take our bad selves" became "Find the prettiest girl, give 'er a whirl"), and after "Right on down to the Ozdust Ballroom," the music and text are different in this earlier version. There is

Example 5.25. "Which Way's the Party?" (Undated, deleted material), mm. 17–21.

then a modulation to A major/F-sharp minor as Fiyero declares, "I'll buy the first round of suds!" (set to quarter note triplets, unusual in this portion of the song), and then musical material from the song's main section returns with new lyrics. In places, the melodic line splits into two parts, meaning that others besides Fiyero are singing, but no characters are identified. A modulation to E-flat minor just before "Part 2" of the song sets the stage for Galinda to perform her con job on Boq. It is musically quite different than the current staged version, more like a recitative and based on quarter note triplets and some different lyrics, but with the same sentiment. Fiyero returns and tells Galinda that he will pick her up at eight, "but don't be late because I won't wait . . . ," and then the segment closes with material from "Which Way's the Party?" The next version of the scene bears the revision date of 20 July 2002. It is comparable to what appears to be the earlier version in terms of which sections appear, but this is a completed score, with the characters identified and more interpretive instructions. The opening of the main tune is marked "Bright; Slightly Swung," with the fast tempo of quarter note = 172. There are places where Schwartz changed rhythms in the vocal lines from the previous version, usually adding more syncopation. The lyrics are basically the same, with subtle changes in the musical treatment, such as an added "the party is here!" for Fiyero to sing out in the top of his range at the end of the final long note. A few modulations have been moved, transitions between sections have undergone subtle changes, and Schwartz added one segment of musical underscoring for the conversation between Galinda and Boq, but this version of the scene gives every indication that Schwartz thought he might have finished it. Most of the music and text, however, changed for "Dancing through Life." In this earlier scene, "We Deserve Each Other" and its music never appears, but Schwartz resurrected it for the Broadway version. An interesting, related sketch in Schwartz's hand is entitled "Which Way's the Party—tag," a brief attempt to contrapuntally combine material from the song with that title and "We deserve each other" with its usual melodic outline. Schwartz wrote at the bottom that "Also—just the 1st + last phrases will work," but this material appears nowhere else in the materials consulted for this study. It does show that Schwartz considered that the "We Deserve Each Other" material might go with "Which Way's the Party?"

One more brief manuscript sketch related to this scene bears the title "Ozdust Chant." Schwartz experiments with working out a contrapuntal section (see example 5.26). The melody in the top staff is similar to what sets Fiyero's line "Let's go down to the Ozdust Ballroom" (OCR, track 6, 2'06"–2'10"), and the chordal structures resemble what appears in the Broadway score in the right hand of the accompaniment. The melodic idea with which Schwartz combines this more familiar material here in the left hand ("Skirts 'n' studs . . .") is unfamiliar, and one must comment that, with the three-part choral writing in the right hand, this section is denser in texture than what one usually hears from Schwartz.

YBR included the deleted song "As If by Magic," replaced by "Something Bad," but that appears earlier in Act 1. Elphaba, Fiyero, and Doctor Dillamond sing "As If by Magic" in Doctor Dillamond's laboratory after success in his experiments to prove the similarity between human consciousness and that of the Talking Animals. The catalyst that causes the desired crystallization is the attraction between Fiyero and Elphaba, who together hold the solution in their hands. The song is in 6/8 with some use of hemiola. The three characters sing short phrases that combine to form the song's melody, as may be seen in the following example (see example 5.27). A familiar sound is Doctor Dillamond bleating as

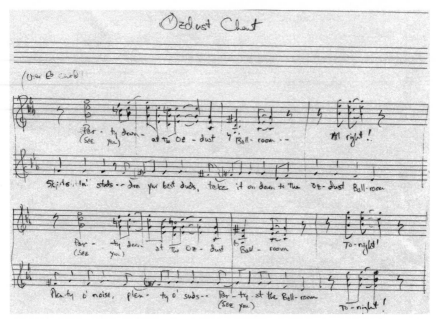

Example 5.26. "Ozdust Chant" (Undated, deleted material), mm. 1–8.

he pronounces the letter *a*. Elphaba sings ten measures of material from "Making Good," so Schwartz tried to unify the score here with repeated material. The song concludes with 24 measures of dance music, and they are suddenly interrupted by three knocks on the door. It does not say this in the score, but earlier scripts show that it is Madame Morrible seeing what is going on, and Doctor Dillamond does not want her to know.

A funeral scene for Dillamond remained in *Wicked* until after the San Francisco run. The music for the scene was a reprise of "Dear Old Shiz" with different lyrics. As a funeral song, it starts in measure 9 of the version heard on the OCR, so it appears that the scene might have been joined with the cast in midsong. The ending musically is different than on the OCR, with text that praises what the professor had done for the school.

The song "One Short Day" appeared in *YBR* with no date of revision, probably in a rendition that dates from between the August 2000 folder and the staged version. The music is closer to what one hears on the OCR, but the lyrics are more like those from three years before. The contrapuntal section that concludes the song begins, like on the OCR, at "Wizomania," and at the conclusion of the song Elphaba sings "two good

Example 5.27. "As If by Magic" (*Yellow Brick Road*), mm. 35–42.

friends," and then Glinda corrects her with "two best friends." As on the OCR, the final chords frame the palace guard's declaration that they may now see the Wizard.

YBR included a version of "A Sentimental Man" bearing the revision date of 1 July 2002. Schwartz rewrote this song before the show opened, with new lyrics and different musical material. The most obvious difference here is that the eighth note is the principal rhythmic value in 6/4, but in the staged version, the 6/8 meter causes the common motion of long-short rhythms from quarter and eighth notes. At some points, the melody is quite similar, such as "I am a sentimental man" (OCR, track 10, 0'43"–0'56"), which in both versions precedes an instrumental statement of the song's main melody. Other segments are different, such as these lyrics from *YBR*: "I know you've come here with a plan to win me over; please, don't bother. I promise, as we say in Kansas, I'll be fair and square with you the way I oughter." These are set to music much like what remains today, but as may be seen in example 5.28, a line where the Wizard describes his parental feelings for Elphaba has different lyrics and music than what is heard on the OCR (0'34"–0'42"), followed by the familiar setting of the title text described above. The Wizard and Elphaba discuss what sign she might perform, and then the Wizard sings material to her

Example 5.28. **"A Sentimental Man"** (*Yellow Brick Road*), mm. 9–12.

very much like the staged version (not on the OCR) except for the change of meter. Also, in *YBR* he says he tests her "allegiance," but in what one hears today he uses the word "adeptness," a major difference in intended meaning.

A version of "The Chance to Fly" appeared in *YBR*, already described above in its earlier form of August 2000. The *YBR* version includes no date of revision on the title page, but later pages bear the date 24 July 2002. The lyrics in this later rendition are different after two years, but it fulfills the same purpose: it leads to Elphaba's hasty rush from the Wizard's throne room. It is an effective musical scene, with the Wizard introducing the opportunities he has to offer for Elphaba, Glinda, and Madame Morrible, and then Elphaba chanting from the Grimmerie to demonstrate that she can make the monkeys sprout wings. The Wizard sings a verse in counterpoint to her chanting a spell (see example 5.29). There is instrumental underscoring for dialog and the transformation of the monkeys, the latter accompanied by augmented chords over various other pitches in perfect fifths and octaves, another indication of the importance of augmented triads with added tones in this score. In a section marked "Romantic!" the Wizard sings a brief trio with Morrible and Glinda, the two women enthralled with how their lives will change by being associated with the Wizard, as may be seen from this conclusion of the

Example 5.29. "The Chance to Fly" (*Yellow Brick Road*), mm. 26–33. **The Wizard sings the top line, and Elphaba chants the second line.**

segment (see example 5.30). They are interrupted when Elphaba leaves hurriedly, and Glinda follows her while the "Wicked" motive sounds a number of times.

The folder of songs from August 2000 described early in this chapter included lyrics for "For Goodness Sake," a song that demonstrated the conflict between Elphaba and Glinda before "Defying Gravity." Brief snippets from this song open the act's finale in the staged version. Schwartz's office yielded a lead sheet for the entire song with melodic lines and chord symbols. Glinda sings the first verse in B-flat minor, based on a scalar ascending motive (like the first three notes) and a stepwise descending passage (see measure 9 in example 5.31). Elphaba's verse is up one-half step; she tears into Glinda for her hypocrisy. In the following section, both sing "I hope you're happy" to similar descending lines

Example 5.30. "The Chance to Fly" (*Yellow Brick Road*), mm. 74–78.

as on the OCR (track 11, 0'05"–0'16"), but the rhythms on the lead sheet are syncopated. In the final version, Schwartz set the lines on consecutive quarter notes, and the following lines have different lyrics than heard on the OCR (for example, instead of "you hurt your cause forever" [track 11, 0'10"ff], the line on this lead sheet is "you've enhanced your reputation") to a similar melodic shape as what one hears today in the show. The remainder of the song is an elaborate duet between the two women based on the opening two verses, yet another song by Schwartz that concludes with counterpoint. As may be seen in example 5.32, Glinda and Elphaba remove their metaphorical gloves here, asserting that they know the "truth" about each other and, a bit after the example ends, calling each other a "fake." It is musically effective, but Schwartz achieved a tone in this song that perhaps would have made the eventual rapprochement between the friends more difficult to believe. In contrast, in the version one sees today they wish the best for each other during "Defying Grav-

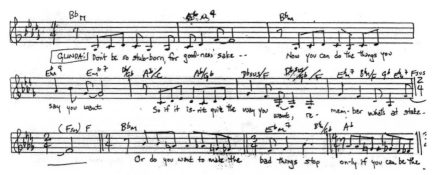

Example 5.31. "For Goodness Sake" (Undated, deleted material), mm. 1–11.

Example 5.32. "For Goodness Sake" (Undated, deleted material), mm. 11–16 of segment after dialog.

ity," even though they seek different paths. The *YBR* text is similar to the version described in the August 2000 version, but there are three people each playing Glinda and Elphaba conferring with each other on how they should proceed, which would certainly have complicated this dramatic moment in the story before the Act 1 finale.

The final song placement for which there were deleted songs in Schwartz's office was the song that became "Wicked Witch of the East," Elphaba's meeting with Nessarose early in Act 2. The first document is a one-page manuscript sketch for a reprise of "Defying Gravity," eight measures of very familiar material ending with "they'll never bring us . . . ," interrupted by Nessarose telling her sister to "Shut up!" so that she can complain about how Elphaba has never used her magical abilities to help her learn to walk. Given the uplifting feeling that "Defying Gravity" has at the end of Act 1, it would have been jarring to hear it stopped midphrase in this manner. There is also a piano/vocal draft of three segments from a song entitled "You've Got to Love Me," Schwartz's next attempt after "Step by Step by Step" in this placement. He has stated that the creators decided Nessarose did not need a major song because they did not want her character to be that important.[83] Their ultimate solution was to have her reprise musical material from "We Deserve Each Other" in "Wicked Witch of the East," but this draft shows that they were already leaning in that direction because the majority of the material in these three short segments (parts 2, 4, and 5 are extant) emanates from "We Deserve Each Other." In Part 2, Nessarose is happy that she can now walk, singing "Step by Step by Step" and pleading to be left to try and walk alone, finally declaring the title text "You've Got to Love Me," her hope that Boq will finally be hers. In Part 4, she is vindictive after Boq has told her that he wants to go to the Emerald City to see Glinda, finally saying that she will put a spell on him. Example 5.33 shows that Schwartz melodically based this segment on "We Deserve Each Other." In Part 5, Nessarose begs Elphaba to save Boq now that he is dying from the effect of her spell, based on the same melodic material. Carol de Giere provides a manuscript of another draft for this scene called the "Elphaba 'Heart' Chant," a contrapuntal passage in which Nessarose pleads for Boq's life after she has shrunk his heart (to the tune of "We Deserve Each Other") as Elphaba sings the chant that turns Boq into the Tin Man.[84]

"Step by Step by Step" in *YBR* is a very different version of the scene. It shares some lyrics with the song described in the previous paragraph, but Schwartz's conception here is completely different. Elphaba has put a spell on the shoes and places them on Nessarose's feet; she walks with difficulty but insists on doing it alone. Schwartz provided halting music

Example 5.33. "Wicked Witch of the East" (Undated, deleted material), mm. 6–9.

to accompany her steps, the notes getting gradually closer together until they are continuous eighths, but Nessarose apparently falls, as may be seen at the end of the following programmatic, instrumental excerpt (see example 5.34). She begins her song with the marking "With a groove, but hesitant," finally building to a marking of "Heavy Funk Rock" as she gains confidence in the song's main segment. There is also a short dance sequence. Frex, their father, is present, and he makes Elphaba promise always to take care of her sister. (In the Broadway version of the show, their father has died before this scene.) Nessarose enumerates her six-step program that will bring her all that she has ever wanted, from finally winning Boq's love to ruling Munchkinland, each step announced on a descending minor second and then described in a larger range. By the end of the song, she has moved from confidence to recklessness, becoming the figure whose death the Munchkins celebrate. She dramatically announces

Example 5.34. "Step by Step by Step" (*Yellow Brick Road*), mm. 6–12.

Example 5.35. "Step by Step by Step" (*Yellow Brick Road*), mm. 59–66.

her conversion in example 5.35. Nessarose is surer of herself here than Elphaba ever is in the show, and this is the kind of music that Elphaba sings. The creators obviously decided that Nessarose did not require such a distinctive moment, and the scene in her chamber with her sister was changed completely.

Conclusion

The Score of Wicked in Context

The score to any piece of integrated musical theater is greater than the sum of its parts because the overall impression is based on the cumulative effect of individual numbers. An impressive song provides a single moment within the work, but the composer will often revisit at least part of it as a motive that recurs or in a longer reprise, and at that point the song shares its impact with another part of the score. Some returning motives appear sufficiently frequently to take on lives of their own, confirming the musical dramatist's intentions at appropriate moments and conferring unity and cohesion. Broadway composers learned the technique from nineteenth-century operas, especially Wagner's encyclopedic use of the *Leitmotiv*, but the German master often profoundly transformed his themes, a technique one finds much less frequently in Broadway scores. A more appropriate operatic model for the kind of motivic unification that Schwartz practiced in *Wicked* would be Bizet's *Carmen*, where themes such as the title character's fate motive, usually recognizable in its original form but sounding at various speeds, appears at significant moments throughout the opera. Schwartz has remarked on the indelible impression that he took from Jule Styne's use of the "I have a dream" motive in *Gypsy*,[85] and the "Wicked" and "Unlimited" motives in Schwartz's score operate similarly. As *Wicked* progresses, the number of important motives increases. None take on as much importance as the two named above, but as has been described above, a number of recognizable snippets of music appear in either the vocal lines, the orchestra, or both, especially during Act 2, and through this web of self-quotations Schwartz encourages the listener to move past the songs and explore the entire score.

Schwartz places himself in select company with his attention to unifying motives in *Wicked*, reminding one of aspects of Broadway scores by Bernstein and Sondheim. *West Side Story* (1957) is famous for how the tritone and minor seventh figure prominently in a number of scenes, and Sondheim provided a very sophisticated reuse of multiple motives in *Sweeney Todd* (1979). Schwartz is less dependent on such small building blocks as intervals, as in Bernstein, preferring to quote melodies and sections of melodies, and one could argue that some of the resulting musico-dramatic unity in *Wicked* is easier to follow by the casual listener than that of Bernstein in *West Side Story*. Schwartz seems more interested in the individual identity of musical numbers than Sondheim is in *Sweeney Todd*, where recurring motives play an even larger role, causing some scenes to be constructed mostly from recurring material. It is true that Schwartz uses almost entirely recurring material in the finale of *Wicked*, where "No One Mourns the Wicked," "For Good," "A Sentimental Man," and other numbers combine in a compelling collage of references, but most other numbers in *Wicked* (except "The Wicked Witch of the East," a musical scene that music supervisor Stephen Oremus described in an interview as dramatically constructed using motives from throughout the show[86]) have their own independent melodic identity that combines with some recurring motives. Sondheim's dramatic finale to *Sweeney Todd* is almost entirely based on recurring material as well, but he uses the technique more readily in the remainder of the show than Schwartz tends to in *Wicked*. In Sondheim's first act, for example, one might consider the song "Kiss Me," sung by Anthony and Johanna (a sequence that includes Anthony's quotation of his earlier solo, "Johanna"), followed by "Ladies in Their Sensitivities," sung by the beadle to Judge Turpin. "Kiss Me" returns immediately in the following quartet that involves these four characters, and then the opening material from the beadle's unctuous introduction to "Ladies" also serves as introductory and later contrasting material in "Pretty Women," the duet for Judge Turpin and Sweeney Todd. During this song, as Sweeney prepares to murder the judge, he quotes a major segment from "My Friends," singing to his razor that one must enjoy the prospect of revenge. Anthony bursts in at the end of "Pretty Women," briefly singing material from "Kiss Me," warning Judge Turpin of his plans to elope with Johanna and interrupting the barber just before he kills his customer. Schwartz does not tend to go to this length in reusing themes for dramatic reasons in Act 1 of *Wicked*, and he seldom uses recurring material with such density as does Sondheim in *Sweeney Todd*.

The effective presence of recurring motives for dramatic reasons is one way to evaluate a Broadway score. Other important considerations in a musical play include the quality of the songs themselves and how well each song contributes to the storytelling. Both are subjective judgments, but effort will be made below to qualify such opinions within the context of Broadway history and the traditional roles of various types of songs.

As the opening number of a musical play, "No One Mourns the Wicked" must grab the audience's attention and clarify what the show is about while identifying most of the main characters. One might compare it to "Tradition" from *Fiddler on the Roof*, a scene that introduces the characters and how important the community believes it is to pass their ways on to the next generation. Since much of the show's story concerns how those traditions are upset by the actions and attitudes of the younger people and changes within the society, "Tradition" provides the audience with some of the required backstory. The same can be said of "No One Mourns the Wicked," which communicates Oz's joy at the death of someone whom they believed to be their arch nemesis and then launches the flashback that begins with Elphaba's birth, her rejection by her father, and her appearance as a young woman ready to attend school. The audience also meets both sides of Glinda, seeing her glibness and polish in her public role and her discomfort when defending her friendship with Elphaba. Madame Morrible does not appear here, but she is a major part of the next scene as the new students arrive at Shiz. The Wizard is an unseen presence, but his dominant role in Oz is established in the number, as is the social importance of conformity. The musical tableau that presents Elphaba's conception and birth demonstrates questions about her paternity and that her coloration made her life difficult from the beginning, just two of the plot points introduced in this packed opening number. The music of "No One Mourns the Wicked" includes the two main motives of the show ("Wicked" and "Unlimited"); other music that recurs (the chorus "No One Mourns," the Wizard's "Have another drink . . . ," and others); and most of the musical styles that will appear in the show, except for a strong statement of the pop idioms that define Elphaba's musical personality, which appear first in "The Wizard and I." "No One Mourns the Wicked" is linked closely with the finale because both take place at the same chronological point in the story, they share some of the same music, and the finale clarifies the meaning of the first scene. The music of the scene varies in style, but the most memorable material is the chorus "No One Mourns," which is somewhat folklike, in a narrow range and regular in rhythm. It is a simple, elegant theme that Schwartz completes with the soaring material that starts with "and goodness knows . . . ," which sounds a bit like a 1930s film finale, perhaps an unconscious reference to the original MGM film that inhabits *Wicked* throughout.

"Dear Old Shiz" briefly and firmly places the show in academia, a time when one is young and full of future possibilities. Many of us can sing a stodgy alma mater, and Schwartz captures that musical quality. The other musical effect that Schwartz presents in the scene is Galinda's solo melisma at the song's end, marking her as different.

"The Wizard and I" is Schwartz's first song of the score that introduces the type of pop music he has written over the years. Broadway tunes seldom become Top 40 hits these days, but effective pop numbers in a score can greatly increase its audience, a phenomenon that Schwartz experienced firsthand in *Godspell* and *Pippin* in the early 1970s. Elphaba represents the outsider who craves fame and attention, and in this "I want" song, she uses the musical language of a pop diva. This song has many cognates in Broadway history. Schwartz himself wrote a fine pop "I want" song in *Pippin* with "Corner of the Sky," but "The Wizard and I" is a more aggressive number with Menzel singing in a full-throated Broadway belt, not unlike parts of the score of *Rent*. Elphaba is the only character in *Wicked* who spends most of her time in this musical neighborhood. Glinda only visits, staying on the lighter side of pop in the songs that feature the real girl that she is ("What Is This Feeling?" and "Popular"), only crossing into the pop diva world in "For Good," and that number is different than "The Wizard and I" and "Defying Gravity," Elphaba's prototypical songs. "The Wizard and I" reaches out to all young women who believe that their dream and popularity are only around the corner, and it might be magically found if they could sing like that and desire something with such intensity.

Very soon after the conclusion of "The Wizard and I," Galinda and Elphaba sing "What Is This Feeling?" It is a natural song placement because it allows these two characters to express many of their feelings musically, and their immediate, mutual dislike has been established in dialog before the number starts. What the song demonstrates is that the students all take Galinda's side and that Elphaba has the spirit to fight on alone. As noted above, the tone of the song is light pop, Galinda's musical language, appropriate because this more describes her world than that of Elphaba. This "falling into hate" song is above all a clever number with a delightful tune set to catchy rhythms. It is not profound, and it shows little of the ambiguity that is so much a part of the show. The musical style of "What Is This Feeling?" is similar to several songs in Schwartz's *Godspell*, such as "Save the People" and "We Beseech Thee." Schwartz continued to produce such songs in *Pippin*, *The Magic Show*, and other shows. The ironic nature of the text gives the number much of its cheeky appeal, a quality that it shares with songs from a number of Broadway shows. Consider, for example, the antagonism between Curly and Jud Fry that Rodgers and Hammerstein explored humorously in "Pore Jud Is Daid" from *Oklahoma!* (1943) or Eliza Doolittle's rant "Just You Wait" from *My Fair Lady* (1956), where she explains her great anger toward Henry Higgins in humorous terms as she imagines her tormenter's suffering. Schwartz does not go quite as far in "What Is This Feeling?" (as noted in the "Deleted and Revised Songs" section of this chapter, however, in previous drafts of this song he had the young women fantasizing about their roommate's death or serious illness), but he does show how witty a little pointed hatred can be in a song between two rivals.

"Something Bad" returns to the gray world of "No One Mourns the Wicked," leaving one to wonder who holds the key to truth in Oz. Through metrical and rhythmic uncertainty and harmonic dissonance, Schwartz puts over his lyrics effectively. Elphaba is not ready to believe Doctor Dillamond, but it is not from the score's lack of cues. The number clarifies the dramatic situation for the audience: some major force in Oz is persecuting the Talking Animals, and as a result some are forgetting how to speak. The effect even seems to be beginning for the brilliant Doctor Dillamond, who bleats unintentionally. One of the musical techniques that Schwartz uses to achieve this ominous effect is frequent noodling of eighth notes, which Sondheim also uses with great effect in *Sweeney Todd* in such songs as "City on Fire" and "The Ballad of Sweeney Todd." The chilling effect of "Something Bad" demonstrates that the youthful optimism of "The Wizard and I" might have been misplaced, and that the antagonism exposed in "What Is This Feeling?" is a minor problem compared to what is coming in this musical play. As noted in the above analysis, Schwartz makes this song pay dividends later in the score when he reuses material in it at moments related to Doctor Dillamond's fate and elsewhere.

The music of "Dancing through Life" is not as important to *Wicked*'s success as the amount of the plot that occurs during this musical scene. As noted, Schwartz and his fellow creators worked on this scene longer than any other in the show, and the composer/lyricist had to subjugate his musical impulses to serve the dramatic needs. After discarding several tunes for this song placement, Schwartz wrote sections of five possible musical settings for "Dancing through Life," allowing his collaborators to choose which to use. The result is a functional song that helps show Fiyero's superficiality of thought and feeling, and how eager his fellow students are to join him in a party. The number's jaunty rhythms carry a sort of 1970s disco spirit, but this is not one of the score's most memorable songs. Schwartz's varied use of "We Deserve Each Other" in the scene provides musical continuity and its only strong musical ties to the remainder of the score. If one were to compare this lengthy musical scene to something like "If I Loved You" from *Carousel* (1945) or Sondheim's lengthy opening sequence from *Sunday in the Park with George* (1984), one finds that the creators of *Wicked* also managed to cobble together a memorable sequence of events that advances the story and builds characters, but in order to do so, perhaps Schwartz had to compose around multiple events in the drama more than Rodgers and Hammerstein or Sondheim did in these other examples.

Schwartz began musically to describe Galinda's true character in "What Is This Feeling?" and he effectively finished the job in "Popular." The lyrics demonstrate how he can define personality in his songs, and here he also inserted political commentary (". . . especially great communicators . . ."). Schwartz's intentional use of the sound of bubblegum rock in this song places it in a style that has appeared often on Broadway since about 1970, including several times in Schwartz's early scores. One will find similar songs in youth-oriented musicals based on popular music such as *Grease* (1972) and *Joseph and the Amazing Technicolor Dreamcoat* (first version, 1968; Broadway premiere, 1982), but Schwartz's song is a bit unusual because of its ironic nature. Andrew Lloyd Webber in *Joseph*, for example, makes rich use of what might be called easy pop, and there are funny moments in the show, but most of the songs are part of the storytelling in a serious plot. The "Song of the Pharaoh" is an apt illustration because it is at one level a hilarious Elvis Presley parody, but at another level it presents the pharaoh's dreams, a serious part of the story.

The effectiveness of "I'm Not That Girl" has already been considered in detail, and the song also plays a telling role in delineating the show's drama. This fine ballad tells the audience how Elphaba feels about the relationship between Galinda and Fiyero, and it also adds depth to Elphaba's character. The dramatic masterstroke is when Glinda sings a few phrases of the song in the second act. One is reminded of the delightful reprise of "People Will Say We're in Love" in Act 2 of Rodgers and Hammerstein's *Oklahoma!* (1943) and Bernstein's reuse of "Tonight" as a quintet later in Act 1 after its first appearance as a ballad.[87]

As noted above, "One Short Day" includes popular-based music that describes Elphaba and Glinda in their day's activities in the Emerald City and then a convincing parody of early 1960s Broadway music in the "Wizomania" section, the two then combined in counterpoint. The song carries significant dramatic content, showing the moment of closest friendship between the two girls before the crisis erupts at the end of Act 1. "One Short Day" may be compared to many other songs that extol the virtues of a town, most of which are about New York City in Broadway musicals, such as "Come up to My Place" in *On the Town* (1944) and "N.Y.C." in *Annie* (1977). Celebration of relationships has also been a frequent theme in songs for the musical theater, including "Friendship" from Cole Porter's *Anything Goes* (1934) and "I Don't Need Anything But You" from *Annie*.

"A Sentimental Man" is a musical con job sung by the Wizard to lure Elphaba and Glinda into his camp. As noted above, Schwartz accesses musical styles from the early twentieth century in describing the Wizard, showing that he does not belong in Oz and allowing him some appeal as a regular guy who just wants to help these young women in the same way that he has "assisted" everyone else in Oz. The Wizard's slick sales job reminds one of other con men of the musical theater, such as Harold Hill of Meredith Willson's *The Music Man* (1957). Hill never sings anything quite so maudlin as "A Sentimental Man" while performing his flimflam operation, seducing his public rather with bravura in such songs as "Ya' Got Trouble" and "Seventy-Six Trombones," but the Wizard puts over just as slick a sales job in "A Sentimental Man" and sings in a musical style from the same historical period that Willson uses to describe Hill's character. As the Wizard reaches the loftier moments of his song, such as the angular writing in "Everyone deserves a chance to fly . . ." (OCR, track 10, 0'27"ff), one might think of Sportin' Life's "There's a Boat Dat's Leavin' Soon for New York" from the end of George Gershwin's *Porgy and Bess* (1935), where he convinces Bess to accompany to him to New York City. Schwartz confronts a number of past ghosts of musical theater history in this number.

"Defying Gravity" has for many in *Wicked*'s audience become the show's signature song, with its title defining the central theme. The musical reasons for its effectiveness have been described in detail above, but the song invites comparison to other Broadway tunes in terms of the way it defines a character and effectively closes an act. Two possible Broadway antecedents are Billy Bigelow's "Soliloquy" from *Carousel* (1945) and Albin's "I Am What I Am" from Jerry Herman's *La Cage aux Folles* (1983). In all three numbers, characters respond in a revealing fashion to conditions that they are not ready to accept. Billy Bigelow can hardly be surprised that Julie has become pregnant, but he is not ready for fatherhood, especially if the child turns out to be a girl. He ends the multisectioned, complicated song with an unfortunate resolve that leads to his death in Act 2. The song does not actually end the act because the townspeople leave for the clambake and Billy joins them, but his decision weighs heavily on the audience as the curtain falls. In *La Cage aux Folles*, Albin has been Georges' lover for years, but Georges does not want him to meet the parents of his son's fiancée, who are famous crusaders against homosexuality. At the end of Act 1, Albin reveals his true identity while dressed as a woman and sings "I Am What I Am" as a proud, enraged anthem against social bigotry and the way his lover has just wronged him. In the same way, Elphaba states her true identity in "Defying Gravity" in the face of social condemnation. Also, like Billy and Albin, she does not care what people think and knows what course she must pursue.

"Thank Goodness" is the first new musical material in Act 2. Schwartz describes Glinda's uncertain feelings with the unusual 5/8 meter, rhythmic displacement, and rests where they might not be expected. The song can be dramatically compared with other numbers in which characters are faced with ambiguous feelings or a decision to be made, such as "Twin Soliloquies" from *South Pacific*, "A Puzzlement" from *The King and I* (1951), "I've Grown Accustomed to Her Face" from *My Fair Lady*, and "I

Have Confidence in Me" written by Rodgers alone for the film version of *The Sound of Music* (1965). Writing musical plays that confront real issues and place characters in moral binds, Rodgers and Hammerstein provide several songs in which characters consider various options; in some ways "Soliloquy" from *Carousel* is another. The song that may be dramatically closest to Glinda's situation is "A Puzzlement" because the king debates with himself about issues that strike right at the heart of his duty to Siam and how he is perceived. It is lonely to make royal decisions, and he is not always sure which basis is most important for making a choice. Glinda is in the process of achieving everything that she has ever wanted, but she knows that Elphaba has been treated unfairly and that at least part of the Wizard's image is a fraud. Both Glinda and the king demonstrate their self-awareness in these numbers, a quality that makes the remainder of each plot possible.

"The Wicked Witch of the East" is a musical scene of great importance. It includes little important musical material that is not heard elsewhere in the show. Much of the scene is sung, but the majority of the music is based upon the "We Deserve Each Other" material that has already been heard in various situations, somewhat like the repetitious recitative material that Andrew Lloyd Webber uses to tie together the major tunes in his shows. *Joseph and the Amazing Technicolor Dreamcoat*, for example, includes a number of delightful parodies of various types of music, but much of the connecting material sung by the narrator and other characters is based on a common minor chordal *ostinato* (i, flat VII, flat VI, V, i . . .). Schwartz does not make his connective tissue in *Wicked* that predictable, but the music associated with "We Deserve Each Other" appears a number of times in the score.

"Wonderful" shares with "A Sentimental Man" its musical origins in American popular music of the first two or three decades of the twentieth century. The song's main tune could easily have been written by any songwriter working on musical comedies or revues in the 1920s and 1930s, making it sound not unlike the MGM musical *The Wizard of Oz*. Schwartz has a good ear for such parodies, and he penned a winning number right here in which we watch Elphaba get caught up in the excitement and almost accept the Wizard's offer. If she did not see Doctor Dillamond, she would have been back in league with the Wizard. This is a scene of climactic confrontation, the conclusion of which sets in motion the events that drive the story to its denouement. One is reminded of the scene in *West Side Story* in which Anita goes to the Jets to try to get word to Tony from Maria, but they do not believe she wants to help and begin to assault her before Doc stops them. The terrified Anita instead tells the Jets that Chino has killed Maria, and that lie helps bring about the show's tragic ending. That scene from *West Side Story* includes only underscoring and no song, however, and Schwartz managed to work important musical content into almost every scene of *Wicked*.

Fiyero and Elphaba escape to an encampment and sing "As Long As You're Mine," a song related to much of the rest of the score because its opening musical gesture is the "Wicked" motive. Unlike most of the songs in the score, "As Long As You're Mine" does not directly move the plot forward except that it confirms the love and physical attraction between the two young people. In the language of musical theater, Elphaba and Fiyero are now a couple because they are singing together, and the lyrics imply that they have consummated their relationship. Similar songs in Broadway musicals that serve to confirm a couple's relationship are too numerous to mention, but one might consider the reprise of "People Will Say We're in Love" from *Oklahoma!* or the reprise of "Goodnight My Someone/Seventy-Six Trombones" and "Till There Was You" from *The Music Man*. *West Side Story* provides another interesting parallel because at about this spot in Act 2, Tony and Maria, another couple in a forbidden relationship, sleep together for the first time after the dream ballet of "Somewhere." They are also aware that their bliss might be short-lived.

Anger and disillusionment have provided powerful grist for composers' mills since early in the history of opera. The "rage aria" was a standard fixture in Baroque Italian operas, and one can find musical numbers displaying anything from disappointment to apoplexy throughout the history of opera and the Broadway musical theater. Elphaba's frustration in "No Good Deed" is palpable, and Schwartz captures her emotions with great intensity. Two examples in other musical plays to which "No Good Deed" can be compared are "Rose's Turn" from *Gypsy* and "Is Anybody There?" from *1776*. The powerful musical scene that Jule Styne and Stephen Sondheim wrote for Ethel Merman is an apt comparison because Rose also looks back on her life and sees failure and disappointment, believing that others have triumphed with her help and she has received little credit. The fact that Rose is more of a villain in *Gypsy* and Elphaba is the heroine of *Wicked* makes little difference because both are main characters bitterly reevaluating their lives. Also, at the end of the song, Elphaba removes herself as heroine of her personal narrative, acknowledging herself to be as wicked as the Ozians believe her to be. Rose, on the other hand, performs her song for herself as the brilliant star that she believes herself to be, and for that moment she has found her glory. John Adams sings "Is Anybody There?" after spending all of his energy pushing for American independence in the Continental Congress, and at this darkest moment he wonders if anyone has heard him. Both Adams and Elphaba seek to be part of great societal change, and here late in each show they feel that they have been defeated.

"For Good," described above as an excellent example of Schwartz's ability to compose using effective speech rhythms, provides a satisfying culmination of the relationship between Elphaba and Glinda. There are few songs within the Broadway canon with which "For Good" may be effectively compared because there are few shows with two strong female characters who also are best friends. Duets that express such deep emotional content in musical plays are usually between a man and a woman, or gay lovers. In the latter category, one could cite the reprise of "With You on My Arm" from *La Cage aux Folles* (sung by Georges and Albin after Georges' son Jean-Michel has sung "With Anne on My Arm," showing his depth of feeling for his fiancée) and "Thrill of First Love" from *Falsettos* (a humorous look at the love/hate relationship between Whizzer and Marvin), but these songs include rich humor along with a depth of feeling. "For Good" is serious throughout. A song involving two strong female characters is "Bosom Buddies" from *Mame*, but it illustrates how bitchy Mame and Vera enjoy being with each other. In "For Good," Elphaba and Glinda have abandoned all pretense and competition and simply spill out their feelings for each other, but their friendship appears to be nonsexual. The couple has been compared to gay lovers (see chapter 9, pp. 294–96), but the women appear to be heterosexual in *Wicked* as both pine after Fiyero and one sleeps with him. "For Good" also operates on a more general level in the show: as confirmation of what the story has been about. Schwartz and Holzman tried to keep their main gaze on the two women and their story in creating *Wicked*, and in this song, faced with probably their last meeting, they confess how their friendship has changed their lives. Another song that seems to summarize a show's main plotline is "Move On" from *Sunday in the Park with George*, where the break between the nineteenth-century George and Dot is mitigated by the rapprochement between the modern George and Dot's spirit. Dot served as the first George's muse, and here she performs the same function for the younger George, helping him see how he might "move on" in his artistic pursuits. "Move On" prepares the audience for the finale by bringing the main relationship to a satisfying close, as does "For Good."

Sondheim and Schwartz then close their shows with a similar spirit: by returning to material heard before. Sondheim reprises "Sunday," the choral number that also ended Act 1. The centuries have already been mixed into one timeless place as Dot has met George's great-grandson and the young artist has returned to the island where his ancestor painted the famous work on which the show is based. The only finale that would make sense at this point is to reassemble magically the tableau based on Seurat's painting that ended Act 1. Similarly, *Wicked* has returned to an earlier point in the show. The flashback has been completed, and now the audience knows why Glinda was so conflicted in the opening number and that Elphaba has been treated unfairly by the Wizard and the other Ozians. Schwartz introduces no music in the finale, creating a web of musical allusions. Although they are unaware of each other, Glinda and Elphaba reprise bits of "For Good" before Elphaba disappears with Fiyero through a rear door. The last musical idea that Schwartz reuses here provides a fascinating intertextual relationship: his evocation of the end of *West Side Story*. What, after all, do these two shows have to do with one another? There are perhaps two levels of meaning to be explored. The first is that Schwartz knew and admired Bernstein and appropriated the famous tritone relationship at the end of *Wicked* as a gesture of homage, and as a bold statement that *Wicked* is Schwartz's own serious musical play, a work that perhaps will help define a generation of the musical theater like *West Side Story* did in its time. (Perhaps Schwartz also calls attention to the fact that he managed to end his story almost entirely with musical scenes, whereas Bernstein did not successfully musicalize Maria's climactic speech while she holds the gun. Bernstein reprises "Somewhere" at the end of the show, but the drama concludes in dialog before this appended finale.) The other level of meaning for Schwartz's evocation of *West Side Story* might refer to the ambiguity that inhabits both stories. The narrative in *West Side Story* takes no sides: the Jets and Sharks, and in a larger sense all of society, are responsible for this tragedy, inspiring an ending that offers little solace. In the 1957 score, the tritone does not sound in the last bar, but Bernstein added it in his 1984 recording (and it remains in more recent scores), taking the ambiguity to the very end of the show.[88] Schwartz and Holzman certainly take sides in *Wicked*, with Elphaba in the right and the Wizard and Madame Morrible in the wrong, but Elphaba has her faults as well, and there is confusion between what is good and what is evil. Schwartz carries this feeling through to nearly the end of the score. He perhaps wants the audience to leave the theater with doubts similar to those caused by *West Side Story*, a desire stated explicitly in his last dramatic measures.

The Music of *Wicked* Goes Public

The American music industry regularly ensures that songs from a hit musical will be available in a multitude of forms. Music publishing giant the Hal Leonard Corporation is often engaged by those who hold the rights to Broadway shows to market, and often to prepare, these varied print items. Hal Leonard, for example, sells parts of the *Wicked* score in various piano and vocal versions, for choirs, orchestras, concert bands, and marching bands, among other formats. Such arrangements have been performed in a wide variety of venues by school, community, and professional groups, bringing excerpts of the score to many who have not seen the show in a theater. The most important published form of excerpts from a show, however, is the "Vocal Selections" for voice and piano, which customarily also includes guitar chords. Stephen Schwartz took a strong interest in this publication for *Wicked*, insisting that they be issued in a version where the piano part is a reduction of the orchestral accompaniment in both hands. This means that the vocal melody does not tend to be in the right hand of the piano, the expected convention in most publications of popular songs. Hal Leonard issued the songs in the form that Schwartz specified,[89] but they also published what they called "Piano/Vocal Selections" that includes a note on the cover: "Standard piano/vocal format with the melody in the piano part."[90] Similar pairs of publications from Broadway shows have appeared for other musicals as well, such as *Avenue Q*.[91]

Both editions of the *Wicked* songs include a "Note from the Composer."[92] He begins by stating that choices have to be made when "translating the score from a show into a book of vocal selections." He found the task more difficult for *Wicked* because of the way the songs advance the show's plot, and he realized that changes needed to be made to some songs for performances done "out of context." Schwartz wrote new lyrics for "No One Mourns the Wicked" and "Defying Gravity"; changed the endings of "Dancing through Life," "Defying Gravity," and "Wonderful"; and removed choral sections, introductions, and "other show-oriented material" from several songs. He also took the opening of "Thank Goodness" and created the song "I Couldn't Be Happier." Schwartz notes that he will provide versions of songs "in the original show format" in response to e-mail requests. He states that the piano accompaniment "is essentially a reduction of what is played by the show orchestra." The differences in his prefatory note between the two versions comes in the paragraph on the piano accompaniment, where he describes both as orchestral reductions, with the "Piano/Vocal Selections" including "adjustments . . . to accommodate the vocal line." He refers his reader to the "Vocal Selections" if they desire a "separate piano accompaniment." Schwartz concludes with some explanation of the chord symbols and expresses his gratitude to Alex Lacamoire, Stephen Oremus, and Mark Carlstein (of Hal Leonard) in the preparation and editing of the music.

The "Piano/Vocal Selections" version, with the song's melody in the right hand of the accompaniment, was prepared by uncredited arrangers, one of whom was George J. Ferencz, a theory professor at the University of Wisconsin at Whitewater who has also worked with Hal Leonard on publications for *Urinetown* and *Avenue Q*.[93] The task for Ferencz and his collaborators in preparing the version with the vocal melody in the right hand was to write that right-hand part, including playable harmonic material for that hand, and alter the left hand as needed. When a female sings in such editions, the melody for the pianist customarily sounds in the same octave as the voice, but it might sound an octave higher (certainly possible when Elphaba belts out material below the staff), and for male soloists the part is usually one octave higher, and sometimes two octaves higher. For some songs, placing the melody in the right hand removes most of the right-hand accompaniment from the other version, meaning that additions may need to be made in the left hand if insufficient accompaniment remains in the left hand to define the harmony. Some tunes provided special problems, but the approach advocated by the arrangers was to maintain as much as possible of what Schwartz had written while still providing the entire vocal melody in the right hand. It is a simple fact that some singers need to hear the melody in the accompaniment to perform the song effectively. It is remarkable to see in Ferencz's sketches and the final published version of the "Piano/Vocal Selections" the ingenuity involved in rendering this functional product, a telling demonstration of the fusion of art and practicality that one often finds in commercial music.[94] This work was done in a white heat in early May 2004 in response to a deadline imposed by Hal Leonard to get the music out as soon as possible. Hal Leonard usually assigns their employees to prepare such arrangements, but at the time, they had too much work and hired freelancers.

Notes

1. David Cote, *"Wicked": The Grimmerie; A Behind-the-Scenes Look at the Hit Broadway Musical* (New York: Hyperion, 2005), 76–87.

2. Carol de Giere, *Defying Gravity: The Creative Career of Stephen Schwartz from "Godspell" to "Wicked"* (New York: Applause Theatre & Cinema Books, 2008), 301–6, includes her most detailed musical comments on *Wicked*.

3. Telephone interview with Herb Braha, 25 February 2008.

4. Paul R. Laird, "The Creation of a Broadway Musical: Stephen Schwartz, Winnie Holzman, and *Wicked*," in *The Cambridge Companion to the Musical*, 2nd edition, ed. William A. Everett and Paul R. Laird, 340–52 (Cambridge: Cambridge University Press, 2008).

5. Personal interview with Stephen Schwartz, New York, 22 March 2005, reported in Laird, "The Creation of a Broadway Musical," 348.

6. "Stephen Schwartz's Update Winter 2001," www.musicalschwartz.com/schwartzscene/schwartz-scene-01-12.htm#spark02 (accessed 29 July 2010).

7. Personal interview with Stephen Schwartz, New York, 22 March 2005, reported in Laird, "The Creation of a Broadway Musical," 348.

8. Telephone interview with Stephen Schwartz, New York, 23 July 2005, reported in Paul R. Laird, "Stephen Schwartz and Bernstein's *Mass*," in *On Bunker's Hill: Essays in Honor of J. Bunker Clark*, ed. William A. Everett and Paul R. Laird, 263–70 (Sterling Heights, MI: Harmonie Park Press, 2007), 266.

9. Personal interview with Stephen Schwartz, New York, 22 March 2005, reported in Laird, "The Creation of a Broadway Musical," 348.

10. Personal interview with Stephen Schwartz, New York, 22 March 2005, reported in Laird, "The Creation of a Broadway Musical," 348.

11. Personal interview with Stephen Schwartz, New York, 22 March 2005, reported in Laird, "The Creation of a Broadway Musical," 348–49.

12. de Giere, 127.

13. de Giere, 296–97.

14. de Giere, 443.

15. de Giere, 445.

16. Carol de Giere describes this month of intense writing for the show, p. 314. It was also for this reading on 28 September 2000 that Stephen Oremus joined the collaborators as the show's music supervisor.

17. As noted in chapter 4, Schwartz and Cole are not completely convinced that the YouTube audio files are from that reading, but the lyrics, which are close to the 14 December 2001 script and the files, were identified on YouTube as "December 2001." They had been removed from the site by March 2010.

18. Internet Broadway Database, www.ibdb.com (accessed 1 September 2010).

19. Robert Vieira, "*Wicked*'s Ground*break*ing Score," *The Schwartz Scene*, no. 18 (Winter 2005), www.musicalschwartz.com/schwartzscene/schwartz-scene-18.htm (accessed 9 April 2010).

20. Schwartz published two versions of vocal selections from *Wicked* with Hal Leonard in 2004. One is the traditional arrangement for such publications with the vocal line in the right hand of the keyboard part. The other includes a more interesting keyboard part without the vocal line reinforced in the right hand. See pp. 204–6.

21. Schwartz admitted in a personal interview (New York, 22 March 2005) that this is an intentional reference to the close of *West Side Story*; reported in Laird, "The Creation of a Broadway Musical," 352.

22. de Giere, 306.

23. Personal interview with Stephen Schwartz, New York, 22 March 2005, reported in Laird, "The Creation of a Broadway Musical," 350.

24. I would like to thank Stephen Schwartz for permission to quote this document.

25. E-mail from Stephen Schwartz to Joe Mantello, 28 October 2002. I would like to thank Stephen Schwartz for permission to quote this message.

26. Schwartz described these motives in our personal interviews in New York on 22 March 2005 and 1 April 2008, and de Giere has also covered them (pp. 304–6).

27. Schwartz has mentioned the influence of Rachmaninov's famous prelude in C-sharp minor in an interview (22 March 2005), and de Giere (p. 303) also mentions it.

28. Vieira.

29. Personal interview with Stephen Schwartz, New York, 22 March 2005, reported in Laird, "The Creation of a Broadway Musical," 347; and de Giere, 305.

30. As will be shown in the section on deleted songs later in the chapter, in what Schwartz called a "predraft" of a "New Opening" for the show, he identified this bitonal fanfare as the "original celebratory vamp." Its combination of C major and E major, when stacked as a single chord, produces an augmented triad (C–E–G-sharp) with an added perfect fifth and major seventh. With the removal of the fifth of the C major chord, an augmented triad with an added seventh remains, a chord that appears at several dramatic moments in *Wicked*.

31. Schwartz's thoughts here appear in Cote, 76.

32. Cote, 76.

33. Cote, 77. Schwartz also states here that he wanted "The Wizard and I" to sound like a song for a young person.

34. Vieira.

35. Personal interview with Stephen Schwartz, New York, 22 March 2005, reported in Laird, "The Creation of a Broadway Musical," 344.

36. Cote, 77.

37. Vieira.

38. Cote, 78.

39. Cote, 78, includes the material from Schwartz provided in this paragraph.

40. Schwartz reported in his quarterly update on his website that he actually only wrote several measures of each version. See *The Schwartz Scene*, no 13 (Fall 2003), www.musicalschwartz.com/schwartzscene/schwartz-scene-13.htm (accessed 7 April 2003). Schwartz notes that he has sometimes approached lyric writing for films in a similar manner, allowing his collaborators to choose which version they prefer. Stephen Oremus reports that Schwartz tended to write a major chunk of songs that he was just trying out, noting that at one point probably at least a verse and the chorus of each of these five versions existed (telephone interview with Stephen Oremus, 28 September 2010).

41. Vieira.

42. Personal interview with Stephen Schwartz, New York, 22 March 2005, reported in Laird, "The Creation of a Broadway Musical," 343.

43. Cote, 79.

44. Cote, 79.

45. Personal interview with Stephen Schwartz, New York, 22 March 2005, reported in Laird, "The Creation of a Broadway Musical," 349–50.

46. Vieira.

47. Personal interview with Stephen Schwartz, New York, 22 March 2005, reported in Laird, "The Creation of a Broadway Musical," 350.

48. Cote, 79, includes Schwartz's memories concerning the writing of "One Short Day."

49. For an interpretation of Elphaba and Glinda as a "queer couple," see Stacy Ellen Wolf, "'Defying Gravity': Queer Conventions in the Musical *Wicked*," *Theatre Journal* 60, no. 1 (March 2008): 1–21. This article is considered in detail in chapter 9 (see pp. 294–96).

50. Cote, 80.

51. Cote, 80. Cote also includes a facsimile of three pages of Schwartz's manuscript for "Defying Gravity" (pp. 81–84).

52. Vieira.

53. The prominence of the ascending octave in this motive (interrupted by the *sol*) moving down a half step after the second *do* provides an eerie resonance with the opening of the "Unlimited" motive, the first three notes of which are the same as the famous "Bali Ha'i" motive that Richard Rodgers made dramatic use of in the score to *South Pacific*. Schwartz of course derived the motive from the opening of the song "Somewhere Over the Rainbow," but his rich use of the motive for musico-dramatic unification in *Wicked* does invite comparison to the important unifying melody in *South Pacific* as well.

54. Vieira.

55. Personal interview with Stephen Schwartz, New York, 14 January 2008.

56. de Giere, 341.

57. Personal interview with Stephen Schwartz, New York, 22 March 2005, reported in Laird, "The Creation of a Broadway Musical," 345.

58. "Stephen Schwartz's Update Winter 2001," www.musicalschwartz.com/schwartzscene/schwartz-scene-01-12.htm#spark02 (accessed 29 July 2010).

59. Personal interview with Stephen Schwartz, New York, 22 March 2005, reported in Laird, "The Creation of a Broadway Musical," 350.

60. Cote, 85.

61. This analysis shows Schwartz's interest in using augmented chords, often with added tones, when musically describing a strange or dramatic moment. This particular chord, an augmented triad with an added major seventh above the root, appears here, as the final chord of the underscoring of "Set Free the Monkeys," at the end of the underscoring for Elphaba and Fiyero's camping scene, and in the underscoring that accompanies Glinda's discovery that Madame Morrible caused Nessarose's death after "March of the Witch-Hunters," among other places. These are four evocative moments to use the chord, but Schwartz does not apply it systematically in *Wicked*, like Richard Wagner uses the "Tristan chord" in his *Tristan und Isolde*. This is, however, an effective harmony that one hears often in the repertory. Indeed, Scott Murphy found an inversion of the chord playing a significant role in Bernard Herrmann's score for Alfred Hitchcock's *Psycho*, and

he describes the chord and its special sound in his "An Audiovisual Foreshadowing in *Psycho*," in *Terror Tracks: Music, Sound and Horror Cinema*, ed. Philip Hayward, 47–59 (London: Equinox, 2009). I would like to thank Professor Scott Murphy, my colleague at the University of Kansas, for his assistance.

62. The credited dance arranger for *Wicked* was James Lynn Abbott.

63. Vieira. Lehmann Engel musically defined the "charm song" as "a song that embodies generally delicate, optimistic, and rhythmic music, and lyrics of light though not necessarily comedic subject matter." See his *The American Musical Theater* (New York: Macmillan, 1975), 87.

64. Cote, 85.

65. Vieira.

66. Cote, 86.

67. Cote, 86.

68. Cote, 86.

69. Vieira.

70. Cote, 87.

71. This seems close to Schwartz's frequent use of an augmented triad with a major seventh (see note 61), but with the two added tones the chord could also be seen as a G-sharp minor triad with an added diminished fourth and minor sixth, and other spellings are possible.

72. Vieira.

73. There is a segment of Kristin Chenoweth and Idina Menzel rehearsing "For Good" with Stephen Schwartz and musical director Stephen Oremus (interspersed with performance footage) in "*Wicked*: The Road to Broadway," an extra feature on disc 3 of *B'Way/Broadway: The American Musical*, directed by Michael Kantor (Educational Broadcasting Corporation and the Broadway Film Project, 2004).

74. Vieira.

75. Vieira.

76. Vieira.

77. Vieira.

78. www.playbill.com/news/article/120640-Yellow-Brick-Road-Not-Taken-Will-Celebrate-Wickeds-Fifth-Anniversary (accessed 24 April 2010).

79. Internet Broadway Database, www.ibdb.com (accessed 10 December 2010).

80. De Giere (p. 503) provided a facsimile of a brief draft for this scene that is fairly close to the version on the OCR.

81. *Wicked: 5th Anniversary Edition*, 2 compact discs, Decca B0012127-72, 2008.

82. Personal interview with Stephen Schwartz, New York, 1 April 2008. An excerpt of Norbert Leo Butz singing this song in rehearsal may be seen on "*Wicked*: The Road to Broadway."

83. Personal interview with Stephen Schwartz, New York, 1 April 2008.

84. de Giere, 353.

85. de Giere, 302.

86. Telephone interview with Stephen Oremus, 5 February 2008.

87. Nigel Simeone has noted that Bernstein and lyricist Stephen Sondheim actually wrote the "Tonight Quintet" before the ballad version that the lovers sing earlier in the show. See Nigel Simeone, *Leonard Bernstein: "West Side Story"* (Farnham, Surrey, England: Ashgate, 2009), 64.

88. This important change may be heard by comparing the end of the 1957 original cast recording (Columbia CK 32603) and the 1985 recording (Deutsche Grammophon 415 253-2), the latter featuring Bernstein's attempt to perform his score with opera singers such as Kiri Te Kanawa and José Carreras.

89. Stephen Schwartz, *"Wicked" Vocal Selections* (Milwaukee, WI: Hal Leonard Corporation, n.d.).

90. Stephen Schwartz, *"Wicked" Piano/Vocal Selections* (Milwaukee, WI: Hal Leonard Corporation, n.d.).

91. The *Avenue Q* score was by Jeff Marx and Robert Lopez. The "Vocal Selections" are available with melody in the piano accompaniment (ISBN: 9780634079191) and with a separate piano accompaniment (ISBN: 9780634091421).

92. Schwartz, *"Wicked" Vocal Selections* and *"Wicked" Piano/Vocal Selections*, 9.

93. www.uww.edu/cac/music/faculty/indpages/ferenczg.html (accessed 27 September 2010).

94. My thanks to George J. Ferencz for allowing me access to some of his work on this project.

CHAPTER SIX
ORCHESTRATION

Stephen Schwartz prepared piano/vocal scores for each number in *Wicked*, the standard for most Broadway composers, who have not as a group tended to orchestrate their own shows. Arranging the music for pit orchestra has always been considered a specialty, partly because it is time consuming and requires a large base of knowledge. In addition, Schwartz and other members of his profession usually find themselves too involved with preparing musical revisions and consulting on other aspects of a show's creation to have time to prepare the orchestrations. Few Broadway composers possess the knowledge and experience to be an effective orchestrator, who should have intimate knowledge of each musical instrument that might be used in a pit orchestra in terms of range, what each instrument does well and what types of writing for each should be avoided, and how to employ special effects on each instrument. An orchestrator also should understand how an instrument blends with other members of the same instrument family and other possible combinations in a pit orchestra; what instrumental combinations effectively support certain voice types; and how one scores effectively for the varied musical styles that might appear in a single score, such as rock, jazz, Latin, gospel, funk, traditional Broadway sounds, and other styles. One can learn some of the basics of such knowledge in a music school, but real expertise develops through years of experience working with various musical ensembles as a musician, copyist, arranger, or conductor. Such tasks function as an apprentice system for Broadway orchestrators, who also often work in film, television, and other types of commercial music.

The arcane nature of the field has made orchestration one of the least understood of the specialties brought together to create a Broadway musical. Few audience members either know or care about the best range for an oboe solo or what artificial harmonics from the string section can add to a special musical moment, and perhaps few listeners would know if a song were well orchestrated, but Broadway professionals know the difference, and orchestration is a major expense in a show's budget.[1] Scholars of theatrical music have started to shed more light on the process of orchestration, including George Ferencz with his work on the most famous of Broadway orchestrators, Robert Russell Bennett (1894–1981),[2] and Steven Suskin, whose *The Sound of Broadway Music: A Book of Orchestrators & Orchestrations* approaches the subject during the so-called "Golden Age" of the Broadway musical.[3]

Robert Russell Bennett learned his craft by playing violin and trumpet from a young age; playing cornet professionally in his father's band from the age of ten; gigging over the years on piano, trumpet, trombone, violin, and organ in various musical ensembles; studying with such figures as Carl Busch (conductor of the Kansas City Symphony) and Nadia Boulanger (one of the most famous composition teachers of the twentieth century); and working professionally in the theater from virtually the moment he moved to New York City in 1916.[4] He helped orchestrate over 300 shows, including many of the most famous of the Golden Age. His long-time association with lyricist Oscar Hammerstein II was a major factor in his Broadway career, and he often worked with Jerome Kern and Richard Rodgers. His influence in the field is substantial.

Suskin provides statements from some famous orchestrators about the actual duties of their profession. Don Walker (1907–1989), primary orchestrator for *Carousel*, *The Music Man*, *Fiddler on the Roof*, and many other shows, called his art "the clothing of musical thought . . . in the colors of musical instruments and/or voices."[5] He divided the musical tasks for realizing a score: composing, or producing "the basic themes of a composition"; arranging, placing those themes "into the desired form"; and orchestrating, or making the arrangement "fit the size and composition of whatever orchestral combination has been selected."[6] Often the composer and the arranger are the same person. Richard Rodgers, Leonard Bernstein, and Stephen Schwartz are examples of Broadway composers who also usually prepared (or prepare) arrangements for their songs, providing a piano/vocal score that included the vocal melody (or melodies) and an appropriate accompaniment for keyboard. Bennett saw his duties as being to take the composer's work "and put his melodies into shape for a performance in the theatre." He thought the orchestrator had to become "part of him [the composer]—the part that is missing."[7] This leaves room for the orchestrator to play varied roles in finishing the music for a show, and it is certain that at times those duties included those more often associated with the composer, especially those who could not provide a fully arranged piano/vocal score. Irving Berlin, an utterly ingenious songwriter, was not an educated musician, requiring aid to write down his melodies.[8] His own taste and ear had the final say on what a song sounded like, but Berlin could not have assisted with orchestration. One might compare Berlin to Leonard Bernstein, who orchestrated his own concert music and could have written his own Broadway orchestrations, but he instead consulted with his orchestrators because there was not time during the pre-production period for him to be part of the main creative team and do the orchestrations.[9] Many composers make suggestions to an orchestrator—how Stephen Schwartz worked with William David Brohn on *Wicked* is described below—but usually the act of deciding which instrument plays what on a particular tune is the work of the orchestrator. Two Broadway composers known to have usually done their own orchestrations were Victor Herbert (1859–1924) and Kurt Weill (1900–1950).[10] Suskin believes that Herbert's scores must have undergone changes by assistants in the hectic weeks before a show opened,[11] and he suggests that Weill did his own orchestrations somewhat out of financial need and that the resulting, merciless work schedule might have helped cause his fatal heart attack at a fairly young age.[12]

What makes the orchestration schedule of a show so demanding? The orchestrator cannot start a job until the piano/vocal arrangements are ready and the song has been "routined" by the director and cast and rehearsed.[13] Composers, lyricists, and book writers typically prepare a prerehearsal score and script, but all content is negotiable during the rehearsal period. Songs are transposed, revised, and thrown out, and new songs appear that were not even conceived before rehearsals started. Most orchestrating, therefore, must be done in the last weeks or days before a show opens, and some will be redone as numbers get altered late in the process. The orchestration might be accomplished in unspeakably long days and through lonely nights, with several copyists (in the precomputer days) to prepare parts after the score has been written. Dance music is not usually written until rehearsals have started, and usually by a dance arranger, not the composer. The dance music also requires orchestration. It is no small wonder that Suskin documents the principal orchestrator and assistants for many shows and often names other musicians who performed uncredited work.[14] Bennett, for example, did very few shows by himself. Suskin consulted business invoices for the orchestrations that exist for Bennett's shows from after 1946, and in that long list, the only show that Bennett did by himself was *The Sound of Music* (1959), and that was because Rodgers made it a point to get every song done in time for Bennett to be able to do the job.[15]

Schwartz has stated more than once that his first choice for the orchestrator of *Wicked* was William David Brohn, who worked in that capacity on *Ragtime*, a score that Schwartz greatly admires.[16] However, in Schwartz's summer 2002 update on his website, he announced that Danny Troob would orchestrate the show.[17] Troob had worked on the Disney film *Pocahontas* for which Schwartz wrote the lyrics to Alan Menken's music, and Schwartz has stated how much he learned about writing for orchestra while working on the Disney films.[18] Obviously, however, Troob did not work on *Wicked*, and Schwartz offered the job to Brohn, who accepted it on the first telephone call from the composer/lyricist.[19]

Brohn has had a long career on Broadway, as can be seen in textbox 6-1, which lists his Broadway credits. (In addition, Brohn has worked on a number of Cameron Mackintosh's projects for London's West End.) Born in Michigan in 1933, Brohn studied double bass and conducting at Michigan State University and New England Conservatory.[20] His conducting teachers included Leopold Stokowski. Brohn played in a number of orchestras and in the 1960s started directing ballet orchestras and tours of musicals. In 1966, he was associate conductor (under Franz Allers) of the *Show Boat* revival at Lincoln Center.[21] He started to orchestrate for Broadway in the 1970s, and he has also worked extensively on incidental music for plays, television, films, and arrangements for recordings by such singers as Mandy Patinkin and Frederica von Stade, and he has also written original music.

Textbox 6.1
Broadway Orchestrations by William David Brohn
(prepared from Suskin and the
Internet Broadway Database)

Gone with the Wind (1973)—additional orchestrations (closed out-of-town)

Rodgers & Hart (1975)—additional orchestrations

Rockabye Hamlet (1976)—additional orchestrations

Timbuktu! (1978)—additional orchestrations

King of Hearts (1978)—orchestrator

Brigadoon (1980)—orchestrator

Marilyn: An American Fable (1983)—orchestrator

The Three Musketeers (1984)—additional orchestrations

Wind in the Willows (1985)—orchestrator

The Boys in Autumn (1986)—orchestrated incidental music for play

Jerome Robbins' Broadway (1989)—orchestrated with Sid Ramin

Miss Saigon (1991)—orchestrator

The Secret Garden (1991)—orchestrator

Crazy for You (1992)—orchestrator

The Red Shoes (1993)—orchestrated with Sid Ramin

Carousel (1994)—orchestrator

Show Boat (1994)—new orchestrations

Ragtime (1998)—orchestrator

High Society (1998)—orchestrator

Minnelli on Minnelli (1999)—orchestrator

Sweet Smell of Success (2002)—orchestrator

Oklahoma! (2002)—additional orchestrations

Wicked (2003)—orchestrator

Mary Poppins (2006)—orchestrator

Curtains (2007)—orchestrator

Ragtime (2009)—orchestrator and arranger

Textbox 6-1 demonstrates that Brohn, like most Broadway orchestrators, has a large range. He has worked on a number of revivals of "Golden Age" musicals with scores by Kern, Rodgers, and Frederick Loewe, and

217

in *Jerome Rodgers' Broadway* he orchestrated the music of a number of significant Broadway composers active from the 1940s through the 1960s. His work on the revue *Rodgers & Hart* involved their songs from musical comedies of the 1920s to 1940s, and *Timbuktu!* was an African American version of the musical *Kismet,* based on the music of nineteenth-century Russian composer Alexander Borodin. *Miss Saigon, The Secret Garden,* and *Ragtime* provide a wide palette of musical styles: *Miss Saigon* has a pop-based score, *The Secret Garden* is grounded in English folk music, and *Ragtime* is a mixture of musical styles cultivated in the United States before World War I. *Minnelli on Minnelli* and *Curtains* made Brohn work in the big band style that dominated Broadway scoring in the 1930s and 1940s, among other styles. At this writing, Brohn is simultaneously represented on Broadway and in the West End by *Wicked* and *Mary Poppins,* making him one of the more prominent orchestrators working today.

Brohn came to *Wicked* fairly late in the show's creation, and there are two other musical collaborators that must be acknowledged first because they had a significant impact on the show's instrumental sound. Schwartz's closest associate in preparing the score for *Wicked* was Stephen Oremus, a major figure in musical theater performance as conductor and music supervisor. He majored in film scoring at the Berklee School of Music, but he has pursued his career in theater music.[22] He has simultaneously served as music supervisor for *Wicked* and *Avenue Q,* which means that he has conducted extensively on Broadway and has traveled to a number of cities to teach these shows to new casts and musicians. His association with *Wicked* began at the initial reading of the first act in September 2000, and he played piano at every subsequent reading and then conducted the show for its first year on Broadway. He was with Schwartz through most of the writing process, assisting in many capacities as he learned the composer's taste and methods. Schwartz usually prepared a full piano accompaniment for a song, but at times he was in too much of a hurry and wrote out only a lead sheet. Schwartz played each song for Oremus, who prepared his accompaniments from that model. Schwartz has traditionally done his own vocal arrangements, but Oremus learned his style and prepared drafts of some that Schwartz would edit. A favorite aspect for Oremus about *Wicked* is Schwartz's synthesis of varied musical styles. He felt comfortable working with Schwartz and believes that he has a special understanding of his music: "I've been a big fan of his work for many, many years, so I knew there was kind of a pop undercurrent in all of the music that he wrote. So it helped that I had been working on a lot of new and modern works like Andrew Lippa's *Wild Party* and *tick . . . tick . . . Boom!* I really got to do a lot of rock/pop arranging . . . "[23]

In our interview, Oremus offered useful thoughts about *Wicked* concerning the orchestra and other matters, and he described his work as music supervisor. He spoke about the sound worlds that he helped Schwartz create for *Wicked*, combining "the grandiosity of the big MGM musical" with "pop" and "otherworldly" elements, along with music for specific characters, such as the Wizard.[24] Oremus and Alex Lacamoire, who also assisted Schwartz with the score as assistant music director,[25] worked out the pop elements and did the arranging for the rhythm section, which includes two guitars, bass, drums, and most of the material for the three keyboards. They accomplished this during the summer of 2003, between the run in San Francisco and the previews in New York. Given the pop sensibility of much of the score, Oremus and Lacamoire contributed significantly to what one hears from the pit. Oremus and Lacamoire also assisted with vocal arranging and incidental music, with Oremus specializing in the former and Lacamoire in the latter. Oremus notes that Schwartz either wrote or approved every note in the score.[26]

Oremus reports that it was never their intention to copy any existing musical styles in their pop scoring but to create a "hybrid" of various styles somewhat unlike what the audience might expect to hear to help serve this "other world" of Oz that the entire creative team intended to evoke.[27] They worked in Schwartz's studio, with both Oremus and Lacamoire playing keyboards and Lacamoire also working on guitar, and they also brought in another guitarist and used synthesized drum sounds, trying to show how the songs could be expanded in a pop sense. Oremus remembers that they worked out five or six songs as recorded demonstrations and scores for guitars, bass, drums, and keyboard parts and presented them to Schwartz and Brohn, who gave them notes. From there the collaboration continued to develop until the orchestrations were complete, what Oremus describes as a "fluid process," with every element dependent upon the needs of the story. Oremus cites as an example of this rich collaboration the third keyboard part, played on a synthesizer, which Brohn largely used to augment the string sound, but Oremus and Lacamoire also made a number of suggestions that sound there.

As the show's music supervisor, Oremus has taken part in many aspects of the preparations, such as cast auditions, choosing orchestral members and designing orchestral placement in a theater, rehearsing the chorus, and other tasks. Of the show's roles, he believes that Elphaba is the most challenging to sing. It is also the hardest role to cast because it requires considerable acting ability. He has found it easier to cast Galinda, but she must be more than just a funny soprano who can belt, because the character becomes more complex as the show progresses. Oremus states that the chorus parts in *Wicked* are demanding because the ensemble sings in a variety of styles ("from *Carmina Burana* to pop"[28]) while having to play college students at Shiz, angry Ozians, and other roles. Oremus notes: "The piece is far more complex than people really understand, both musically and dramatically. Everything that we've done musically has been to serve the story."[29]

In auditions, Oremus has observed that the talent pool is deepest in the United States, with different circumstances in London, Australia, and Japan, but he emphasizes that they have found good casts everywhere that the show has been mounted. He has worked with local music directors to hire musicians and to rehearse the cast and orchestra. Oremus insists that new music directors experience the show firsthand as they learn it. In the winter of 2008, for example, Oremus resumed conducting the New York production so that the Australian conductor could experience the show with him, and from there he sent the new conductor to observe in London.

During one of my discussions with Schwartz, Brohn was in his apartment for work on the orchestration of *Séance on a Wet Afternoon*, allowing a discussion with both on their work on *Wicked* and *Séance*. (They shared orchestration credits on Schwartz's 2009 opera, a project that the composer called his "postgraduate work" in orchestration.[30]) Schwartz spoke with admiration about the sounds that Brohn produces from a limited Broadway orchestra:

> I could say to him for the beginning of the second act of *Wicked*, for example, "I'd like it to feel like the opening of the fourth act of *Boris Godunov*. I don't know exactly what Mussorgsky is using there, but that's what this section feels like to me." And he would say, "Oh, that's high piccolos," and somehow achieve that effect using our orchestra.[31]

Brohn recalls that the process of orchestration for *Wicked* was close to the Broadway norm, with the exception that Oremus and Alex Lacamoire first worked out the parts for the rhythm section. He took what had been written for the rhythm section and then produced the remainder of the orchestration from the piano/vocal score. Brohn admits that he would not have been "on the top of the list that people call when they're looking for a pop orchestrator," causing more of "a two-way street between the collaborators."[32] Another area that Schwartz and Brohn discussed was the use of synthesizers in the show. There are three in the pit on Broadway, including one that is part of a special conventional piano that is also MIDI-capable and can be played as a synthesizer.[33] Andy Barrett programmed the synthesizers; Brohn remembers that he "took copious notes" in his two sessions with Barrett.[34] Brohn thinks that the way they used synthesizers in *Wicked* has helped to produce a new Broadway sound; Schwartz believes that the new element is the way they have combined synthesizers and the guitars with the remainder of the orchestra. The composer does not like to use a synthesizer to imitate acoustic instruments, but often in *Wicked* they must enhance the sounds of the strings or brass. Elsewhere, however, Schwartz states that "the synthesizers are there to be synthesizers and make those effect-laden sounds that are specifically designed for the synthesizer. I'm a particular fan of sparkly Roland sounds, for instance."[35] Comments on the way synthesizers have been incorporated in the *Wicked* orchestra will be part of the following analysis, made possible by the rare opportunity to consult the full score produced for the original cast recording (OCR).[36]

The orchestra for *Wicked* is largest in the New York City production, where there are 23 musicians.[37] In the pit there are two violins, a viola, a cello, two trumpets, two trombones, two horns, four reeds, three keyboards, two guitars, a bass, and a drummer (although this percussionist does far more than play drums!), with another percussionist and harp player located in their own rooms elsewhere in the theater. In most theaters where *Wicked* has run, it has been necessary to displace some musicians from the pit because of the lift in the center of the stage that raises Elphaba during "Defying Gravity." In the Broadway production, they discovered that they could not get enough sound out of the harp when it was in the pit.[38] It required separation from the remainder of the instruments so that they could boost its volume through the soundboard.

The orchestra in San Francisco included an electro-acoustic harp, but the player they wanted in New York worked only on acoustic harp.[39] The international and touring productions of *Wicked* at first used eighteen musicians, including one more synthesizer. Oremus spoke about the smaller orchestra: "We just lost a couple of things . . . the orchestral reduction is a fine representation of what we did initially, and it would take your layman many hours of listening to really discern the difference. We made sure that everything was very, very carefully reduced so that the show's sound is still represented well."[40] A modern, if less desirable, twist on the show's "orchestra" occurred in Osaka. The show's accompaniment was prerecorded, and the production functioned without a conductor. A trained technician coordinated the use of digital loops of vamps and started the accompaniment of a song at the right moment. Oremus reports that some Japanese theaters do not have pits and they have pioneered this technology. This was after the 18-member orchestra had been used in the Tokyo production and the cast recorded a Japanese cast album with a live orchestra, including expanded string sections![41]

Suskin provides useful descriptions of typical instruments that one finds in a pit orchestra, noting musical tasks that work well on particular instruments and citing examples in the Broadway repertory.[42] Given his extensive coverage, our introduction to the pit orchestra will be limited to identification of the families of instruments and the most common members of each that Broadway orchestrators often use. In the parlance of commercial music, the woodwind family is the "reeds," a category that includes the flute despite its lack of a reed. The most common "reeds" in pit orchestras include the flute (often along with the smaller piccolo and larger alto flute), the B-flat clarinet (and often the larger bass clarinet and sometimes the smaller E-flat soprano clarinet), the oboe (and frequently the larger English horn), the saxophone (with the alto and tenor the most frequent to appear in pits, but the soprano and baritone also appear), and the bassoon. Musicians who play reeds often perform on more than one—they earn more for doubling, and few pit orchestras have more than four or five woodwind specialists. An orchestrator usually will prepare parts for several instruments in each book, with the musician playing that book responsible for each instrument. A brass section in a pit will usually include one or more of the following instruments: trumpets (with a common doubling on the mellower flugelhorn), French horns, trombones, and sometimes a tuba. The string section in the pit has shrunk over the years, especially with the advent of the synthesizer, often used to produce string sounds. (Purists can easily tell the difference, but economics often dictate that at least some of the string section will emanate from a keyboard.) Shows with a string section draw from the violin, viola, and cello; the string bass is a member of the rhythm section. The harp is another stringed instrument that appears in pits, but it has become less common over the years. Possible doublings for strings include one musician playing violin and viola, or a violinist who also plays mandolin or electric violin. The rhythm section includes keyboard instruments, drums and other percussion, bass string instruments, and plucked string instruments, forming a crucial part of almost any pit orchestra in any period, but especially for more recent musicals using popular music. Keyboards today might include acoustic piano or synthesizer, but in the past the electric piano might have been present. Synthesizers dominate some modern pit orchestras, providing timbres from every section and sound effects. The combination of drums and cymbals, usually called a "trap set," is found in most pit orchestras, but there might be any number of other percussion instruments as well, sometimes played by a second percussionist. A bass player might use an acoustic string bass, an electric bass with frets, or a fretless electric bass, depending upon the desired timbres and effects. (All three appear in *Wicked*, as will be described below.) The choice of guitars and other plucked string instruments again depends upon the desired sounds, but electric guitars and various acoustic instruments are possible, as well as the banjo and mandolin.

The *Wicked* orchestra on Broadway embraced a wide palette of instruments played by the 23 musicians that would make possible everything from an approximation of a symphony orchestra (such as the ballroom introduction to "Wonderful" in Act 2) to a variety of popular sounds, such as the bubblegum rock of "Popular" and the disco-inspired sound of the Ozdust Ballroom in "Dancing through Life." Brohn employed the basis for the Broadway pit orchestra as it had existed for decades, in addition to the modern rhythm section. He wrote four reed books. The first is for a flutist who plays five instruments: standard C flute, piccolo, alto flute in G, alto recorder (for a moment in "Popular"), and pennywhistle (briefly for the rustic sound that Schwartz desired in "Thank Goodness"). The second reed book is for an oboist who also plays English horn and bass oboe. The latter, also known as a baritone oboe, is a large oboe that sounds one octave lower than the written pitch and has a range one octave lower than the conventional oboe. It seldom appears in any instrumental ensembles, but Brohn makes frequent use of it in *Wicked*. Considering the dearth of saxophones in the score, he might have turned to it as another available sound from the reeds that could be produced by the oboist. (Oboe is an instrument that woodwind doublers often play, but one who concentrates on clarinet and saxophone does not usually have the same ability on oboe that a specialist might. Brohn probably wanted a real oboist and then broadened his possibilities of timbre with a bass oboe.) The third and fourth reed books for *Wicked* are spread more generally among the woodwind family. The third is for a clarinetist who plays the B-flat clarinet, E-flat soprano clarinet, bass clarinet, and soprano saxophone. All three of the clarinets make frequent appearances, and the soprano saxophone is used in a few places for its bright, rich color. The fourth book is indicated throughout the score as "Bassoon," with the four other woodwinds marked in as needed: baritone saxophone, clarinet, bass clarinet, and flute. This musician plays bassoon and baritone saxophone frequently, serves as one of the two clarinets when needed, and plays flute when the flutist is already playing. It is unusual for a Broadway score to include no alto or tenor saxophones, and there are several numbers in *Wicked* where no saxophones play. Brohn's general conception of the reeds is more orchestral than one sometimes hears out of a Broadway pit.

The brass parts include far less variety. The two horns are sometimes muted and also played while stopped with the right hand. Both trumpet players also play flugelhorn in several numbers, and Brohn calls for a wide variety of mutes used to change the timbre. The two trombones are also at times muted. The percussion section for *Wicked* includes an amazing variety of instruments. The following list was taken from a document in Schwartz's office that included the instrumentarium for the sake of percussionists provisioning the show outside of New York: two 26-inch timpani, with gauges; glockenspiel; gran cassa; crotales; mark tree; vibraphone; bell tree; mounted ratchet; xylophone; two suspended cymbals; large tam-tam; chimes; finger cymbals; triangles; congas, with smaller bongos as an adequate substitute if there are space problems; small rainstick; eight shakers; small box shaker; large box shaker; caxixi, an African talking drum; sleighbells; Flextone; agogo bell; three gourd shakers; framedrum; bulbhorn; siren; slide whistle; bell plane; tambourines; highwood (perhaps the highest temple block or woodblock); small cricket; shell maraca; shell windchimes; small Indian bells; tin maraca; shaman rattle; vills, thick ethnic finger cymbals; nutshaker; one Tibetan goatbell; two singing bowls; wooden bowl; a Plugs Percussion trine; sandpaper blocks; waterphone with bass bow; birdflappers, various lengths of balsa strips; wand; ankle bells; nutrattles; and an arrangement of magic tinkle sounds. Stephen Oremus reports that Gary Seligson and Andy Jones both played major roles in developing the wide variety of percussion sounds in the score. Seligson was especially important in establishing the "groove" for each song, and Jones was effective in finding unusual sounds.[43]

Schwartz and Brohn commented on how they broke new ground in the ways that this orchestration mixes guitars and synthesizers with the remainder of a pit orchestra. Since they worked on the scoring for the rhythm section, Oremus and Lacamoire were part of this process. Full evaluation of how guitars have fit into the Broadway pit goes well beyond the scope of this study, but the variety of sounds and effects desired from the two guitarists in *Wicked* is remarkable. The first guitarist plays electric guitar, six-string acoustic guitars both with nylon strings and steel strings, banjo, and mandolin. The second guitarist plays electric, six-string acoustics with both types of strings, twelve-string acoustic, and banjo. Possible timbres are multiplied on each of these instruments by playing with fingers or various types of picks, often indentified in the score. Many other effects are notated as well, including such possibilities as: the "E-Bow" (a handheld, battery-powered attachment that allows a surprising, sustained sound on a plucked guitar along with other effects[44]); the "Seek Wah" (a guitar pedal that combines a 1960s wah pedal inductor with an analog sequencer, providing a combination of *tremolo* and a "wah-wah" sound); and rock's famous "power chords" (a perfect fifth, sometimes with the octave above the root as well, often played with distortion on electric guitar). Guitars sound as melodic and chordal instruments in the score in a large variety of textures.

As noted above, the first keyboard player in the pit performs on a conventional piano that is attached to a synthesizer, and two other keyboardists play synthesizers. The programming for the electronic instruments was a huge job because they each produce a wide array of sounds, from the recognizably electronic to timbres intended to reinforce an acoustic family of instruments, such as the brass or the strings, as well as sounds intended to augment the percussion section, the latter including celesta and sometimes mallet percussion instruments. There are combinations of sounds that occur more than once in the score and earned their own moniker, such as "Glinda's Suitcase," and many other effects notated in the score, some of which will be named in the following analysis. The piano also doubles various instruments and takes on a variety of roles, but it is not often an individualistic sound in the pit orchestra.

The orchestra includes a string quartet: two violins, a viola, and a cello. Even by amplifying these instruments through a soundboard and doubling them with a synthesizer set on a string stop, Brohn could not produce a symphonic string sound from such a small section, but there are many sounds provided by the strings. They remain the best choice for certain types of melodies, such as the cello sound associated with the "Unlimited" motive, made louder by doubling with synthesizer and other instruments. Rapid violin scales are a time-honored way to build excitement into a new section of a song—especially during a modulation—and string harmonics are among the eeriest sounds in the orchestra. As will be shown in the following analysis, Brohn uses his small string section to good advantage throughout *Wicked*. At one point, Brohn had scored for electric violin in "As Long As You're Mine," but he later changed the line to the acoustic instrument, and there is no further use of electric violin.

The bass player plays three different instruments: string bass, Fender bass, and fretless bass. (The score also includes multiple references to "electric bass," but these lines would probably be played on the Fender bass.) The string bass, often called the "stand-up bass," can fit well with the string quartet, but the player often plucks it for the sound commonly heard in jazz and other types of vernacular music. The Fender bass has been standard in many types of popular music since its appearance in the middle of the twentieth century. Jaco Pastorius (1951–1987), bass player with Weather Report, introduced the fretless bass, which offers a different timbre than a bass with frets because a finger stops the strings rather than a fret. Stephen Oremus reports that Schwartz was especially interested in the appearance of a fretless bass in the score.[45] The orchestral score includes identification of the desired type of bass at any given moment.

Suskin provides some analysis of orchestration, describing two pieces each by several of the most important Golden Age orchestrators, going through each number and describing how the orchestration changes, sometimes drawing attention to an especially satisfying moment.[46] The analysis below of the orchestration of *Wicked* has been based to an extent on Suskin, with adjustments in terms of details and leaving out repetitious material. The main intention here is to comment on Brohn's major instrumental focus for a song and to mention the most interesting moments of orchestration. Sometimes these telling moments demonstrate an attempt to paint in music what is happening in the text, and other times it is simply an interesting sound or timbre. As noted above, the score consulted for this study was from the recording session for the original cast recording (OCR) of *Wicked*, but in places it turned out to be different than what is on the recording, usually with entrances for one or more instruments cut, perhaps when the orchestration in a particular moment was too loud for the singer or so that another, more important line could be heard. The analyses below of each number are cued to time indices on the OCR so that the reader might hear what is described.

The opening track, "No One Mourns the Wicked," includes different sections that Brohn approaches with varied effects.[47] A fascinating sound emerges at 0'19", where the orchestra provides machinelike patterns for the gears that the monkeys turn at the opening of the show. Brohn produced this with repeated, rapid figures in high woodwinds (piccolo, E-flat clarinet, oboe) and first keyboard, clicks in the first guitar, plucking in the violins and harp, and a "high wood" effect in the percussion (perhaps a high-pitched temple block or woodblock). A shimmer accompanies the "Unlimited" motive; Brohn starts that effect at 0'34" with the rapid alternation between two notes in the flute and clarinet parts, sixteenth notes in the harp, the second keyboard on a "Sparkling Rhodes" setting (a digital sound similar to the Rhodes piano, a popular type of electric piano), and *tremolo* in the upper strings. The "Unlimited" theme enters at 0'39" in first horn, both trombones, viola, cello, third keyboard marked "celli (large symphonic section)," joined by first trumpet at 0'44". A quick, satisfying effect takes place at 1'12", where the choir declares "The Witch of the West is dead," followed immediately by a boom from the large bass drum, the bass drum in the trap set, and a low tone cluster on the first keyboard. The following long notes in the choir on "dead" (starting at 1'18") and "news" include an active, rhythmic accompaniment from all winds. Glinda's first vocal entrance (1'40", "Let us be glad . . .") is accompanied by an orchestral shimmer built from vibraphone (marked "motor fast"), guitar 1 with an E-Bow, and *tremolo* in the second and third keyboards and strings. When she sings "You know who" (1'55"), the vibraphone and piano imitate her melody during her rest, maintaining the high sounds associated with Glinda as she plays her public persona. Just before the choir starts "No One Mourns the Wicked" (notated as the start of a new song in the score), Glinda is accompanied by a chord in the full orchestra (2'13") as she reaches her climax, soaring up to an *a"* three times. Brohn then changes the sound completely (2'26") with fuller scoring, ominous notes in bells and chimes, a rock beat in the trap set, melodic doubling in instruments (Glinda had not been doubled in the orchestra), and heavy use of guitar. An effect perhaps added at the recording session—it is not in the score—is harp *glissando* just as Glinda sings "And goodness knows . . ." at a modulation (2'49"), a common effect in commercial music. A major break in the number takes place at 3'38", where Glinda starts to tell Elphaba's story. A harp *glissando* leads into the brief waltz sung by Elphaba's parents before Frex leaves. The waltz is set up by downbeats in the bass and accompaniment by two guitars (with the nylon acoustic providing a subtle sound), and then single instruments (guitar and bass clarinet) double the vocal lines with a counter-melody in the English horn, providing an innocent sound before Melena admits her lover. The musical seduction mandates a major change in timbre, and similar sounds return in the Wizard's later numbers. Brohn uses trombones, appropriate percussion effects, one of the guitarists on banjo, and fillers on bass clarinet. The third keyboard for two bars plays a bass line marked "Slightly woozy Tuba." There are other short doublings of the vocal line in instruments such as the xylophone, one of several novelty effects that lend a vaudeville-like sound. Brohn raises the energy level in the birth scene (4'38") with constant eighth notes in the bassoon and cello *pizzicato* (plucked notes), and he pulls out all of the stops when the midwife and Frex discover the baby's color (4'51"), with *glissandi* in the piccolo, clarinet, horns, first trombone, banjo, and second keyboard, and a chromatic run in the cello. The loud chord in the next measure, as the voices scream "Ah," includes "wild glisses" in the harp. As the singers report Elphaba's color in eighth notes, Brohn brings in the brass and bassoon to double on the word "unnaturally," which sets up effectively the loud chord on "Green!" The voices strike it first, and in the second half of the measure, much of the orchestra enters. The heavy orchestration for the remainder of the number is similar to what was heard earlier in "No one mourns . . . ," but now with two electric guitars and a strong rock beat in the drums. In the last minute of the first track of the OCR, one can hear how Brohn layered the full orchestra over the rock sound that Oremus and Lacamoire provided in the rhythm section.

The musical segment in the score called "Elphaba's Entrance" sounds on the OCR at the beginning of track 2, "Dear Old Shiz." Brohn opens with a moment that sounds like Stravinsky or Debussy, with arpeggios in the clarinet, harp, and second keyboard, and a descending quarter note motive in various woodwinds and strings and a number of bell sounds in the percussion. The alma mater is sung without accompaniment.

"The Wizard and I" (track 3) opens with more than a minute of recitative as Madame Morrible predicts a future that Elphaba craves and the main character responds. Brohn varies the typical chordal accompaniment of such a section by opening with a brass chorale and some woodwinds, and the strings gradually become more involved. The percussion offers metallic sounds for contrast and punctuation. Elphaba's first verse of the tune starts at 1'16", with constant eighth notes in the first guitar and a strong bass line in the second keyboard marked "Brite, sunny Rhodes" and "Fender Bass," and a shimmer from upper strings and the third keyboard. Brohn gradually adds more parts, including several instruments (bassoon, second horn, two flugelhorns, and second trombone) jumping in with the dominant rhythm at the end of the verse (2'01") to propel the song into the next verse as Elphaba holds a long note on "I." The second verse (2'08") has a similar accompaniment but with a more active bass line and a stronger rock beat in the guitars. It is also an occasion in the score with the use of "Seek Wah," here in the first electric guitar part from 2'03" to 2'45" in a series of instrumental fill-ins, some doubled by harp and second keyboard set on "High Shimmer." At 2'46" Elphaba begins her fantasy about how the Wizard might change her coloring to something more conventional in sung declamation that approaches recitative. Brohn changes the orchestral sound with sparkling eighth notes in the alto flute, clarinet, and second keyboard, a little bass line, and metallic sounds from the mark tree. Other instruments join as notable variety ensues in the orchestration while Elphaba dreams, with a special effect under the word "degreenify" (3'14"): *glissandi* in the second trombone and timpani and *tremolo* in the strings. The guitar sound returns at 3'18" as Elphaba imagines that she agrees to the Wizard's fanciful procedure, and the song feels more like the two verses she has already sung. At 3'35", where Elphaba has her "Unlimited" vision, there is a sound called "Magical Shimmer" in the third keyboard along with sixteenth-note arpeggios in the harp, piano, and upper strings. The "Unlimited" theme that Elphaba sings is doubled by electric guitars (the first also imitates her line for a moment), with the second guitar marked "Sitar-like sound," referring to the amplified, plucked string instrument from India. The shimmer stops at 3'54" as Elphaba sings "it sounds truly crazy" followed by orchestral chords, and then, at 4'11", where Elphaba sings her long note on "me" before the final, exhilarating verse, there is a *crescendo* in the orchestra with rhythmic chords in the winds, sixteenths in the upper strings, brass, and a rock beat in the drums. The whole orchestra plays at 4'20" with counter-melodies, held chords, and driving quarter notes that are very heavy in the bass and drums. When Elphaba sings "esteem" at 4'42", Brohn adds exhilarating sixteenth notes in the strings. Many instruments play the melody in the last two measures, dominated by the first trumpet in a high register.

Schwartz often speaks of the fact that he writes "piano tunes" and "guitar tunes," referring to a song's dominant style of the accompaniment. He traces this distinction back to early moments in his career. In *Godspell*, for example, songs such as "Turn Back, O Man" and "All for the Best" are piano tunes because they have an active accompaniment that works best on a keyboard instrument. "On the Willows" is a guitar tune with simple arpeggios in the accompaniment.[48] "The Wizard and I" is less clearly intended for piano or guitar, but the rhythm section plays an important role the first two times through the verse, with the orchestral instruments adding color. "What Is This Feeling?" (track 4) is more securely a guitar tune because the accompaniment is dominated by guitars playing repeated eighth notes and other instruments offering similar material, especially the keyboards, which often imitate guitar patterns. Galinda and Elphaba sing an opening recitative accompanied by chords in the woodwinds as they write letters to their parents. At 0'13", Brohn accompanies Galinda's lyric "rise" with a rapid upward gesture in the flute. Once the tune starts at 0'40", until 1'56" when the chorus enters with contrasting material, everything of importance in the accompaniment, besides the drums, is in the guitars or is in imitation of them. Brohn wrote extensive material for woodwinds and brass, but most of it was deleted for the recording, probably because it was too heavy. When the chorus enters ("Dear Galinda . . . ," 1'56"), woodwinds double the voices, and there are short, accented notes in the strings. As Galinda answers her friends ("These things are sent to try us . . . ," 2'08") in her public, soprano voice, Brohn backs her quasi-angelically in the flute, harp, and strings, and with a single, ironic note in the chimes that is not in the score, meaning that it was perhaps added at the recording session. Once the contrapuntal section in the voices begins (2'14"), the guitar-dominated accompaniment returns, but now with the parts in the other instruments present as well, providing a driving eighth-note background to the end of this song. Even though Elphaba also sings, this number exists more in Galinda's world with a style of accompaniment for her in private moments, also heard in "Popular."

"Something Bad" (track 5) is in a completely different mood. Brohn also makes rich use of guitars in this song, with the winds playing a significant but subtle role, providing interesting timbres. Schwartz's accompaniment from the piano/vocal version included many eighth-note arpeggios and alternation between two adjacent pitches, also in eighth notes, the kind of noodling that one associates with scores by Minimalist composers, especially Philip Glass or Steve Reich. Glass, for example, makes extensive use of this technique in his opera *Akhnaten* (1983), and in general oscillating eighth notes in a minor key carry a brooding feeling. Schwartz used the sound often in his opera *Séance on a Wet Afternoon.* Brohn co-orchestrated the opera with Schwartz, and together they produced several segments that hearken back to "Something Bad." Brohn set the rising arpeggios at the opening of this song in *Wicked* subtly for low strings, the first keyboard in a low range, second guitar (marked 12-string acoustic in the score, but changed by hand to steel-string acoustic), bass clarinet and B-flat clarinet in a low range, English horn, alto flute, and African talking drum, later adding trombones with cup mutes, mandolin, and more keyboards. When Doctor Dillamond starts to sing about the "owl in Munchkin Rock" (0'18"), Brohn darkly doubles his vocal line with a bass clarinet a third lower and adds a violin harmonic and second keyboard on a harpsichord stop. (Although a typical instrument for early music, the harpsichord's timbre often suggests a ghoulish feeling in popular culture, as heard for example in the theme song for the 1960s television show *The Addams Family*). At this point, the arpeggios have been replaced by oscillation between two pitches, heard here in the woodwinds. Marked by hand over the first keyboard part is "w/Hoot," but the electronic effect is drowned out by the simultaneous artificial harmonic in the violin. The cello part here is *ponticello*, a strained sound produced by placing the bow close to the bridge, and at 0'41" other string parts play *ponticello* on noodling eighth notes. When Dillamond bleats at 0'45", the weird accompaniment from alto flute, clarinet, bass clarinet, mandolin, harp, harmonics in the strings, and a synthesized celesta setting is most effective. Brohn accents Dillamond's second accidental bleat (1'11") in the orchestra with metallic sounds from synthesizer and percussion. The score also calls for talking drum, inaudible on the OCR.

Brohn's challenge in "Dancing through Life" (track 6) was to create an atmosphere of abandon in the orchestra to support Fiyero's hedonistic philosophy. Schwartz has stated that his music for the song was inspired by dance tunes associated with Sting. One might consider, for example, songs from the artist's first solo album *The Dreams of the Blue Turtles* (1985), such as "Fortress around Your Heart," or from his second album *Nothing Like the Sun* (1987) the songs "We'll Be Together," "Fragile," or "Be Still My Beating Heart."[49] These models would suggest that Schwartz imitated the melodic style, the range of the voice and vocal quality, the extensive use of riffs in the accompaniment, and the repetitious trancelike nature of the tune's rhythmic quality, similar to the disco and club scenes of the 1970s and 1980s. The orchestration for "Dancing through Life" definitely started with Oremus and Lacamoire because the rhythm section dominates the proceedings. Fiyero's pop recitative during the first 30 seconds of the song includes accompaniment by acoustic guitar on steel strings and chords in the keyboards, one of which imitates an electric piano. It is the kind of restrained instrumentation one often hears at the beginning of a dance song before the main "groove" starts. As the verse begins at 0'30", the orchestra offers a metallic, strained sound with one electric guitar marked "w/delay/swell" and the first keyboard indicated with "Chorus Pno." When Fiyero reaches the second verse (0'56"), the second keyboard's setting is "B-3 Org." (an imitation of the Hammond B-3, an electronic organ ubiquitous in gospel, jazz, and rock of the 1960s and 1970s, and a sound often used in synthesizers), the drummer plays constant quarter notes on the cymbals, and there is finally a bass line, but it is not yet very active. At 1'12", the end of the second verse, a prominent bass line (based on the instrumental riff that opened the song in the treble register) starts in bass and second and third keyboards, propelling forward the third verse (1'17") and much of the remainder of the segment of this long number. The B-3 sound plays a prominent role with several *glissandi* and other sounds familiar to those who listened to dance music in the late 1970s and 1980s. There are fillers from the woodwinds and brass, and the entrance of string *tremolo* at 2'43" adds to the ambience. The next major change takes place when Galinda suggests that Boq should ask Nessarose to the dance (3'11") accompanied by long chords in the strings, first keyboard on a harp setting, second keyboard supplying the sound called "Glinda's Suitcase" on repeated eighth notes, and other effects that produce a high, metallic sound that helps make Galinda sound insincere. When Boq answers Galinda in a spoken line, her melody for "Oh really, you would do that for me?" appears in the first guitar and third keyboard on a setting called "Music Box." The short duet for Fiyero and Galinda (3'52") sounds over similar accompaniment associated with Fiyero earlier in the song. The most interesting orchestral effect in the small scene between Elphaba and Nessarose is the oboe counter-melody (4'23"), a textbook use of the instrument's plaintive quality as Nessarose pleads with her sister. More instruments enter at "We deserve each other . . . ," the climax of her line. Elphaba goes off to thank Galinda for helping Nessarose (4'58"), and the orchestra briefly quotes the melody of "I loathe it all" from 1'23" of "What Is This Feeling?" (track 4), appropriate as the rivals meet and Galinda prepares her trick with the hat (5'07"). The orchestra returns to disco mode, initiating "The Ozdust Dance" (5'33"), a separate number in the score but a continuous part of track 6 on the OCR. The orchestra here is a fuller version of the earlier disco sound with heavy use of the winds in melodic roles, such as at 5'33" where the new Ozdust theme sounds in multiple octaves in the oboe, clarinet, bassoon, first horn, first keyboard (marked "piano with rock pno layer"), and second keyboard (in a Rhodes imitation), accompanied by *tremolo* in the strings and third keyboard and with heavy rock drums, mark tree, and suspended cymbals. The scoring is even denser at the end of the section. Brohn again calls upon the oboe in a melancholy role at 6'33", just after Boq has admitted to Nessarose that he has not been fair to her. The oboe plays a transformation of his theme as Nessarose says "I know why . . . ," musical confirmation of their misunderstanding. The characteristic use of oboe in this number is another way that Brohn layered other instruments on top of the heavy rhythm section parts in *Wicked*.

Much of the orchestration for "Popular" (track 7) is reminiscent of "What Is This Feeling?" and fits well with the bubblegum pop sound that Schwartz intended here. Brohn draws the accompaniment of Galinda's opening recitative (0'13") from chords in the strings and woodwinds and fill-ins from various treble sounds (harp, celesta, etc.). The "Harpsiclav" in the second keyboard (0'25") is especially effective. The classical nature of the brief brass chorale cadence that accompanies Galinda saying "I know, I know exactly what they need" captures Galinda's poised assurance. Another fine moment is the *glissando* in the harp and the long sound from the mark tree that decorates Galinda singing "succeed." String *tremolo* at 0'52" under the word "lead" builds excitement for the chorus, which starts at 1'01" with punctuation from the kind of high, metallic sounds (xylophone, triangle, first keyboard on "Piano/Marimba," and third keyboard on "Wurlitzer Piano") that Brohn tends to associate with Galinda. As she starts the refrain for the second time, constant quarter notes sound in various instruments, a typical sound for much of the remainder of the number, and the second keyboard provides a strong bass line in imitation of "Fender Bass Guitar." An interesting change between the score and the OCR is the deletion of all instruments under the line "Think of it as personality dialysis," despite the heavy use of percussion, guitars, three keyboards, and bass provided in the score. It is a funny line that Schwartz surely wanted heard, perhaps causing the change. At 2'51", as Galinda tells Elphaba she is beautiful after her "makeover," the strings and harp produce a nearly classical sound in strong contrast to most of the rest of the number. Brohn uses more of this campy, ironic classicism at 3'07", after Elphaba has left. Galinda sings "you protest your disinterest" over alto recorder and oboe, and then "I know clandestinely" accompanied by muted strings, with a striking return to the number's more typical instrumentation through to the end.

The contrast between "Popular" and "I'm Not That Girl" (track 8) is about as strong as any two consecutive numbers in the score, and Brohn matches the affect of each tune beautifully with his orchestration. Although a lovely ballad, "I'm Not That Girl" is also rueful. Brohn uses sweet sounds that lend a touch of irony to Elphaba's strong case of envy. The opening timbres remain nearly continuous in the song, except in the B section (1'15", "Ev'ry so often . . ."). The simple opening includes oboe on a long note, single notes in the glockenspiel, harmonics in the acoustic guitar with steel strings, a syncopated line of single notes in the harp, the second keyboard set on "Dulcimer—(very soft hammers)," the third keyboard on "Kalimba" (a modern version of the African *mbira*, or thumb piano), and a high harmonic in the cello. A percussionist adds a few strikes on the finger cymbal (not in the score). In the second set of four measures (0'11"), a few more instruments join the mix, but the overall sound changes little. The rainstick indicated in the score in the eighth measure, just before Elphaba enters, is deleted. This austere orchestration shows how Brohn can use his Broadway orchestra for a chamber music sound, polishing Schwartz's ballad to a high sheen. The strings enter on long notes at the second statement of A (0'48"), adding poignancy. For the B section, Brohn opts for a slightly more robust orchestration, adding alto flute, clarinet, bassoon, harp, first keyboard on "Bottle Piano" (with a handwritten note for Andy Barrett, who programmed the synthesizers, "This is a very distant and dream-like Piano with loads of echo"[50]), and upper strings rapidly alternating between two pitches above a subtle bass line played by cello. At 1'31", with the return of the A section, Brohn brings back nearly the tune's original scoring. As Elphaba sings "She who's winsome," the score indicates that trumpets should enter with Harmon mutes, but this seems to have been cut from the OCR. At 1'42", the cello enters with a brief counter-melody. The final repetition of A begins at 2'12", where the most prominent addition is long notes on various octaves of *e* in the strings, a minor counter-melody in the oboe at 2'22", and a bit more soft noodling in the woodwinds to complete one of Brohn's most consistent and effective charts in the show.

After the intimacy of "I'm Not That Girl," "One Short Day" (track 9) functions as a major production number with an orchestral sound not unlike sections of "Dancing through Life" and "Popular." Schwartz wrote a song with propulsive energy, another of his "guitar tunes" with huge chords ripped from the 12-string acoustic guitar by the second guitarist through much of the song. The rhythm section plays the dominant role here, another number where Oremus and Lacamoire would have written quite a bit before Brohn started to work. The song begins in earnest at 0'26", where one hears "chatter" from the percussion (mostly cymbal and tambourine, the latter not listed in the score), acoustic and electric guitar, and material from all three synthesizers. When Elphaba and Galinda begin to sing about the sights to see (0'46"), there is less "chatter" as strings, flute, and oboe form a subtler accompaniment, but still with a great deal of energy. (As Carol de Giere points out, a witty quotation takes place in the flute and oboe [1'06"–1'13"] with reference to the song "Optimistic Voices" ["You're out of the woods, you're out of the dark . . ."] from the MGM film, heard just as Dorothy and her friends come out of the poppy field and start to run to the Emerald City.[51]) More instruments join in as that section proceeds, and the A material returns at 1'17" with the fullest instrumentation heard to that point in the song, including large chords from 12-string acoustic and electric guitars. A complete change ensues when the *Wizomania* segment begins (1'43"). As noted in chapter 5, Schwartz imitated such 1960s Broadway composers as Jerry Herman here. Brohn assists the effect with woodwinds, brass, and strings playing along with the vocal rhythm with short notes on "Who's the mage/Whose major," and then removing most of the instruments during Schwartz's chromatic treatment of "itinerary is making all Oz merrier." Both effects repeat. Novelty percussion instruments such as the slide whistle, cowbell, and agogo bell help build the vaudeville-like sound, and the string section's sixteenth note runs at "Whose enthuse . . ." (1'56") also sound typical of the style. When Schwartz's contrapuntal combination of "One short day . . ." and "Who's the mage . . ." begins at 2'09", Brohn divides the orchestra between instruments supporting each line. The winds rhythmically interact with the *Wizomania* material and the main melody of "One Short Day," treated here with rhythmic augmentation, sounds in the glockenspiel, harp, first violin, and viola. It is a striking but confusing sequence that lasts only 12 seconds. Schwartz earlier had provided another eight measures of the *Wizomania* tune in counterpoint, but it was cut as the song quickly reaches its intimate moment as the girls acknowledge their friendship before the orchestra provides the big finish.

Except for the synthesizers, "A Sentimental Man" (track 10) might have been orchestrated in a similar manner 70 years before. Schwartz designed the Wizard's music to sound like a throwback to an earlier time, and Brohn followed suit here with the way he uses the instruments. Much of the tune has the character of a recitative, and Brohn accompanies the opening phrases with chords in the strings, the third keyboard set on "Mellow Strings," and chords in the harp. At 0'07", just before the Wizard says the word "father"—a maudlin gesture from the con artist—a chime sounds, added after the score was prepared. (The date of revision on this number is 10 October, but there were several changes in the orchestration before the recording was made in November.[52]) Immediately thereafter, the brass enters subtly for the phrase "that's why I do the best I can . . . ," answered by two clarinets as the phrase continues. At 0'20", Brohn removes the strings in favor of winds for "Elphaba, I'd like to raise you high," with violins and viola then doubling the Wizard's melody at the climax (0'25") of "'cause I think ev'ryone deserves the chance to fly." Other additions on the OCR not in the score include ascending scales in the strings and other upward gestures on "fly" (0'31"ff). The tune concludes with chordal accompaniment and a final instrumental tag. The score consulted for this study includes more material at the end that was cut as Schwartz and his collaborators revised the song for the new Wizard, Joel Grey.

The instrumental accompaniment of "Defying Gravity" (track 11) revolves around the many power chords in the electric guitars. The chorus occurs first from 1'52" to 2'08", and each time it is accompanied by a series of power chords and arpeggiated eighth notes in a high range in the piccolo and other instruments. The third significant gesture is a riff in the bass line, heard first in the trombones, first and second keyboards, cello, and electric bass at 0'32". Glinda pleads with Elphaba to reconsider her decision at 0'42", accompanied by strings and winds; Elphaba answers that she must instead change her desires. As she sings "more" at 1'10", the bass riff sounds along with a power chord on C-sharp. The other motive described in chapter 5 (see pp. 147) that occurs several times in "Defying Gravity" (ascending *do-sol-do*, descending *ti-sol-do*) sounds here in the third keyboard (marked "Sparkly") in a high range, foreshadowing the arpeggiated eighth notes. The ascending *do-sol-do* of this motive is the same as the three notes from a power chord. Elphaba explains herself in recitative at 1'17" ("Something has changed in me . . ."), accompanied primarily by electric guitar and first and second keyboard; Brohn wrote lines for the winds and strings as well but then marked those *tacet* until measure 52 (1'49"), where Elphaba sings "and leap," launching the next section. Heavier accompaniment of the recitative would have dulled the effect of the powerful buildup from upward gestures in the piccolo, bass oboe, and guitars that leads into Elphaba's first chorus. At 1'52", the arpeggiated eighth notes occur in the piccolo, first and third keyboards, and violins.

The power chords are not in the score, with rests notated here for guitar, but they appear on the recording. The intervals that produce the power chords also appear in the left hands of the first and second keyboards. Glinda sings her warning to Elphaba about "delusions of grandeur" at 2'06" as more instruments enter, and Elphaba pushes right ahead at 2'10" into what becomes a convincing rock tune dominated by electric guitar, drums, and electric bass with syncopated chords in the other instruments. The chorus with title text occurs the second time at 2'37", this time with power chords notated in the second guitar and arpeggiated eighth notes in the same instruments as at 1'52". (The score simply refers the instruments back to the previous measure numbers.) The shimmer that accompanies the "Unlimited" motive sounds here in harp and keyboards with string *tremolo* (doubled by the third keyboard) as Elphaba invites Glinda to join her. When Elphaba sings "Unlimited," the oboe doubles her. The duet passage begins at 3'25" with a *crescendo* in the large suspended cymbal and other instruments before the women start to sing the chorus together at 3'29" accompanied by power chords and arpeggiated eighth notes. Glinda drops out at 3'39", leaving the last line for Elphaba alone, and then statements of the bass riff accompany Elphaba asking if Glinda will come with her. At 3'47", the woodwinds and violins plaintively imitate the bass riff in a high register as Elphaba realizes that she is alone. At 3'53", as Glinda wishes her friend well, a handwritten notation in the score states that everything should be one-half step lower, from A major to A-flat; the OCR here is in A-flat. Four bars later (the next page) the score is also in A-flat. Brohn based most of the remainder of "Defying Gravity" on materials that have been described, but one must recognize the orchestral excitement as Elphaba sings her final chorus. Robert Vieira cites the soaring horn as Elphaba counsels those looking for her to "look to the western sky" (4'37").[53] A new effect occurs at 5'15", as Elphaba throws down her gauntlet, "And nobody in all of Oz . . . ," where rich string *tremolo* prepares the final *crescendo*, reaching the climax at 5'28" where most of the orchestra sounds around the B-flat power chord. This is a B-flat minor chord, and in the coda Schwartz resolves the number in D-flat major, ending Act 1.

Act 2 includes less music than Act 1, but the numbers exist in a broad spectrum of musical styles, mandating that Brohn prepare varying orchestrations. Schwartz intended the opening number "Thank Goodness" to show folk influence, which strongly contrasts with the vaudeville nature of "Wonderful." Glinda's brief reprise of "I'm Not That Girl" includes a different orchestration than the first occurrence of Schwartz's poignant ballad. As love, lust, anger, and frustration boil over in the middle of the act, Schwartz's score takes a popular turn in "As Long As You're Mine," "No Good Deed," and "March of the Witch-Hunters," the last two songs based on the same musical material. "No Good Deed" is an especially fine example of how Brohn scores for orchestra on top of an active rhythmic section. "For Good" is a ballad, but also an emotional duet for pop divas that required careful attention from the orchestrator. The finale is a combination of music heard previously in the show, and another example of Brohn's fine ear for musical effect.

As noted in chapter 5, Act 2 musically opens where Act 1 ended. Brohn uses different effects in the orchestration, calculated here to emphasize the fear that marks this number. The song opens with the bass riff from "Defying Gravity," harmonized homorhythmically by many instruments. There are two electric guitars; the first plays several power chords in the opening measures. The *do-sol-do* motive that appears in "Defying Gravity" also occurs here in the glockenspiel, harp, and second and third keyboards. There is also an assertive, folklike gesture reminiscent of Bartók in the strings (0'09"), with hints of it in the winds as well. The marking is "con forza." These are four or five note gestures, each of which would fit in a 5/8 measure, the dominant meter of "Thank Goodness." Schwartz placed this section in 4/4, however, and the folklike ambience tells the audience that this segment might sound like the end of Act 1, but it is not entirely similar. At 0'14", the chorus enters with material based on "No One Mourns the Wicked," here with words that show that the Wicked Witch has been terrifying the population for a substantial period. Brohn places several ominous devices in the orchestra: rapid piccolo scales, constant sextuplets in the upper strings (which change to sixteenth notes at 0'25"), a strong rock beat in the drums, and chimes. Vocal solo lines enter at 0'36", handled here as recitative with chords in the orchestra and *tremolo* in the strings, building to the chorus singing "with her calumnies and lies" at 0'42", backed by strident quarter notes in the orchestra. Oremus, Lacamoire, and Brohn underline the loud, dissonant choral statement of "lies" (0'46") with power chords in the second guitar, sixteenth notes in the strings and third keyboard, and a piccolo trill on each beat. The climax of this opening segment occurs at "Save us from the wicked!" (0'49") with heavy string *tremolo*, more power chords, and brass doubling the voices, which compellingly move in parallel perfect fourths, fifths, and octaves. There is a gradual *diminuendo*, preparing the complete change of mood in "Thank Goodness."

"Thank Goodness" (track 12) exists in four different sections in the score. "Act II Opening," considered above, is the first minute and 11 seconds of track 12. "Thank Goodness (Part I)" is the material from 1'11 to 1'43, and the next two sections proceed from 1'43" to 4'02" and from 4'02" to the track's end. Brohn helps establish the folklike atmosphere of "Thank Goodness" with several devices: placing the flute player on pennywhistle at the opening of the song (later switching the line to piccolo); using mandolin and banjo; using a tambourine among the percussion instruments; and using synthesizer settings of folk instruments such as "Hurdy Gurdy" (1'11"), "Musette" (5'47"), "Jew's Harp" (6'14"), and "Highland Bagpipe Drone" (6'14"). The song features a preponderance of light, high sounds, the likes of which are associated with Glinda throughout the show: synthesized celesta, glockenspiel, piccolo, harp, and triangle strikes. Contrast occurs when Madame Morrible spins her false tale about what transpired in the Wizard's throne room at the end of Act 1. At 2'42", when Morrible starts her recitative, the second keyboard plays on a "Harpsichord" setting, adding to the gothic ambience that surrounds her character.[54] The only other instruments that accompany this line in the score are trumpet and bass, but a string sound (probably in the third keyboard) was added after the score was prepared, perhaps to emphasize the melody under the singer. As Madame Morrible announces "Glinda the Good" (3'01"), more winds accompany. Brohn provides some delicious instrumental effects during Morrible's tale, such as woodwinds jumping to a high register and a "slight squawk" in the E-flat clarinet as Morrible declaims "squeal" (3'07") and stopped horns, pedal tones in the trombone, and playing *ponticello* in the strings with *tremolo* to emphasize "lurking surreptitiously" (3'14"). Brohn manages a Middle Eastern quality under the various solos that report rumors about the Wicked Witch (3'19"), with piccolo, E-flat clarinet, stopped horn, dry and single notes in the harp, more *tremolo* in the strings played *ponticello*, muted brass, and tambourine along with other effects in the percussion. As Glinda works through her ambiguous feelings during the fifth minute of the track, Brohn provides a tentative, light orchestration, with more instruments and a *crescendo* at

4'54" as Glinda appears to be over her angst, and the song heads toward its joyful conclusion. At 5'11", winds begin to double the outline of her melody, adding the first violin at 5'21", bringing orchestral confirmation to her new certainty. The accompaniment gradually becomes denser, with the full ensemble engaged at 5'47".

"Wonderful" (track 13) opens with the "Ballroom Transition," that number in the score that accompanies the change of scene between Nessarose's chambers in Munchkinland and the Wizard's throne room in the Emerald City. It constitutes the first 37 seconds of track 13 on the OCR. It sounds as much like traditional orchestral music as any excerpt in the show, somewhat resembling orchestrations that Robert Russell Bennett did for the shows of Rodgers and Hammerstein and Lerner and Loewe. The trumpet carries the melody, doubled by other instruments. The orchestra thins out as the transition begins for the Wizard's song, announced by the horn playing Elphaba's "Unlimited" theme. Schwartz wrote "Wonderful" with vaudeville and Tin Pan Alley songs from the early twentieth century in mind, and Brohn effectively followed his conception with traditional orchestration and novelty percussion. The Wizard begins his recitative at 0'46"; Brohn accompanies it chordally with strings and a few winds through 1'11", a typical Broadway sound. When the Wizard declares "Then suddenly . . . ," the strings play *tremolo* for one bar, lending appropriate weight. As the Wizard croons "soon" (1'31"), Brohn underlines it with a piano sound in the first keyboard, a strike of the small triangle, and glockenspiel. Joel Grey hams up his rendering of "carried away" (1'37"), and Brohn joined in the fun with sixteenth note gestures in the woodwind instruments. When the chorus of "Wonderful" starts (1'48"), Brohn provides lively vaudeville effects: *tremolo*, hi-hat cymbal, small cricket, triangles, woodblock, small siren, xylophone, banjo, and trombone on a jazzy solo with Solotone mute. These and other sounds are also part of the underscoring as the Wizard explains his cynical points between 2'37" and 2'55", including a delightful version of the "Wonderful" opening for banjo played with a felt pick. Similarly detailed effects may be heard through the end of the song, such as the change from string accompaniment to brass during a recitative passage when the Wizard starts to sing "The most celebrated . . . ," and then the dramatic *tremolo* under "celebration throughout Oz" (4'02"). At 4'10", where the Wizard again sings "Wonderful," Brohn wrote an active march accompaniment for flutes and oboe that was cut from the score, probably because it was too heavy. The tune ends with full orchestra in a ragtime mode, the prominent first keyboard actually set on "Ragtime Piano," the second keyboard on "Tuba" and later "3 trumpets," the melody in the trumpets, rich counter-melody in the strings, lots of notes in the xylophone, and the reed players playing piccolo, oboe, and soprano and baritone saxophones.

Brohn demonstrates his ability to provide a varied orchestration to the same number in Glinda's reprise of "I'm Not That Girl." He uses different instruments and more variety of timbres than appeared in Elphaba's setting in the first act. As the more flamboyant personality of the pair, perhaps Brohn thought that Glinda required a wider palette to communicate her level of suffering over losing Fiyero. The track opens with flute, bassoon, harp, and first keyboard (probably on acoustic piano), and the introduction closes with long notes in the clarinet, the sparkly "Glinda's Suitcase" on second keyboard, and muted strings in the third keyboard and upper strings. Glinda enters at 0'12" along with both guitarists on acoustics with nylon strings, the second keyboard set on "Sombre Rhodes," and long notes in the third keyboard and strings. Woodwinds gradually enter, and there is a poignant moment at 0'23" where the solo clarinetist plays the theme of "I wasn't born for the rose and pearls" with accompaniment by English horn and bassoon. Glinda does not sing this line. The irony is that Glinda was "born for the rose and pearls," but Fiyero has left her. Once Glinda sings "girl I know" (0'31"), the orchestration remains sparse, with only high sounds in the guitars, the second keyboard on "Celesta," and long notes in the viola. Brohn provides an imaginative reenvisioning of the song in this brief reprise.

The rhythm section dominates the scoring for "As Long As You're Mine." Oremus and Lacamoire provided for heavy use of two electric guitars, drums, and cymbals, and there are also appropriate sounds from the synthesizers. Brohn wrote complementary parts for other instruments, some of which were cut, but the winds and strings add little of significance to the orchestral sound in this song. There are many power chords in the electric guitar parts, often with just the fifth, but more with the fifth and octave as the song proceeds. There is a fine example of the E-Bow with electric guitar at 0'08", a line that sounds somewhat like a theremin or *ondes Martenot*. A fascinating sound from the second keyboard is the "Bell Piano," which produces a distant, strained sound timbre with considerable echo. It enters first at 0'16" and sounds often during the course of the song. At 0'47", as Elphaba starts the chorus, the guitars become even more prominent. The unchanging rock accompaniment for this song is appropriate as Elphaba and Fiyero declare their mutual desire.

"No Good Deed" is another song with an active rhythmic section, but Brohn adds important material for winds and strings. The basic sound of the accompaniment is set at the beginning. The triplet figures in the flute, clarinet, first keyboard on piano, second keyboard set on "Hard EP [likely Electric Piano]," third keyboard playing "Strings" and "Berlioz Bell," and upper strings with cello provide tremendous energy; rapid notes sound through most of the piece, changing to sixteenths at 1'03". Descending quarter notes in stepwise motion are important at the opening and recur in the song as well (not always in stepwise motion), sounding at the outset in the horns, electric guitars (with and without E-Bow), harp, and first and second keyboards. These lines stop for the first time at 0'09" to prepare the vocal entrance at 0'13". There are also prominent long notes in the trumpets, in two-measure phrases and ending with fanfare-like sixteenth notes. The trombones open with *glissandi*, an effect they perform often in this number. The opening minute and 15 seconds of the song, through Elphaba's first recitative, remains remarkably similar in the accompaniment with the major changes being the modulations. The settings on the keyboards do change, but with minimal impact on the overall sound. The electric guitars play many power chords in "No Good Deed," a sound strongly associated with Elphaba.

There are a number of distinctive places in the remainder of the orchestration. At 1'28", where Elphaba sings "creed," the chimes play a descending motive of three quarter notes (with the intervals of major second, minor third) that becomes an important motive in the song. Immediately thereafter, power chords in the first guitar emphasize her line that begins with "My road of good intentions . . . ," and at 1'37", just after the title of the song, a major point of punctuation is produced in the orchestra with power chords and heavy drums. Elphaba's introspective section begins at 1'43" as she names those who have been lost or hurt. The orchestration changes completely, but the three-note descending line of quarter notes remains in winds and strings and first guitar with E-Bow, accompanied by constant sixteenth notes in the second keyboard set on "Tine Pno" (a "tine" is the thick wire struck by a neoprene hammer to produce the sound in an electric piano). As Elphaba calls out Fiyero's name for the first time at 1'55", the first keyboard enters on the constant sixteenths and there is *tremolo* in the strings (along with first keyboard), and then her vocal explosion on "Fiyero" at 1'59" includes a power chord in the second guitar and the "Wicked" motive presented prominently in the winds and first keyboard. This is the first moment in the song when there are no continuous fast notes. At 2'07", Elphaba begins a recitative section based on speech rhythms under which the orchestra produces a series of driving dotted quarter-eighth note rhythms through a variety of interlocking patterns. A major climax occurs at 2'25", when Elphaba sings "why" over a powerful series of quarter notes in the orchestra played by first guitar with E-Bow, first trumpet, first keyboard, strings (and third keyboard) with *tremolo*, and accompanied by a power chord on each eighth note for two measures in second guitar. Elphaba then repeats part of the chorus and concludes with her declaration of wickedness over the orchestra playing similar effects to those already described. "No Good Deed" carries an almost operatic intensity and switches between recitative and more arialike sections like a *scena* in an Italian opera. Brohn uses the orchestra convincingly in support of Schwartz's vision.

The song continues in "March of the Witch-Hunters." The accompaniment opens with a snare drumroll followed by the three-note motive in a number of instruments, and then the orchestra falls into a marching quarter note pattern. The chorus enters at 0'04" with new melodic material, and the melody of "No Good Deed" appears with new words at 0'14", accompanied throughout the first passage by power chords in both guitars and typical march figures from the remainder of the orchestra. Boq's recitative, a tirade against Elphaba, is lightly accompanied, first by woodwinds and second keyboard set on "Aggressive Clarinet" (which sounds a bit like a harpsichord), and with punctuation of brass fanfares. When he mentions the lion, the third keyboard provides a pitched lion roar at 0'49", more sound effect than musical accompaniment. At 1'00", the chorus returns with more quarter notes in the orchestra, but also sixteenth notes in the first keyboard and sextuplets in the upper strings, producing some of the most frenzied sounds in the show at an appropriate moment.

"For Good" opens on the recording with Elphaba singing "I'm limited" to Glinda, using her signature motive to convince her friend to help repair what ails Oz. This segment, which lasts until 0'36", is not in the score consulted for this study. The accompaniment includes primarily high sounds, but without the continuous "shimmer" of sixteenth notes that usually sounds with this motive. One hears harp, probably a celesta setting from one of the keyboards, horns, and bells, with horns and perhaps other brass instruments playing the "celebration throughout Oz" motive that has appeared several times in the show as Elphaba tells Glinda "now it's up to you." "For Good" opens with a recitative and chorus for Glinda and then the same material for Elphaba; Brohn conceived of varied accompaniment for the two singers. This number, however, is about the two pop divas presenting their final big moments, and Brohn provides appropriate orchestration while keeping the orchestra out of the way. The orchestral introduction opens with a triadic motive in the oboe and second keyboard on "Sombre Rhodes" (0'36") followed by brief statements in other solo instruments, including the same motive in the viola. At 0'51", Glinda's recitative is accompanied by harp and third keyboard on the ethereal "Glinda's Suitcase" setting, already heard several times in the show. Glinda sings the significant words "But I know I'm who I am today . . ." at 1'27" with bassoon, horns, and piano entering to underline the text. Glinda's refrain starts at 1'36" with fuller instrumentation but still the high sounds that have dominated her accompaniment in the show: alto flute, acoustic guitar with nylon strings, harp, piano, second keyboard on "Sombre Rhodes," muted strings doubled by the third keyboard, and triangle strikes. As Glinda ends her segment at 2'13", the opening triadic motive sounds in the clarinet and first and second keyboards. Elphaba enters with her recitative at 2'16" with thicker accompaniment of drums, two guitars (nylon and 12-string), harp, all three keyboards, strings, and bass with the first real bass line in the song. Brohn later adds bass oboe, but it is not a strong presence. Elphaba's chorus is at 2'59", when the first guitarist switches to electric (marked "a la Lap Steel") and more winds enter. The recitative dialog is at 3'28", with more activity in the drums, guitars, and strings. The remainder of the song has little that is distinctive or new, but the joint chorus at 3'52" includes effective interjections from xylophone and suspended cymbal, and Brohn gets the orchestra out of the way nicely at 4'14" as they sing "I do believe . . ." and then includes an attractive *crescendo* at 4'40" on the word "change," an effect that just evaporates as isolated effects and the main triadic motive sounds in various instruments before the end of the song.

The orchestral score of the "Finale" shows evidence of many revisions, such as pages where Elphaba sings to Fiyero that she no longer has the powers she once had, and Fiyero answers her with "Then all that you can do, I guess, is do the best you can" over the trumpet solo of the melody associated with the text "A celebration throughout Oz" that actually opens the finale on the OCR. By removing Fiyero's line, the trumpet solo offers ironic confirmation that Elphaba got her celebration, but not for the reason she might have hoped. The song "No One Mourns the Wicked" starts at 0'07" with words appropriate to the occasion, but it is restrained emotionally and accompanied by woodwinds, strings (doubled by third keyboard), and guitars. At 0'20", an extended oboe solo begins based on the music associated with "And goodness knows, the wicked's lives are lonely . . . " The score notes that flute doubles the oboe, but it is inaudible. Chords in winds and strings accompany. A loud E in timpani, guitars, cello, and bass prepares the statement of "Good news!" in the chorus, and then the score shows a major cut that included a solo on the melody of "No one mourns . . ." in piccolo and later E-flat clarinet with keyboards, but the OCR jumps to a washed-out statement of "Good news!" in the chorus. Glinda sings "Who can say . . ." at 0'51", with high chordal accompaniment in the winds and strings, and Elphaba joins her at 1'01" with violins and viola doubling them, confirming the importance of their duet on "Because I knew you . . . " They sing "change" together at 1'19" with a *crescendo* in the orchestra, not unlike toward the end of "For Good," which grows into the final three statements of "Wicked!" where the woodwinds and brass double the voices. The harp plays a number of *glissandi* in the final measures while the low *A-sharp* (the *West Side Story* moment) sounds heavily in the electric guitars with distortion, harp, second keyboard (set on "Tuba + Trombs."), and with punctuation in the tam-tam. The final chord includes string *tremolo*, doubled in the third keyboard.

Wicked as we know it today is unthinkable without its orchestration. Assembling the totality of a musical play is the result of extensive collaboration between several specialists, and the sense of cooperation also exists within the various specialties. For the music, Stephen Schwartz was the primary creative spirit, but he worked with Oremus, Lacamoire, Brohn, and others as they bridged the vast gap between the piano/vocal version and the orchestral score, one of the final steps in deciding what this version of the Land of Oz would sound like in the Gershwin Theatre. As has been shown, the process of orchestration was not unlike Schwartz's composition of the score, because the collaborators made numerous changes, including between producing the score and the recording session. The next step was the reorchestration to prepare for smaller pit ensembles on tours and international productions, but that would be the subject of another study.

Notes

1. Gottfried reports that orchestration for a show might have cost as much as $100,000 in 1977. See Martin Gottfried, *Broadway Musicals* (New York: Abradale Press/Harry N. Abrams Inc., 1984), 47.

2. George J. Ferencz, ed., *The Broadway Sound: The Autobiography and Selected Essays of Robert Russell Bennett* (Rochester, NY: University of Rochester Press, 1999).

3. Steven Suskin, *The Sound of Broadway Music: A Book of Orchestrators & Orchestrations* (Oxford: Oxford University Press, 2009).

4. See Ferencz, and Suskin, 24–32, for information on Bennett's career.

5. Suskin, 3.

6. Suskin, 3.

7. Suskin, 3–4.

8. Laurence Bergreen, *As Thousands Cheer: The Life of Irving Berlin* (New York: Da Capo Press, 1990), 57–58.

9. Sid Ramin, who orchestrated *West Side Story* with Irwin Kostal, described how they worked with Bernstein at a conference on Bernstein in Boston at Harvard University from 12 to 14 October 2006. They consulted closely with the composer before starting their work and then did the work according to the detailed verbal specifications he offered. They then went over the finished work with Bernstein, who suggested changes as he found them necessary. See also Suskin, 62–63, and Nigel Simeone, *Leonard Bernstein: "West Side Story"* (Farnham, Surrey, England: Ashgate, 2009), 85–92.

10. bruce d. mcclung and Paul R. Laird, "Musical Sophistication on Broadway: Kurt Weill and Leonard Bernstein," in *The Cambridge Companion to the Musical*, 2nd edition, ed. William A. Everett and Paul R. Laird, 190–201 (Cambridge: Cambridge University Press, 2008), 193.

11. Suskin, 176.

12. Suskin, 177.

13. Gottfried, 46.

14. Suskin, 314–607.

15. Suskin, 29.

16. Personal interview with Stephen Schwartz, New York, 22 November 2008.

17. "Stephen Schwartz's Summer 2002 Update," www.musicalschwartz.com/schwartzscene/schwartz-scene-01-12.htm#spark08 (accessed 29 July 2010).

18. Personal interview with William David Brohn, New York, 22 November 2008.

19. Personal interview with Stephen Schwartz and William David Brohn, New York, 22 November 2008.

20. Jon Alan Conrad, "Brohn, William David," *Oxford Music Online* (accessed 29 July 2010).

21. Jerome Kern and Oscar Hammerstein II, *Show Boat*, Music Theater of Lincoln Center, RCA Victor 09026-61182-2, 1966, reissued 1992.

22. Telephone interview with Stephen Oremus, 5 February 2008.

23. Telephone interview with Stephen Oremus, 5 February 2008. *tick . . . tick . . . Boom!* was by Jonathan Larson, who also wrote *Rent*.

24. Telephone interview with Stephen Oremus, 5 February 2008.

25. Carol de Giere, *Defying Gravity: The Creative Career of Stephen Schwartz from "Godspell" to "Wicked"* (New York: Applause Theatre & Cinema Books, 2008), 375.

26. Telephone interview with Stephen Oremus, 5 February 2008.

27. Telephone interview with Stephen Oremus, 28 September 2010. The material in this paragraph all comes from this source.

28. Telephone interview with Stephen Oremus, 5 February 2008.

29. Telephone interview with Stephen Oremus, 5 February 2008.

30. Personal interview with Stephen Schwartz, New York, 22 November 2008.

31. Personal interview with Stephen Schwartz, New York, 22 November 2008.

32. Personal interview with William David Brohn, New York, 22 November 2008.

33. Telephone interview with Stephen Oremus, 28 September 2010.

34. Personal interview with William David Brohn, New York, 22 November 2008.

35. Personal interview with Stephen Schwartz, New York, 22 November 2008.

36. I would like to thank Stephen Schwartz and Michael Cole for making this orchestral score available for me to consult.

37. Suskin provides a fascinating section (pp. 234–50) on how the creative team arrives at the number of musicians in a pit orchestra. The process has traditionally involved input from the composer, music director, orchestrator, and producer, with musical and economic decisions being balanced with such requirements as the minimum number of musicians that must be used in a particular theater according to the union contract and "house musicians" who must be involved in every production in their theater. Suskin reports (p. 236) that the minimum number of musicians in the six largest houses on Broadway in 2008 was 19. This almost certainly applies to the Gershwin Theatre where *Wicked* plays, one of the largest of Broadway theaters.

38. Telephone interview with Stephen Oremus, 5 February 2008.

39. Oremus notes that the New York orchestra is the only one with a live harpist; elsewhere the sounds are produced on synthesizer (telephone interview with Stephen Oremus, 28 September 2010).

40. Oremus described here the touring versions of the show in 2008. A touring version of *Wicked* in Kansas City in late 2009 included only fourteen musicians in the pit, with no strings. The company traveled with the conductor, three keyboard players, guitarist, and drummer, and the other nine players were hired locally. According to the program, the orchestrations had been adapted by Christopher Jahnke. In an e-mail message from 12 December 2009, Schwartz acknowledged that the touring pit orchestras had been reduced in size for economic reasons. Oremus notes that whether or not the tour uses the 18-member orchestra or the smaller version without live strings is a local business decision (telephone interview with Stephen Oremus, 28 September 2010).

41. Telephone interview with Stephen Oremus, 28 September 2010.

42. Suskin, 214–29.

43. Telephone interview with Stephen Oremus, 28 September 2010. Oremus also notes that the touring version of the show uses a much smaller group of percussion instruments, with some sounds produced through more traditional means and others transferred to synthesizers.

44. Oremus reports that he agreed with Schwartz and Lacamoire that the E-Bow should be used in the *Wicked* score (telephone interview with Stephen Oremus, 28 September 2010).

45. Telephone interview with Stephen Oremus, 28 September 2010.

46. Suskin, 260–81.

47. Brohn received contractual credit for *Wicked*'s orchestrations. Therefore, in this analysis, his name will usually be used as the creator of these orchestrations and instrumental effects, but, as shown above, Brohn acknowledges the contributions of Stephen Schwartz, Stephen Oremus, Alex Lacamoire, and other musicians to the overall effect, a collaborative process that Oremus also described.

48. Personal interview with Stephen Schwartz, 14 January 2008.

49. For more on Sting and his music, see Christopher Gable, *The Words and Music of Sting* (Westport, CT: Praeger, 2009).

50. Stephen Schwartz, "I'm Not That Girl" orchestral score with orchestrations by William David Brohn, dated 18 September 2003, 8.

51. de Giere, 306.

52. The liner notes of the OCR (Decca Broadway B0001682-02, 2003) state that the recording was made on 10 November 2003, but de Giere (pp. 449–55) reports three days of sessions.

53. Robert Vieira, "*Wicked*'s Ground*break*ing Score," *The Schwartz Scene*, no. 18 (Winter 2005), www.musicalschwartz.com/schwartzscene/schwartz-scene-18 .htm (accessed 9 April 2010).

54. Vieira mentions this "piquant use of harpsichord" as well.

CHAPTER SEVEN
CRITICAL RECEPTION AND PUBLIC ACCEPTANCE

The critical response to *Wicked* was widely varied, ranging from unqualified raves involving most every aspect of the show to sarcastic pans. A useful study concerning critical responses to popular shows has been offered by Jessica Sternfeld in her book *The Megamusical*. For example, she has studied the critical reaction to Lloyd Webber's shows in detail, finding that critics attacked his works for two main reasons.[1] The first was for their huge success: Lloyd Webber simply became the most popular composer of musicals, making him the biggest target. Other critics would praise Lloyd Webber's shows while simultaneously bemoaning the audience's taste and intelligence, suggesting that people only enjoyed his works because they were simplistic and included great spectacle. The first reason would not have applied to *Wicked* because none of its creators had enjoyed anything like Lloyd Webber's level of success on Broadway in the last decade before *Wicked* opened. Critics writing about *Wicked*, however, did at times question the audience's taste and level of intelligence. One cannot expect a critic to foresee how successful a show might be, and in the case of *Wicked*, most critics could not have known how well the show would appeal to young women or how devoted many fans would be to the score. Still, in light of *Wicked*'s status as one of Broadway's biggest hits of this young century, it is instructive to consider the collective efforts of those who professionally critique Broadway shows.

Ben Brantley of the *New York Times* expressed great admiration for the work of Kristin Chenoweth, finding that her "undiluted star power . . . provides the essential helium in a bloated production."[2] Brantley

Photo 7.1. Sign at the Gershwin Theatre, where *Wicked* opened on 30 October 2010, courtesy of Doug Laird.

was not convinced by the show's political satire, which he believed to be too heavy-handed. He described Schwartz's songs as "generically impassioned," remarking on their similarity to the anthems in *Les Misérables*. The critic praised many production elements and several actors, but in the end he states that the show "does not, alas, speak hopefully for the future of the Broadway musical." Only Kristin Chenoweth managed to do that in *Wicked*, according to Brantley, and he found that his interest in the production wandered when she left the stage.

Howard Kissel of the *New York Daily News* was one of the primary naysayers for *Wicked*, calling it "an interminable show with no dramatic logic or emotional center."[3] The "strength" was the actors, but Kissel felt that they could only do so much with a score that lacks "emotional subtext" and a book that failed to "tell the story clearly." He disliked the production elements that he named and stated that, unlike *The Wizard of Oz*, "Nothing about *Wicked* is magical." He concluded with the suggestion that Broadway should spend less money on shows and work more diligently on emotional context. Those who like *Wicked* would find it difficult to accept Kissel's notion that the show has no "emotional center," because many find it in the relationship between the two witches.

Clive Barnes, writing for the *New York Post*, offered a mixed evaluation, finding it "a kid's show with aspirations" that would provide most audience members something to enjoy.[4] He liked Chenoweth and Menzel and praised several others in the cast, and he believed that the production team was so successful that others involved should "keep well out of the way." Barnes did not think that Schwartz and Holzman added to the show's quality, calling the music "oppressive . . . and banal." He described the book as "complex, if foolish," but left his reader with the basic idea that *Wicked* was worth seeing.

The critics for New York City's three major dailies pinpointed the aspects of *Wicked* that most critics praised: the performances of Chenoweth and Menzel as both actors and singers. Approval of the remainder of the cast also suffused the *Wicked* reviews, and they demonstrate in miniature how mixed the comments about production elements tended to be. How definitively these three critics rejected the score and book was stronger than the larger body of writers, some of whom found the writing effective and creative. Perhaps Brantley, Kissel, and Barnes simply did not fit the profile for which Schwartz wrote his score.

Linda Winer of *Newsday* wrote a detailed review of *Wicked*. She thought the witches' story to be the best part of the show, along with the actors who portray them. She found the spectacle overwhelming and the set ugly, along the lines of what designer Eugene Lee did years before for *Sweeney Todd*. She called Schwartz's score "uneven and ambitious," with some numbers uncomfortably close to Sondheim's *Into the Woods*, an unusual assertion for a score that only convincingly approaches Sondheim's style in Glinda's reflective passages in the Act 2 opener.[5] Writing for the *New York Sun*, Jeremy McCarter was positive about the cast and the show's sense of spectacle, commenting that even with the huge production, "*Wicked* never loses its soul."[6] He believed that it succeeds because of the efforts of the cast and director Joe Mantello. The book he termed "generally solid," and the music was "uneven at best," but McCarter found the show worthy overall.

There were a number of other reviews on Halloween in the New York daily press. Dan Callahan of the *New York Blade* believed that "Friends of Dorothy" (a reference to gay men) should see the show because of Menzel and Chenoweth, but he thought the creators tried to tie the show too closely to the famous film *The Wizard of Oz*, meaning that it needed a new second act and a "darker conclusion."[7] Terry Teachout's detailed essay in the *Wall Street Journal* included considerable praise for a number of aspects, and he overall highly recommended the show as "funny and touching," despite the flaws that he articulated. He believed that Schwartz had changed little as a composer since *Godspell*, but he also offered that "I'm Not That Girl" is "the most poignant new Broadway ballad to come along in ages."[8] Teachout's review demonstrates how seriously critics tended to take the new show, perhaps an encouraging aspect of the reviews for the creators, even in reviews that were less than positive.

Additional reviewers, some from out of town, added their input once the dust had settled from the morning-after reviews. Michael Phillips of the *Chicago Tribune* wrote about *Wicked* and *The Boy from Oz*, calling both "mediocre," but they "nearly get by on star power," with Menzel and Chenoweth in *Wicked* and Hugh Jackman in *The Boy from Oz*. He allowed that *Wicked* might run for one or two seasons because of its stars.[9] Charles Isherwood of *Variety* wrote the kind of lengthy, pithy review that one expects in that journal. He called the production "lumbering" and "overstuffed," and, like Ben Brantley, Isherwood seemed most impressed by Chenoweth, but he liked Menzel as well. He praised Holzman for clarifying the novel's plot but still called the show "a bewildering thicket of themes, characters and throwaway gags." He found Schwartz "an ill fit" for the show and disliked a number of the production elements. Outside of the two witches, he saw little reason for *Wicked* to be successful.[10] In the *Village Voice*, Michael Feingold called the show "a hideous mess," and after condemning what he saw as the show's political correctness and other sins, he asked, "What audience could enjoy this congealed mixture—is there a Ph.D. program in critical theory that admits five-year-olds?"[11] Feingold's review is as full of insulting hyperbole as one might expect to see in several pans.

David Hurst, writing in *Next Magazine*, raved about *Wicked*, calling it "a magical new musical for which the adjective 'fabulous' seems to have been invented." In a short essay, he praised Holzman's adaptation of the novel, Schwartz's "gorgeous score," production elements, and the cast. He predicted a long run.[12] John Lahr of the *New Yorker* acknowledged the show's standing ovation, attributing it to one of Schwartz's lines in the song "Dancing through Life": "Life is painless/For the brainless." Lahr liked the sets, costumes, Holzman's book, and the two witches, but he labeled the show "an exercise in high camp," and of the songs, "not one of them is memorable."[13] Lahr replayed the role of many critics who panned shows like *Cats* and *Phantom of the Opera* in the 1980s, finding little to admire and blaming the show's popularity on the audience's lack of taste and sophistication. John Simon of *New York* joined Lahr, setting the tone for his pan in his first paragraph by calling the show "flat," "heavy," "long," and "boring."[14] Lahr and Simon were not going to form part of the adoring audience that has caused *Wicked* to run so long.

John Heilpern of the *New York Observer*, however, might have stood in line for tickets. He noted, "*Wicked* manages to be both quite cynical and very innocent simultaneously—an impossible feat." He praised the two witches, the "clever, mostly exhilarating score," and most of the remainder of the show, concluding by recommending that his readers "book early for Christmas. *Next* Christmas."[15] Christopher Byrne of *Gay City News* was not as impressed as Heilpern, offering that one might have to attend *Wicked* again "to understand why a musical that has so many elements that could make it great never fulfills its promise."[16] Byrne was enthralled with the show's political satire (comparing it to *Knickerbocker Holiday*) and did

Photo 7.2. Large *Wicked* advertisement in Times Square next to those of its competition, courtesy of Doug Laird.

not think the creators quite pulled it off, but he believed that the show had more "substance" than most musicals. He approached each element in considerable detail and took a longer view of the show than many reviewers, for example noting that Schwartz's score "bears hearing several times," and he wanted to experience the cast album. Byrne ultimately found the show disappointing, but he did so in one of the best-considered reviews one might read.

Writing in *Backstage*, Ron Cohen dared his reader to carry "what resistance you can" to the show, but he insists that it "will eventually wear you down, overwhelm you, and genuinely impress you." He cited the "powerhouse score" and believed the songs to be an important part of telling the story.[17] In one of the show's most positive reviews, Rex Reed of the *New York Observer* called it "an irresistible extravaganza of music, magic, artistry and enchantment" with a "delightful score."[18] Jonathan Warman reviewed the show for *HX Magazine* and offered pointed criticism, especially about Schwartz's score, which sounded "lazy" to him when compared to the music from *Pippin*.[19] David Cote in a brief essay in *Time Out New York* offered praise for most aspects of the show except the score, which he found unmemorable.[20] A few weeks later, Barry Bassis briefly reviewed the show for the *New York Resident*, also praising the two leads and stating that Schwartz wrote "showstoppers" for both witches, but Bassis did not believe that the show's score measured up to what Harold Arlen and Yip Harburg had written for the film.[21] In a late review from early December in *West Side Spirit*, Christopher Moore was impressed with most aspects of the show, but he was lukewarm on the score, which "lacks memorable show tunes but delivers in key moments."[22] A review article five months after the show opened by Linda Armstrong in *New York Amsterdam News* was an unqualified rave, citing a "brilliant script," a score by a "musical genius," and "the audience cannot help but be swept away by this play."[23]

These many, decidedly mixed reviews document the show's reception in New York by critics from the time that it opened and for several months thereafter. Harder to document, of course, are the reasons for the public's reaction, but plausible explanations for the show's popularity can be offered. Perhaps most important is the connection with *The Wizard of Oz*, possibly the most famous American fantasy ever written. Even without the iconic film, L. Frank Baum's novels about Oz have resonated with American children for over a century, and their popularity can still be observed among young readers today. The MGM musical starring Judy Garland then gave Oz a strong presence on the silver screen, and the Arlen/Harburg score gave the story an unforgettable soundtrack. Gregory Maguire tapped into a strong current in American popular culture when he wrote *Wicked*, providing the show's creators with a fine premise. Winnie Holzman brought to the book a great talent for representing the feelings of teenagers in a way that reaches out to an audience, and in Elphaba and Glinda she helped bring to life two believable young characters that speak volumes to young women. Their friendship and rivalry reaches across the generations in appeal, and their competition for the same young man is archetypal. The highly successful original cast album brings into focus the score's appeal. Schwartz's music for the show evinces a wider range than most critics acknowledged, as demonstrated in the discussion of the music in chapter 5. Clearly he included enough of a popular nature for the score to land squarely in the ear of the youth market and those with sympathy toward popular music, but he also drew upon other influences and made sure that each song grows organically out of the plot. The album's success is partly dependent upon what the music sounds like, but also on the music's ability to help the listener relive the show outside of the theater. For these and certainly other reasons, *Wicked* has found its audience, while some of the reasons for the show's appeal were lost on a number of prominent critics.

Notes

1. Jessica Sternfeld, *The Megamusical* (Bloomington: Indiana University Press, 2006), 71–77.

2. Ben Brantley, "There's Trouble in Emerald City," *New York Times*, 31 October 2003, E1, 31.

3. Howard Kissel, "The Girl from Oz: It's Such a 'Wicked' Waste of Talent," *New York Daily News*, 31 October 2003, 57.

4. Clive Barnes, "Broom Shtick: *Wicked* Witches Most Entrancing," *New York Post*, 31 October 2003.

5. Linda Winer, "Bewitched and Bothered, Too: Bewildering *Wicked* Tries to Be Both Cute and Dark; So Witch Is It?" *Newsday*, 31 October 2003, B2.

6. Jeremy McCarter, "The Golden Girls," *New York Sun*, 31 October 2003, 17.

7. Dan Callahan, review, *New York Blade*, 31 October 2003, 27.

8. Terry Teachout, "View: Hooray for the Girls from Oz," *Wall Street Journal*, 31 October 2003, W13.

9. Michael Phillips, "Brick Road Leads to Mediocre Musicals," *Chicago Tribune*, 2 November 2003, Sec. 7, 17.

10. Charles Isherwood, "More Bothered Than Bewitched by *Wicked*," *Variety*, 3 November 2003, 30, 44.

11. Michael Feingold, "Green Witch, Mean Time," *Village Voice*, 5 November 2003, 77.

12. David Hurst, "*Wicked*," *Next Magazine*, 7 November 2003, 42.

13. John Lahr, review, *New Yorker*, 10 November 2003, 127.

14. John Simon, "Ding-Dong: *Wicked* Tells the Backstory of the Witches of Oz, but It's Lifeless; *Golda's Balcony* Is the Perfect Merging of Playwright, Actress, and Character," *New York*, 10 November 2003, 100.

15. John Heilpern, "The Good, the Bad and the *Wicked*: Dueling Witches Raise the Roof," *New York Observer*, 10 November 2003, 21.

16. Christopher Byrne, "Witches' Brouhaha: Ambitious Musical Loses Courage of Convictions in Second Act," *Gay City News*, 13 November 2003, 23, 32.

17. Ron Cohen, "Wicked," *Backstage*, 14 November 2003, 48.

18. Rex Reed, "And Toto, Too," *New York Observer*, 17 November 2003, 22.

19. Jonathan Warman, "*Wicked*: These Gals from Oz Are Intriguing, but Not Always So Tuneful," *HX Magazine*, 28 November 2003, 61.

20. David Cote, "*Wicked*," *Time Out New York*, 6 November 2003, 145.

21. Barry Bassis, "Pair of Witchy Women Take Stage in *Wicked*," *New York Resident*, 24 November 2003, 42.

22. Christopher Moore, "With Worthy Witches, *Wicked* Works Wonders," *West Side Spirit*, 4 December 2003, 24.

23. Linda Armstrong, "Broadway Play Is Wonderfully 'Wicked,'" *New York Amsterdam News*, 4 March 2003, 40.

CHAPTER EIGHT
BEYOND NEW YORK
Wicked Hits the Road

Producers have long craved tours for valuable theatrical properties, and successful shows sometimes are presented as "sit-down" productions for months or years in other cities. These new versions are likely to be replicas of what audiences see in New York, or at least to the extent that is possible on the road and in other venues. The producers of *Wicked* have opened two North American touring companies; sit-down productions in Chicago, Los Angeles, and San Francisco; and international versions in London's West End, Australia, Japan, and Germany. The last three productions have each been seen in more than one city, and those in Japan and Germany involved translations of the libretto. A "nonreplicated" production (one not based on the Broadway version) has opened in Helsinki, involving another libretto translation into Finnish. Each international version has included the challenge of taking the *The Wizard of Oz*, a thoroughly American story, to another culture. The London production will be described below in detail as a case study of taking *Wicked* on the road.

In chronological order, *Wicked* productions have opened outside of New York City in the following locations:[1]

The First National Tour premiered in Toronto at the Canon Theatre on 21 March 2005, and the tour continues to make stops varying in length from less than two weeks to more than two months at cities throughout North America. The touring show "has broken the house record in every single city in which it's played."[2]

261

The Chicago production opened at the Ford Center for the Performing Arts—Oriental Theater on 13 July 2005, where it became the longest running and highest grossing Broadway musical in Chicago theatrical history. It closed on 25 January 2009 after 1,500 performances. The total audience in Chicago was 2.9 million people, and the box office gross was $206 million.[3] The stage at the Oriental Theater is smaller than at the Gershwin Theatre in New York City, causing the production to be redesigned, but the effect of the show in Chicago remained very similar.[4]

The West End production opened at the Apollo Victoria Theatre on 27 September 2006, where it was still running in the summer of 2010 after more than 1,500 performances and total box office gross sales of more than GBP 100 million.[5] After seeing this production in July 2008, it was remarkable to witness how fully London and its tourists have embraced the show.

The Los Angeles production opened at the Pantages Theatre on 21 February 2007. The cast included John Rubinstein—the original Pippin on Broadway in 1972—as the Wizard and Carol Kane as Madame Morrible, a role that she has also played in other productions. A later Madame Morrible was Jo Anne Worley, known for her performances on *Rowan & Martin's Laugh-In* in the 1960s and 1970s. *Wicked* closed in Los Angeles on 11 January 2009 after 791 performances, a total attendance of 1.15 million, and gross ticket sales of over $90 million.[6] This production then moved to San Francisco.

The Tokyo production opened at the Dentsu Shiki Theatre on 17 June 2007. This was the first production for which the libretto was translated: Schwartz reports that the task was simpler than it would prove to be in German because song lyrics need not rhyme in Japanese. This lack of rhyme may be observed on the fifth anniversary OCR, which includes tracks in Japanese of "Popular" and "Dancing through Life."[7] The lyrics are almost entirely in Japanese, but Glinda does sing the English words "popular" and "popularity" in the former song. Schwartz also reports that the notion of Glinda changing her name could not be explained to Japanese audiences, so it was dropped for this version. Miyuki Numao was the original Glinda opposite Megumi Hamada as Elphaba. The show closed in Tokyo on 6 September 2009 after a run of more than two years, and the production then transferred to Osaka.[8]

The German production of *Wicked* opened in Stuttgart at the Palladium Theater on 15 November 2007. One challenge was what to call the show in German. Schwartz reports that there is no real word for "wicked" in German,[9] which seems far-fetched in such a rich language, but my exploration of the concept with German professor Dr. Karin Pagel-Meiners demonstrated that most German words that might express the idea actually bear different first meanings, and certainly no similar word in German carries the double meaning that "wicked" has come to in English slang, where it also means "good."[10] (Also, in the German version of "As Long As You're Mine" ["Solang ich dich hab"], Elphaba concludes by using the English word when she admits that for the first time she feels "wicked."[11]) The creators finally settled on the German title of *Wicked: Die Hexen von Oz*, following the English title with "The Witches of Oz." Schwartz notes that part of the appeal of this title was that *Hexen* bears some of the double meaning in German, both positive and negative, that "wicked" bears in English. (Dr. Pagel-Meiners also confirmed this.[12]) Schwartz admits that translating the lyrics into German was an enormous challenge, but he was satisfied with the result that they worked out with translator Michael Kunze. Schwartz looked for the same results with the German lyrics that he knew from the English, and he discovered that the word *liebenswert* (literally "worthy of love" and used for "popular") did not bring the laughs that its English counterpart did. They changed the word to *heissgeliebt* (literally "hotly loved"), and then the lines drew the reaction that Schwartz expected.[13] The show closed in Stuttgart on 29 January 2010 and transferred to Oberhausen.[14]

The Melbourne production opened at the Regent Theatre on 12 July 2008. Amanda Harrison, who originated the role of Elphaba in Australia, had already worked extensively in musical theater both there and in the West End.[15] Lucy Durack, the original Australian Glinda, has worked primarily in her native country.[16] *Wicked* closed in Melbourne on 9 August 2009,[17] after which it moved to Sydney.

San Francisco, where the show's pre-Broadway out-of-town tryout had taken place in the spring of 2003, had its premiere of a sit-down production of *Wicked* at the Orpheum Theater on 6 February 2009. In the week that ended 15 February 2009, the show grossed $1,459,610, a new record for San Francisco theaters.[18] The production moved from Los Angeles, but the San Francisco cast was different, assembled from actors

Table 8.1. Summer 2010 Schedule for Two National Touring Companies of *Wicked*

Dates	Venues
5/26/10–6/27/10	Dallas, Music Hall at Fair Park
6/16/10–7/11/10	St. Louis, The Fabulous Fox
6/30/10–7/25/10	Houston, Hobby Center
7/14/10–8/8/10	Milwaukee, Uihlein Hall
7/28/10–8/29/10	Columbus, Ohio Theater
8/11/10–9/19/10	Minneapolis, Orpheum Theater

who had been in other productions, including Teal Wicks as Elphaba, Kendra Kassebaum as Glinda, and Carol Kane as Madame Morrible.[19] A replacement for Kane was noted actress Patty Duke.[20] This production closed on 5 September 2010 after 660 performances.[21]

The Second National Tour opened at the Barbara B. Mann Performing Arts Hall in Fort Myers, Florida, on 7 March 2009.[22] It also continues to play throughout the United States and in Canada. The twin tours bring the show to a striking number of cities during the course of a year, and as of November 2010 there were announced bookings through September 2011. Table 8.1 provides the schedule for both tours during summer 2010.[23]

The Australian production, with much of the same cast that had played in Melbourne, opened at Capitol Theatre in Sydney on 12 September 2009.[24] Scheduled to run for exactly a year until 12 September 2010, the production transferred to Brisbane in January 2011.[25]

The Japanese production opened in Osaka at the Shiki Theater on 11 October 2009.[26]

The German production opened at the Metronom Theater in Oberhausen on 5 March 2010.[27] Willemijn Verkaik, who originated the German role of Elphaba in Stuttgart, also initiated the role in Oberhausen.[28]

The first "nonreplicated" version of *Wicked* (not based on the Broadway production) opened at the Helsinki City Theater on 26 August 2010. Schwartz worked with Sami Parkinnen on the translation of the lyrics into Finnish.[29] The director of the Finnish production is Hans Berndtsson. A "nonreplicated" Danish production in Copenhagen is also planned.

Wicked in London

The West End production of *Wicked* began its rehearsals on 24 July 2006, taking place at the 3 Mills Film Studios, one of the few places sufficiently large to assemble the enormous show.[30] The executive producer for the British production is Michael McCabe, who began his career in theater ticket sales and then joined an advertising firm before founding Michael McCabe Associates in 1989, which specializes in marketing commercial theater ventures. From there McCabe's career as producer developed as he moved from the position of marketing director of *Mamma Mia!* in fourteen different productions around the world to its associate producer from 1998 to 2004.[31] Since working on *Wicked*, he has been on the producing team for other shows on Broadway and in the West End. The creative team's goal in London was to replicate the Broadway production, but with the knowledge that there would need to be changes for the British audience. Schwartz has written that for the show's international versions Glinda's opening monolog needed to be expanded, such as identifying the witch-hunters who had killed the Wicked Witch of the West and talking about how they killed her, details better known in the United States.[32] Months before *Wicked* opened in London, reporter Matt Wolf stated that the commercial chances for the show there seemed strengthened by the creative team's intention to make the political message more obvious than it had been in the original Broadway version.[33] Certainly there was reason to be concerned about how the public might embrace the show because *The Wizard of Oz* stories are more popular in the United States than in the United Kingdom. Broadway producer David Stone has called the tales part of the "DNA of America,"[34] and Nicola Christie compared the popularity of L. Frank Baum's tales in the United States to the importance of *Alice in Wonderland* in the United Kingdom.[35] One of McCabe's challenges was to make the British public care about this American story. The adaptation of *Wicked* for the British audience provides confirmation of Bruce Kirle's idea that musicals always remain works in progress, with even famous book musicals being altered in subsequent productions because of changes in personnel and audience tastes.[36] Schwartz and his fellow creators might have been able to use the Broadway production elsewhere in the United States and Canada, but in London substantive changes were required.

Photo 8.1. The entrance to the Apollo Victoria Theatre, across the street from Victoria Station, where *Wicked* opened on 27 September 2006, courtesy of the author.

The theater chosen for *Wicked* was the Apollo Victoria on Wilton Road, close to Victoria Station. The house opened as a cinema in 1932, designed by E. Wamsley Lewis, with decorations inside in an underwater motif. It originally held an audience of 2,500 but closed in 1976. After reopening with the current name, *Starlight Express* ran there for years following major renovation for the show's huge set, which resulted in the removal of 1,000 seats. The Apollo Victoria reopened in 2002 with 2,200 seats.[37]

Serious commercial buzz for *Wicked* began as tickets went on sale in early March. One journalist reported shortly thereafter that the show "will be virtually critic-proof" because GBP 100,000 worth of tickets were sold during the first hour that the box office was open, and by 10 March the advanced sale had reached GBP 1.7 million.[38] One of the factors driving ticket sales in April was the news that Idina Menzel would recreate her role as Elphaba for the first four months of the London run. Her singing was known from the OCR, and the British press provided considerable hype. Baz Bamigboye, a gossip columnist and arts reviewer for the *Daily Mail*, wrote about Menzel with great admiration, calling her a "power-house performer . . . the like of which has not been seen on a London stage in a very long time."[39] Menzel was reimbursed handsomely for her work in the West End, with her salary reported as $30,000, or GBP 16,000, per week, making her the highest paid actress in London theatrical history.[40]

The British press continued to print stories about the coming show through the spring and summer in anticipation of the fall opening, some of them no doubt spurred on by McCabe's publicity machine. Reporter Susan Mansfield interviewed novelist Gregory Maguire and wrote a lengthy article on his work on the novel and his feelings about the musical. A noteworthy moment came when Maguire said that Schwartz told him the following at their first meeting concerning the project: "Your characters have immense moral struggles and they know themselves, they're very passionate, nothing will be lost by having them rush to the edge of the stage in front of 1,700 people and sing their soliloquies. Most stories can't carry such a thing."[41] The novelist believes that Schwartz's show retains the most important scenes from the novel, especially "how we demonise our enemies in order to justify violence against them." This feeling would have played well with many in a United Kingdom growing tired of Prime Minister Tony Blair and his cozy relationship with President George W. Bush in the United States, who was deeply unpopular in the United Kingdom at that point.

The identity of who would play Glinda became known in May. As Baz Bamigboye reported on 12 May, Australian actress Helen Dallimore would make her West End debut after prevailing through eight auditions. She told the reporter how she would try to adapt the role for the British audience: "In America, Glinda was sort of a valley girl. Here she'll have an English accent. I believe I'll be playing her like an upper-class English twit."[42] In another report, McCabe commented on his first impression of Dallimore: "It was a joy when she walked into the room; none of us knew who she was and she was absolutely fantastic."[43] Playing opposite Menzel, Dallimore became a memorable presence in the production praised by most critics; although, as will be shown, there were some who found her singing wanting next to the formidable Menzel. Jasper Rees reported in August that Madame Morrible would be played by noted British actress

Miriam Margolyes, perhaps best known in recent years outside of England as Professor Sprout in the *Harry Potter* films, and the Wizard would be Nigel Planer, who plays Neil Pye on the BBC comedy *The Young Ones* and has also appeared in a number of West End musicals.[44] Fiyero would be played by Adam Garcia, who had played the role in a 2002 workshop performance but had not been chosen for the Broadway production. Garcia is an Australian actor and tap dancer who has worked extensively in the West End.[45]

Previews for *Wicked* at the Apollo Victoria began on 7 September, with the premiere set for 28 September. The show would face stiff competition. In addition to *Wicked*, Robert Colville reported the following schedule for announced openings of West End musicals: *Cabaret* (10 October), *Monty Python's Spamalot* (16 October), *Dirty Dancing* (24 October), *Porgy and Bess* (9 November), and *The Sound of Music* (14 November),[46] the latter after the successful reality television program *How Do You Solve a Problem Like Maria?* where Connie Fisher had been chosen as the

Photo 8.2. Sign on the Apollo Victoria Theatre over the London buses that stop in front of Victoria Station, courtesy of the author.

star for the new production. Advance sales for *Wicked* continued apace: Matt Wolf noted that they had hit a total of GBP 5 million slightly more than a week before the premiere.[47]

Critics provide some details of the memorable premiere on Thursday, 28 September. There was considerable jostling by the audience trying to get into the Apollo Victoria, but Ian Shuttleworth stated that this was because the management had failed to open all of the doors, perhaps trying to create more excitement, if a bit dangerously.[48] The audience greeted Idina Menzel with a roar just for walking on stage, and every major number received extensive applause. Some critics were surprised at how much people in the audience seemed to already know about the show, but fans had surely already learned much through the OCR and various Internet sources. A few critics noted that not all of the sound problems had been solved by opening night because they had trouble understanding lyrics, and several complained how loud the music was in the theater.

The London media provided many reviews of *Wicked* over the next few weeks, and the results were decidedly mixed. Of the 22 reviews consulted from the print media for this study, 4 ranged from mostly positive to raves, 14 included positive comments but also included major reservations about one or more aspects of the show, and 4 were primarily negative. A number of the critics, even some who panned the show, stated that they believed *Wicked* would be critic proof. A survey of their commentary illustrates how the London critical establishment greeted the show, and as a group they do not seem to have differed greatly from the way New York critics wrote about *Wicked*. Their favorite aspects of the evening included the production itself and the actors, especially Menzel, Dallimore, and Margolyes. Some of the strongest praise went to Margolyes—clearly a British favorite—even from some critics who found little to like about the show. Appraisal of Schwartz's score was uneven, from the highly positive to the outright dismissive.

Four reviews appeared on the day the show opened, obviously produced from previews. Sheridan Morley of *The Express* found *Wicked* "a truly eccentric affair," but he thought the show would do well "for its sheer spectacle."[49] Nicholas de Jongh, writing for the *Evening Standard*, was unimpressed by the music but raved about "the experience of a magical mystery tour through the fantasy land of Oz that talks and holds attention." He concluded, "*Wicked* works like a dream."[50] Patrick Marmion of the *Daily Mail* enjoyed the production but felt differently about the lyrics and the overall tone of the show. He said Schwartz's texts to the songs "take banality to galactic proportions," adding to what he found to be "one of the show's excruciating ironies is that while asserting the importance of being earnest it is wilfully moronic."[51] The *Daily Telegraph*'s Charles Spencer admitted that he had never liked the Oz story, but he called *Wicked* an "unexpectedly witty, enjoyable though far from flawless show."[52] Spencer found "wit" in Schwartz's lyrics, and he admired the "big gloopy power ballads" that allowed the singers to strut their stuff. He thought that the show deserved more of an audience than just adolescent girls.

Critics whose reviews appeared the morning after the premiere ran the gamut from pans to raves. Benedict Nightingale, writing for *The Times*, concluded, "I'd rather see *The Wizard of Oz* 20 times than this ersatz show once."[53] Paul Taylor of *The Independent* enjoyed "the delicious Miriam Margolyes" but disliked virtually everything else.[54] Michael Billington in *The Guardian* offered a more balanced view. He enjoyed the first act but disliked the "moralising" in the second act, admitting that the show was performed well with fine actors and included a worthwhile score. His conclusion, however, showed his ultimate disappointment: "It seems all too typical of the modern Broadway musical: efficient, knowing and highly professional but more like a piece of industrial product than something that genuinely touches the heart and mind."[55] The positive reviews came from Peter Law of *Greater London, Kent, and Surry Counties Publications* and Siobhan Murphy of the *Metro* (London). Law called Menzel "quite simply spellbinding" and offered this unqualified praise: "The musical adaptation of the prequel to the classic *The Wonderful Wizard of Oz* is chock-a-bloc with special effects, magical costumes, soaring sing-a-longs and witty in-jokes." He was not completely convinced by the story, which he found superficial, and he stated that the "line between good and evil never really blurs."[56] Murphy described it as a spectacular show with a heart: "This is slick, big bucks theatre that, amid all the hugely expensive special effects and costumes, still manages to be funny, poignant and politically astute."[57]

The next set of reviews ran on Sunday, 1 October. Tim Walker of the *Sunday Telegraph* penned one of the show's most glowing reviews. He believed that it worked on different levels: "as blockbuster family entertainment, and, thanks to Stephen Schwartz's Sondheimian lyrics, sophisticated comedy and even thought-provoking drama. It's sexy, sassy and sensational." He was most impressed with "a musical that manages to be both populist and intelligent at the same time."[58] Mark Shenton of *The Express on Sunday* had reservations about the show's size and thought it "rather overcrowded in the narrative department." It was basically a positive review, however, because he believed that *Wicked* "taps into a genuine public appetite for spectacle, art and heart, and this demanding, sometimes commanding musical provides it in spades."[59] Clifford Bishop in the *Sunday Times* thought Schwartz's score uneven, but he praised how Winnie Holzman told the story, including the way she used "the high-school comedy, to win a younger, straighter, less sentimental demographic than most other musicals." He concluded that *Wicked* "often succeeds only by defying its own musical limitations."[60] Kate Bassett, from *The Independent on Sunday*, was impressed with "a piece of glittery showbiz harbouring a political message akin to *The Crucible*," but she found the score "bland" and the choreography "lame."[61] Writing in *The Observer*, Susannah Clapp was dismissive: "If you fancy being bawled at by a woman with a green face and hit over the head by a galumphing moral, go to see *Wicked*."[62] Georgina Brown of the *Mail on Sunday* had a similar impression: "It's anything but spellbinding. The score is insipid, the production witless, charmless, brainless and tedious."[63]

Reviews continued for more than another week. Alastair Macauley, writing in the *Financial Times*, called the plot "inventive and suspenseful" and liked the show's message, but he thought it was best when nobody sang and finally called it "fun, but forgettable."[64] Jane Edwardes of *Time Out London* provided a mixed review, enjoying Menzel, Dallimore, and the effect of the Act 1 finale, but also stating that "the ending is a terrible cop out, and rather like the Wizard himself, there's something very conventional lurking behind the spectacle."[65] Mark Shenton, who reviewed *Wicked* for *The Express on Sunday*, also offered his opinion in *What's On in London*, where he declared that the show offered "plenty to enjoy" even though "there's a better, more intricate and densely-layered musical bursting to get out from under the mechanical baggage of this spectacular production."[66] Sharon Garfinkel in the *Tribune* praised the "sizzling production" and "sterling performances" but still said that she would rather watch the 1939 film because it is "not only preferable, but far more wicked."[67] Matt Wolf, critic for the *International Herald Tribune*, saw the show's potential for the female audience, commenting that "it is likely to enchant teenage girls well into their middle age and beyond."[68] He also thought that the London audience was so busy admiring Menzel's performance that they missed *Wicked*'s message. William Russell of the *Herald* was disappointed that some of the lyrics were covered by the orchestra. He found *Wicked* "superbly staged by Joe Mantello," but "the songs are unmemorable, Schwartz's lyrics uninspired."[69] He did enjoy the cast and thought that "friends of Dorothy will adore it." *The Sun*'s Bill Hagerty enjoyed the "tremendous energy crackling through Joe Mantello's production, plus a handful of magical performances." The score did not work for him: "I've heard more memorable melodies on a mobile phone."[70]

Ian Shuttleworth, editor of *Theatre Record*, commented with surprise about the huge disparity of opinion one noted about *Wicked* among the British critics. One reviewer gave the show five stars, and one gave it none. In his own reflection on the show, Shuttleworth found himself liking it more in retrospect. He mentions two critics, Nicholas de Jongh and Alastair Macauley, who considered the music the least important part of the show, but Shuttleworth appreciates "Schwartz's unashamed tendency towards the idioms of pop rather than those of the contemporary stage musical."[71] He also thought that the show's political message, involving a self-righteous leader, carried resonance for contemporary Britain.

Despite the lukewarm response to *Wicked* from West End critics, the producers clearly hoped for box office magic because they spent GBP 7 million on the production, and the public rewarded their optimism handily. By 6 October, *Wicked* had sold GBP 5.5 million in tickets.[72] On 23 October, reports showed that the show had the highest weekly gross sales ever in the West End at GBP 761,125, with 18,000 people in attendance.[73] By the end of January 2007, that weekly gross record had grown to GBP 873,020, and the house continued to be 95% full for most performances, a high figure in the West End.[74] Producer Michael McCabe noted in an interview in April that usually 60% of the West End audience was over the age of 35, but they had found for *Wicked* that 50% was under 35, so they budgeted heavily for online advertising to draw the youth audience and made video clips of the show available on the Web.[75] Such efforts helped the show's success to continue, with weekly grosses remaining at GBP 538,000 per week in January 2008, the month that the

West End production paid off its original investment.[76] As of 23 June 2008, *Wicked* had enjoyed sales of GBP 50 million.[77]

McCabe and his collaborators found a memorable British actress to play Elphaba, which *Wicked* patrons started to discover in November 2006. Kerry Ellis first signed on as Idina Menzel's understudy, and her contract stipulated that she would take over the role when Menzel left. The American star began to have throat problems in November, and Ellis went on for her.[78] In December, Baz Bamigboye reported that some fans were going to see the show three times per week in hopes of seeing Ellis play the role for Menzel,[79] which she did nine times before taking the role over herself at the beginning of February 2007.[80] Ellis had previously served as understudy for Eliza Doolittle in Cameron Mackintosh's 2001 production of *My Fair Lady*, and then she played in the musicals *We Will Rock You* and *Les Misérables*.[81] Later, Ellis played Elphaba in the Broadway production from June to November 2008.[82]

Press coverage of *Wicked* and related matters in London remained strong through the holiday season. Edward Seckerson, a noted reviewer

Photo 8.3. *Wicked* **advertising amidst the hustle and bustle inside Victoria Station, courtesy of the author.**

of recordings, turned his attention to OCRs as buyers worked on their Christmas lists, and he included *Wicked*, which had been available as a compact disc for three years at that point, but interest had peaked in London with the popular production. He described Schwartz's music "as operatic retro pop" and singled out "I'm Not That Girl" and "For Good" as examples of the types of songs that Schwartz had written early in his career.[83] In one of those end-of-the-year lists that the press loves, Louise Jury in *The Independent* provided her version of "Theatreland's Top 100 Players." The top figure was Andrew Lloyd Webber, but Stephen Schwartz made the list, a novelty for a theater composer who had not to this point enjoyed great success in the United Kingdom for any show besides *Godspell*.[84] An anonymous reporter placed *Wicked* in the tradition of British holiday entertainment by suggesting that the show was a good alternative to panto, children's musicals that have been part of British holiday entertainment for decades. This writer hated panto as a child but noted that *Wicked* might be good for family entertainment at that time of year because it "is a great big luscious Broadway extravaganza with two strong female leads and a lot of power ballads. But there's medicine in with the sugar." He also states that the show has inspired "one of London's most fervent cults."[85]

The popularity of *Wicked* with the public was demonstrated to an extent with the announcement of the Whatsonstage.com Theatregoer Awards in February. The public's vote named *Wicked* the best new musical, Idina Menzel won for best actress in a musical, Miriam Margolyes won for best supporting actress in a musical, and the show earned best set design.[86] *Wicked* did not enjoy similar success in the Laurence Olivier Awards, the West End equivalent of the Tony Awards. The show was nominated in the categories of director, lighting design, set design, and costume design, but it did not win any. *Wicked* was notably missing from the nominations as best new musical or in any acting categories, including best performance in a supporting role in a musical, an area in which many critics thought Miriam Margolyes distinguished herself.[87]

One notes that *Wicked*'s fate in the West End has been quite similar to what has happened on Broadway: the public has embraced the show with open arms, but the critics and theatrical establishment have kept the show at arm's length. In an article that helps place the British *Wicked* in a useful context, Dominic Maxwell in October 2007 wrote in *The Times* about what makes musicals run well in London.[88] He noted that theaters in the West End now sell more tickets than are sold on Broadway, and the intense competition in London tends to mean that a show will either be a major success or a flop—there is little middle ground. Examples of recent shows that had disappeared quickly were *The Drowsy Chaperone*, *Daddy Cool*, and *Menopause the Musical*, the first of which was successful on Broadway. Maxwell suggested a number of ways that a producer can help a show do well. The article was written in a tongue-in-cheek style but was intended seriously, and much of it rings true. In the West End, women often decide which shows to attend, and female group ticket packages are important, so advertising must appeal to females. Maxwell offered that one must be able to explain a show in a single sentence, believing this quality to be more important in London than in New York. He thought this was one of the problems with *The Drowsy Chaperone*, which he described as entertaining but too complicated to grasp quickly in conversation. A show's logo is important, with the success that *Cats* had with its two eyes being the most famous example. The producers must give audience members a reason to return to the show, and a good way to do this is to bring in stars to play major roles as the run progresses. The initial advertising budget must be huge: in the area of GBP 1 million for large theaters and GBP 600,000 to 700,000 in smaller theaters, with continuing weekly budgets of between GBP 25,000 and 30,000 per week. A producer must set the show's budget without planning to sell out every night; Maxwell suggests that *The Drowsy Chaperone* would have run longer if the producer had deeper pockets. The cast must remain in top form every night with someone watching performance quality. He also described how the producers of *Billy Elliott* leave survey sheets in seats to try to get feedback from the audience. Good reviews are important, but they need not be in the print media. *Wicked*, for example, derived great word-of-mouth support from an enthusiastic review by Phillip Schofield, a trusted host on ITV's *This Morning*. Maxwell also counseled producers to conceive new ideas on how to market a show, citing the recent use of television reality shows as a way to find cast members. Maxwell closed by saying that a good idea for a show was not as important as the show having a sound structure, a point that Stephen Schwartz has often made.[89] *Wicked*, through planning or good fortune, triumphed in most of these arenas, and for that reason it has enjoyed a solid run in the tough West End market.

Wicked Touring Production in Kansas City, 28 November 2009

One of the national touring companies played in the Music Hall in Kansas City, Missouri, in November and December of 2009. It was the show's second visit to Kansas City and afforded an opportunity to take detailed notes during the show. The following paragraphs include a description of minor staging points that are difficult to remember after viewing the show, some significant moments where the music comments upon the action, and observations on what the touring production is like. The show worked well in this sizable venue (capacity of 2,400), even from near the back of the large balcony.

The flying monkeys were on the stage from the beginning of the music identified in the score as "Monkey Groove" (OCR, track 1, 0'19"); one squeaked as he turned the crank that moves the dragon and the remainder of the gear assembly in the front of the set. (The set of *Wicked* depicts the inside of a large clock, with the rear of the face at the back of the stage. With the dragon projecting outward from the proscenium, it is clear that the set's inspiration comes from the Clock of the Time Dragon that plays a major role in Maguire's original novel, but there are few references to the device in the show besides the set.) As Glinda's metallic bubble descended from the fly-space, it emitted a profusion of bubbles, and lighting effects added to her spectacular entrance. She sang her entire solo passage in the air, finally touching the floor at center stage at "on your own" (track 1, 3'08"). Glinda's narration of Elphaba's conception and birth ensued. As the disguised Wizard and Elphaba's mother Melena began their tryst, they embraced but did not descend to the stage floor before she became visibly pregnant. Melena had her back to the audience at center stage and then turned around ready to give birth. Toward the end of the number, Glinda had returned to her bubble and ascended eight or ten feet as she performed her solo line above the chorus (5'43"), and then after an Ozian asked her if she were actually friends with the Wicked Witch, she signaled for her bubble to descend and offered the narrative that began the flashback. At the end of this first scene, Elphaba's silhouette, huge in size, appeared at the back of the stage in the reverse clock face. She burst in from the back, ready to start at Shiz University, just as Glinda said that they "were very young" when they were friends at school.

The scene for Shiz University took place in the slightly modified middle of the stage, where most individual scenes in *Wicked* take place. The staging for the scene included two large paintings of a human and a goat hanging from the fly-space, and when Elphaba made Nessarose's chair return to her from Madame Morrible's hands, there were various lighting and stage effects, including projected gears and the dragon in motion, showing the clock's participation in telling the story. (In Maguire's novel, the Clock of the Time Dragon could reenact events for an audience.) The smaller orchestra for the tour could not provide adequate presence during the "Unlimited" section of "The Wizard and I" (track 3, 3'35"), especially in the sixteenth notes that provide the shimmer.

The staging of the song "What Is This Feeling?" began with Galinda and Elphaba on opposite sides of the stage, and they remained alone until the chorus actually started to sing. The ensemble came rushing onto the stage in two groups, dancing and singing in support of Glinda until the end of the song. In this version, Elphaba actually tweaked Galinda's face at the end of the song rather than just scaring her.

An effective moment of underscoring took place in the scene with "Something Bad," once Madame Morrible had entered and was in conversation with Elphaba and Doctor Dillamond. The instrumental music included material from "The Wizard and I," perhaps illustrating that Madame Morrible is Elphaba's ticket to her dreams, not Doctor Dillamond.

The cart that brought Fiyero onto the stage for the first time in the touring version was small, hardly large enough to hold him. The students sat around on stage with their books studying but then discarded these props gleefully as they began "Dancing through Life." The number progressed through several small scenes assembled quickly behind the dancing cast members. The set included panels that often slid in from the sides, decorated with the gears that dominated the set, and such pieces were used in this number to create small areas like Nessarose's room, where she sang to Elphaba as she got ready for her date with Boq. At the Ozdust Ballroom, Boq and Nessarose danced together as he pushed her wheelchair around from the back to the front in the middle of the stage, just before Elphaba made her entrance in the black, peaked hat. She danced uncomfortably for several moments without music as Fiyero and Galinda spoke, and once Galinda joined her, Elphaba allowed her to look foolish dancing alone for a moment. While Galinda danced, the music began once again, and then Elphaba joined her. For a moment Galinda's two main friends seemed to challenge her choice as she danced with Elphaba, but then the entire cast commenced doing the "Elphaba." As the cast gathered as a group at the scene's conclusion, Elphaba was enjoying herself in the middle, apparently for the moment part of the group.

It was notable how silly Galinda acted in Act 1 of *Wicked*, obviously played this way for laughs but also perhaps making more dramatic her transition to the more mature "Glinda the Good" at the show's close. Her antics form a deliberate part of the show's arc, but it is striking that it is such broad comedy. *Wicked* includes a wide range of expression, which delights some but confuses others, and it might explain some of the negative critical reactions. Many of Galinda's sillier shenanigans took place during "Popular," such as her clueless attempts to use her new wand, finally asking if it is turned on. An effective moment in the underscoring came when she placed a flower in Elphaba's hair and the orchestra played material from "I'm Not That Girl," a tune not yet sung.

When Elphaba unintentionally used her magic in the classroom to place everyone in a trance in order to save the lion cub, those affected by the spell broke into coordinated stage movement, one of those moments in *Wicked* that at first might not be thought of as dance but perhaps included the collaboration of choreographer Wayne Cilento. Fiyero and Elphaba rushed out with the caged lion cub, and the underscoring before "I'm Not That Girl" began just as Elphaba ran across the stage to grab Fiyero's hand. He had become angry that she would not allow him to speak, and she wanted to prevent him from leaving. As Elphaba sang at center stage, Galinda and Fiyero appeared together behind her, not on a bridge above Elphaba as happens in the Broadway version.

The set included a 12-by-12 array of lights projected on the floor at center stage used for various effects during the show, in the next scene suggesting a patterned floor at the train station where Elphaba's friends have come to see her off to the Emerald City. Such arrangements of lights appeared several times during the show in various places and at different angles. The cinematic nature of the staging became clear at the end of the scene when Elphaba invited Glinda to the Emerald City with her, and the light array disappeared from the floor and everything became green in an instantaneous transition to the Wizard's city. A bit of stage action that illustrated Glinda's personality was her curtsy after she announced her new name, expecting applause for her gesture.

The *Wizomania* sequence illustrated once again how much of *Wicked* takes place at center stage. Elphaba and Glinda rushed in to see the show after a curtain descended to delineate the smaller stage. The curtain opened to show the musical segment heard on the OCR as part of "One Short Day" (track 9, 1'44"). The Wizard's large mechanical head and its accompanying contraption then appeared in the same spot with Chistery atop it, where he stayed for much of the sequence. As Elphaba gave the monkeys wings, the stage was bathed in red light. After Elphaba escaped and Glinda followed her, the limited staging possibilities of the touring production were accommodated by having Elphaba take the broom that she finds off stage left to block the door from the guards. (On Broadway the broom levitated in place.) The broom then "floated" back on stage after Elphaba made it fly. The bright lighting that framed Elphaba at the end of "Defying Gravity" emanated from spotlights in the auditorium as well as from the top and bottom of the stage area. Act 1 was 92 minutes in length.

As Act 2 opened, the Ozians sang "Everyday more wicked . . ." in front of the large scrim that bears the map of their land, and then the scrim opened as a platform came forward for Glinda, Fiyero, and Madame Morrible. This scene, dominated by the song "Thank Goodness," included coordinated stage movement for the crowd that came to Glinda's celebration.

At the outset of Scene 2, in Nessarose's chamber in Munchkinland, Elphaba appeared mysteriously in her sister's wardrobe through a lighting effect. The accent color for the scene was red, such as in the upholstery, and Nessarose and her shoes were lit with the color after Elphaba used her magic to allow her sister to walk. Other staging effects involved Boq's transformation into the Tin Man. After Elphaba cast her spell, he fell asleep in a large chair with his back to the audience, allowing the actor to change costumes unseen.

The engagement ball for Glinda and Fiyero followed immediately. It was suggested with orchestral underscoring (track 13, 0'00"–0'45") and brief stage movement before the Wizard's mechanical head came forward at center stage. The audience first saw the side with the head, and then the device turned around as Elphaba entered, suggesting that we were now in the Wizard's private chamber. Musical effects that jumped right out of the pit were those that emphasized the vaudevillian nature of the song "Wonderful," such as the overdone piano arpeggio on the dominant seventh chord under "balloon" (1'45") to set up the next section. Unlike some earlier versions of the script, the Wizard did not take possession of Elphaba's broom, which blocked her escape, until later in the song. When the Wizard sang "A celebration throughout Oz . . . ," it was abundantly clear that this had been derived from "The Wizard and I." The Wizard then released the monkeys at Elphaba's request. Two monkeys appeared in front of the stage suspended by wires, and more flew behind the bars while others danced on the stage and projections of flying monkeys appeared elsewhere on stage and on the surrounding walls.

Elphaba and Fiyero immediately came on stage with a lantern and made their way to the front as Glinda sang "I'm Not That Girl." The couple sang "As Long As You're Mine" while kneeling in each other's arms. In this tour version, the orchestral accompaniment included considerably less percussion than one hears on the OCR. At the conclusion of the song, a projection across the back of the set showed a house flying, and Elphaba announced that she knew that Nessarose was in trouble and must go help her.

Elphaba's arrival at the scene of her sister's death sparked her confrontation with Glinda and their "catfight," presented here with Glinda executing similar, campy martial moves with her large wand that Kristin Chenoweth popularized in the Broadway version. One might criticize this as another possible breach of tone in *Wicked*. A physical fight between the two main characters ranks as a dark moment, but the creative team chose to play it for laughs with Glinda twirling her wand in a send-up of martial arts films. Such role-playing, however, is consistent with Glinda's character. If she must fight with her best friend, Glinda will make believe that she has some sort of legendary prowess. Her actions drew many laughs, and the scene did not seem to distract from the act's dramatic progression. After Fiyero arrived to rescue Elphaba from the situation, Glinda encouraged her friend to flee as well and picked Elphaba's hat up and tossed it to her before she left.

While Elphaba sang "No Good Deed," the staging was memorable. There were monkeys on stage with her at the start of the song. Air was blown onto center stage to make her clothes move, and the lighting changed color. Bright lights from the floor shone in Elphaba's face.

In the next scene back in the Emerald City, the song continued as "March of the Witch-Hunters." Boq sang his two verses from stage left. When he revealed why the Lion would like to kill Elphaba, one only saw the Animal's tail as Boq tried to pull him into view. Everyone on stage froze while Glinda and Madame Morrible discussed the cyclone, with movement resuming after Morrible finished telling Glinda that she must pretend to take part in the crowd's desire for blood.

Schwartz managed a lovely, nuanced moment in the scene where Elphaba received the message from Fiyero and allowed Glinda to believe that he was dead. As Elphaba read the note, the "Wicked" motive sounded in the winds. At this point, it appeared that Elphaba's fate had been sealed, and the motive seemed to bring her journey to a close. A striking image from later in the scene occurred during "For Good," sung at center stage and partially lit from behind the large clock face at the rear of the stage, casting the clock's shadow across the floor. This backlighting occurred elsewhere in the show as well, but here it was richly symbolic of the passage of time and how events beyond their control have affected their friendship.

Dorothy threw the bucket at Elphaba and "melted" her behind a curtain with the event backlit and viewed as shadows on the curtain. The sequence happened quickly, and then the Wizard's throne room had already been set up a bit stage right of the melting so that Glinda and Chistery could move the curtain and Glinda could proceed immediately into the throne room. After the Wizard's departure, Glinda removed Madame Morrible from her position, but in this version she only spoke condescendingly to her former mentor without the American Sign Language Kristin Chenoweth used to spell out "p-r-i-s-o-n" in the Broadway version.

In the final scene, Glinda and Elphaba were on stage at the same time but were unaware of each other. As they sang a bit of "For Good," Glinda was about halfway up in her bubble and Elphaba was center stage on the floor, just before she and Fiyero departed through the clock face as the show ended. The second act in the tour version was 60 minutes in length.

Notes

1. An important source for basic information on *Wicked* in its various productions is *Wicked: Around the World in One Short Day* (New York: The Araca Group, 2008). Although largely a book of photographs, the book includes a brief essay on each production through the time of its publication, and pictures appear of prominent actors who have appeared in *Wicked*.

2. "The History of *Wicked*," www.wickedthemusical.com.au/about/history .html (accessed 20 June 2010).

3. http://leisureblogs.chicagotribune.com/the_theater_loop/2009/01/count down-to-the-close-of-chicagos-wicked.html (accessed 20 June 2010).

4. This is based on my own observation, having seen the show both in New York and Chicago.

5. "Wicked Celebrates £100m Box Office Milestone," www.uktheatre tickets.co.uk/article/19841507/Wicked-celebrates-%C2%A3100m-box-office -milestone (accessed 20 June 2010).

6. "Los Angeles *Wicked* to Close 1/11/09," http://losangeles.broadway world.com/article/Los_Angeles_Wicked_to_Close_11109_20080402 (accessed 20 June 2010).

7. CD 2, tracks 6 and 7 on *Wicked: 5th Anniversary Special Edition*, Decca B0012127-72, 2008.

8. "The History of *Wicked*."

9. *Wicked: Around the World in One Short Day*, ii.

10. Telephone interview with Dr. Karin Pagel-Meiners, Lawrence, KS, 10 June 2010.

11. This may be heard on track 4, "Solang ich dich hab," of the compact disc *Wicked: 5th Anniversary Special Edition*.

12. Telephone interview with Dr. Karin Pagel-Meiners, Lawrence, KS, 10 June 2010.

13. *Wicked: Around the World in One Short Day*, ii.

14. www.musical-friends.de/index.php?page=Thread&threadID=1048 (accessed 20 June 2010).

15. http://broadwayiswicked.com/tag/amanda-harrison (accessed 20 June 2010).

16. www.lucydurack.com (accessed 20 June 2010).

17. http://melbourne.citysearch.com.au/arts/1137659764545/Wicked+Is +Leaving+Town! (accessed 20 June 2010).

18. "The History of *Wicked*."

19. http://sanfrancisco.broadwayworld.com/article/Photo_Flash_Cast_of_ WICKED_San_Francisco_20090217 (accessed 20 June 2010).

20. http://articles.sfgate.com/2009-03-23/entertainment/17215954_1_coeur -russian-hill-aunt-eller (accessed 20 June 2010).

21. http://wickedtour.net/page/2 (accessed 19 November 2010).

22. www.broadwayworld.com/article/Wicked_to_Launch_2nd_National_ Tour_in_March_2009_20080522 (accessed 20 March 2010).

23. www.wickedthemusical.com/page.php#WickedCitiesOnTour (accessed 20 June 2010).

24. "Wicked Opens in Sydney," www.aussietheatre.com.au/index.php?option =com_content&view=article&id=209:wicked-opens-in-sydney&catid=44:general &Itemid=67 (accessed 20 June 2010).

25. www.wickedthemusical.com.au/news/news.html (accessed 20 June 2010).

26. "The History of *Wicked*."

27. "The History of *Wicked*."

28. www.musicalworld.nl/actueel/verkaik_verhuist_met_wicked_mee_naar_ oberhausen (accessed 20 June 2010).

29. www.broadwayworld.com/article/TV_Around_the_BroadwayWorld_ WICKED_in_Helsinki_20100905 (accessed 13 September 2010).

30. Nicola Christie, "It's Wicked," *The Independent*, 17 August 2006.

31. www.michaelmccabe.net/about_michaelmccabe.html (accessed 12 June 2010).

32. *Wicked: Around the World in One Short Day*, ii.

33. Matt Wolf, "Hot Hits from Broadway," *Evening Standard*, 24 January 2006. Whether or not this actually happened is unclear, but if it did, it did not result in the obvious addition of many lines to the show. It does follow that the writers may have thought they could get away with more political commentary outside the United States.

34. Mark Shenton, "Spellbinding," *The Express on Sunday*, 1 October 2006.

35. Christie, "It's Wicked."

36. Bruce Kirle, *Unfinished Business: Broadway Musicals as Works-in-Progress*, Theater in the Americas (Carbondale, IL: Southern Illinois University Press, 2005), especially pp. 1–40, Kirle's first chapter entitled "Celebrating Incomplete- ness," and pp. 75–126, his third chapter called "Unfinished Business."

37. Richard Andrews, *The London Theatre Guide* (London: Metro Publica- tions, 2002), 32.

38. Ruth Leon, "Backstage with Ruth Leon," *The Express*, 10 March 2006.

39. Baz Bamigboye, "Beeb's Desert Hit List," *Daily Mail*, 21 April 2006.

40. See Guy Adams, "Pandora: Broadway Star Set to Scoop up a Wicked Transfer Fee," *The Independent*, 2 May 2006, and Ann Caird, "Letter: Briefly . . . Overpriced Actors," *The Independent*, 5 May 2006.

41. Susan Mansfield, "Other Side of the Rainbow," *The Scotsman* (Edinburgh), 29 April 2006. The next quotation from Maguire is also from this source.

42. Baz Bamigboye, "Mum's the Word for Hectic Keira," *Daily Mail*, 12 May 2006.

43. Shenton, "Spellbinding."

44. Jasper Rees, "Something Wicked This Way Comes—Theatre," *Sunday Times*, 20 August 2006.

45. www.adamgarcia.net (accessed 21 June 2010).

46. Robert Colville, "A Glittering Season of Musicals," *Daily Telegraph*, 20 September 2006.

47. Matt Wolf, "Broadway Hit Casts Its Spell Over Here: It's Making a Million a Week in New York. Now, Says Matt Wolf, *Wicked* Is the Hottest Ticket in a Packed West End Autumn of Musicals," *Daily Telegraph*, 20 September 2006.

48. Ian Shuttleworth, "Prompt Corner," *Theatre Record*, 26/20 (24 September–7 October 2006): 1143.

49. Sheridan Morley, "Witches in Need of Magic Touch," *The Express*, 28 September 2006.

50. Nicholas de Jongh, "We Must All Be Off to See This Wicked and Wonderful Vision of Oz," *Evening Standard*, 28 September 2006.

51. Patrick Marmion, "Patrick Marmion First Night Review," *Daily Mail*, 28 September 2006.

52. Charles Spencer review in the *Daily Telegraph*, 28 September 2006, consulted in *Theatre Record*, 26/20 (24 September–7 October 2006): 1154.

53. Benedict Nightingale, "Wicked—Theatre," *The Times*, 29 September 2006.

54. Paul Taylor, "Reviews—Theatre," *The Independent*, 29 September 2006.

55. Michael Billington, "Theatre: Musical Moralising Taints the Magic of Oz: *Wicked* Apollo Victoria London," *The Guardian*, 29 September 2006.

56. Peter Law, "Wicked—The Untold Story of the Witches of Oz," *Greater London, Kent, and Surry Counties Publications*, 29 September 2006.

57. Siobhan Murphy review in the *Metro* (London), 29 September 2006, consulted in *Theatre Record*, 26/20 (24 September–7 October 2006): 1155.

58. Tim Walker, "A Terribly Long Secret Theatre," *Sunday Telegraph*, 1 October 2006. Walker revisited the show about a year later and stated that he still agreed with his rave from a year before. See Tim Walker, "Arts/Theatre: Heart of Darkness," *Sunday Telegraph* (2 September 2007).

59. Mark Shenton, "Lavish Show with a Real Touch of Magic," *The Express on Sunday*, 1 October 2006.

60. Clifford Bishop review in the *Sunday Times*, 1 October 2006, consulted in *Theatre Record*, 26/20 (24 September–7 October 2006): 1155.

61. Kate Bassett, "Theatre: The Old Vic Cometh Back," *The Independent on Sunday*, 1 October 2006.

62. Susannah Clapp, "Review—Critics—Theatre—Make Mine a Double: Conor McPherson's Latest Play Full of Drinks Is Intoxicating, while at the Old Vic Kevin Spacey and Eve Bert Go Head to Head in Peerless Fashion," *The Observer*, 1 October 2006.

63. Georgina Brown review in the *Mail on Sunday*, 1 October 2006, consulted in *Theatre Record*, 26/20 (24 September–7 October 2006): 1156.

64. Alastair Macauley, "Arts: *Wicked* Victoria Palace Theatre London; The Critics," *Financial Times*, 3 October 2006.

65. Jane Edwardes review in *Time Out London*, 4 October 2006, consulted in *Theatre Record*, 26/20 (24 September–7 October 2006): 1156.

66. Mark Shenton review in *What's On in London*, 5 October 2006, consulted in *Theatre Record*, 26/20 (24 September–7 October 2006): 1157.

67. Sharon Garfinkel review in the *Tribune*, 6 October 2006, consulted in *Theatre Record*, 26/20 (24 September–7 October 2006): 1156.

68. Matt Wolf review in the *International Herald Tribune*, 11 October 2006, consulted in *Theatre Record*, 26/20 (24 September–7 October 2006): 1157.

69. William Russell review in the *Herald*, 13 October 2006, consulted in *Theatre Record*, 26/20 (24 September–7 October 2006): 1157.

70. Bill Hagerty, "Wizard Performers but Woeful Songs—Something for the Weekend," *The Sun*, 13 October 2010.

71. Shuttleworth, 1143.

72. Tom Teodorczuk, "Musicals Battle to the Tune of GBP 37m," *Evening Standard*, 6 October 2006.

73. *The Independent*, "Witches Work Box Office Magic," 23 October 2006.

74. Louise Jury, "Wicked! Theatreland Is Alive to the Sound of Ringing Tills," *The Independent*, 30 January 2007.

75. Robin Eggar, "Youth Enters Stage Right—Report," *Sunday Times*, 8 April 2007.

76. *Daily Mail*, "Wicked Witch with a Magic Touch," 28 March 2008. Ellis played the role in New York from 17 June to 9 November 2008.

77. *Evening Standard*, "*Hairspray* Makes Profit in Record 29 Weeks," 23 June 2008.

78. Baz Bamigboye, "Something Wicked This Way Coughs," *Daily Mail*, 24 November 2006.

79. Baz Bamigboye, column, *Daily Mail*, 22 December 2006.

80. Tom Teodorczuk, "Something Wicked This Way Comes for Understudy Kerry," *Evening Standard*, 10 January 2007, and Dan Evans, "Weekend Theatre," *The Express*, 2 February 2007.

81. Teodorczuk, "Something Wicked."

82. *Daily Mail*, "Wicked Witch with a Magic Touch," and Internet Broadway Database, www.ibdb.com (accessed 4 December 2010).

83. Edward Seckerson, "Go on with the Shows—Musicals," *Sunday Times*, 17 December 2006.

84. Louise Jury, "Theatreland's Top 100 Players," *The Independent*, 29 December 2006.

85. *Evening Standard*, "Magical Alternative to Panto," 7 January 2007. (Many of these British articles and reviews were consulted from the service NewsBank, which provided no author for this article.)

86. *The Guardian*, "Theatre: Public Gives *Wicked* a Vote of Confidence," 10 February 2007, and Anita Singh, "The Hills Are Alive with Many Theatre Prizes for Connie Fisher and *The Sound of Music*," *Western Mail*, 10 February 2007.

87. www.officiallondontheatre.co.uk/olivier_awards/past_winners/view/item98375/Olivier-Winners-2007 (accessed 14 June 2010).

88. Dominic Maxwell, "Born to Run and Run—Arts," *The Times*, 22 October 2007.

89. Personal interview with Stephen Schwartz, New York, 1 April 2008.

CHAPTER NINE
WICKED IN CONTEXT

Meaning and *Wicked*

Most forms of entertainment operate simultaneously on more than one level. One's perception of the various strata will depend on maturity, level of sophistication, and life experience. Explored in chapter 1, for example, were possible interpretations of L. Frank Baum's *The Wonderful Wizard of Oz*. Children will be satisfied with the fantasy itself, the way that the story tickles the imagination. Those interested in the influence of history on American literature will be drawn to Baum's possible allegory involving William Jennings Bryan and American Populism of the 1890s, and postmodernists find possible feminist, gay, and environmental perspectives, among other possibilities. Clearly a work that offers such a variety of possible interpretations will appeal to more people in the long run and remain meaningful to future generations.

The same applies to works in musical theater. Shows commonly include treatments of positive themes that resonate with a large segment of the public, much in the same way that Hollywood studios churn out films that provide the "feel-good" experience that many anticipate at the local multiplex. Often these themes are buried in the fiber of a show, behind the story that first greets the audience. Scholars use these subtextual themes to compare shows that at first might seem quite different, as may be seen in Raymond Knapp's *The American Musical and the Formation of National Identity*, among other studies.[1] For example, under Knapp's section entitled "Defining America," in various subcategories Knapp approaches

Little Johnny Jones (1904), *The Cradle Will Rock* (1938), *Oklahoma!* (1943), *Guys and Dolls* (1950), *The Music Man* (1957), *Hair* (1968), and *Assassins* (1990), and there is a similarly diverse list of musicals under "Managing America's Others."

Such larger themes help determine what might be called a show's shelf life: when a musical is "about something" that we continue to celebrate or recognize, it is more likely to remain in the repertory. One common theme in musicals concerns the formation and maintenance of a community, certainly an important theme in American history, which has been filled with tales of immigration and settlement. In each of these new places (at least new for settlers), people, often from diverse backgrounds, have had to sink new roots and discover how to form a community. Diverse musicals that have somehow celebrated the formation or maintenance of a community have included *Oklahoma!*, *Brigadoon* (1947), *Wonderful Town* (1953), *Godspell* (1971), *Cats* (1982), and *The Lion King* (1997), to name but a few. Another broad, significant theme in the history of almost any country is generational change, both the way that cultural values pass from one generation to another and how a younger generation changes traditions advocated by parents and grandparents. Shows that have approached this theme have included *The King and I* (1951) and *Fiddler on the Roof* (1964), musicals that treat other major themes as well, but in both, life changes as the torch passes to a new generation. Another favorite message in musicals is the importance of dreams and goals in one's life, a theme treated in *Man of La Mancha* (1965) and *Joseph and the Amazing Technicolor Dreamcoat* (1968). Given the significance of race in American society, it is hardly surprising to see race and ethnicity as significant themes in American musical theater. Knapp includes *Show Boat* (1927), *Porgy and Bess* (1935), *West Side Story* (1957), and *Fiddler on the Roof* in his consideration of these themes, but to that could be added *South Pacific* (1949), in which Rodgers and Hammerstein confronted race in the United States just before the Civil Rights Era. The "Other," a person or group that does not fit comfortably in mainstream society, has been a frequent topic of musicals. Stephen Sondheim, for example, has made the "Other" a central presence in most of his shows, as one can see in the title character in *Sunday in the Park with George* (1984) or in any of the main characters in *Assassins*.[2] In Andrew Lloyd Webber's *Phantom of the Opera* (1988), the title character also is misunderstood and living outside of society. The theme of making the best use of each day may be observed in *On the Town* (1944), *Carousel* (1945), and *Candide* (1956). In each show, the theme is approached differently, but it is a significant part of the core message. A theme of social criticism that has appeared in several musicals is how we rely on celebrities and their portrayal in the media to help bring meaning to our own lives, which one sees in such shows as *Chicago* (1975), *Evita* (1979), and *Hairspray* (2002). A theme in many shows is what one might call the redemption of love, with couples overcoming adversarial conditions to be united just before the curtain falls, but in these shows one person in the couple has been "redeemed" by love, or saved from a darker nature, such as Harold Hill in *The Music Man*, removed from his shady career as a con man by the love of Marian Paroo.

Which of these themes are of special importance in *Wicked?* The most important is probably the "Other," obvious in the character of Elphaba, who does not fit in because of her unusual color and becomes a victim of racial prejudice. Elphaba dreams of doing something important, but she does not succeed. (Glinda has her dreams as well and achieves them, but by the end of the show she is full of regrets for the way things have turned out.) *Wicked* includes a statement of the possibility of redemption by love in the relationship between Fiyero and Elphaba. Fiyero is at first infatuated with Glinda, but he falls in love with Elphaba and shows her how to move past her odd coloring and love herself, and they end the show together happily despite adverse circumstances. It is an unusual take on the dream of "happily ever after" that is so common in musical theater, but it allows Elphaba's fans to cheer for her at the end of the show.

More than most shows, *Wicked* carries themes that involve moral and political commentary. Some have found that load too burdensome or believe it to be unconvincing in a musical that also includes a substantial amount of comedy and light moments in the score, but others have described the show as refreshingly serious for a musical.[3] *Wicked's* creators did not shy away from controversy or political interpretations. The Wizard is a tyrant who has united his adopted land by making the Talking Animals into a group of scapegoats, and his apparently sincere desire to serve as a surrogate father for the Ozians does not disguise his brutal methods. He might be compared to any strong, divisive leader, but the Wizard's actions bear resemblance to the liberal interpretation of President George W. Bush and his administration as they pursued policies that led to the Second

Iraq War. (Liberals, for example, sometimes believe that the Bush administration exaggerated claims about possible weapons of mass destruction in Iraq to justify the invasion.) The show could not have been inspired by that event, however, because *Wicked* was well on its way to full creation by the time the United States invaded Iraq on 20 March 2003.

Elphaba's advocacy for the Talking Animals makes her one of Broadway's more memorable agitators. The Wizard and Elphaba are the most politicized major characters in *Wicked*, but others are involved as well. Glinda spends most of the show as an ambitious apologist for the Wizard, willing to overlook egregious acts while pursuing her own agenda. Glinda even takes part in the terror campaign when she is at her most vulnerable, suggesting to the Wizard and Madame Morrible that they use Nessarose to lure Elphaba out of hiding just after she has lost Fiyero. Madame Morrible works shamelessly with the Wizard, encouraging his excesses and willingly performing some of his dirty work. Doctor Dillamond is the victim of oppression who is already a member of the despised group, and he further places himself in harm's way by speaking out. We discover the Wizard's soft side when he is unable to have the goat put to death, and Doctor Dillamond's mute presence at the Wizard's palace stops Elphaba from joining forces with the Wizard in Act 2. Fiyero finds himself transformed by Elphaba and her cause, drawn to this outcast rather than the popular Glinda and joining his new love's crusade. These political and moral considerations drive the plot, motivating characters and influencing their actions. There are other major aspects of the plot, such as the friendship between Glinda and Elphaba and their romantic triangle with Fiyero, but the competing visions for Oz advocated by the Wizard and Elphaba cannot be minimized. The character of Elphaba makes no sense without her cause, and Glinda's journey from a superficial, ambitious young woman to the humble "Glinda the Good" at the curtain is in reaction to her friend and what Elphaba has taught her about the Wizard. The moral and political conflict also mandates the Wizard's departure, Madame Morrible's arrest, and the self-exile of Elphaba and Fiyero.

Wicked's uncompromising dependence on this struggle over politics and morality is rare in Broadway history and places it in interesting company in the genre's history. *Deep River* (1926) was a vivid, realistic portrait of the life of Creoles and African Americans in 1835 New Orleans, far ahead of its time and probably unsuccessful, at least in part, because of its progressive nature.[4] *Show Boat* (1927) constitutes an interesting comparison with *Wicked* because of its serious attention to racism and the relationship between the races in the South between 1887 and 1927. For its time it was bold, but politics are more important in *Wicked* than in *Show Boat*. Politics played a huge role in some shows of the 1930s, when the Great Depression caused leftist writers and directors to use the musical theater as a tool for social criticism. *Of Thee I Sing* (1931) and *Let 'Em Eat Cake* (1933) by George and Ira Gershwin, George S. Kaufman, and Morrie Ryskind both included political satire, perhaps making each show's political component more important than what occurs in *Wicked*. *Let 'Em Eat Cake* (involving the same characters as its predecessor) had more of a sense of bitterness and was not successful. *As Thousands Cheer* (1933) by Moss Hart and Irving Berlin was another satirical success, poking fun at the economic troubles and political foibles of the time. *Pins and Needles* (1937), a revue produced by the International Ladies' Garment Workers' Union at the old Princess Theater, renamed the Labor Stage Theater, was decidedly leftist, but it also included sufficient humor to run for 1,108 performances. Perhaps the most political musical of the 1930s was Marc Blitzstein's *The Cradle Will Rock* (1938), created by the Federal Theater Project, but the controversy it engendered caused its ban by this New Deal agency, and the show, which resembled Communist agitprop theater, ran independently in memorable fashion. The political content of some musicals in the 1930s exceeded what one finds in *Wicked*.

Politics became less important on Broadway after the 1930s, but one still sees shows that are forerunners of *Wicked*. Rodgers and Hammerstein wrote serious musical plays but made more use of real human emotions and dramatic situations than political commentary. Perhaps their most political shows were *South Pacific* (1949) and *The Sound of Music* (1959). Both of the couples in *South Pacific* are affected by race, and the captain's aversion to Nazism in *The Sound of Music* is an important plot point that was downplayed in the popular film from 1965. *West Side Story* (1957) was a show based in the contemporary reality of racism, juvenile delinquency, and gang wars. The creators emphasized social commentary rather than politics. *Cabaret* (1966) was rooted in German politics of the early 1930s, with many references to the growing power of the Nazis. Various fractures in American society in the 1960s boiled over on Broadway in *Hair* (1968), a musical bathed in the politics of youthful rebellion that rivals

Wicked in terms of its plot's dependence upon politics. Stephen Sondheim's musicals include rich emotionalism and often cynicism, but politics is not frequently a major presence in his shows. *Assassins* (1990) includes many political references, but Sondheim's real intention in the show is to explore the "Other" in the lives of people who felt they had been denied the American Dream and then acted out by shooting a president. A show that includes considerable political commentary for which Stephen Schwartz wrote the lyrics is *Rags* (1986), which was based on the plight of Jewish immigrants in New York City before World War I. It ran four performances.

If *Wicked* should be considered a megamusical, it includes more political meaning than most other representatives of this genre. Andrew Lloyd Webber has shown far more interest in emotional stories and religious symbolism in his shows, but *Evita* (1979) involves Argentine politics and Juan Perón's heavy-handed governance. Politics and morality appear more prominently in the shows by Claude-Michel Schönberg and Alain Boublil, with the fervent revolutionary zeal heard from many characters in *Les Misérables* (1987) and the attention paid to children fathered by American soldiers during the Vietnam War in *Miss Saigon* (1991). Unlike *Wicked*, however, where politics drives the story, one can imagine *Miss Saigon*, with its strong plot based on Puccini's *Madama Butterfly*, without such emphasis on Amer-Asian children in Vietnam.

Another way to assess the unusual amount of thought-provoking material in *Wicked's* plot has appeared in the book *The Wicked Truth: When Good People Do Bad Things* by Suzanne Ross,[5] a detailed application of the show's situations and themes to the philosophy and theories of René Girard.[6] A historian and scholar of French literature, Girard came to the United States in 1947 and earned a Ph.D. at Indiana University in 1950. His teaching career has taken him to Duke, Bryn Mawr, Johns Hopkins, SUNY-Buffalo, and Stanford, and he is one of the founders of the Colloquium on Violence and Religion. Girard's work has embraced moral philosophy in reference to how people and societies unify against those identified as enemies. According to Ross, he defines "myths" as "stories that get told by winners to deliberately conceal the loser's story."[7] Winners have the opportunity to tell what they see as the truth, thereby hiding the loser's or victim's story. A society may be unified by identifying a scapegoat who will be sacrificed for the greater good. According to what Ross calls the "Sacrificial Formula," once society has identified a goal that it believes to be good, "then any means, even those of oppression and violence, can be justified."[8] Those who have invested in this thinking believe that there are two types of violence: good violence, which good people direct against bad people, and bad violence, directed in the opposite direction.[9] Girard insists that all violence is bad and that the ends never justify the means, and that once a society has decided to use violence against those it has identified as evil, the society will likely be using the same methods that it associates with those that are "evil."

Suzanne Ross found *Wicked* to be an ideal object lesson for Girard's ideas.[10] The Wizard came to Oz, found himself in power, and consolidated his position and the people's unity by identifying the Talking Animals as scapegoats. Because he has convinced the Ozians that the group is evil, he can justify any persecution or violence directed at them. Madame Morrible has embraced the Wizard's thinking fully, which in her mind justifies Nessarose's murder so that they can bring Elphaba out of hiding and capture her. Elphaba spent the early part of her life worshipping the Wizard and hoping she might work with him so that she could change people's feelings about her, especially her father's. When she discovers that the Wizard has no magical powers and that he needs her more than she needs him, she vows to destroy him, seeing the world from within her own myth and believing that violence against the Wizard will be justified because he is evil, just as the Wizard and Madame Morrible believe that whatever they must do to capture Elphaba is justified. At the end of the show, Fiyero's suffering and Glinda's insistence allows Elphaba to remove herself from the myth she created and see that violence against the Wizard cannot work. She has come to resemble the one that she hates. Glinda begins the show as one who fully embraces her own myth and understands how to use it to ensure her own power and popularity. As she learns more about the Wizard and the truth about the Talking Animals, she manages to move outside of her myth and remove the Wizard and Madame Morrible from their positions of power in Oz. This is what Elphaba had wanted to do, but the fact that she had become one of the Ozian scapegoats made it impossible for her to accomplish it. Ross covers all of these points, and others, with copious details, referencing almost every facet of the plot and frequently quoting the script and lyrics. It is remarkable to see how *Wicked* can be approached with such a fine-toothed comb in what is basically a treatise on moral philosophy. The creators of *Wicked* wrote a musical, but in the process they also presented archetypes of human thinking and behavior, the likes of which have inspired thinkers like René Girard.

Interpreting the Main Characters and Female Empowerment

A scholarly article on *Wicked* that has drawn considerable attention and comment is Stacy Wolf's "'Defying Gravity': Queer Conventions in the Musical *Wicked*," which appeared in the *Theatre Journal* in 2008.[11] Wolf described how the show utilizes the conventions of the traditional musical, certainly the focus of a creative team that includes Schwartz, who has patterned most of his shows after the genre's usual expectations. Wolf focused on the duets between Elphaba and Glinda, which she believes make the two friends a "queer couple" because their relationship, developed within the songs, follows the arc of many heterosexual couples in musicals. Wolf noted how traditional musicals often present a story in which the lead man and woman progress from an adversarial relationship to lovers.[12] An obvious example is *Oklahoma!*, where Curly and Laurie haggle through unresolved issues in the songs "The Surrey with the Fringe on Top" and "People Will Say We're in Love" in Act 1, but by the end of the show they have met at the altar. Wolf traced the relationship between Elphaba and Glinda from "What Is This Feeling?" which demonstrates their adversarial relationship, through "For Good," a song of reconciliation where Wolf saw a queer "marriage" between Elphaba and Glinda that, given the political situation in Oz, can only take place in private. Wolf carefully stated that she was not suggesting that Elphaba and Glinda are lesbians,[13] but that the way their relationship is portrayed marks them as a musical couple as surely as Curly and Laurie are in *Oklahoma!* Wolf believed that the show "infuses the formula with newly gendered and queered content and relationships that are in large part responsible for its enormous theatrical and financial success."[14]

Theatrical scholarship frequently includes possible readings of a musical, and Wolf's essential argument that Elphaba and Glinda can be seen as a "queer couple" is a possible interpretation given the number of songs that they sing together, the content of those songs, and Elphaba's obvious identification with the "Other" that is so much a part of queer theory as applied to musicals.[15] Wolf does, however, introduce a few inaccuracies concerning the story and the music. She opened her article by declaring the queer nature of "What Is This Feeling?" because of the way the passage that starts, with the title text sounding like two characters falling love, but then the feeling turns out to be "loathing."[16] However, in the opening recitative, Galinda is clearly upset by her roommate and her coloring, and Elphaba dismisses Galinda by using "blonde" as an epithet, providing the segment of the song that Wolf found so revelatory with a different meaning than she suggested. The author also offered that Galinda alters her name to show how much Elphaba has changed her.[17] I have not seen this suggestion in any script draft, nor in the final version, where it is clear that Galinda drops the first *a* from her name in hopes of impressing Fiyero, whom she perhaps sees as potentially drawn to Elphaba. Just a few moments later, Glinda declares to Elphaba that it was silly to change her name. Wolf described Elphaba's "Unlimited" motive and how Glinda shows her understanding of her friend because "they both sing Elphaba's signature phrase in several different songs."[18] The "Unlimited" material, however, appears in "The Wizard and I," "Defying Gravity," and the introduction to "For Good," as well as some purely instrumental versions. In the first song, only Elphaba is on stage. In "Defying Gravity," the green girl sings the "Unlimited" material alone; after it, Glinda does not sing until the line "If we work in tandem." In "For Good," Glinda does not sing until the actual song starts; Elphaba has a solo for the entire introduction alone. In "Defying Gravity," Wolf also offered that after Elphaba and Glinda sing the "Unlimited" motive together, the two sing "in tight harmonies, to the last line of the song,"[19] but Elphaba has extended solo passages late in the song. The author labeled "I'm Not That Girl"—a powerful number that might debunk her designation of Elphaba and Glinda as a "queer couple"—as "a slightly nauseating and conservative, male-centered choice in a show that otherwise privileges women and their strength and autonomy,"[20] and for Wolf what was most important about the song is how it links the women because they both sing it, rather than how it shows their desire for a heterosexual relationship with Fiyero. Wolf found that the staging of "As Long As You're Mine" demonstrates the song's unimportance because the two characters are kneeling, a weak position as opposed to Elphaba soaring at the end of Act 1 and Glinda making her initial entrance from the fly-space, and she also cites the song's "inspecific lyrics," quoting from the first several lines.[21] Their position on stage also might suggest that they just made love, a possibility suggested in the second scenario from 21 November 1999 that resulted from the collaboration of Schwartz, Holzman, and Marc Platt.[22] In addition, the lyrics that Wolf quoted do lack specificity concerning the relationship between Fiyero and Elphaba, but later in the song Elphaba celebrates "lying beside you, with you wanting me," and they both sing "I'll wake up my body and make up for lost time." In the language of popular song, these lyrics suggest sexual activity.

Although some may disagree with Wolf's classification of Elphaba and Glinda as a "queer couple," Wolf convincingly described *Wicked*'s theme on the empowerment of women. She stated that the show's most powerful political statement is that "two women form a primary relationship and sing and dance together."[23] She went further in her final conclusion, hoping that *Wicked* "might simultaneously please its audience and guide them to want a queer and feminist Broadway musical theatre."[24]

In another article, Wolf substantively explored the show's "girl power" theme. It is obvious to state that *Wicked* empowers women, but this is a difficult concept to quantify or qualify. Wolf made something of an attempt to do so in her article "*Wicked* Divas, Musical Theatre, and Internet Girl Fans," which appeared in *Camera Obscura* in 2007.[25] She covered some of the same ground there that she did in her article on "Queer Conventions," but she also looked in detail at websites with chat boards where young fans of the show had posted messages concerning *Wicked*. Wolf noted that many of these young women were interested in careers in musical theater, meaning that they identified closely with the performers who have played Elphaba and Glinda on Broadway and in other productions, and they commented, sometimes at length, concerning their feelings about a particular actor in a role. They also stated whether they were personally more like Elphaba or Glinda, or if their personality were a combination of the two. (David Cote also addressed this kind of material in *The Grimmerie*, including a test for someone to determine which main character they more resemble.[26]) Wolf described the stage door ritual that some of these young fans observed and how they reported on meeting the actors afterward. It is not hard to discover how much young women like *Wicked* because one hears the delighted screams at performances, but Wolf approached this aspect of the show with insight in her article. Stephen Schwartz has stated that the show "was certainly not geared toward trying to attract any specific segment of an audience, be it teenagers or any other."[27] By luck or by design, however, *Wicked* has certainly reached the teenaged, female audience.

If I may be permitted some personal commentary, I have had the opportunity to see *Wicked* through the eyes of a young woman who has explained to me why the show means so much to her. My daughter Caitlin was born in 1994 and fell in love with L. Frank Baum's books as a young girl in Kansas. She discovered *Wicked* as a "tweener" in 2005 when her father began to study Stephen Schwartz. She has had the opportunity to see *Wicked* four times, and the compact disc that we share of the show was one of the first discs she put on her iPod. She knows the score well (and can sing it much better than her father!). Her enthralled reaction to *Wicked* emanates from how it interacts with one of her favorite stories and how much she loves the music, but also from the deep level with which she identifies with the characters. She states simply that she knows those characters and could be one of them. She can easily point to friends with personality traits of Elphaba, Glinda, and Fiyero. Despite the fact that the story is a fantasy, its characters seem real to the show's young fans, a tribute to how well Winnie Holzman was able to render Elphaba and Glinda in their friendship. The story includes some of the rituals and experiences of the teen years—dances, makeovers, crushes, best friends, popularity, and ostracism—bringing a welcome touch of reality to the fantastic world of Oz. Baum's stories have never been this realistic or this hip. The process is assisted by Schwartz's score, which includes several songs that young fans love.

Teenaged fans are unlikely to name "female empowerment" as one of the reasons that they like *Wicked*, but it is difficult to cite another Broadway show where two female characters have such important roles, and where the roles they play are so important in the society represented in the musical. The entire show revolves around Elphaba and Glinda—indeed, there are few moments when at least one of them is not on stage—and almost every action by the less important characters in some way involves one or both of the women. They are also two of the most important figures in Oz, rivaled only by the Wizard, and by the end of the show, he has lost what power he had.

One can usually gauge a character's importance in a musical by the number of songs in which the person is involved. A remarkable aspect of

Wicked is how many of the songs are sung by women. Textbox 9-1 summarizes the characters that sing or speak during the music in each of the major songs, including the 19 on the OCR plus "The Wicked Witch of the East." The information for this textbox came from the piano/vocal score, not the OCR, meaning that some characters are named below that are not heard on the OCR, which does not include all of each number. The eight characters considered "major" for the purposes of this textbox are Elphaba, Glinda, Boq, Doctor Dillamond, Fiyero, Madame Morrible, Nessarose, and the Wizard.

Textbox 9.1
Main Characters Who Sing or Speak during the Music for Each Major Song in Wicked (Characters Who Have Only a Few Lines Are Listed in Parentheses)

Act 1

"No One Mourns the Wicked"—Glinda, Wizard

"Dear Old Shiz"—(Galinda)

"The Wizard and I"—Elphaba, Madame Morrible, (Galinda)

"What Is This Feeling?"—Elphaba, Galinda

"Something Bad"—Doctor Dillamond, Elphaba, (Madame Morrible)

"Dancing through Life"—Fiyero, Galinda, Boq, Nessarose, (Elphaba, Madame Morrible)

"Popular"—Galinda, (Elphaba)

"I'm Not That Girl"—Elphaba, (Fiyero)

"One Short Day"—Elphaba, Glinda

"A Sentimental Man"—Wizard, (Elphaba, Glinda, Madame Morrible)

"Defying Gravity"—Elphaba, Glinda, (Madame Morrible)

Act 2

"Thank Goodness"—Glinda, Madame Morrible, (Fiyero)

"Wicked Witch of the East"—Elphaba, Nessarose, Boq

"Wonderful"—Wizard, Elphaba

"I'm Not That Girl" (reprise)—Glinda, (Madame Morrible, Wizard)

"As Long As You're Mine"—Elphaba, Fiyero
"No Good Deed"—Elphaba
"March of the Witch-Hunters"—Boq, (Glinda, Madame Morrible)
"For Good"—Elphaba, Glinda
"Finale"—Glinda, (Elphaba, Fiyero)

Wicked is not a show for those who only wish to hear male characters involved in musical numbers. Textbox 9-2 shows how many major and minor appearances each main character makes during the most important musical numbers in the show. A "major sung segment" is defined as at least a verse or extended segment of a song where a character sings a solo or duet. "Minor participation" is only a few sung or spoken lines at some point in the number, sometimes including lines spoken over underscoring.

Textbox 9.2
Number of Major Sung Segments and Minor Sung or Spoken Lines for Main Characters in Wicked

Boq—3 major sung segments
Doctor Dillamond—1 major sung segment
Elphaba—11 major sung segments, minor participation in 4 numbers
Fiyero—2 major sung segments, minor participation in 3 numbers
Glinda—10 major sung segments, minor participation in 4 numbers
Madame Morrible—2 major sung segments, minor participation in 6 numbers
Nessarose—2 major sung segments
Wizard—3 major sung segments, minor participation in 1 number

The score of *Wicked* is a study in female empowerment. Elphaba and Glinda dominate the singing in *Wicked*, with 21 major sung moments between them, and the female characters have 25 such moments as opposed to 9 for the male characters. When moments of minor participation are factored in, the score is 39 to 13 in favor of the female characters. The only songs dominated by male characters in the show are "Something Bad," the opening of "Dancing through Life," "A Sentimental Man," and "Wonderful," and two of those also include major participation by Elphaba. Fiyero starts "Dancing through Life," but many characters and the chorus have important parts as the song proceeds. All three of Boq's sung moments are major, but each is part of a larger number. If empowerment in a show comes from participation in musical numbers, *Wicked* must be one of the most female-dominated shows in Broadway history.

The Megamusical

The term "megamusical" has become accepted by the Broadway audience and scholars. The most complete study of the concept is *The Megamusical* by Jessica Sternfeld,[28] and she includes *Wicked* "as a prime example of the third generation of the megamusical" that combines "elements of its ancestors . . . with a current sensibility."[29] Sternfeld describes the show's forerunners in the genre in great detail, including such works as *Cats*, *Les Misérables*, and *Phantom of the Opera*. For Sternfeld, a typical megamusical is based upon an epic story that is often set in the past, is sung through (or at least has few lines of dialog), has large and complicated sets and is full of special stage effects, and is publicized as an event that one must experience rather than as just a show.[30] Sternfeld continues her definition with the requirement that megamusicals make a great deal of money, often internationally, and that they tend to find mixed success with critics.[31]

Wicked seems to correspond to the majority of Sternfeld's definition. With its association with *The Wizard of Oz*, it is a fantasy from the past, and the story has epic qualities with events that determine the fate of its fictional world. The show is not even close to sung through, having long dialog sections, but also extended musical scenes of considerable power. The sets are large and complicated, but outside of Elphaba's flight at the end of Act 1, the show has few moments where the set seems as dominant as in *Phantom of the Opera* or the huge, interlocking towers on either side of the unforgettable stage where *Les Misérables* took place on Broadway. Sternfeld does refer to the dragon that juts out from over the stage, the many gears, and the show's flying monkeys,[32] but these parts of the set and other effects do not overwhelm the human element of the show. *Wicked* certainly corresponds to Sternfeld's definition in the area of publicity, and, as shown in chapter 8, it has become an international phenomenon, but not to the extent of the three iconic megamusicals named above. *Wicked* has been greeted with huge financial success and has had a mixed critical reception, the latter shown in chapters 7 and 8.

Sternfeld summarizes some of the reviews of *Wicked*, noting the objections of such critics as the *New York Times'* Ben Brantley, but in her own commentary she suggests that there are sufficient elements within the show to feel a human presence. While noting that the plot is "quite complicated," she states that it "does carry the audience from the comic numbers to the emotional peaks and back again."[33] She praises Elphaba's progression as the character gradually embraces her "supposedly wicked side" between her makeover in "Popular" and the end of Act 1 with "Defying Gravity." Sternfeld believes that some of the show's success derives from the inclusion of humor; an "earthbound comedic tone set earlier makes Elphaba seem like a real person, not an idealized romantic heroine, so that by the time she belts out these high notes [in "Defying Gravity"] she has reached the top but not gone over it."[34]

Wicked will forever be known as a megamusical. As Sternfeld suggests, the show's financial windfall has been partially due to the way the story and characters have imprinted on the audience, including the girls whose posts on the Web were studied by Stacy Wolf. The show's mixture of an effective score, a satisfying story based on one of America's favorite fictional tales, compelling stage effects, and realistic, touching human elements with which audience members identify has helped make it popular. This group of successful factors has not impressed critics in the same way that it has audiences, a condition that Sternfeld observed in several megamusicals. A question arises: Who is right, the critics or the audience? Critics naturally see more shows than the average audience member, but their own expertise about theater varies. In the end, a critic offers one opinion; the audience offers many each night. The critic's opinion is easy to document because it is published; the public's opinion can only be viewed in aggregate by looking at how many tickets a show sells, how many productions finally open around the world, and how many tours are launched and for how long they run. Broadway history is often told through the critical lens; we use reviews to try to understand why shows succeed or fail and to gauge the contemporary reaction. This study itself has included a generous sampling of *Wicked* reviews from both New York and London. Perhaps, however, it is time to recognize in our Broadway histories the ephemeral nature of reviews, the one-sidedness of the opinion, and how it reflects a stance from the past.

One could suggest that the major story on *Wicked* now is not the mixed opening-night reviews, but the millions who have enjoyed the show since 2003. Their delight with the show was in part made possible by the rigid sense of self-criticism applied to developing the music and literary material by the creators, an effort that has been documented in this study. If one wants to believe the adoring audience—perhaps an appropriate yardstick in the unapologetically commercial world of Broadway—it would seem that the strenuous efforts by Schwartz, Holzman, Platt, and others were worth it.

Notes

1. Raymond Knapp has largely adopted this approach in his two major studies: *The American Musical and the Formation of National Identity* (Princeton, NJ: Princeton University Press, 2004), and *The American Musical and the Performance of Personal Identity* (Princeton, NJ: Princeton University Press, 2006). Joseph P. Swain's study *The Broadway Musical: A Critical and Musical Survey*, 2nd edition (Lanham, MD: Scarecrow Press, 2002; 1st edition: Oxford: Oxford University Press, 1990), approached the repertory thematically, choosing single shows as representatives of such types as "Morality Play," "Myth," and "Ethnic Musical."

2. See Jim Lovensheimer, "Stephen Sondheim and the Musical of the Outsider," in *The Cambridge Companion to the Musical*, 2nd edition, ed. William A. Everett and Paul R. Laird, 205–19 (Cambridge: Cambridge University Press, 2008).

3. See chapters 7 and 8 for a survey of critical opinion on *Wicked* in both New York City and London.

4. A useful introduction to all shows in Broadway history (through 2000) may be found in Gerald Bordman, *American Musical Theatre: A Chronicle* (Oxford: Oxford University Press, 2001).

5. Suzanne Ross, *The Wicked Truth: When Good People Do Bad Things* (Glenview, IL: The Raven Foundation, 2007).

6. Joel Grey provided an interesting perspective on *Wicked* when he called it "a thinking man's Disney kind of show" in "*Wicked*: The Road to Broadway," an extra feature on disc 3 of *B'Way/Broadway: The American Musical*, directed by Michael Kantor (Educational Broadcasting Corporation and the Broadway Film Project, 2004).

7. Ross, 211.

8. Ross, 211.

9. Ross, 212.

10. Schwartz has acknowledged that the writers were aware that *Wicked* involved "ethical and moral issues" when they were working on it, ideas that would allow a religious perspective on the show if one chose to pursue it. See Judith M. Sebesta, "Interview with Stephen Schwartz," *Baylor Journal of Theatre and Performance* 3, no. 1 (April 2006): 75.

11. Stacy Ellen Wolf, "'Defying Gravity': Queer Conventions in the Musical *Wicked*," *Theatre Journal* 60, no. 1 (March 2008): 1–21. Wolf also addresses the queer nature of female duets in musical theater in her article "'We'll Always Be Bosom Buddies': Female Duets and the Queering of Broadway Musical Theater," *GLQ: A Journal of Lesbian and Gay Studies* 12, no. 3 (2006): 351–76. In this article, however, Wolf merely mentions *Wicked*; she draws her primary examples from *Mame, Guys and Dolls,* and *West Side Story.* Wolf's essays on *Wicked* also appear in her book *Changed for Good: A Feminist History of the Broadway Musical* (New York: Oxford University Press, 2011).

12. Wolf, 9.

13. Wolf, 5.

14. Wolf, 6.

15. Lovensheimer approaches this in his "Stephen Sondheim and the Musical of the Outsider," 205–19. For more complete considerations of gay perspectives on the musical, see John M. Clum, *Something for the Boys: Musical Theater and Gay Culture* (New York: St. Martin's Press, 1999), and D. A. Miller, *Place for Us: Essay on the Broadway Musical* (Cambridge: Harvard University Press, 2000).

16. Wolf, 2.

17. Wolf, 2.

18. Wolf, 12.

19. Wolf, 16.

20. Wolf, 19.

21. Wolf, 19.

22. In Schwartz's first scenario, he simply notes that Elphaba and Fiyero shared a "love scene" (Carol de Giere, *Defying Gravity: The Creative Career of Stephen Schwartz from "Godspell" to "Wicked,"* [New York: Applause Theatre & Cinema Books, 2008], 507), but the scenario from 21 November 1999 states, "They've just made love for the first time." See Scenario (entitled *Wicked* Outline 11/21/99) produced by collaboration between Schwartz, book writer Winnie Holzman, and producer Marc Platt, 21 November 1999, unpublished, 10.

23. Wolf, 20.

24. Wolf. 21.

25. Stacy Wolf, "*Wicked* Divas, Musical Theatre, and Internet Girl Fans," *Camera Obscura* 65 (2007): 39–71.

26. David Cote, *"Wicked": The Grimmerie; A Behind-the-Scenes Look at the Hit Broadway Musical* (New York: Hyperion, 2005), 68–69.

27. Sebesta, 76.

28. Jessica Sternfeld, *The Megamusical* (Bloomington: Indiana University Press, 2006).

29. Sternfeld, 350.

30. Sternfeld, 1–3.

31. Sternfeld, 3–4.

32. Sternfeld, 349.

33. Sternfeld, 350.

34. Sternfeld, 350.

APPENDIX
Notes on the *Wicked* December 2001 Workshop Video Files on YouTube

As a musical conceived in the digital era, it is inevitable that files of *Wicked* during the period of its genesis would appear on websites such as YouTube, where they would be popular with anyone interested in the show's earlier versions. There are two ways to look at these resources. If all one wishes to do is compare these audio files with the OCR or with the show as it appears in theaters today, the comparisons are fairly obvious for anyone who knows the recording or the show. However, when the goal is to try and place these excerpts into the creative history of the show as developed in chapters 4 and 5 of this study, problems emerge. The YouTube files were identified on the site as from December 2001, which would most likely indicate the major reading that month on the 14th rather than the less important reading on the 7th. Stephen Schwartz and his assistant Michael Cole were not certain that the YouTube files emanate from the 14 December reading. (In two e-mail messages on 10 January 2010 from Michael Cole, Stephen Schwartz's assistant, neither Schwartz nor Cole could be certain that these clips were from December 2001. The material above describing Schwartz's and Cole's reactions to the audio files came from these e-mails.) Both state unequivocally that Idina Menzel played the part of Elphaba in these files, and 14 December was her first major reading in the role. Schwartz, however, did not believe that the narrator's voice was the person that he knew performed in that reading, and he also was not sure if the actor playing Doctor Dillamond was correct. Because he knew that Menzel is on the recordings, however, his "best guess" is that the files were from 14 December 2001, unless it was a later reading in Los Angeles. The material about these files below was compiled in January 2010 when the files were available on YouTube; they have since been removed, but they transmitted useful information about the show's genesis.

The script and songs performed on the files were not identical with any sources consulted for this study, but most of the songs and the spoken lines were at least similar to the 21 November 2001 script and score for the chorus made available by Michael Cole, analyzed in considerable detail in chapters 4 and 5. That source, however, only included chorus parts from *Wicked*, meaning that there was considerable material on the YouTube clips not available in this source. The audio files, however, were not identical to the 21 November 2001 source, perhaps reflecting changes that Schwartz and Winnie Holzman made to the script and score between 21 November and 14 December, when a great deal of work occurred on the show. The files studied on YouTube in January 2010 included the following numbers, described below more or less in the order that the songs appear in the show. The way that the files were numbered on YouTube could not be reconciled with the usual order of songs. The following descriptions focus on material in the clips that does not appear in the show today.

"No One Mourns the Wicked": This lengthy segment was in two audio clips. Unfamiliar lyrics from the opening of the song began "Ring every bell!" a way of celebrating the Wicked Witch's death that Schwartz later deleted. Madame Morrible delivered the Wizard's orders on how the celebration should proceed, including burning effigies of the Wicked Witch. Madame Morrible announced the official time that the witch died, instead of Glinda as in the Broadway version, and she also stated that the witch-slayers were in the palace for their rewards. Morrible traced the Wicked Witch's "path to wickedness" by pointing to an arrow on a map of Oz, a silly moment that also appears in the 21 November 2001 script. The Scarecrow came out of the palace to make a statement, describing the witch's writhing and how the moon turned green. The Scarecrow then sang "No One Mourns the Wicked" as a solo with some different lyrics and no choral answer. Glinda then appeared. Someone quickly asked her if she were the Wicked Witch's friend, and both she and Madame Morrible answered the question. Morrible said that they both knew her before her true wickedness was really known, and Glinda offers that the Wicked

Witch did not intend for things to end this way. Morrible put a different spin on her statement, and then Glinda sang "No one mourns . . ." with an interjection by Madame Morrible. Glinda started to tell Elphaba's story, as in the final version, but here Morrible interjected that Elphaba had every advantage, including her father as governor of Munchkinland. The flashback then began. Frex, Elphaba's father, appeared to start his annual tour of the provinces, and then the familiar tableau of Elphaba's conception and birth began. The remainder of this opening number was similar to what is described in *The Yellow Brick Road Not Taken* segment of chapter 5 (see pp. 168–70).

"Making Good": This file opened with Elphaba singing her "Un-limited" material, apparently to Nessarose at the train station before they leave together for Shiz University. Much of the remainder of the song was similar to that described as part of *The Yellow Brick Road Not Taken* in chapter 5 (see pp. 170–71).

"Popular": This rendition was fairly similar to the final version of the song with a few interesting additions. Galinda at one point asked Elphaba if she might be able to borrow her sister's lovely shoes. When Galinda turned Elphaba to the mirror to tell her that she is beautiful, the underscoring was from the accompaniment to "I'm Not That Girl," as in the Broadway score.

"I'm Not That Girl": This file began from the point where Elphaba points out to Fiyero that he is bleeding and then went much like the final version. After Elphaba sang the song through the first time as audiences know it today, the scene changed to the train station with Galinda begging Elphaba to come home with her for the break over underscoring from "I'm Not That Girl," but Elphaba insisted that she needed to help Doctor Dillamond with his experiment. The train left and then Elphaba sang what is known today at the end of the song, the final time through the A section where she repeats "Don't wish, don't start . . ."

"As If by Magic": This file was very similar to the version from *The Yellow Brick Road Not Taken* (see pp. 183–85).

"Dear Old Shiz (Dillamond's Funeral)": This rendition included the music known from "Dear Old Shiz" on the OCR, but with different words for Dillamond's funeral, an event deleted from the script following San Francisco. The words here were slightly different than those in *The Yellow Brick Road Not Taken*.

"One Short Day": This song appeared in two files on YouTube, the first very close to the song as it appears in *The Yellow Brick Road Not Taken* but with some differences in the contrapuntal section where the main tune combines with "Wizomania." The second file, "One Short Day (Extended)," was corrupted and would not play fully, but it was musically similar to the song in the first file.

"A Sentimental Man": This rendition was much shorter than the version in *The Yellow Brick Road Not Taken*, including only the first thirteen measures.

"Defying Gravity": This file bore considerable resemblance to the Broadway version. The opening material between Elphaba and Glinda and then Elphaba's first time through the song were similar, and then a guard demanded that the door be opened. Elphaba started chanting from the Grimmerie and Glinda tried to make her stop, and the song's continuation sounded fairly familiar to those who know the OCR, but with some different lyrics.

"I Couldn't Be Happier": This file was corrupted and one could only hear the first 2:22 of the promised 7:49, which was similar to the 21 November 2001 script described in chapter 4 (see p. 66), but Glinda's lyrics were different than that source, changed to the material about the "fairy tale plot" as heard in the current stage version. Material from this scene later became part of "Thank Goodness."

"We Deserve Each Other": This segment appeared in two files on YouTube. Schwartz and his collaborators made many adjustments to this second act scene between Elphaba and Nessarose, but in this excerpt it was notable to see how much of the final version was there nearly two years before the show opened. Elphaba opened by telling her sister that she had used every possible spell to try and help the Talking Animals, but Nessarose interrupts her to say that she needs her sister's help, singing material close to what made it in the stage version. Elphaba opened the Grimmerie and started to chant, causing her sister's shoes to glow red. Nessarose walked, called Boq, and sang some of "We Deserve Each Other" until Boq saw Elphaba, who hides, unlike in the final version. Boq sang familiar material to those who know the Broadway show about how he must go to the Emerald City to tell Glinda how he feels about her, and Nessarose had a similarly savage reaction as she does in the stage version. Boq then sang material later cut in a desperately high range about how he would like to see them "parting as friends," but Nessarose put a nasty spell on him to try to make him love her. Elphaba returned to the scene in time to see Nessarose's spell take effect, and Elphaba chanted another spell to save Boq's life. While she put on the spell, Nessarose sang another verse to the "We Deserve Each Other" music, but with different lyrics than those heard today. In the second file, Boq has been turned to tin and Nessarose blames it on Elphaba. Boq ran out screaming before Nessarose sang material unknown today about the "girl in the mirror," an unhappy version of herself, concluding with "We deserve each other," suggesting that she will remain in the governor's palace with the man she loves who is now made of tin. This entire scene is similar to the 21 November 2001 script.

"Wonderful": This file was fairly similar to the 21 November 2001 script and also shared a good bit of material with the stage version. The Wizard referred to himself as a "Kansas hick" rather than "cornfed hick." His dialog with Elphaba was quite different than what is heard today. He explained what happens to animals where he lived before Oz, singing a waltz about how he has kept the animals "from the ax and the sausage grinder." The file ended suddenly as the Wizard tossed Elphaba the key to the monkey's cage.

"Just for This Moment": This is an alternative title for "As Long As You're Mine." The rendition started with Glinda's brief reprise of "I'm Not That Girl." The song between Fiyero and Elphaba had the same lyrics as the 21 November 2001 script, lyrics that changed substantially before the stage version.

"Catfight": This was a scene of dialog where Glinda and Elphaba argue and fight at the site of Nessarose's death, only to be interrupted by the Wizard's guards and then Fiyero. It was reminiscent of the 21 November 2001 script.

"No Good Deed": This song was fairly close to what one hears on the OCR but with some different lyrics that also appear in the 21 November 2001 script. There was also another version from a workshop labeled "No Good Deed (Extended)" that began with the guards putting Fiyero on the poles in the cornfield before Elphaba sang the same version of the song.

"March of the Witch-Hunters": Much of this rendition sounded familiar, combining material known in the Broadway version with some that appears in the 21 November 2001 script. The main difference that does not appear in the show today is that Dorothy and her three friends from Oz appeared.

"For Good (Extended)": This opened with dialog heard in the 21 November script, and the song was very much like what appears on the OCR.

"Finale": This file opened with Glinda ordering Madame Morrible's arrest, as in the 21 November script. The major difference between this version and what one sees in the theater today was a scene with Fiyero and Elphaba together in the Badlands. Elphaba sang to Doctor Dillamond, trying to help him learn to speak again. As noted in chapter 4 (p. 70), this was a scene in the show that Schwartz fought to retain, but Joe Mantello opposed it.

BIBLIOGRAPHY

Main Sources

Adams, Guy. "Pandora: Broadway Star Set to Scoop Up a Wicked Transfer Fee." *The Independent*, 2 May 2006.

Andrews, Richard. *The London Theatre Guide*. London: Metro Publications, 2002.

Armstrong, Linda. "Broadway Play Is Wonderfully 'Wicked.'" *New York Amsterdam News*, 4 March 2003, 40.

Auxier, Randall E., and Phillip S. Seng, eds. *The Wizard of Oz and Philosophy: Wicked Wisdom of the West*. Popular Culture and Philosophy, vol. 37. Chicago and LaSalle, IL: Open Court, 2008.

Bamigboye, Baz. Column. *Daily Mail*, 22 December 2006.

———. "Beeb's Desert Hit List." *Daily Mail*, 21 April 2006.

———. "Mum's the Word for Hectic Keira." *Daily Mail*, 12 May 2006.

———. "Something Wicked This Way Coughs." *Daily Mail*, 24 November 2006.

Barbour, David, and David Johnson. "Hocus Pocus: Envisioning the Fantastical Land of Oz for Broadway's *Wicked*." *Entertainment Design* 38, no. 2 (February 2004): 16–23.

Barnes, Clive. "Broom Shtick: *Wicked* Witches Most Entrancing." *New York Post*, 31 October 2003.

Bassett, Kate. "Theatre: The Old Vic Cometh Back." *The Independent on Sunday*, 1 October 2006.

Bassis, Barry. "Pair of Witchy Women Take Stage in *Wicked*." *New York Resident*, 24 November 2003, 42.

Bergreen, Laurence. *As Thousands Cheer: The Life of Irving Berlin*. New York: Da Capo Press, 1990.

Bernstein, Leonard. *West Side Story*. Original cast recording. Columbia CK 32603. 1957.

———. *West Side Story*. Studio recording. Deutsche Grammophon 415 253-2. 1985.

Billington, Michael. "Theatre: Musical Moralising Taints the Magic of Oz; *Wicked* Apollo Victoria London." *The Guardian*, 29 September 2006.

Bishop, Clifford. Review in the *Sunday Times*, 1 October 2006, consulted in *Theatre Record*, 26/20 (24 September–7 October 2006): 1155.

Bordman, Gerald. *American Musical Theatre: A Chronicle*. Oxford: Oxford University Press, 2001.

Brantley, Ben. "There's Trouble in Emerald City." *New York Times*, 31 October 2003, E1, 31.

BroadwayWorld. "Los Angeles *Wicked* to Close 1/11/09." http://losangeles .broadwayworld.com/article/Los_Angeles_Wicked_to_Close_11109_ 20080402 (accessed 20 June 2010).

Brown, Georgina. Review in the *Mail on Sunday*, 1 October 2006, consulted in *Theatre Record*, 26/20 (24 September–7 October 2006): 1155–56.

B'Way/Broadway: The American Musical, directed by Michael Kantor. Educational Broadcasting Corporation and the Broadway Film Project, 2004: "Episode Six: Putting It Together (1980–2004)."

Byrne, Christopher. "Witches' Brouhaha: Ambitious Musical Loses Courage of Convictions in Second Act." *Gay City News*, 13 November 2003, 23, 32.

Caird, Ann. "Letter: Briefly . . . Overpriced Actors." *The Independent*, 5 May 2006.

Callahan, Dan. Review. *New York Blade*, 31 October 2003, 27.

Carter, Tim. *Oklahoma! The Making of an American Musical*. New Haven, CT: Yale University Press, 2007.

Christie, Nicola. "It's Wicked." *The Independent*, 17 August 2006.

Clapp, Susannah. "Review—Critics—Theatre: Make Mine a Double; Conor McPherson's Latest Play Full of Drinks Is Intoxicating, While at the Old Vic Kevin Spacey and Eve Bert Go Head to Head in Peerless Fashion." *The Observer*, 1 October 2006.

Clum, John M. *Something for the Boys: Musical Theater and Gay Culture*. New York: St. Martin's Press, 1999.

Cohen, Ron. "*Wicked*." *Backstage*, 14 November 2003, 48.

Colville, Robert. "A Glittering Season of Musicals." *Daily Telegraph*, 20 September 2006.

Conrad, Jon Alan. "Brohn, William David." *Grove Music Online*, www.oxford musiconline.com (accessed 29 July 2010).

Cote, David. "*Wicked*." *Time Out New York*, 6 November 2003, 145.

————. *"Wicked": The Grimmerie; A Behind-the-Scenes Look at the Hit Broadway Musical*. New York: Hyperion, 2005.

Daily Mail (London), "Wicked Witch with a Magic Touch," 28 March 2008.

de Giere, Carol. *Defying Gravity: The Creative Career of Stephen Schwartz from "Godspell" to "Wicked."* New York: Applause Theatre & Cinema Books, 2008.

de Jongh, Nicholas. "We Must All Be Off to See This Wicked and Wonderful Vision of Oz." *Evening Standard*, 28 September 2006.

Earle, Neil. *"The Wonderful World of Oz" in American Popular Culture: Uneasy in Eden*. Lewiston/Queenston/Lampeter: The Edwin Mellen Press, 1993.

Edwardes, Jane. Review in *Time Out London*, 4 October 2006, consulted in *Theatre Record*, 26/20 (24 September–7 October 2006): 1156.

Eggar, Robin. "Youth Enters Stage Right—Report." *Sunday Times* (London), 8 April 2007.

Engel, Lehmann. *The American Musical Theater*. New York: Macmillan, 1975.

Evans, Dan. "Weekend Theatre." *The Express*, 2 February 2007.

Evening Standard (London), "*Hairspray* Makes Profit in Record 29 Weeks," 23 June 2008.

Evening Standard (London), "Magical Alternative to Panto," 7 January 2007.

Feingold, Michael. "Green Witch, Mean Time." *Village Voice*, 5 November 2003, 77.

Ferencz, George J., ed. *The Broadway Sound: The Autobiography and Selected Essays of Robert Russell Bennett*. Rochester, NY: University of Rochester Press, 1999.

"For Good." An extra feature on disc 3 of *B'Way/Broadway: The American Musical*, directed by Michael Kantor. Educational Broadcasting Corporation and the Broadway Film Project, 2004.

Gable, Christopher. *The Words and Music of Sting*. Westport, CT: Praeger, 2009.

Gardiner, Martin, and Russell Nye. *The Wizard of Oz and Who He Was*. East Lansing, MI: Michigan State University Press, 1957.

Garfinkel, Sharon. Review in the *Tribune*, 6 October 2006, consulted in *Theatre Record*, 26/20 (24 September–7 October 2006): 1156.

Geer, John G., and Thomas R. Rochon. "William Jennings Bryan on the Yellow Brick Road." *Journal of American Culture* 16, no. 4 (Winter 1993): 59–64.

Gottfried, Martin. *Broadway Musicals*. New York: Abradale Press/Harry N. Abrams Inc., 1984.

Hagerty, Bill. "Wizard Performers but Woeful Songs—Something for the Weekend." *The Sun* (London), 13 October 2006.

Heilpern, John. "The Good, the Bad and the *Wicked*: Dueling Witches Raise the Roof." *New York Observer*, 10 November 2003, 21.

"The History of *Wicked*," www.wickedthemusical.com.au/about/history.html (consulted multiple times).

Hurst, David. *"Wicked." Next Magazine* (New York), 7 November 2003, 42.

Internet Broadway Database, www.ibdb.com (consulted multiple times).

Isherwood, Charles. "More Bothered Than Bewitched by *Wicked*." *Variety*, 3 November 2003, 30, 44.

Jury, Louise. "Theatreland's Top 100 Players." *The Independent* (London), 29 December 2006.

———. *"Wicked!* Theatreland Is Alive to the Sound of Ringing Tills." *The Independent* (London), 30 January 2007.

Kern, Jerome, and Oscar Hammerstein II. *Show Boat*, Music Theater of Lincoln Center. RCA Victor 09026-61182-2. 1966, reissued 1992.

Kirle, Bruce. *Unfinished Business: Broadway Musicals as Works-in-Progress*. Theater in the Americas. Carbondale, IL: Southern Illinois University Press, 2005.

Kissel, Howard. "The Girl from Oz: It's Such a 'Wicked' Waste of Talent." *New York Daily News*, 31 October 2003, 57.

Knapp, Raymond. *The American Musical and the Formation of National Identity*. Princeton, NJ: Princeton University Press, 2004.

———. *The American Musical and the Performance of Personal Identity*. Princeton, NJ: Princeton University Press, 2006.

Lahr, John. Review. *New Yorker*, 10 November 2003, 127.

Laird, Paul R. "The Creation of a Broadway Musical: Stephen Schwartz, Winnie Holzman, and *Wicked*." In *The Cambridge Companion to the Musical*, 2nd edition, edited by William A. Everett and Paul R. Laird, 340–52. Cambridge: Cambridge University Press, 2008.

———. "Stephen Schwartz and Bernstein's *Mass*," in *On Bunker's Hill: Essays in Honor of J. Bunker Clark*, edited by William A. Everett and Paul R. Laird, 263–70. Sterling Heights, MI: Harmonie Park Press, 2007.

Law, Peter. *"Wicked*—The Untold Story of the Witches of Oz." *Greater London, Kent, and Surry Counties Publications*, 29 September 2006.

Leon, Ruth. "Backstate with Ruth Leon." *The Express* (London), 10 March 2006.

Littlefield, Henry M. "The Wizard of Oz: Parable on Populism." *American Quarterly* 16, no. 1 (Spring 1964): 47–58.

Lovensheimer, Jim. *South Pacific: Paradise Rewritten*. Oxford: Oxford University Press, 2010.

———. "Stephen Sondheim and the Musical of the Outsider." In *The Cambridge Companion to the Musical*, 2nd edition, edited by William A. Everett and Paul R. Laird, 205–19. Cambridge: Cambridge University Press, 2008.

Macauley, Alastair. "Arts: *Wicked*, Victoria Palace Theatre London; The Critics." *Financial Times*, 3 October 2006.

Maguire, Gregory. *A Lion among Men*. New York: William Morrow, 2008.

———. *Son of a Witch*. New York: ReganBooks, 2005.

———. *Wicked: The Life and Times of the Wicked Witch of the West*. New York: ReganBooks, 1995.

Mansfield, Susan. "Other Side of the Rainbow." *The Scotsman* (Edinburgh), 29 April 2006.

Marmion, Patrick. "Patrick Marmion First Night Review." *Daily Mail* (London), 28 September 2006.

Maxwell, Dominic. "Born to Run and Run—Arts." *The Times* (London), 22 October 2007.

McCarter, Jeremy. "The Golden Girls." *New York Sun*, 31 October 2003, 17.

mcclung, bruce d. *Lady in the Dark: Biography of a Musical*. New York: Oxford University Press, 2007.

mcclung, bruce d., and Paul R. Laird. "Musical Sophistication on Broadway: Kurt Weill and Leonard Bernstein." In *The Cambridge Companion to the Musical*, 2nd edition, edited by William A. Everett and Paul R. Laird, 190–201. Cambridge: Cambridge University Press, 2008.

"Michael Blakemore Biography (1928–)," www.filmreference.com/film/19/Michael-Blakemore.html (accessed 28 July 2010).

Miller, D. A. *Place for Us: Essay on the Broadway Musical*. Cambridge: Harvard University Press, 2000.

Moore, Christopher. "With Worthy Witches, *Wicked* Works Wonders." *West Side Spirit* (New York), 4 December 2003, 24.

Morley, Sheridan. "Witches in Need of Magic Touch." *The Express* (London), 28 September 2006.

Murphy, Scott. "An Audiovisual Foreshadowing in *Psycho*." In *Terror Tracks: Music, Sound and Horror Cinema*, edited by Philip Hayward, 47–59. London: Equinox, 2009.

Murphy, Siobhan. Review in the *Metro* (London), 29 September 2006, consulted in *Theatre Record*, 26/20 (24 September–7 October 2006): 1155.

Nightingale, Benedict. "*Wicked*—Theatre." *The Times* (London), 29 September 2006.

Phillips, Michael. "Brick Road Leads to Mediocre Musicals." *Chicago Tribune*, 2 November 2003, sec. 7, 17.

Rahm, Suzanne. *The Wizard of Oz: Shaping an Imaginary World*. Twayne's Masterwork Studies No. 167. New York: Twayne Publishers, 1998.

Reed, Rex. "And Toto, Too." *New York Observer*, 17 November 2003, 22.

Rees, Jasper. "Something Wicked This Way Comes—Theatre." *Sunday Times* (London), 20 August 2006.

Ross, Suzanne. *The Wicked Truth: When Good People Do Bad Things*. Glenview, IL: The Raven Foundation, 2007.

Russell, William. Review in the *Herald*, 13 October 2006, consulted in *Theatre Record*, 26/20 (24 September–7 October 2006): 1157.

Schwartz, Stephen. "Stephen Schwartz's Update Fall 2000." www.musical schwartz.com/schwartzscene/schwartz-scene-01-12.htm#spark01 (accessed 28 July 2010).

———. "Stephen Schwartz's Update Winter 2001." www.musicalschwartz.com/ schwartzscene/schwartz-scene-01-12.htm#spark02 (accessed 29 July 2010).

———. "Stephen Schwartz's Update Spring 2001." www.musicalschwartz.com/ schwartzscene/schwartz-scene-01-12.htm#spark03 (accessed 29 July 2010).

———. "Stephen Schwartz Update Fall 2001." www.musicalschwartz.com/ schwartzscene/schwartz-scene-01-12.htm#spark05 (accessed 7 April 2010).

———. "Stephen Schwartz Update Spring 2002." www.musicalschwartz.com/ schwartzscene/schwartz-scene-01-12.htm#spark07 (accessed 7 April 2010).

———. "Stephen Schwartz Update Summer 2002." www.musicalschwartz.com/ schwartzscene/schwartz-scene-01-12.htm#spark08 (accessed 7 April 2010).

———. "Stephen Schwartz Update Fall 2002." www.musicalschwartz.com/ schwartzscene/schwartz-scene-13.htm (accessed 7 April 2010).

———. "Stephen Schwartz Update Spring 2003." www.musicalschwartz.com/ schwartzscene/schwartz-scene-01-12.htm#spark11 (accessed 7 April 2010).

———. *The Schwartz Scene*, no. 13 (Fall 2003), www.musicalschwartz.com/ schwartzscene/schwartz-scene-13.htm (accessed 7 April 2010).

———. *Wicked*. Original cast recording. Compact disc, Decca B0001682-2. 2003.

———. *Wicked: 5th Anniversary Edition*. 2 compact discs, Decca B0012127-72. 2008.

Sebesta, Judith M. "Interview with Stephen Schwartz." *Baylor Journal of Theatre and Performance* 3, no. 1 (April 2006): 73–78.

Seckerson, Edward. "Go on with the Shows—Musicals." *Sunday Times* (London), 17 December 2006.

Shenton, Mark. "Lavish Show with a Real Touch of Magic." *The Express on Sunday* (London), 1 October 2006.

———. Review in *What's On in London*, 5 October 2006, consulted in *Theatre Record*, 26/20 (24 September–7 October 2006): 1156–57.

———. "Spellbinding." *The Express on Sunday* (London), 1 October 2006.

Shuttleworth, Ian. "Prompt Corner." *Theatre Record*, 26/20 (24 September–7 October 2006): 1143.

Simeone, Nigel. *Leonard Bernstein: "West Side Story."* Farnham, Surrey, England: Ashgate, 2009.

Simon, John. "Ding-Dong: *Wicked* Tells the Backstory of the Witches of Oz, but It's Lifeless; *Golda's Balcony* is the Perfect Merging of Playwright, Actress, and Character." *New York*, 10 November 2003, 100.

Singh, Anita. "The Hills Are Alive with Many Theatre Prizes for Connie Fisher and *The Sound of Music*." *Western Mail* (Cardiff, Wales), 10 February 2007.

Spencer, Charles. Review in the *Daily Telegraph*, 28 September 2006, consulted in *Theatre Record*, 26/20 (24 September–7 October 2006): 1154.

Sternfeld, Jessica. *The Megamusical.* Bloomington: Indiana University Press, 2006.

Street, Douglas. "The Wonderful Wiz That Was: The Curious Transformation of *The Wizard of Oz*." *Kansas Quarterly* 16, no. 3 (Summer 1984): 91–98.

Suskin, Steven. *The Sound of Broadway Music: A Book of Orchestrators & Orchestrations.* Oxford: Oxford University Press, 2009.

Swain, Joseph P. *The Broadway Musical: A Critical and Musical Survey*, 2nd edition. Lanham, MD: Scarecrow Press, 2002; 1st edition, Oxford: Oxford University Press, 1990.

Taylor, Paul. "Reviews—Theatre." *The Independent* (London), 29 September 2006.

Teachout, Terry. "View: Hooray for the Girls from Oz." *Wall Street Journal*, 31 October 2003, W13.

Teodorczuk, Tom. "Musicals Battle to the Tune of GBP 37m." *Evening Standard* (London), 6 October 2006.

———. "Something Wicked This Way Comes for Understudy Kerry." *Evening Standard* (London), 10 January 2007.

The Guardian (London), "Theatre: Public Gives *Wicked* a Vote of Confidence," 10 February 2007.

The Independent (London), "Witches Work Box Office Magic," 23 October 2006.

Vieira, Robert. "*Wicked*'s Ground*break*ing Score." *The Schwartz Scene*, no. 18 (Winter 2005), www.musicalschwartz.com/schwartzscene/schwartz -scene-18.htm (consulted multiple times).

Walker, Tim. "Arts/Theatre: Heart of Darkness." *Telegraph* (London), 2 September 2007.

———. "A Terribly Long Secret Theatre." *Sunday Telegraph* (London), 1 October 2006.

Warman, Jonathan. "*Wicked*: These Gals from Oz Are Intriguing, but Not Always So Tuneful." *HX Magazine* (New York), 28 November 2003, 61.

Wicked. Broadway Across America. Program from the National Tour, Kansas City, November 2009.

Wicked. December 2001 Workshop. www.youtube.com (consulted multiple times).

Wicked: Around the World in One Short Day. New York: The Araca Group, 2008.

"*Wicked*: The Road to Broadway." Extra feature on disc 3 of *B'Way/Broadway: The American Musical*, directed by Michael Kantor. Educational Broadcasting Corporation and the Broadway Film Project, 2004.

"Wicked Celebrates £100m Box Office Milestone." www.uktheatretickets.co.uk/article/19841507/Wicked-celebrates-%C2%A3100m-box-office-milestone (accessed 20 June 2010).

"Wicked Opens in Sydney." www.aussietheatre.com.au/index.php?option=com_content&view=article&id=209:wicked-opens-in-sydney&catid=44:general&Itemid=67 (accessed 20 June 2010).

Winer, Linda. "Bewitched and Bothered, Too: Bewildering *Wicked* Tries to Be Both Cute and Dark; So Witch Is It?" *Newsday* (Long Island), 31 October 2003, B2.

Wolf, Matt. "Broadway Hit Casts Its Spell Over Here: It's Making a Million a Week in New York. Now, Says Matt Wolf, *Wicked* Is the Hottest Ticket in a Packed West End Autumn of Musicals." *Daily Telegraph* (London), 20 September 2006.

———. "Hot Hits from Broadway." *Evening Standard* (London), 24 January 2006.

———. Review in the *International Herald Tribune*, 11 October 2006, consulted in *Theatre Record*, 26/20 (24 September–7 October 2006): 1157.

Wolf, Stacy Ellen. "'Defying Gravity': Queer Conventions in the Musical *Wicked*." *Theatre Journal* 60, no. 1 (March 2008): 1–21.

———. "'We'll Always Be Bosom Buddies': Female Duets and the Queering of Broadway Musical Theater." *GLQ: A Journal of Lesbian and Gay Studies* 12, no. 3 (2006): 351–76.

———. "*Wicked* Divas, Musical Theatre, and Internet Girl Fans." *Camera Obscura* 65 (2007): 39–71.

Other Websites

http://articles.sfgate.com/2009-03-23/entertainment/17215954_1_coeur-russian-hill-aunt-eller (accessed 20 June 2010).

http://broadwayiswicked.com/tag/amanda-harrison (accessed 20 June 2010).

http://leisureblogs.chicagotribune.com/the_theater_loop/2009/01/countdown-to-the-close-of-chicagos-wicked.html (accessed 20 June 2010).

http://melbourne.citysearch.com.au/arts/1137659764545/Wicked+Is+Leaving+Town! (accessed 20 June 2010).

http://sanfrancisco.broadwayworld.com/article/Photo_Flash_Cast_of_WICKED_San_Francisco_20090217 (accessed 20 June 2010).

http://wickedtour.net/page/2 (accessed 19 November 2010).

www.adamgarcia.net (accessed 21 June 2010).

www.broadwayworld.com/article/TV_Around_the_BroadwayWorld_
WICKED_in_Helsinki_20100905 (accessed 13 September 2010).

www.broadwayworld.com/article/Wicked_to_Launch_2nd_National_Tour_in_
March_2009_20080522 (accessed 20 March 2010).

www.gregorymaguire.com/about/about_interview.html (accessed 30 January
2010).

www.lucydurack.com (accessed 20 June 2010).

www.michaelmccabe.net/about_michaelmccabe.html (accessed 12 June 2010).

www.musical-friends.de/index.php?page=Thread&threadID=1048 (accessed 20
June 2010).

www.musicalworld.nl/actueel/verkaik_verhuist_met_wicked_mee_naar_
oberhausen (accessed 20 June 2010).

www.officiallondontheatre.co.uk/olivier_awards/past_winners/view/item98375/
Olivier-Winners-2007 (accessed 14 June 2010).

www.playbill.com/news/article/120640-Yellow-Brick-Road-Not-Taken-Will
-Celebrate-Wickeds-Fifth-Anniversary (accessed 24 April 2010).

www.wickedthemusical.com/page.php#WickedCitiesOnTour (accessed 20 June
2010).

www.wickedthemusical.com.au/news/news.html (accessed 20 June 2010).

Unpublished Scenarios and Scripts

Scenario by Stephen Schwartz from September 1998 (also published in Carol de
Giere, *Defying Gravity: The Creative Career of Stephen Schwartz from "Godspell" to "Wicked."* New York: Applause Theatre & Cinema Books, 2008, pp.
503–9).

Scenario (entitled *Wicked* Outline 11/21/99) produced by collaboration between
Stephen Schwartz, book writer Winnie Holzman, and producer Marc Platt,
21 November 1999.

Wicked: A New Musical, Based on a Novel by Gregory Maguire, Book by Winnie Holzman, Music and Lyrics by Stephen Schwartz, Producer: Marc Platt,
First Complete Draft, 12 March 2001.

Wicked: A New Musical, Based on a Novel by Gregory Maguire, Book by Winnie Holzman, Music and Lyrics by Stephen Schwartz, Producer: Marc Platt,
First Complete Draft [*sic*], 21 November 2001.

Wicked Script—workshop draft. October 2002.

Wicked Rehearsal Script, 31 March 2003.

Wicked, Pre-New York Rehearsal, as of 28 July 2003.

BIBLIOGRAPHY

Wicked, Pre-New York Rehearsal Script, 25 August 03.
Wicked, New York Rehearsal Script, 16 September 03.
Wicked, New York Rehearsal Script, 5 October 2003.
Wicked Broadway, Revised Performance Script, 5 December 2006.

Musical Sources

Wicked: Songs for First Act (dated 30 August 2000).
Deleted songs from *Wicked* dating between 2000 and 2003 (most of the drafts undated).
Deleted songs prepared for *The Yellow Brick Road Not Taken*, a benefit performance on 27 October 2008 (songs bear various dates of revision, mostly from fall 2008).
Holograph scores of freelance arrangements prepared for Hal Leonard "Piano/Vocal Selections" by George J. Ferencz: "As Long As You're Mine," "Defying Gravity," "For Good," "I Couldn't Be Happier," "No Good Deed," "Wonderful."
Wicked: A New Musical, Based on a Novel by Gregory Maguire, Book by Winnie Holzman, Music and Lyrics by Stephen Schwartz, Producer: Marc Platt, First Complete Draft [*sic*], 21 November 2001 (includes choral parts from the score).
Wicked: A New Musical, Music & Lyrics: Stephen Schwartz, Book: Winnie Holzman (undated score of entire show with revision dates between 25 March and 15 October 2003).
Wicked (orchestral score prepared for the original cast recording).
Wicked: Piano/Vocal (undated score of entire show with revision dates between March 2004 and 21 January 2005).

Interviews

Herb Braha, by telephone, 25 February 2008.
William David Brohn, personal, 22 November 2008.
Winnie Holzman, by telephone, 29 March 2005.
Stephen Oremus, by telephone, 5 February 2010.
———, by telephone, 28 September 2010.
Dr. Karin Pagel-Meiners, by telephone, 10 June 2010.

Stephen Schwartz Interviews

Personal, New York, 22 March 2005.
By telephone, 23 July 2005.

Personal, Kansas City, MO, 26 June 2006.
Personal, Schroon Lake, NY, 20 July 2007.
Personal, New York, 14 January 2008.
Personal, New York, 18 March 2008.
Personal, New York, 19 March 2008.
Personal, New York, 1 April 2008.
Personal, New York, 22 November 2008.

Unpublished Documents and Correspondence

Cole, Michael. E-mail message to author from 27 March 2005.
————. E-mail messages to author from 10 January 2010.
Doran, Greg. Letter to Stephen Schwartz, undated.
Ferencz, George J. E-mail message to author, 26 October 2010.
Nunn, Trevor. Letter to Stephen Schwartz, 21 May 2001.
Oremus, Stephen. Several e-mail messages to author in 2008 and 2010.
Prince, Harold. E-mail to Stephen Schwartz, 26 March 2001.
Schedule of *Wicked*'s creation, accessed in Stephen Schwartz's office, 20 March
    2008.
Schwartz, Stephen. E-mail message to author, 12 December 2009.
————. E-mail message to Joe Mantello, 28 October 2002.
Stroman, Susan. Letter to Stephen Schwartz, 25 June 2001.
Unpublished notes consulted in Stephen Schwartz's office, 20 March 2008.
Wicked production schedule, 29 October 2002.

INDEX

Songs from *Wicked*, including those cut from the show, appear in quotation marks without further comment. Songs from other sources are briefly identified. Other musicals, films, plays, and books are also briefly identified. Page numbers referring to artwork (examples, textboxes, tables, and photos) are italic.

ABOUT THE AUTHOR

Paul R. Laird is professor of musicology at the University of Kansas, where he teaches courses on music of the Baroque and twentieth century, American music, and the history of musical theater and directs the Instrumental Collegium Musicum. He holds a Ph.D. in music from the University of North Carolina at Chapel Hill. Laird's previous books have included *Towards a History of the Spanish Villancico* (1997), *Leonard Bernstein: A Guide to Research* (2002), *The Baroque Cello Revival: An Oral History* (2004), and *Leonard Bernstein's Chichester Psalms* (2010). With William A. Everett, Laird was coeditor of both editions of *The Cambridge Companion to the Musical* (2002, 2008), and they coauthored *The Historical Dictionary of the Broadway Musical* (2008). His articles, chapters, and reviews have appeared in numerous journals and edited collections. Laird lives in Lawrence, Kansas, with his wife, Joy, and his daughter, Caitlin.